PUBLICATIONS

OF THE

NAVY RECORDS SOCIETY

VOL. 129

THE HAWKE PAPERS

A Selection: 1743–1771

THE NAVY RECORDS SOCIETY was established in 1893 for the purpose of printing unpublished manuscripts and rare works of naval interest. The Society is open to all who are interested in naval history, and any person wishing to become a member should apply to the Hon. Secretary, c/o the Public Record Office, Chancery Lane, London WC2A 1LR. The annual subscription is £15, which entitles the member to receive one free copy of each work issued by the Society in that year, and to buy earlier issues at much reduced prices.

SUBSCRIPTIONS and orders for back volumes should be sent to the Hon. Treasurer, c/o Binder Hamlyn, 8 St Bride Street, London EC4A 4DA.

THE COUNCIL OF THE NAVY RECORDS SOCIETY wish it to be clearly understood that they are not answerable for any opinions and observations which may appear in the Society's publications. For these the editors of the several works are entirely responsible.

Sir Edward Hawke, Knight of the Bath, in 1748

(from a mezzotint by J. MacArdell after G. Knapton, reproduced by permission of the National Maritime Museum)

THE HAWKE PAPERS

A Selection: 1743–1771

edited by

RUDDOCK F. MACKAY, D.Litt.

PUBLISHED BY SCOLAR PRESS
FOR THE NAVY RECORDS SOCIETY
1990

Published by
SCOLAR PRESS
Gower Publishing Company Limited
Gower House
Croft Road
Aldershot
Hants GU11 3HR

Gower Publishing Company
Old Post Road
Brookfield
Vermont 05036
USA

British Library Cataloguing in Publication Data
Hawke, Edward Hawke, *1705–1781*
    The Hawke papers: a selection, 1743–1771. – (Publications
of the Navy Records Society), V. 129
    1. Great Britain, Royal Navy   Hawke, Edward
    I. Title   II. Mackay, Ruddock F. (Ruddock Finlay)
    III. Navy Records Society   IV. Series
    359.331092

Library of Congress Cataloging-in-Publication Data
Hawke, Edward Hawke, Baron, 1705–1781
    The Hawke papers: a selection, 1743–1771 / edited by Ruddock F.
Mackay
    p. cm. — (Publications of the Navy Records Society; vol. 129)
    ISBN 0–85967–830–X
    1. Hawke, Edward Hawke, Baron, 1705–1781. 2. Great Britain —
History, Naval — 18th century — Sources. 3. Great Britain. Royal
Navy — Biography. 4. Admirals — Great Britain — Biography.
    I. Mackay, Ruddock F. II. Series.
    DA87.1.H34H38   1990
    359'.0092—dc20
    [B]   90–38654
    CIP

ISBN 0–85967–830–X

Printed in Great Britain by
Billing & Sons Ltd, Worcester

CONTENTS

vii

MAPS AND ILLUSTRATIONS

Frontispiece: Sir Edward Hawke, Knight of the Bath, in 1748 (from a mezzotint by J. MacArdell after G. Knapton, reproduced by permission of the National Maritime Museum).

PREFACE

In 1970 the main personal collection of Admiral Hawke's service papers was acquired by the National Maritime Museum. This major acquisition was enhanced in 1984 when the seventh Earl of Rosse deposited his collection of Hawke's private papers at the Museum so that microfilm copies could be made there for the benefit of scholars. The editor of this volume gratefully took advantage of the opportunity thus afforded to transcribe from the originals a number of items for inclusion here.

The editor also extends his thanks to the Trustees and staff of the National Maritime Museum, remembering in particular the friendly assistance of Dr R. J. B. Knight and Dr R. A. Morriss; the Public Record Office at Kew (where much of the transcription was done) and its staff, amongst whom Dr N. A. M. Rodger gave indispensable help; the Trustees and staff of the British Library for access to the Bridport (Alexander Hood) Papers; and especially to the general editor of this series, Mr A. N. Ryan, whose patience and guidance were a constant support. Crown copyright material is reproduced by permission of Her Majesty's Stationery Office.

It was agreed that, in this volume, alternative references should be given in the List of Documents where the text, for instance a dispatch from Hawke to the Admiralty, was represented both at the Public Record Office and at the National Maritime Museum. In that List, it will be inferred, about half of the references are to original documents. Usually Hawke had copies made of his out-letters which survive in his letter books; but on occasion he decided not to have a copy made. When, on the other hand, the Admiralty wrote to him, a copy was almost always retained; and on receiving such a letter the Admiral usually had a copy written into a letter book, but he made a number of judicious exceptions. In *his* collection of service papers, it is the copies which comprise a fairly complete source of reference. This is supplemented by the originals, mostly to be found in Lord Rosse's collection—and some of these are unique. Where both an original and a copy of a document were found, discrepancies were rare. On occasion a copy permitted completion of a damaged original.

With a few designated exceptions, documents are presented with their spelling and punctuation modernized. The Council permitted the editor to insert explanatory comments in square brackets before or after certain documents. The life dates of officers, where available, are given in the index. Now that the Compact Edition of the *Dictionary of National Biography* has made Sir John Laughton's outstanding series of eighteenth-century naval biographies more widely and easily accessible, it was thought useful to asterisk names in the index where such a biography exists.

Before the change of the calendar in 1752, the documents are dated in Old Style; but in introductions and footnotes the year is always given in New Style.

GLOSSARY OF ABBREVIATIONS
IN THE FOOTNOTES

Ady	Admiralty
D.N.B.	*Dictionary of National Biography*
Ld	Lord

For details of an officer's career:

L	lieutenant
CR	commander
C	post captain
RA	rear-admiral
VA	vice-admiral
A or Adm.	admiral

For archival references, see the preamble to the List of Documents and Sources.

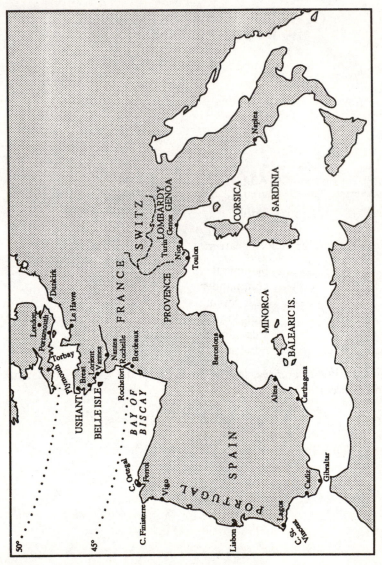

Places in Europe mentioned in the text

GENERAL INTRODUCTION

The eighteenth century saw Britain rise to a degree of maritime dominance which was remarkable, especially when account is taken of the greater population and military potential of her chief rival, France. Moreover, France could usually count on Spain as an ally. At sea the British dominance was asserted during the protracted conflict of 1739–48 and triumphantly re-emphasized during the Seven Years War (1756–63). Yet the contingent nature of British sea power was, not long afterwards, strikingly illustrated in the American Independence War. On this occasion France, being free of continental preoccupations, could concentrate on the maritime and colonial sphere and give Britain a taste of disaster. The series of French wars, dating from the late seventeenth century, ended with the Revolutionary and Napoleonic conflicts between 1793 and 1815. France was heavily committed to warfare on land and Britain, through her substantial control over European waters, made it impossible for Napoleon to achieve a secure domination of Europe. As one would expect from such an account, the main decisive British sea victories between 1739 and 1815 belong to the first, second, and fourth above-mentioned periods of conflict. Yet while Horatio Nelson, the outstanding battle-winner of the final period, is universally remembered, Edward Hawke, who in 1747 and again in 1759 commanded in engagements decisive for the wars concerned, is almost universally forgotten. True, the peace of 1815 left the British Navy for long without a rival; but the Seven Years War, which left so deep an impress on North American and Indian history, was arguably the most successful war that Britain ever fought.

Hawke was born in 1705—in London, it is thought. However, there seems to be no documentary record of the event, despite the fact that his father, also named Edward, was a barrister of Lincoln's Inn and his mother stemmed from the Yorkshire gentry. Hawke's father died in 1718 but his mother's brother, Colonel Martin Bladen (a Commissioner of Trade and Plantations from 1717 to 1746) placed his nephew Edward in the Navy as a volunteer in 1720. Hawke passed for lieutenant in 1725 and, after serving on the east coast of North America and in the, then, pestilential West Indies, he was commissioned on 11 April 1729. Promotions ensued, firstly to master and commander in 1733 and then to post captain in 1734. In 1735 he returned to England in command of the *Flamborough* of 20 guns.

Until 1739, when war broke out with Spain over the question of trade in the West Indies, Hawke was on half pay in England. In 1737 he had embarked on his happy marriage with Catharine Brooke. Four of their children would survive infancy—three sons and a daughter.

From the autumn of 1739 to the end of 1742, Hawke commanded the markedly-aging *Portland* (50) in the West Indies. He was engaged in trade protection there, but during two of the annual hurricane seasons he went to Boston to refit his ship. In practice, the enemies which engrossed much of his attention were the tempests and fevers characteristic of the West Indian service. The Spanish privateers worrying the British traders in the area proved most elusive. Early 1743 found Hawke back in England; and it is at this stage that the documents of Part I begin.

Taking into consideration the fact that Hawke not only served the Navy in one capacity or another for half a century, but also commanded in several important campaigns and was finally First Lord of the Admiralty, it was clear that a great deal of relevant material would have to be excluded from a single volume. Therefore in sifting the documents at the Public Record Office and the National Maritime Museum (which holds the main collection of Hawke Papers), and the British Library, the editorial approach was aimed at providing (*a*) useful illustration of every stage of Hawke's career possessing obvious importance; (*b*) a connected sequence of documents for his outstanding campaign of 1759 so that it could be read as a narrative; (*c*) something on his peacetime command at Portsmouth between 1748 and 1754 as a linking period between two wars; and (*d*) finally, documentation of his term as First Lord sufficient to afford a useful conspectus without becoming disproportionate in length. For it can hardly be denied that Hawke was a great commander of fleets in wartime before he was anything else.

In August 1743 Hawke sailed in the *Berwick* (70) for the Mediterranean. At the age of 39 (providing something of a parallel with Nelson at Cape St Vincent half a century later) he was soon to have his first experience of a fleet action and respond, physically and morally, in a highly positive fashion. On 11 February 1744 the emergence of the French and Spanish fleets led to the inconclusive Battle of Toulon. Thomas Mathews[1] tried, with scant success, to bring the Mediterranean Fleet into action against the allies as they headed away southwards in a line ahead. Amid the disorder and poor morale characterizing the British attack, one British captain distinguished himself from the rest. Hawke shrugged off the general fear of breaking the line, heightened in this instance by Mathews's contradictory signals, and bore down to within pistol shot of the nearest oncoming enemy ship. After hot exchanges the *Poder*, a Spanish ship of 64 guns, struck to the *Berwick*. Yet, despite his brave and successful initiative, Hawke was apparently on the verge of being passed over, in 1747, for a flag on the active list. Fortunately King George II refused to allow him to be 'yellowed'. Thanks to his intervention, documents of even greater moment exist for inclusion in Part II of this volume.

In July 1747 Hawke hoisted the flag of a Rear-Admiral of the White as the commanding officer at Plymouth. At this time the Western Squadron represented the Navy's principal strategic and fighting force, but there was no indication that Hawke was likely to join it. The squadron had recently been commanded with success by Anson[2] at what became known as the First Battle of Cape Finisterre. When, in June 1747, Anson became First Lord of the Admiralty, he handed over the Western Squadron to his experienced second-in-command, Sir Peter Warren[3]. Early in August, however, Warren put into Plymouth, suffering from scurvy. He asked for Hawke to be appointed as his second-in-command and, while he was

[1] Mathews: L 1699, C 1703. Distinguished himself at C. Passaro, 1718. After 1724, lived at his family seat and was passed over for his flag. Commissioner at Chatham 1736–42. With France becoming hostile, he was abruptly advanced to VA and c.-in-c., Mediterranean 1742–4 (A 1743). Court-martialled after Battle of Toulon (11.2.44). Cashiered Oct. 1746.

[2] Anson: L 1716, CR 1722, C 1724. Famous circumnavigation, 1740–4. RA 1744, VA 1746, A 1748. A Ld of Ady 1744–51, 1st Ld 1751–6 and 1757–62 (died in office). Successful administrator and strategist. Commanded Western Squadron 1746–7 (winning First Battle of C. Finisterre) and 1758. Baron 1747. Adm. of the Fleet 1761.

[3] Warren: L1723, C 1727. Commodore, Leeward Is., 1744–5. Amassed much prize money. Naval c.-in-c. at taking of Louisbourg, 1745 (RA 1745). Anson's second-in-command at First Finisterre battle, 1747. Made K.B. and VA. Commanded Western Squadron from May 1747 to end of the war in 1748 but, owing to his ill-health, Hawke deputized for him from Aug. 1747 to Feb. 1748.

recovering ashore, as his deputy in command of the Western Squadron. Reluctantly, the Admiralty agreed.

Until 14 October, Hawke duly cruised in the Bay of Biscay, seeking to intercept French shipping. On that day, in the meridian of Cape Finisterre, he intercepted a strongly escorted convoy bound for the West Indies. There ensued a chase action subsequently known as the Second Battle of Cape Finisterre. Of the eight, mostly powerful, French ships of the line covering the convoy, six were captured. It was the crowning and conclusive British sea victory of the war. French naval strength was reduced below what might serve as a basis for recovery. However, France's superiority on the continent of Europe produced a stalemate which, in October 1748, found expression in the Treaty of Aix-la-Chapelle. Meanwhile in consequence of his victory Hawke had been made a Knight of the Bath, promoted to Vice-Admiral of the Blue and, in July 1748, appointed in succession to Warren in the chief command at Portsmouth.

The documents of Part III arise from his time at Portsmouth. Until 1752 his administrative work continued on a fairly continuous basis. After that, there was a marked reduction in general naval activity and, apart from presiding occasionally at courts martial, Hawke was on half pay until the beginning of 1755. Letters to the Admiralty testify to his poor health in 1754—probably attributable to his long service at sea. In any case, he had good reason to meditate on the question of diet and the other likely determinants of health during prolonged cruises.

Problems of manning and health emerge in Part IV(a) where, in 1755, the still-undeclared Seven Years War begins. The documents relating to the war are arranged chronologically in six subdivisions, (a) to (f); and questions of health and food supply receive much illustration during the campaign of 1759, documented in Part IV(e). However, the conclusive victory achieved by Britain over France and Spain, with all its long-term political and cultural consequences for North America and India, was of course due to a considerable list of contributory factors. Important among these were French preoccupation with land warfare in Europe, the limited direct involvement of the British in continental operations, the overwhelming size of the British mercantile marine and the great reserve of experienced seamen which it provided, Britain's financial strength (itself largely derived from trade), and the political influence at Westminster of the merchant class which did much to ensure a level of expenditure on the Navy normally unmatched by France and Spain. Yet, many naval campaigns in this series of French wars illustrate the fact that, even under generally favourable circumstances, a decisive victory at sea could prove very elusive. In 1759, however, such a victory was won on a dark November day in a manner uniquely thrilling, amid the little-known rocks and shoals of a turbulent Quiberon Bay. The battle was the sequel to a tenaciously sustained close blockade of Brest where the French were building up a naval force. This was intended to escort a French army of invasion from Quiberon Bay to western Scotland.

In the perspective of the long series of French wars fought under sail it was, and still is, argued that a more open type of blockade would, in 1759, have been just as effective in preventing invasion while avoiding the wear and tear entailed by a close blockade. Against this, it has been held that a more complete elimination of French trade and seaborne supply was achieved by having the main British battlefleet so persistently stationed, even during the winter months, close to the French ports in the Bay of Biscay; also that the moral effect, together with the lack of exercise at sea imposed upon the French fleet and its many inexperienced seamen, had much to do with the fact that Hawke, confident of his fleet's superior all-round seamanship and gunnery, did not hesitate to pursue the French as they fled into the presumed sanctuary offered on 20 November by a tempestuous and darkening Quiberon Bay. It may at least be certainly concluded that a clear margin of overall superior strength, such as was lacking in the American War, but did exist in the Seven Years War, was an indispensable prerequisite of a policy of close blockade.[1]

Allowing that it is difficult to dissociate the victory at Quiberon from the remarkable blockade that preceded it, credit must go to Anson and the various organs of supply under his ultimate control for overcoming so successfully the difficulties inherent in blockade on a novel scale of duration, intensity and danger. The documents show that Hawke, too, kept a hold on the measures needed to mitigate scurvy, typhus and the other scourges liable to afflict eighteenth-century seamen on a long campaign.

[1] The subject of the 'Blockade of Brest, 1689–1805' has been reconsidered (in English) by A. N. Ryan in Martine Acerra et al. (eds), *Les Marines de Guerre Européennes XVII–XVIIIᵉ siècles* (Paris: Presses de l'Université de Paris-Sorbonne, 1984). Mr Ryan is also editing a new bibliography of British naval history, due in 1993. Meanwhile, for the period treated in this volume, the reader may refer to the relevant chapter in Robin Higham (ed.), *A Guide to the Sources of British Military History* (Berkeley: Univ. of California Press and London: Routledge & Kegan Paul, 1971) and, for a recent bibliography bearing on the Seven Years War, to N. A. M. Rodger, *The Wooden World* (London: Collins, 1986).

While documentation of 1759 occupies much of Part IV, items are supplied for other notable episodes of Hawke's service during the Seven Years War. In Part IV(*b*) will be found his replacement of the unhappy Byng[1] in the Mediterranean in 1756; in (*c*) his role in the inconclusive Rochefort expedition of 1757 may be followed; in (*d*) there are papers concerning his raid on the Basque Roads in 1758 and his subsequent clash with the Admiralty; and then, after the major subsection (*e*) appertaining to 1759, comes (*f*) with documents relating to Hawke's final spells of wartime service in 1760 and 1762.

Lastly, Part V provides documentation of Hawke's term as First Lord of the Admiralty from late 1766 to early 1771. Here the main editorial aim was to provide a balanced overall impression of the business transacted by the Board. In particular, items bearing on the seaworthiness of the ships and their readiness for the next war readily qualified for inclusion. Of Hawke's own performance it should be said that, while he never displayed exceptional administrative ability, he was assiduous in his attendance at the Board;[2] and it can be seen that the documentary record implies no diminution, during his regime, in attention to the work of the Navy Board including the timber problem, in willingness to investigate technical and dietary suggestions, or in a general disposition to act with humanity and good sense.

Towards the end of Hawke's time at the Admiralty, a dispute about the sovereignty of the Falkland Islands dramatically revealed the extent to which the ships laid up in ordinary had been quietly deteriorating. By September 1770 the possibility of war, not only with Spain but with a France bent of naval revenge, was leading to British naval mobilization. However, by early 1771 the Spanish had agreed to withdraw from the islands on the understanding that the sovereignty question was left open and would be discussed on a future occasion. The recent recrudesence, in 1982, of the Falklands question will doubtless add to the interest of the final sequence of documents in Part V.

In January 1771, when the Falklands crisis was already past its peak, Hawke resigned as First Lord on grounds of ill health. In 1776 he was ennobled as Baron Hawke of Towton. He died in 1781. Not only had he been a humane, uncomplicated man but the greatest

---

[1] Byng: L 1732, C 1727, RA 1745. Sat on Mathews's court martial, 1746. VA 1747, A 1756 and c.-in-c., Mediterranean. Abandoned Minorca and, in 1757, was shot on quarterdeck of the *Monarch* (formerly the French *Monarque*, taken by Hawke in 1747).

[2] For details see R. F. Mackay, *Admiral Hawke* (Oxford: Clarendon Press, 1965) p. 324.

naval commander of his generation. At a time of national misfortune, Horace Walpole wrote of his passing: 'Lord Hawke is dead and does not seem to have bequeathed his mantle to anybody'.

PART I

1743–6

SENIOR CAPTAIN:
THE BATTLE OF TOULON AND AFTER

INTRODUCTION

Having completed his spell of four years in West Indian and North American waters, Hawke was appointed in June 1743 to the newly constructed *Berwick* (70)—a considerable advance on the *Portland* (50) which was, indeed, broken up that same year. The *Berwick* lay at Deptford and Hawke was to see that she was manned and provisioned, ostensibly for service in the Channel[1]. However, because Britain had been at war with Spain, while keeping a watchful eye on France, since 1739, manning proved difficult. The documents soon illustrate this [2–7]. They also include Hawke's account of careening at Boston [6]. On board the *Berwick*, the perennial health problem soon comes to the fore [7].

In September Hawke sailed for the Mediterranean in company with the *Dorsetshire* (80). By October Hawke was reporting to her captain (who was senior to him) that his crew was suffering badly from fevers and scurvy [8]. After a spell in Mahon the *Berwick* finally joined Mathews's fleet in Hyères Bay, near Toulon, on 11 January 1744.

Meanwhile France, having been engaged on land in the Austrian Succession War since 1740, was deciding to join forces openly with the Spanish against the British; and by 8 February a combined French and Spanish fleet had set sail from Toulon. In light winds they stood to the southward. On 11 February the partial engagement known as the Battle of Toulon took place. To the professional satisfaction of the historian, if not necessarily of the accused, the battle was eventually followed by a series of courts martial held in England in 1745–6. Of particular interest for the light which they shed on Hawke's conduct during the battle were the trials of Captains Robert Pett and George Sclater, especially the former. The

3

official dispatch of any admiral after a complex engagement, let alone that of Mathews with his concern for self-justification, was unlikely to afford the lively impressions of Hawke's conduct which, with some variation, emerge from the excerpts given from the verbatim evidence. Hawke's own reticence may have been due, at least in part, to characteristic modesty; but he probably did not wish to underline the fact that he must, on his own initiative, have broken the (admittedly disorderly) line of battle [16].

Part I also includes papers relating to Hawke's subsequent service in the Mediterranean. On several occasions he was given command of detached squadrons. This experience would prove valuable when, in 1747, supreme responsibility was suddenly thrust upon him. From August 1744 onwards his orders emanated from a new commander-in-chief in the Mediterranean, Sir William Rowley.[1]

1. *Instructions from the Lords of the Admiralty to Hawke*

15 June 1743

Whereas we have appointed you Captain of His Majesty's Ship the *Berwick* at Deptford, which ship we have ordered to be fitted out for Channel service, manned with her highest complement, victualled with four months' provisions of all species except beer, and of that as much as she can conveniently stow, floored with water, and stored accordingly; you are hereby required and directed to cause all possible diligence to be used in completing her for the sea, and when she shall be in a readiness, you are to proceed with her to Longreach, and having there taken in her guns and gunner's stores, repair to the Nore and remain there till further order, taking care to keep your provisions, stores and water always complete till you proceed to sea.

You are to procure what men you can. Given, etc.

2. *Hawke to Thomas Corbett,*[2] *Secretary of the Admiralty*

Berwick, Deptford
28 June 1743

Sir,

We are making all the dispatch we can in fitting the *Berwick*. I have got Captain Trevor's[3] list of the people turned over on board

---

[1] Rowley: L 1708, C 1716, RA 1743, VA 1744. C.-in-c., Mediterranean, Aug. 1744 to July 1745; censured for his partial conduct of a court of inquiry. A 1747; and a Ld of the Ady 1751–6 and 1757. Adm. of the Fleet 1762.

[2] Corbett: a clerk at the Ady 1715–23; Chief Clerk 1724–8; Deputy Secretary 1728–41; Secretary of the Ady 1741–51.

[3] Trevor: L 1711, C 1732.

of us. As yet only fifty-seven of them have appeared at the Clerk of the Cheque's, and we have but thirty-two out of that number to do any duty on board, and the best part of them came at the latter end of last week. We treat them with all the indulgence that can possibly be allowed, in order to induce them the more readily to come on board to their duty.

We have got the standing rigging overhead and set up. I shall take care to keep everybody employed to fit her as fast as possible.

Hitherto, I have not had it in my power to obey their Lordships' orders in fitting out any tenders, as not having a sufficient number of men for one; but as soon as I can man one and reserve a few men to go on with the fitting the ship, I shall send her out directly, and at the same time shall acquaint you where she is stationed, taking care to observe their Lordships' directions on that head ...

3. *Hawke to Corbett* (holograph)

Berwick, Deptford
7 July 1743

Sir,

I have received your letter of today's date, and in answer to it am to acquaint you that I shall use my utmost endeavours to get the ship to Longreach as soon as possible. We have had but very little assistance from the *Strafford*'s men as yet, they just coming on board to their musters and going away from the ship immediately afterwards; and it was not in our power to prevent it, as the ship lies alongside the hulk. We have not had above twenty of them, one day with another, to do any duty on board.

I have with some difficulty got thirty-one men, including petty officers, on board the tender appointed for us, which I propose sending out on Saturday to the northward, as their Lordships directed, but I intend to send ten men more in her if I can get them in time. I have this day sent a lieutenant and a gang to a rendezvous to procure men. I should have put their Lordships' orders in execution before in regard to sending out a tender and appointing a rendezvous had it been in my power, but it was not; and I have not slipped any opportunity of forwarding the ship as much as was in my power. She is almost rigged and we shall not lose a moment's time in fitting of her; and I am likewise to acquaint you that we are ready to receive the Marines whenever their Lordships shall please to order them on board. I am etc.

4.   *Hawke to Corbett*

Berwick, Deptford
20 July 1743

Sir,

I beg you will be pleased to acquaint their Lordships that the Marines were brought on board last Friday. They all seem to be very likely young fellows and are well clothed. I have not yet received any account from the lieutenant who went out in the tender; and, as to my lieutenant who went out in the tender; and, as to my lieutenant who is at the rendezvous, he tells me that seamen are very scarce in and about London, and that most of the men who enter voluntary with him are landmen.

We go on in fitting the ship as fast as possible, and have got on board our ground tier and cables, and are now getting off our anchors and officers' stores. And she will be ready to fall down to Longreach by the middle of next week, when the tide will fall out right to carry her down. I am etc.

5.   *Hawke to Corbett*

Berwick, Longreach
29 July 1743

Sir,

I have your letter of the 27th instant with their Lordships' order of the same date and shall punctually observe them both to the best of my power.

I am extremely concerned that their Lordships should think me in any way dilatory in fitting out the ship. I can assure them very faithfully that I have not been wanting in using my best endeavours with the men that I have had, and hope their Lordships will not believe me to be so very inactive if they will do me the favour to reflect that one cannot keep one's men on board at Deptford as at Chatham, so consequently can't fit the ship so soon, and that this has been the case with other officers before me who have fitted at Deptford, and who undoubtedly would have been as much pleased as myself to have had it in their power to have complied strictly with their Lordships' commands. I shall take all the care I possibly can that none of the pressed men deserts, and shall not be wanting in my endeavours to get the ship to the Nore with all the dispatch I can, and shall discharge the gunner agreeable to their Lordships' orders of yesterday's date. I shall continue to lie on board. I am etc.

P.S.   Our lower deck guns will not be ready to be shipped off for us before tomorrow. They have not wanted for timely notice.

Minute: Answers a complaint of his being dilatory in fitting the ship.

6.   *Hawke to Corbett*

Berwick, Nore
22 August 1743

Sir,

I beg you will be pleased to acquaint their Lordships that, the wind coming fair this morning, we got under sail immediately and arrived at the Nore about 2 o'clock this afternoon, and moored the ship, and discharged the pilot with the Yacht's men, and the tender belonging to the Regulating Captain.

This afternoon the Clerk of the Cheque sent me off both your letters of the 19th instant with the four several orders of their Lordships ... In the order [of the 16th] I am directed to proceed with the ships under my command and the tender to Spithead, as soon as she should arrive. She is come to the Nore this night and has brought me thirty pressed men ... I shall take care strictly to observe their Lordships' order of the 20th not to impress any seamen out of ships coming from the Mediterranean.

In answer to your letter of the 19th in regard to the careening of ships at Boston in New England, I am to acquaint you that the method we took to clean the *Portland* was by hauling her to the end of a wharf where we secured the ship by shoring of her quarter and bow, and the middle part of her with spur shores from the whales of the ship to the wharf. There is but one wharf where this can be done (which is called White's Wharf). At the other wharves the water don't come high enough to them to permit a ship of that burthen to lie alongside of them. But even the cleaning [of] a ship at this place must be done with great caution by securing of her in such a manner before it's high water, that neither her head nor her stern may run the risk of breaking loose when the tide of ebb sets down. For should this happen, the ship in all likelihood may break her back, her head being aground at half ebb and her stern in seven fathoms of water, if she should swing off. And I am to observe that no ship so big as a 50 should attempt to lay ashore here unless she is a long full-floored ship, as the *Portland* was. There is no wharves for heaving of ships down at Boston; and if they have a mind to do it, it must be done by vessels according to the ship's burthen. As to 20-gun ships, they generally haul ashore there on the Ways, which is a fine long beach where the tide leaves them dry.

All sorts of stores are very dear there, excepting masts of all kinds, pitch, tar, and turpentine. They have numbers of warehouses that can be hired at any time to lodge a ship's stores in ...

But though we made a shift to clean there in the *Portland*, I think no ship bigger than one of our 40-gun ships should clean there, now they being bigger than what they were formerly ...

7. *Hawke to Corbett*

Berwick, Nore
23 August 1743

Sir,

... I beg their Lordships' permission to acquaint them that among the pressed men sent me down by the Regulating Captains, there are several of them very little, puny, weakly fellows that have never been at sea and, I think any officer must allow, can be of little or no service. The reason why I did not complain of them before was because I was willing to get the ship to the Nore as soon as the winds offered fair. This is likewise the case with regard to the men that are come from the *Princess Royal*, there being several of them poor little sickly fellows that are of no service and are more properly to be termed boys than men; and though a few of these are serviceable aboard a ship, yet a number of them distress a large ship like this greatly; and, what is worse, most of these poor creatures are now sick. But I shall not presume to put them on shore, unless their Lordships will be so good as to give me leave. But there are several of them that, should they stay on board, will breed a sickness in the ship. I beg their Lordships will be so kind as to permit me to send the sick men to the hospital.

I beg their Lordships' pardon for mentioning this affair, but I thought it my duty to do it, for when a ship is so very badly manned, she can be but of very little or no service. I am etc.

8. *Hawke to Captain George Burrish[1] of the DORSETSHIRE*

Berwick at sea
27 October 1743

Sir,

The surgeon of His Majesty's Ship the *Berwick* under my command has this morning acquainted me that we have 123 working men ill. Out of that number, eighty-four have fevers. Six or eight of these are dangerously ill. The rest of them are mostly troubled with the scurvy. The greatest part of these men fell ill since we left Gibraltar, particularly within these two or three nights past; and, what is worse, the men falling ill by tens and twenties every day, we have too great reason to fear it will go quite through the ship's company.

We can no ways account for the men falling ill so fast, otherwise than that a great number of them are lately come from the East Indies and others of them are raw men, picked up by the press gangs in London, and are poor puny fellows; and the ship being new and green is consequently damp, notwithstanding all my endeavours to keep her clean and dry, which I have taken care to do ever since we

---

[1] Burrish: L 1726, C 1733. Court-martialled after Battle of Toulon and cashiered (1745).

have been out ...

I am therefore to beg you will be pleased to consider whether it will be most for the service to make the best of our way to Mahon by our orders, there to put our sick people on shore, or to continue with you. Whichever it is, I shall be satisfied, as I am sensible you will do for the best, and I beg that you will be persuaded that I am, etc.

[For Hawke's conduct at the Battle of Toulon on 11 February 1743/4, see Document 16 below.]

9. *Line of Battle*

Berwick in Hyères Road
9 July 1744

The *Rupert* to lead with the starboard and the *Stirling Castle* with the larboard tacks on board.

Rates	Ships	Guns	Commanders
4	*Rupert*	60	Capt. John Ambrose[1]
3	*Burford*	70	Richd. Watkins[2]
3	*Cambridge*	80	Chas. Drummond[3]
3	*Berwick*	70	Ed. Hawke
3	*Bedford*	70	Hon. Geo. Townshend[4]
4	*Dunkirk*	60	Chas. Purvis[5]
3	*Stirling Castle*	70	Tho. Cooper[6]

[1] Ambrose: L 1728, C 1734. Cashiered in 1745 but soon restored. Superannuated RA 1750.
[2] Watkins: CR 1741, C 1743. Superannuated RA 1763.
[3] Drummond: L 1711, C 1736. Superannuated RA 1747.
[4] Townshend: L 1736?, C 1739. In 1745 (like Hawke before him) he was detached in command of a squadron on the Italian coast. Again a commodore in the Mediterranean, he was court-martialled in 1747 and reprimanded for irresolution off Corsica. Commodore and c.-in-c., Jamaica, 1748–52. RA 1755 and again c.-in-c., Jamaica, 1755–7. This ended his active service. VA 1758, A 1765.
[5] Purvis: L 1735, C 1740. Superannuated RA 1756.
[6] Cooper: L 1719, CR 1735, C 1738. Effective as commodore off Genoa 1745. Commissioner at Chatham 1755–61.

10.   *Line of Battle*

Berwick [off Toulon]
17 July 1744

The *Royal Oak* to lead with the starboard and the *Dunkirk* with the larboard tacks on board.

Rates	Ships	Guns	Commanders
3	*Royal Oak*	70	Capt. Edmd. Williams[1]
4	*Romney*	50	Hen. Godslave[2]
3	*Cambridge*	80	Chas. Drummond
3	*Berwick*	70	Ed. Hawke
3	*Princessa*	70	Robt. Pett[3]
3	*Kingston*	60	John Lovett[4]
4	*Dunkirk*	60	Chas. Purvis

11.   *Instructions from Rowley to Hawke*

Torbay in Mahon Harbour
11 January 1744/5

You are hereby required and directed to take under your command His Majesty's Ships named in the margin [*Royal Oak, Nassau, Leopard, Lowestoft*], whose captains have directions to follow your orders, and proceed towards the coast of Italy, and so off Cape delle Melle, without loss of time in order to join and take under your command His Majesty's Ships the *Dartmouth, Chatham,* and *Antelope* which are cruising that way; which as soon as you have done, you are to deliver my enclosed orders to Captain Crookshanks,[5] who is thereby directed to leave that station and join me with the utmost expedition with any packets he may have for me from Mr Villettes,[6] His Majesty's Resident at the Court of Turin, or Mr Birtles,[7] His Majesty's Consul at Genoa; as likewise to bring me

[1] Williams: L 1708, C 1734. Court-martialled and placed on half pay 1745, but later superannuated RA.

[2] Godslave: L 1738, CR 1740, C 1741. Superannuated RA 1756.

[3] Pett: L 1727, C 1740. Court-martialled in 1745 but acquitted. Commissioner of the Victualling (at Plymouth, 1759).

[4] Lovett: L 1734, CR 1741, C 1741.

[5] Crookshanks: L 1734, C 1742. Cashiered in 1747 for failing to engage the Spanish *Glorioso* (74) which was taken by others after a series of actions.

[6] Villettes: British Resident at Turin 1741–9; British Minister at Berne 1749–62.

[7] Birtles: British Consul in Genoa in the 1740s and 1750s.

particular accounts with the best intelligence he can get of the disposition and progress of the French and Spanish troops on the coast of Genoa ...

You are with the force under your command to annoy and, to the extent of your power, endeavour to destroy the French and Spanish troops, together with any magazines that may be lodged within any towns, villages, or passes belonging to the Republic of Genoa's territories ...

And whereas I have given Captain Crookshanks orders to intercept all vessels laden with ammunition, stores, and provisions going to Genoa (should the French and Spaniards be marching along their coast or in possession of any of their towns), you are hereby required and directed, on seizing any such vessels so loaded as aforesaid to send them under such convoy as you shall judge proper to this port ...

12. *Line of Battle*

Berwick in Vado Bay
29 January 1744/5

The *Royal Oak* to lead with the starboard and the *Chatham* with the larboard tacks on board.

Rates	Ships	Guns	Commanders
3	*Royal Oak*	70	Capt. Edmd. Williams
4	*Antelope*	50	Arthur Scott[1]
3	*Berwick*	70	Edwd. Hawke
4	*Leopard*	50	Lord Colville[2]
3	*Nassau*	70	Essex Holcombe[3]
4	*Chatham*	50	James Young[4]

[1] Scott: L 1739, C 1743. Commissioner at Chatham 1754–5. An Extra Commissioner 1755–6.

[2] Colville: L 1739, C 1734. Commodore at Halifax 1757 and 1760–2. RA 1762.

[3] Holcombe: L 1730, C 1740. Superannuated RA 1755.

[4] Young: L 1739, CR 1742, C 1743. Commanded *Intrepid* which, when damaged in the action off Minorca in 1756, was said by Byng to have hampered the rear division. Served at Rochefort in 1757 and off Brest in 1759. As commodore, commanded the rear division at Quiberon Bay. RA 1762, VA 1770. C.-in-c., Leeward Is. 1775–8. A 1778.

13.   *Rowley to Hawke*

Torbay, Mahon Harbour
9 February 1744/5

Sir,

I received your letter dated 31st January last, in Vado Bay, and I am very glad to hear your squadron are in good health and in good order, as that will always give me the greatest pleasure, though you have not been so fortunate as to meet with any of the enemy's ships or embarkations.

Captain Crookshanks and the *Roebuck* arrived here yesterday.

I very much approve of your resolution of going towards Villafranca to endeavour to intercept the embarkations that I have an account are daily going there. I would never have you above four or five days from your station; but govern yourself as the wind blows to run backwards and forwards, and sometimes stretch out eight or ten leagues to sea, keeping your ships when the weather will permit two or three leagues asunder, as they may make a better stretch and your number be not known.

By the best intelligence I can get, there is but two men of war at Toulon fit to go to sea,[1] but notwithstanding that, I recommend to you to keep a very good look-out that you are not surprised on the coast. By keeping your cruisers out, you may gain intelligence by ships coming up, if any of them are coming up the Straits.

You may depend upon my keeping a watchful eye over the enemy's ships and sending you timely notice of what passes ...

14.   *Hawke to Rowley*

Berwick off Cape de Noli
23 February 1744/5

Sir,

... I sailed from Vaya Bay the 3rd instant and run down as low as Antibes, and sent Captain Young in the *Chatham* to look into that port and Villafranca where he saw a great number of small vessels in each, by which I should judge the embarkation was got into those places, if there was ever any such thing designed ... The weather has

---

[1] After 1744 the French government embarked on a major diversion of funds from the navy to the army. Once the idea of invading England in concert with a Jacobite rising had been abandoned, it was decided not to maintain a large battle-ready fleet. See E. H. Jenkins, *A History of the French Navy* (London: Macdonald and Jane's, 1973) p.113.

been so extremely bad ...

This afternoon, seeing four sail of ships in the offing and believing them to be Frenchmen, I gave chase to them with the ships that were nearest to me, two of my squadron being then becalmed inshore. So soon as we got near enough to make them plain, they made the signal to us, upon which I made the signal to speak with them, not knowing what news or intelligence they might have got that was proper for me to know; and the wind being at that time against them, I believed you would pardon my taking that freedom ...

15. *Hawke to Rowley*

Berwick off Cape delle Melle
5 March 1744/5

Sir,

... It's currently reported at Genoa that Captain Ambrose has taken a prize off Cape St Vincent worth upwards of an hundred thousand pounds.

We spoke with a Dutch ship some time ago, who told us that seven sail of French men of war were gone from Cadiz to the West Indies. The *Northumberland*[1] was one, and went commodore. The rest of the French ships, he said, went for Brest but were to put into Lisbon, if they learnt we had any squadron cruising in the Bay of Biscay.

I am not all sorry that you are so good as to say you will relieve me soon, for we have scarcely had anything else but a constant series of bad weather since we have been upon this station, which has rendered us incapable of doing anything material for the service. However, until it shall be your pleasure to do so, I am perfectly well satisfied and shall always be, in obeying your commands, if I can only be so happy as to execute them agreeable to your pleasure.

My brother officers make great complaints to me of the badness of their sails and rigging. To speak truth, though most of the ships' sails were new that were bent to their yards when we came out, yet we have split them over and over again and reeved so much rope that we have now no more to reeve, which has partly been owing to the sails and rope being very bad, as well as to the weather.

Captain Holcombe acquainting me by letter that his boatswain was dead and desiring that I would appoint someone in his room, I

---

[1] The *Northumberland* was a ship of 70 guns captured by the French in 1744.

gave an order to my best boatswain's mate (who was a boy with me
under Captain Durrell[1] in the *Scarborough*) to act as boatswain of
her till you should think to appoint whom you should think proper.
I am in hopes, if his captain should give him a good character, it will
in some measure entitle him to your favour, men of that profession
being very scarce that are good for anything ...

16.   *Court Martial of Captain Robert Pett of the PRINCESSA,
President Sir Chaloner Ogle,[2] aboard the PRINCE OF ORANGE,*

Deptford
November 1745

[From September 1745 Hawke had been kept available to give
evidence at the long series of courts martial arising from the Battle of
Toulon, fought in January of the previous year. The series ended
only in October 1746 when Mathews himself was cashiered. In the
event, Hawke was called in evidence only at the trial of Robert Pett
who was acquitted.]

1st day, 19 November 1745
Captain Tom,[3] late lieutenant of the *Norfolk*, called in and sworn ...
Q. [by prosecutor]   How soon did the *Berwick* engage the *Poder*
after the admiral bore down, and did the *Berwick* engage nearer than
the *Princessa* and *Somerset* had done?
A.   I can't recollect, but the *Berwick* engaged the *Poder* some
time after the *Norfolk* left off firing. The *Berwick* went down to
leeward to the *Poder* and went close under her stern, and went up
again on his lee side and hauled his wind upon her lee bow, and there
engaged her till her main mast fell and her fore topmast, I believe ...

2nd day, 21 November 1745
James Moore, master of the *Norfolk*, called in and sworn ...
Q.   How soon did the *Berwick* engage the *Poder* after the admiral
bore down and did the *Berwick* engage nearer than the *Princessa* and

---

¹ Durrell (or Durell): C 1720 in which year Hawke served with him as a volunteer in
the West Indies. As a lieutenant Hawke was again with him in 1732, this time aboard
the *Scarborough* (24) on the N. American station. In 1740 Durrell shared in the
capture of the *Princesa* (the *Princessa* of Document 10). He died later in that year.
² Ogle: L 1702, CR 1703, C 1708 and took prizes in the Mediterranean. Knighted in
1723 for operations against N. African pirates. RA 1739, c.-in-c., West Indies 1742–5.
VA 1743, A 1747. Adm. of the Fleet 1749.
³ Tom: L 1732, CR 1745. Though never posted captain, he is correctly addressed as
'Captain Tom' here, by virtue of having been given a small command. The *rank* of
commander was not established till 1794.

Somerset had done?

A. The *Berwick* was not above an hour engaged with the *Poder*, if so much. She engaged nearer than the *Princessa* and *Somerset* had done, for she engaged her close on board that a stone might be thrown on board from the one to the other.

Q. Did the *Poder* strike to the *Berwick* because she engaged her much nearer than the other ships had done?

A. Yes, I believe so.

Q. What ships engaged the *Poder* on the 11th February?

A. The *Princessa, Somerset,*[1] *Dragon, Bedford, Berwick*, and I believe the *Kingston* fired some shot at her, but not near enough ...

4th day, 25 November 1745

The Prisoner was brought in by the marshal, and the witnesses ordered to be called in.

Captain Watson[2] of the *Dragon* called in and sworn ...

Q. Did the *Poder* strike to the *Berwick* because she engaged her much nearer than the other ships had done?

A. I cannot think that entirely because the ship was a great deal disabled in my opinion before the *Berwick* bore down ...

Captain Hawke of the *Berwick* called in and sworn ...

Q. How soon did the *Berwick* engage the *Poder* after the admiral bore down? And did the *Berwick* engage nearer than the *Princessa* and *Somerset* had done?

A. We engaged the *Poder* about two hours. We had her fire half an hour before we bore down close to her. We began to engage her close about 2 o'clock or a little after, and continued to engage her till about ¼ after 4 before she struck. When she first fired at us, she was upon our quarter. I don't know whether she [the *Berwick*] engaged nearer than the *Princessa* and *Somerset* had done. The *Princessa* appeared to me to engage her very near, but whether as near as us, I can't say. We engaged her very close at last ...

Q. What ship of the enemy might be opposed to you before you engaged the *Poder*?

A. The *Neptune*[3] as I took her to be.

---

[1] The *Somerset* was commanded by George Sclater who, like Robert Pett, was tried in 1745 and acquitted.

[2] Watson: L 1735, C 1738. Commanded the *Princess Louisa* (60) at both Finisterre battles in 1747. RA 1748 and c.-in-c., Newfoundland and N. America. C.-in-c., E. Indies (on Hawke's refusal) 1754–7. VA 1756. Co-operated with Clive in 1757 but died on 16 Aug.

[3] The *Neptune* (70) would be taken by Hawke's squadron on 14 Oct. 1747.

Q.   Did you never engage with her or any other ship but the *Poder*?

A.   Yes, we engaged with the *Neptune* ahead of her and had part of the fire of a French ship ahead of her. When we first brought up, we had the *Neptune* abreast of us and the French ships ahead of us upon our bow, and as they shot ahead the *Poder* came up ...

Q.   I suppose the *Poder* shot ahead of the *Somerset* and those ships nearer the *Namur* [Admiral Mathews] when you engaged her?

A.   Yes, she came up to us.

Q.   What were those ships between you and the *Somerset*?

A.   The *Kingston, Bedford, Dragon,* and *Somerset.*

Q.   When the *Princessa* first began to engage the *Poder* before you hauled up in a line of battle, or just as you were about doing it, where were those four ships you mention?

A.   Bearing down with us.

Q.   Then from the time the *Princessa* left off engaging the *Poder* till you began to engage her, what were those ships adoing?

A.   I don't know because I did not make it my observation ...

PART II

JULY 1747–JULY 1748

THE SECOND BATTLE OF CAPE FINISTERRE

INTRODUCTION

In May 1747 the Western Squadron under Anson had overwhelmed the comparatively weak escort of a joint (French) Canada-bound and eastbound convoy. The convoy escaped. The French then set about preparing a much stronger escort for a convoy to sail from Rochelle to the West Indies.

Meanwhile Hawke's sudden removal from Plymouth to effective command of the Western Squadron is recorded [19–22]. In view of the minimal instructions addressed by the Lords to Hawke personally [21], there was a *prima facie* risk that he might not report his proceedings directly to the Admiralty. The risk became a certainty when the unwell Warren apparently misunderstood their Lordships' instructions to him on this subject. [22] He held such wide powers [23] that Hawke could hardly question the order to report directly to Warren [23–4]; and he duly complied [27, 29–30]. The dangers became apparent before long. [28]

Despite the conclusive nature of Hawke's victory on 14 October, the occasion was marked by yet another court martial. Hawke found he had no choice but to ask for the trial of Thomas Fox [49], a senior captain, for 'misconduct and misbehaviour' during the battle. The evidence is of outstanding historical interest, not least through its being given so soon after the event—much sooner, for instance, than that relating to the Battle of Toulon. One feature was that several of Fox's fellow captains, conscious of the fact that they had initiated the process of accusation [39a], thought it appropriate to place their view of his conduct against their own picture of the battle as a whole. In consequence, there survives much verbatim evidence about the development of the action, Hawke's personal role, and the conduct of a number of his captains. The extant body of evidence about

21

Hawke's more dramatic victory in 1759 is not at all comparable. Two courts martial were necessarily held on captains who had lost their ships, but they were relatively perfunctory.

It emerges especially from the minutes of Fox's trial that, even if Hawke had been unexpectedly and fortuitously appointed to command the squadron, all his captains, with the apparent exception of Fox, went into battle fully expecting that 'every man' would (as on a later occasion) 'do his duty'. The contrast with the confusion and indecisiveness seen at the Battle of Toulon could hardly be more striking. The tactical sequence of chase, then line, then chase again, followed by the signal for a close engagement, resembled that of Anson's victory the previous May. It was admirably designed to overcome L'Etenduère's close-hauled defensive line because a sufficient number of the pursuing British ships could, by dint of superior seamanship, get to windward of the enemy. Then the French were caught successively, from rear to van, in a devastating cross-fire as the individually less powerful British ships overtook them. It is doubtless significant that, on 21 August, Hawke was already contemplating use of the chase, if a force amounting to 'an enemy's fleet' was encountered. [29]

As for the convoy, Hawke's action in sending the *Weasel* sloop to the West Indies [39] contributed to the capture of a considerable number of the French merchantmen on that station.

The court martial having been completed on 21 December, Hawke was available for another cruise. On 8 January 1748 he sailed from Spithead wearing his flag in the *Kent*; and he was soon cruising with seven of the line in the western approaches to France and Spain. By the 22nd Warren was sufficiently recovered to be able to take over the chief seagoing command. The main feature of the cruise was the absence of any significant enemy movements by sea. Therefore no space has been given to the relevant records which are naturally of a repetitive kind. Having persisted at sea through the winter and beyond, Warren and Hawke finally anchored with the squadron at Spithead on 24 July 1748.

17. *Instructions from the Lords of the Admiralty to Hawke*

17 July 1747

By the Lords Commissioners ... to Edward Hawke, Esq, Rear-Admiral of the White, Plymouth.

Whereas you will herewith receive a commission appointing you Rear-Admiral of the White Squadron of His Majesty's Fleet, you are hereby required and directed to hoist your flag on board such ship of His Majesty at Plymouth as you shall judge proper and to give all necessary orders for the dispatch of His Majesty's ships that come into that port, or are already there under orders for fitting or refitting, till farther order. Given etc.

B[EDFORD][1]
A[NSON]
B[ARRINGTON][2]

18. *Hawke to Corbett*

Plymouth Dock
21 July 1747

Sir,

Be pleased to acquaint the Lords Commissioners of the Admiralty that I have this day the honour of their Lordships' orders of the 17th and 18th instant and, in obedience thereto, intend to hoist my flag tomorrow morning on board the *Gloucester*, Captain Philip Durell,[3] when I shall take care to observe and follow every part relating to that order, as well as to dispose of the Deal men on board of the *Eagle*, Captain Rodney,[4] in His Majesty's ships that are going to sea. I am etc.

[1] John Russell succeeded his brother as Duke of Bedford in 1732. He joined Carteret in opposition to Sir Robert Walpole. On Carteret's retirement, joined the ministry led by Henry Pelham and, in 1744–8, was an active and successful 1st Ld of the Ady. Sec. of State (southern dept) 1748–51. Until his death in 1771, he remained an important politician with a following.

[2] William Wildman, 2nd Viscount Barrington: a Ld of the Ady 1746–9 and 1754.

[3] Philip Durell: L 1731, C 1742, RA 1758 and Saunders's second-in-command at Quebec 1759. VA 1762.

[4] Rodney: L 1740, C 1742, RA 1759 and bombarded invasion craft at Le Havre. C.-in-c., Leeward Is. 1761–3: reduced Martinique, captured St Lucia, Grenada and St Vincent. VA 1762 and baronet 1764. MP 1751–5 and 1759–74; he ruined himself by

19. *Instructions from Hawke to John Hay*[1]

29 July 1747

[Hawke usually kept full copies of the orders issued by him as a flag officer. This early example is given entire, partly to illustrate the form which he would normally follow, and partly because of the curiosity that it is addressed to John Hay. Hawke's newly acquired and subsequently notorious secretary, using the standard form 'By command of the Admiral', is issuing the order to himself.]

By Edward Hawke, Esq., Rear-Admiral of the White, etc.

By virtue of the power and authority to me granted by the Right Honourable the Lords Commissioners for executing the office of Lord High Admiral of Great Britain and Ireland to call and assemble courts martial as often as it shall be necessary, and also, in the absence of the Judge Advocate of His Majesty's Fleet and his Deputy, to order some fit person to officiate in their room; you are hereby empowered and directed to take upon you the office of Deputy Judge Advocate to administer oaths and take the affadavits of the evidences in support of a charge exhibited against Lieutenant Cope of His Majesty's sloop *Fly*, to inform the court, prosecute the person to be tried in His Majesty's name, and to attend at the said court martial for the more orderly proceeding of the same. And for so doing, this shall be your order.

Given under my hand on board His Majesty's ship *Mars* in Hamoaze the 29th July 1747.

E.H.

To Mr John Hay, hereby appointed
to act as Deputy Judge Advocate
    By command of the Admiral,

        J.H.

spending some £30,000 on an election of 1768. Adm. in 1778. Again c.-in-c., Leeward Is 1780–2. On the way out, crushed Langara's squadron and relieved Gibraltar. Defeated French under Comte de Grasse off Dominica at Battle of the Saints 1782, and was made a baron. (See David Spinney, *Rodney* (London: Allen & Unwin, 1969); also Rodger, *Wooden World*, pp. 323–7.)
  [1] Hay: Purser. Hawke's secretary 1747, 1755–9, 1760–2. Augustus Hervey saw him (in July 1756) as a spiteful man—'a dirty secretary whom Sir Edward was ever cursed with'. Indeed, in 1777 Hay attempted to blackmail the Admiral. (See Mackay, *Hawke*, pp. 339–42.)

20.   *Hawke to Corbett*

Plymouth Dock
31 July 1747

Sir,

Captain Durell sailed the 29th in the forenoon. The same day, Captain Cookson[1] arriving in the *Fly*, I gave directions for a court martial to be held on his lieutenant, agreeable to their Lordships' orders, and have appointed Mr John Hay of this place to act as Deputy Judge Advocate ...

21.   *Instructions from the Lords of the Admiralty to Hawke*

5 August 1747
By the Lords Commissioners ... to Rear-Admiral Hawke,
Plymouth,
per express ¼ past 7 p.m.

You are hereby required and directed to put yourself under the command of Sir Peter Warren, Knight of the Bath, Vice-Admiral of the White Squadron of His Majesty's Fleet, and follow his orders for your farther proceedings. Given etc.

A[NSON]
B[ARRINGTON]
D[UNCANNON][2]

22.   *Instructions from the Lords of the Admiralty to Warren*

5 August 1747
By the Lords Commissioners ... to Sir Peter Warren, Plymouth,
per express at ¼ past 7 p.m.

Having ordered Rear-Admiral Hawke to put himself under your command, we do hereby require and direct you to take him under your command accordingly and order him to proceed with His Majesty's ships named ... to the ships you have left cruising in the Bay of Biscay and put into execution such orders as you shall think proper to give him, he sending us constant accounts of his proceedings. Given etc.

---

[1] Cookson: L 1739, CR 1747. 'Captain Cookson' was never posted. From 1743 there was a list of commanders for purposes of seniority but not of pay or half pay. (Daniel Baugh (ed.), *Naval Administration 1715–1750*, N.R.S. vol. 120 (1977) pp. 41–2). See also Part I, n.27 above.

[2] Duncannon: Politician. MP 1742–58. A Ld of Ady 1746–56.

A[NSON]
B[ARRINGTON]
D[UNCANNON]

23. *Instructions from Warren to Hawke*

Yarmouth in Plymouth Sound
8 August 1747

By Sir Peter Warren, Knight of the Bath, Vice-Admiral of the White Squadron of His Majesty's Fleet, commander-in-chief of a squadron of His Majesty's ships and vessels employed in the Channel, in the Soundings, or wherever else His Majesty's service shall require.

Pursuant to an order from the Right Honourable the Lords Commissioners of the Admiralty bearing date the 5th instant, directing you should serve in the squadron under my command; you are hereby required and directed according, to put yourself under my command and follow all such orders as you shall from time to time receive from me for His Majesty's service, sending me weekly accounts of the state and condition of the squadron and acquainting me with your proceedings, as often as opportunity offers, for their Lordships' information. For which this shall be your warrant. Given etc.

P. WARREN

24. *Further Instructions from Warren to Hawke*

Yarmouth in Plymouth Sound
8 August 1747

[These instructions closely reflect those issued by the Admiralty to Warren on 20 July 1747. Warren duly supplied Hawke with a copy of the latter on 8 August.]

Whereas the Right Honourable the Lords Commissioners of the Admiralty have been pleased, by their commission and instructions bearing date 20th July last, to put His Majesty's ships named in the list hereunto annexed under my command to form a squadron as well to oppose and frustrate the designs of the enemy, as to protect the trade of His Majesty's subjects; and whereas their Lordships have thought proper by their instructions to me dated the 5th August 1747 that you should serve under me in the said squadron, and that I should be employed for the present in dispatching such of them as are now fitting at Portsmouth, Plymouth, or elsewhere, in order to my joining you with them, or to their being sent to you as soon as may be.

You are therefore hereby required and directed to take all the ships in the beforementioned annexed list under your command ... and whereas the ships named in the margin [*Monmouth, Windsor, Hunter* dogger, tender] are ready to proceed to sea and others will soon be so, both from this port and Portsmouth, and that [the *Prince Frederick, Augusta, Centurion, Gloucester, Portland, Amazon, Viper* sloop] are now cruising in the Bay (according to the rendezvous here given you) for four East India ships and two men of war, which I had intelligence were preparing to sail from Port Lorient. You are therefore to hoist your flag for the present on board any ship of the squadron that you shall think proper and proceed with all such of them as are ready at this port, or that you may meet at sea or elsewhere, and join those in the Bay without loss of time, and cruise diligently with the said ships, or so many of them as you shall judge proper, on such station or stations as shall be most expedient for protecting the trade of His Majesty's subjects and also, according to good intelligence, for meeting with, intercepting, and destroying the convoys of the enemy, outward and homeward bound, for suppressing their privateers, and annoying their commerce as much as possible.

You are, for their Lordships' information, to give me as frequent accounts as you can conveniently of your proceedings, and when you shall think it at any time proper to alter the rendezvous according to any intelligence you can procure, which you are at liberty to do, to leave one of your sailing frigates or sloops at the rendezvous which you shall go from, in order to her acquainting any ship or ships which may be sent to join you where you are most likely to be found; and also, when you have an opportunity, to let me know upon what station or stations you intend to cruise, for my keeping a correspondence with you and reinforcing the squadron with clean ships.

You are at liberty to send detachments from you, whenever you judge it necessary, to cruise on separate stations for the better meeting with the ships of the enemy and to give their commanders such orders as you think proper for that purpose.

You are also at liberty to send such ships of your squadron as shall be foul or sickly into port and to order their captains to return to you, or act otherwise, as you shall judge best for His Majesty's service.

You are to continue at sea so long as your provisions and water will last, or as you shall judge necessary for His Majesty's service, according to what intelligence you shall get of the enemy, and then return into port with all or part of your squadron, proceeding with all those above the fourth rate to Portsmouth and sending such of the rest as you think fit into Plymouth, and to leave orders with those which you shall keep at sea or send thither after your coming into port to cruise diligently on such station as you shall judge best for His Majesty's service. For which this shall be your order. Given etc.

P. WARREN

You will please to observe that such ships as you may have occasion to send in, that do not want fitting or cleaning and are only to boot-hose-top and victual, are to do it in Plymouth Sound and then join you again if you find it necessary, giving me an account of their proceedings for their Lordships' information.

Enclosure:

24a.   LIST OF THE SQUADRON AND THE TIME LAST CLEANED

[This list is copied from one sent to Warren by the Admiralty on 20 July 1747.]

Rates	Ships	Guns	When last cleaned	Rates	Ships	Guns	When last cleaned
2	St George	90	3 April 47	4	Centurion	54	29 May 47
2	Prince George	90		4	Bristol	50	30
3	Devonshire	66	16 March 46	4	Oxford	50	
3	Yarmouth	64	19	4	Gloucester	50	July
3	Edinburgh	64	17	4	Portland	50	12
3	Monmouth	64	30 May 47	5	Ambuscade	40	23 May
3	Prince Frederick	64	29	5	Hector	44	
3	Kent	64		6	Amazon	24	28 July 47
3	Hampton Court	64		6	Siren	24	15 April
4	Nottingham	60	15 March 46	6	Grand Turk	20	Aug. in dock
4	Defiance	60	17	6	Inverness	24	
4	Windsor	60	28 May 47	6	Shoreham	24	
4	Princess Louisa	60	15 March 46	6	Bellona	30	11 July 47
4	Augusta	60	31 May 47	Sloop	Viper	10/14	
4	Eagle	60	27 July	Sloop	Weasel	10/18	
4	Lion	60		Sloop	Falcon	10/14	
4	Falkland	50		Fire	Vulcan	6/8	7 April 47
4	Hampshire	50		Ships	Dolphin	6/8	

ANNEXED TO THE INSTRUCTIONS

The rendezvous is between the latitudes of Belle Isle and Ushant, from ten to thirty or forty leagues to the westward.

Given under my hand on board His Majesty's ship *Yarmouth* in Plymouth Sound, the 8th August 1747.

P. WARREN

25. *Hawke to Corbett*

Windsor, Plymouth Sound
10 August 1747

Sir,

I have received your letters of the 5th and 6th instant and delivered them with everything else relating to the service to Mr Vanbrugh,[1] except what relates to the court martial, which I have left with Captain Watson, as I propose sailing this evening if the wind will permit me, in pursuance to the orders I have received from Sir Peter Warren [now on his way to Portsmouth]. I have hoisted my flag on board the *Windsor* and shall take with me the *Monmouth* and *Hunter* dogger, in order to make the best of my way to join the ships that are cruising to the westward. I am etc.

P.S.   If their Lordships should please to order me any particular ship to hoist my flag on board of, I hope they will indulge me with Mr Bladen of the *Edinburgh* to be, with Mr Hobbs[2] of the *Mars*, my lieutenant.

Minute: 12 August. Own receipt and let him know the Lords will have due regard to his requests when a ship is appointed

26. *Instructions from Hawke to Lieutenant John Lendrick*[3]

Windsor at sea
19 August 1747

Whereas by the death of Captain Robert Hay[4] there is a vacancy of captain on board His Majesty's sloop the *Viper*; you are hereby required and directed immediately to take upon you command of the said sloop and follow such orders as you shall receive from me till further orders. And I do hereby strictly charge and command all the officers and company of the said sloop to behave themselves

---

[1] Vanbrugh: C 1710. Commissioner at Plymouth from 1739 till he died in office in 1753. His unduly passive concept of his duties is discussed in Daniel Baugh, *British Naval Administration in the Age of Walpole* (Princeton University Press, 1965) pp. 291–3.

[2] Hobbs: L 1741, CR 1755, C 1756. From July 1756 to Feb. 1758 he was Hawke's flag captain in the *Ramillies*.

[3] Lendrick: L 1746, CR 1756, C 1758. Evidently an excellent officer (see Document 27), but promotion was slow in coming to him. He may have suffered from Warren's mistaken instruction to Hawke that he should report to *him* for their Lordships' information (see Corbett's minute, Document 28). Again served with distinction during the blockade of Brest in 1759.

[4] Robert Hay: L 1739. Acting commander in Aug. 1747.

jointly and severally in their respective employments with all due respect and obedience to you, their said commander for the time being; and you to observe likewise and execute as well the General Printed Instructions as such orders and directions as you shall from time to time receive from me and any other superior officer for His Majesty's service. For which this shall be your order. Given etc.

27.   Hawke to Warren

Windsor at sea
20 August 1747

Sir,

I have the pleasure of acquainting you that I sailed the Sunday evening after you from Plymouth in company with the *Monmouth* and dogger, and run down the Channel. The next morning we got sight of several vessels to which we gave chase, but upon getting up with them found them all to be Dutch. None of them could give us any intelligence worth notice. On Wednesday, in the afternoon, I had the good fortune to join the *Prince Frederick, Augusta, Centurion,* and *Gloucester.* Captain Norris[1] acquainted me that he had that morning detached the *Bellona* and *Amazon* in order to look into Brest to pick up what intelligence they could and then to return to him. The same day he sent the *Viper* to your late rendezvous with orders to cruise in those latitudes where, if he met with any of the ships belonging to your squadron, he was directed to let the captains know that it was Captain Norris's orders they should immediately repair to the present rendezvous; and was also ordered to acquaint Captain Douglas[2] of the *Vigilant*, if he met with him, it was the directions of the Lords Commissioners of the Admiralty that he should return to Spithead where he would find farther orders. On this service Captain Hay was to cruise ten days and then return to this station.

Thursday the 13th, being about sixteen leagues to the westward of Belle Isle, we gave chase to a sloop in the afternoon. The *Prince*

[1] Harry Norris: Younger son of Adm. of the Fleet Sir John Norris. C 1740. Served at Cartagena 1741; successful on detached command off St Tropez 1742. Commanded *Prince Frederick* at First Finisterre 1747. RA 1756, VA 1759.

[2] James Douglas: L 1732, C 1744. Served under Hawke 1757 (Rochefort). In 1759 Saunders (who incidentally valued his command of nautical French) sent him home with dispatches after the fall of Quebec; and he was duly knighted. Commodore and c.-in-c., Leeward Is 1760–1 and briefly Jamaica 1762 (N.A.M. Rodger (ed.), *The Naval Miscellany Vol. V*, N.R.S., vol. 125 (1984) pp. 244–50.) RA 1762, VA 1770, A 1778. Baronet 1786.

Frederick took her. She proved to be French, belonging to the Company at Port Lorient, and came from thence the day before, bound to Senegal. She is laden with provisions, pitch, tar, shot and gunpowder. I made a division of the people (being but sixteen), ordering some on board of each ship, that they might be examined separately. Upon comparing ours with the rest of the ships' intelligence. I find the prisoners all (except one Spaniard who positively affirms the contrary) agree in this: that seven sail of merchant ships begun to sail from Port Lorient the 5th instant N.S. in divisions, two or three ships at a time, one division following another at the distance of two or three days. Two men of war which convoyed them (some say four) sailed as the centre division without any other ships in company. They began to sail five days after the *St Antoine* put to sea.

Upon my joining Captain Norris with the squadron, I supplied Captain Bonfoy[1] with twenty tun of water out of the *Monmouth* and *Windsor* to enable him to stay out some time longer.

Since I have been upon this station, we have spoke with everything we chased. They have hitherto proved to be mostly Dutch. Some Swedes, a Portuguese, etc., agreeable to the enclosed list.

Yesterday morning, seeing two sail in N.W., I made the *Monmouth* and *Centurion* signals to chase. Upon getting up with them, I found they were the *Viper* sloop and the *Hector* French South Seaman (but last from the Canaries where she had landed all her money, which was 1,600,000 pieces of 8/8) bound for Rochelle. Captain Hay met with her the day after he had parted from Captain Norris. I am really concerned to tell you that Captain Hay was killed after he had engaged her with the greatest bravery imaginable for two and a half hours, although she was so greatly superior to him, as being a ship of above 500 tons and 60 men with 28 guns mounted. His lieutenant [John Lendrick], who appears to me to be a diligent, careful, good officer and a man of spirit, followed the example of his brave captain and had the good fortune to take her after he had engaged her for about half an hour longer. I have given him an order to act as captain of her till further orders, which I hope will prove fortunate to him, as I think he deserves to be preferred. At present they have found but nine chests of dollars in her, but I am apt to believe, by making a very strict search after everything is out, she will produce a great many more.

By this accident the *Viper* was rendered incapable of proceeding

[1] Bonfoy: Commanded the *Augusta* (60) and cruised with Hawke till early September. L 1738, CR 1744, C 1745.

to your former rendezvous, agreeable to Captain Norris's directions; and as she wants several things to be done to fit her for the sea again, I have thought proper to send her in with her prize and the sloop we had taken before, as also the *Hunter* dogger, which proves only an incumbrance to us as she came out foul, goes but badly, and had her mainmast sprung, which I ordered our carpenter to fish. For should I keep her here, we should certainly lose company if it came to blow, and by that means she may be taken. Captain Norris complaining to me that his men fell down fast with scurvy, and that his ship was foul and leaky, and as these vessels were in want of a ship to protect them till they got into Plymouth, I thought it would be right to order him to see them safe in and then proceed to Portsmouth to clean and refit.

By several letters taken out of the *Hector* (the duplicates of which you have enclosed) I find the owners of her have been tampering with the Dutch to bring home the money from the Canaries in one of their ships of war, as she could not be searched by the English, and [the Dutch] would perform this service for three or four per cent.

I am every day in hopes of being joined by some of our ships. When the *Frederick* is gone, I shall have only the *Monmouth, Centurion, Augusta, Windsor* and *Gloucester*. I propose sending a frigate, when any shall join me, to look into Rochelle Road to try to get some intelligence from thence. When I have done that, I believe I shall change my rendezvous for a short time. If I return here again, I shall not fail to observe your directions on that head.

I flatter myself you will do me the justice to believe that I have nothing so much at heart as the faithful discharge of my duty, and in such manner as will give satisfaction both to the Lords of the Admiralty and yourself. This shall ever be my utmost ambition, and no lucre of profit or other views shall induce me to act otherwise. Being with truth and regard etc.

28. *Hawke to Corbett* (holograph)

Windsor at sea
20 August 1747

Sir,

I take this opportunity to acquaint their Lordships that I have ordered His Majesty's ship the *Prince Frederick*, Captain Norris, Portsmouth to clean and refit. By him I have sent the proceedings, with the state and condition of the squadron under my command, as likewise all the intelligence we have collected since I have been out,

to Sir Peter Warren and beg leave to refer their Lordships to him for
their farther information. I am etc.

Minute: 28 August. Let him know I have communicated it to their
   Lordships who command me to acquaint him they expected he
   would have sent them such particular accounts of his proceedings, agreeable to the orders they gave to Sir Peter Warren for
   that purpose, and that for the future they direct him to do it by
   every opportunity that offers.

   Acquaint Sir Peter Warren with the purport of his letter and
   that the Lords desire to be informed whether he directed him to
   send their Lordships constant accounts of his proceedings
   agreeable to their order to Sir Peter of the 5th instant, and if he
   had not done it to do it forthwith.

[Writing to the Admiralty on 30 August, Warren admitted that
Hawke had been instructed 'to transmit all the intelligence' that he
could gather to him, Warren, 'for their Lordships' information'. He
would now 'direct him by the first opportunity to send such immediately to their Lordships.']

29.   *Hawke to Warren*

Windsor at sea
21 August 1747

Sir,

   Yesterday at noon I dispatched the *Prince Frederick* and *Viper*
sloop, with the *Hunter* dogger, *Hector* French South Seaman, and a
French sloop, the first to clean at Portsmouth after seeing the four
latter safe into Plymouth.

   I was joined the same night by the *Portland*[1], *Amazon*, and
Grand Turk, who brought me the enclosed intelligence which I think
of consequence enough to be transmitted to you by express; and
withal to acquaint you that the ships under my command are all
foul, excepting two, which are the worst goers, by which means I
should make but a bad figure, should I fall in with an enemy's fleet
and be obliged to chase them.

   From what intelligence I have picked up, it is my opinion that the
French are collecting a number of ships of war at Brest to convoy
their merchant vessels from Rochelle and Bordeaux. If you shall

---

[1] The *Portland* (50) was not Hawke's former command but a ship completed in
1744.

judge in the same manner, I believe you will think it necessary that I should have some clean ships sent out to me with the utmost expedition and with peremptory orders to join me without first cruising on any other station. As I am to detach the *Amazon* with this express, I have only the *Grand Turk* to send out for intelligence, and as I can spare no other ship to support her I don't think it advisable to send her by herself.

I am informed by Captain Faulkner that the *Bellona* left him in the night, the gammoning of his bowsprit and his fore channels being gone, from which I conclude he went for Plymouth to have them repaired.

My squadron at present consists of the *Monmouth, Portland, Gloucester, Windsor, Augusta, Centurion* and *Grand Turk*. I have only to add that I am with the greatest regard etc.

30. *Hawke to Warren*

Windsor at sea
7 September 1747

[This letter in Hawke's own hand was sent on to the Admiralty where it was minuted at the head: 'Recd. from Adml Warren the 22nd and then read. A copy was returned to him 24th Sept.']

Sir,

Since I wrote to you last, which was by Captain Faulkner of the *Amazon*, I have nothing very material to acquaint you with: only that I was joined by the *Falkland* the 24th of last month. A day or two after, finding I had been upon this station eighteen days and spoke with several neutral vessels, which I judged might give the enemy information of me, I thought it would be best to go from hence for a few days. Accordingly on the 27th of August I gave Captain Rowley[1] of the *Grand Turk* orders to continue cruising here, in order to inform such captains as should be sent out to join me that it was my directions they should cruise here till my return. Then I made the best of my way with the seven sail I had under my command for Cape Ortegal. In our way thither we chased a ship and

---

[1] This was Joshua Rowley, eldest son of Sir William. He was first commissioned in July 1747 and only in temporary command of the *Grand Turk* (24). (See also p. 126, n. 3)

a snow for a whole day. Upon getting up with them, they proved to be the *Old Noll* and *Blake* privateers belonging to Liverpool.

The 30th we made Cape Ortegal and stood well in with the land under an easy sail, in order to give the people on shore reason to believe we were cruising off there. This I thought a proper method to prevent the enemy's avoiding us. For, being obliged to return hither directly by reason of some of the ships being under a necessity of soon going into port, it was probable I might meet with some of them upon the station, while they believed me to be upon another.

Most of the ships in my squadron have had the best part of their beer condemned as sour and stinking, though but lately received from South Devon at Plymouth, occasioned by the cask being badly cleaned as well as its being ill brewed. As the health of the ships' companies depends chiefly on this article, it would be of great service if you would be so good as to think of some means to remedy this inconvenience for the future. Otherwise the ships will not be able to stay out the time appointed.

We have now been on this station these three days without meeting the *Grand Turk* or any other ship belonging to us.

The greatest part of the ships with me are very short of water, occasioned chiefly by the badness of the beer, which lays me under the necessity of sending in the *Centurion* and *Augusta*, who are both very foul, having been out of port twelve weeks, and the *Centurion*'s people beginning to grow very sickly. Then I shall have with me only the *Monmouth, Windsor, Gloucester, Portland*, and *Falkland*; and if we should not be joined in a fortnight by some of our clean ships, we shall be obliged to return into port all together.

Upon considering this rendezvous, I find it to be attended with some inconvenience as to the ships joining, especially in bad weather, for there is a constant swell tumbles in here; if a ship should chance to be between the latitudes of Belle Isle and Ushant, and to the eastward of her account, she may run a great risk of being on shore on the East or West Penmarks, without being able to see the land. For this reason we have taken the liberty to alter that rendezvous and to make it in the latitude of Belle Isle, from thirty to fifty leagues to the westward of it, which I think will answer the purpose as well and be a surer means of finding each other.

By the intelligence you will receive herewith, it seems to me pretty clear that there is a large fleet of merchant ships and vessels making up at Rochelle, bound to the West Indies. I should think that the most effectual method to intercept them would be by cruising with a squadron (if we can't have two) between the latitudes of 48.00 and 44.00 N. at a tolerable distance to the westward. By taking this measure, if they should gain intelligence of us, they could never well know how to avoid us. But of this, you will be the better judge.

I must beg leave to add that I shall be glad to see a number of clean ships, with one for myself, and if I have the honour of seeing you with them, it will still be a greater pleasure to, Sir, etc.

P.S.   The *Amazon* has this moment joined us, but brings no news.

31.   *Instructions from the Lords of the Admiralty to Hawke*

8 September 1747
By the Lords Commissioners ... to Edward Hawke, Esq.,
Rear-Admiral of the White Squadron ... Sent by the *Lion*.

[In the event, this mode of conveyance proved rather unreliable. On 15 October, the day *after* his battle with L'Etanduère, Hawke belatedly received these instructions from the *Lion*'s captain, Arthur Scott, who had joined the squadron on 26 September [34] but had mislaid the papers concerned [38 and 39 (final paragraph)].]

Whereas we have given leave to Sir Peter Warren to resign the command of the Western Squadron for the recovery of his health and have thereupon judged fitting to put the ships and vessels named in the enclosed list under your command; you are hereby required and directed to take the said ships and vessels under your command accordingly, their captains being hereby required and directed to observe and obey your orders; and you are to hoist your flag from time to time on board such one of them as you shall think proper.

You are to cruise diligently with the said ships, or so many of them as you shall think fitting, and to dispose of the whole either jointly or separately on such other station or stations in the mouth of the Channel, Soundings, Bay of Biscay, and adjacent parts, as may best answer the ends of protecting the trade of His Majesty's subjects, taking or destroying the ships of war, privateers, and other ships and vessels of the enemy, meeting and intercepting their convoys outward and homeward bound, and annoying them by all other means in your power; and for your more particular direction in the disposition of your said squadron, we refer you to our additional instructions of this date.[1]

When you shall be joined by the ships named in the margin [*Devonshire, Hampton Court,[2] Yarmouth, Edinburgh, Lion, Princess Louisa, Eagle, Nottingham, Defiance, Tilbury, Oxford, Romney,* and *Vulcan* and *Dolphin* fireships] which are coming out to you from Portsmouth and Plymouth, you are to send such of the ships now with you into port to clean as are in want of it; and you are from time to time, as any of your squadron shall want cleaning, to send them into port in like manner, directing their commanders to return and join you with all possible dispatch. And when you send any ships to clean, you are to order the third rates to Portsmouth and the inferior rates to Plymouth. Given etc.

VERE BEAUCLERK[3]
ANSON
W. ELLIS[4]

Enclosure:

---

[1] These additional instructions are given in full in H. W. Richmond, *The Navy in the War of 1739–48* (Cambridge University Press, 1920, 3 vols) iii, p. 102—the source being Adm. 2/70, p. 558.

[2] In the event, the *Hampton Court* (70) went to Lisbon.

[3] Ld Vere Beauclerk was the 3rd son of the 1st Duke of St Albans. C 1721, RA 1745, VA 1746, A 1748. A Ld of Ady 1738–42 and 1744–9.

[4] Welbore Ellis: Politician. MP 1741–94 (except 1790–1); baron 1794. Held many different offices with limited competence. A Ld of Ady 1747–55.

31a.   LIST OF SHIPS AND VESSELS UNDER THE COMMAND OF REAR-ADMIRAL HAWKE

Admiralty Office
8 September 1747

Rate	Ships	No. of		
		Men	Guns	
3	*Monmouth*	480	70	[At sea with Hawke]
	Kent	480	70	Sailed 24 August from Spithead
	Hampton Court	480	70	[Ditto]
	Edinburgh	480	70	[Ditto]
	Devonshire	520	66	[Ditto]
	Yarmouth	500	64	[Ditto]
4	*Windsor*	400	60	[Still Hawke's flagship]
	Augusta	400	60	[At sea with Hawke]
	Eagle	400	60	Sailed the 4th inst from Plymouth
	Tilbury	400	60	[Ditto]
	Princess Louisa	400	60	[Ditto]
	Nottingham	400	60	[Ditto]
	Defiance	400	60	[Ditto]
	Lion	400	60	At St Helens yesterday
	Centurion	375	50	[At sea with Hawke]
	Gloucester	300	50	[Ditto]
	Portland	300	50	[Ditto]
	Falkland	300	50	Sailed the 20th August from Plymouth
	Oxford	300	50	Sailed the 4th inst from Plymouth
5	*Hector*	250	44	Sailed the 21st August from Spithead
	Romney	250	44	Sailed the 4th inst from Plymouth
	Rainbow	250	44	At Spithead
6	*Amazon*	160	24	[At sea under Hawke's orders]
	Grand Turk	160	24	[Ditto]
	Shoreham	160	24	Sailed the 16th July from Plymouth
	Inverness	160	22	At Spithead
Fireships				
	Vulcan	45	6.8	At St Helens yesterday
	Dolphin	55	6.8	[Ditto]

32.   *Instructions from Hawke to Captain Faulkner of the*
AMAZON

Windsor at sea
11 September 1747

Whereas I think it proper for His Majesty's service to leave this
station and to proceed directly for another, appointed by the Hon.
Sir Peter Warren, for the more immediate meeting with and interception of the enemy's ships and vessels, outward and homeward
bound; you are therefore hereby strictly required and directed to
cruise diligently in, or [as] near, the latitude of Belle Isle as you
possibly can, keeping between thirty or forty leagues to the westward of it, taking care to keep a very good lookout for the Hon. Sir
Peter Warren, whom I expect every hour to join me in His Majesty's
ship *St George* with four or five sail more ...

During the time you shall be on this station, if you should chance
to meet with any number of the enemy's ships of war or convoys,
you are to follow them till you shall be able to judge the course they
may steer, as likewise their number and strength, and then make the
best of your way to join me [in the direction of Cape Finisterre]
agreeable to the rendezvous you will receive herewith, taking particular notice of the winds from the time of your first seeing them till
you have met with me. If you should not meet with me there, you
will find a frigate left by me ...

33.   *Line of Battle and Instructions to the Squadron*

27 September 1747

[Captain Fox having joined Hawke on 26 September with seven of
the line and other vessels, Hawke hoisted his flag aboard the *Devonshire* which had been Warren's flagship when he was Anson's second-
in-command earlier in the year. On the 27th, a copy of the following
document was delivered to every ship therein mentioned, excepting
the *Falcon* sloop, to which a copy was given on the 29th. The number
of guns attributed to the listed ships conforms with that indicated
previously on Warren's list [24a], but not in all cases with the recent
Admiralty list [31]. Hawke found it necessary to send the *Oxford* and
Falkland into port before the day of battle (14 October). Otherwise,
this was his line of battle on that day. Of the captains, only Barradall
(soon to be sent into port), Bentley, Saumarez, Harrison, and Watson
had served with Anson at the first Finisterre battle in May; and, like
their admiral, none of them had succeeded in getting into action,

owing partly to the smallness of the enemy squadron and partly to tactical factors. Hanway, in the *Windsor*, had engaged. Otherwise, only the *Devonshire* (Rear-Admiral Warren and Captain Temple West), *Defiance*, and *Yarmouth* had fought in Anson's battle—both the latter then being likewise under different commanders (Captain Thomas Grenville and Captain Peircy Brett).]

The *Kent* to lead with the starboard and the *Princess Louisa* with the larboard tacks on board.

Frigates	Rates	Ships	Captains	Guns
Hector	3	*Kent*	Fox[1]	64
	4	*Eagle*	Rodney	60
Dogger		*Falkland*	Barradall[2]	50
(tender)		*Defiance*	Bentley[3]	60
		Portland	Steevens[4]	50
Falcon sloop		*Nottingham*	Saumarez[5]	60
Dolphin [fireship]	3	*Edinburgh*	Cotes[6]	64
Grand Turk: to		*Devonshire*	Admiral; Moore[7]	66
repeat signals		*Yarmouth*	Saunders[8]	64
Vulcan [fireship]	4	*Windsor*	Hanway[9]	60

[1] Fox: L 1728, CR 1734, c 1737. In June 1747 he commanded a squadron which intercepted a large fleet of returning French West Indiamen (abandoned by their escort). He was court-martialled for his conduct on 14 Oct. 1747 and dismissed from his ship (See Document 49). Soon restored; made a superannuated RA in 1749.

[2] Barradall: L 1732, C 1744.

[3] Bentley: Anson's flag captain at first Finisterre Battle. Served with distinction at Second Finisterre and Battle of Lagos 1759. Knighted. An Extra Commissioner 1761–4; yet RA 1762, VA 1770.

[4] Steevens: L1729, C 1742. With Harland (below) he captured the *Magnanime* (74) in Jan. 1748. RA 1758, when he was Pocock's second-in-command, India. Remained there as c.-in-c. 1760–1. With Coote, took Pondicherry; died in May 1761.

[5] Philip Saumarez: L 1737, C 1743. Killed at Second Finisterre.

[6] Cotes: L 1734, C 1740. Commanded detached squadrons 1746 and 1748 (when he took some ships in a Spanish convoy). RA 1755, VA 1758; c.-in-c. Jamaica 1752–5 and 1757–60.

[7] John Moore: L 1738, C 1743. Commodore and c.-in-c. Leeward Is 1759–60; Guadeloupe taken and lost. C.-in-c. in the Downs 1762–3; RA 21.10.62. VA 1770, A 1778. Created baronet 1766 and was c.-in-c. Portsmouth 1767–9.

[8] Saunders: L 1734. Accompanied Anson on his circumnavigation 1740–4; C 1741. Distinguished himself at Second Finisterre. MP 1750–75. Treasurer of Greenwich Hospital 1754–66; also Controller of the Navy 25.11.55–24.6.56. RA 1756 and Hawke's second-in-command, Mediterranean; c.-in-c. Jan. to May 1757. VA 1759 and naval c.-in-c. at capture of Quebec. C.-in-c. Mediterranean 1760–2. K.B. 1761. A Ld of Ady 1765–6; 1st Ld 15.9.66–11.12.66 (when he was succeeded by Hawke).

[9] Hanway: L 1739, CR 1742, C 1744. Commodore and c.-in-c. Plymouth 1759–60. Commissioner at Chatham 1761–71.

		Gloucester	Durell	50
Shoreham		Tilbury	Harland[1]	60
		Oxford	Callis[2]	50
		Lion	Scott	60
	3	Monmouth	Harrison[3]	64
Romney	4	Princess Louisa	Watson	60

N.B. As I may often have occasion to detach ships from the squadron, you are to observe what ships are absent at any time, that when the signal may be made for the line of battle, you may close and form the line with the ships that remain in company.

[Hawke lists the signals which he will fly if he wishes to speak with a particular ship. For instance, the *Kent*'s signal is a white flag at the main topmast head.]

For all other signals, I refer you to the General Printed Sailing and Fighting Instructions, with the Additional Signals thereunto annexed, and such other signals and instructions as you shall receive from me.

34.   *Hawke to Corbett* (holograph)

Devonshire at sea
5 October 1747

Sir,

I received your letter dated the 28th August last [reflecting the minute which completes Document 28 above] by the *Princess Louisa*, Captain Watson, acquainting me that it is their Lordships' directions I should, for the future, send them an account of my proceedings without referring them to Sir Peter Warren. I was led into this error by apprehending that Sir Peter Warren, from whom I had received my orders, was in town and would immediately communicate my dispatches to the Admiralty Board. However, I shall take particular care for the time to come to send their Lordships

[1] Harland: L 1742, C 1746, RA 1770, VA 1776, A 1782. With Steevens (above) took the *Magnanime* (74) in Jan. 1748. He was Keppel's second-in-command 1777–8 (including Ushant). A Ld of Ady 1782–3.

[2] Callis: L 1731, CR by 1742 when, by expending the fireship *Duke*, he destroyed five Spanish galleys (on orders of Harry Norris, p. 31, n. 1) at nominally-neutral St Tropez. Posted in consequence 1742. Commanded *Culloden* (74) at Lagos 1759. Soon after retired as superannuated RA.

[3] Henry Harrison: L 1706, C 1740. Prominent at Second Finisterre. RA 1756, VA 1758, commanding at Plymouth till his death in 1759. (See Document 230 for Hawke's request for a new commanding officer.)

constant accounts of my proceedings by every opportunity that offers; and as this omission did not proceed from any design, I flatter myself their Lordships will be so good as not to interpret it to my disadvantage.

In my last, I acquainted Sir Peter Warren that I had left the station off Cape Ortegal and was returned to that off Belle Isle, in hopes I should the sooner be joined by the clean ships that were coming out. I had then with me the *Monmouth, Windsor, Gloucester, Portland* and *Falkland,* having been obliged to send the *Centurion* and *Augusta* into port to clean and refit, as they had been out three months and were very foul and in want of water and provisions. As soon as I should be joined by any clean ships, I proposed to go to the same or some other station, as directed by the intelligence I should receive.

Accordingly, on 10th September in the evening, I joined Captain Watson in the *Princess Louisa* with the *Nottingham, Defiance, Eagle* and *Romney.* Captain Watson brought me a packet from Sir Peter Warren with copies enclosed of all the intelligence your Lordships had sent him. After considering them, I judged it would be best, as I had then a tolerable force with me, to make the best of my way into the latitude of 45.00 North off Cape Ortegal, so as to lie in the fair track for intercepting the enemy, should they sail from Basque Roads to the westward.

On the 11th in the morning, the wind being easterly, I left orders with Captain Faulkner of the *Amazon* to cruise for Sir Peter Warren and gave him a sealed rendezvous of the station I was going to, as well as that off Cape Finisterre, that the senior officer of whatever ships he should join might know where to find me. After this I made all the sail I could to the southward and got into the station the next day, where I continued cruising eight days, which was the time prescribed by Sir Peter Warren in his rendezvous for his continuance both off Belle Isle and Cape Ortegal. While we were cruising there, Captain Bentley of the *Defiance* took a small French ship bound to Rochelle, which being of little value, having but a few fish on board, I gave him leave to sink her that she might not be an encumbrance to us.

During this time, not having heard anything of Sir Peter Warren and believing he might have pushed on to Cape Finisterre, which was the last rendezvous he had appointed, I thought it most likely that I should meet with him there. Therefore the 19th in the morning, I made sail with the squadron under my command for that rendezvous; but the winds coming contrary and having very light breezes for some days, and calms, occasioned our making it the 26th of last month before we could get in sight of that cape. The same day we were fortunate as to join the *Devonshire, Yarmouth, Edinburgh, Kent, Tilbury, Lion, Oxford, Hector, Shoreham, Grand Turk, Dolphin, Vulcan,* and *Hunter* dogger.

Captain Fox delivered to me all Sir Peter Warren's dispatches, as likewise all the intelligence he had collected, both from Captain Mostyn[1] and others since he had been out, and by what I am able to judge from them all I think the principal point first to be followed is: to use our utmost endeavours to intercept the convoy bound out from Rochelle. For this purpose I have taken upon me to keep the *Windsor, Portland, Monmouth, Falkland,* and *Gloucester* some time longer, having supplied them with water and some species of provisions out of the other ships. It is true it might occasion all of us going to port sooner than we might else have done; but as it is of material consequence to the nation that we should be full a match for the enemy in case of meeting with them, I am in hopes what I have done will meet with their Lordships' approbation.

Captain Fox acquainted me that, upon his joining of Captain Mostyn in the *Hampton Court,* he had found her bowsprit sprung very bad and was obliged to send him to Lisbon to get a new one, giving him orders to return to the rendezvous off Cape Finisterre. For this reason, I have there left the *Falcon,* Captain Campbell,[2] to cruise for him with a rendezvous where he may find me, as well as to gain intelligence of the enemy.

Being told upon my joining these ships that Captains Baird[3] and Mackenzie[4] were sent to look into Rochelle Road, I waited three or four days in expectation of being joined by one or other of them; but

---

[1] Savage Mostyn was said by subordinates to be aptly named for his 'tyranny and despotism' (Rodger, *Wooden World,* p. 72). L 1734, CR 1739, C 1739. Served under Vernon at Cartagena 1741. Controller 1749–55. RA 1755, VA 1757. Second-in-command of Western Squadron under Hawke and his successors 1756. A Ld of Ady Apr.–July 1757. Died Sept. 1757.

[2] John Campbell: Before joining, was an apprentice in a coastal vessel. Circumnavigated with Anson; L 1742. CR 1747 of *Falcon,* a sloop of 10 guns. C 23.11.47. Off Brest in 1759 he commanded the *Essex* (64) and then the *Royal George* (100), in which Hawke wore his flag at Quiberon Bay. RA 1778; Keppel's first captain at Ushant and loyal to him through the subsequent recriminations. VA 1779 but not employed by Sandwich. Governor of Newfoundland 1782–6. Maintained a dry Scottish simplicity of speech and manners.

[3] Baird: L 1738, C 1747.

[4] Mackenzie: L 1740, C 1747. Fought a successful frigate action in the Channel 1758; commanded *Defiance* (60) at Havana 1762. Commodore and c.-in-c. Jamaica 1770 (Document 461). RA 1777, VA 1779.

not meeting with either, on the 1st instant I sent the *Romney*,[1] as she is a ship of force and goes well, to look into Basque Road, with directions if she met with either Captain Baird or Mackenzie to send one of them to me.

The 3rd instant I joined the *Rainbow, Weasel,* and *Viper.* Captain Baird [of the *Rainbow*] told me that Captain Mackenzie, being a good deal damaged in an action with a French privateer, was returned to England to refit. By the intelligence he got while he was off Rochelle, the enemy are still in port. I propose, therefore, cruising between the latitudes of 45.00 and 47.00 N., in the meridian of Cape Ortegal, for them. This seems to me to be the most likely track for them. Accordingly I am now making the best of my way for those latitudes where I hope we shall have the good fortune to meet with them, as I am convinced the enemy can at present have no certain intelligence of us.

The winds being easterly and to the northward are likely to prevent us getting to the above station so soon as we might otherwise have done, but I shall do everything in my power to put myself in their way and shall keep all the ships out with me while I have any hopes or probability of meeting with them ...

To conclude, I am sorry to be under the necessity of informing their Lordships that my cruise must be very much shortened for want of water. The squadron has been at an uncommon expense of it, as very great quantities of beer, said to have been received both from Plymouth and Portsmouth, have been condemned by [survey as stinking, sour and unfit to drink, occasioned] by its being badly brewed and the casks not cleaned. The case of the *Monmouth* is very particular for, a few days after she left Plymouth, she was obliged to condemn about seventy butts of beer.

Captain Kerley of the *Grand Turk* having complained to me that his ship is very leaky and wants water etc., as she goes but badly I have sent her in with the *Oxford* to Plymouth. I am etc.

---

[1] The *Romney* (50) was commanded by the Hon. William Bateman (L 1744, C 1745, an Extra Commissioner 1756–61, Controller of the Storekeeper's Accounts 1761–83) who reported in a letter to Hawke of 10 Oct. (which did not reach him till 4 Nov.) that he had sighted L'Etanduère's squadron about 90 miles S. of Ushant: 'This day we descried from our masthead a large fleet to leeward consisting of a hundred and fifty or two hundred sail, amongst them nine or ten large ships, standing with an easy sail to the N.W. with the wind at W.S.W.' (N.M.M., HWK/9).

35. *Hawke to Warren* (holograph)

Devonshire at sea
6 October 1747

Sir,

The Lords of the Admiralty having sent me an order to send the *Oxford* into Plymouth to sheath and fill, in order for her going to the West Indies, gives me the opportunity of paying my regards to you and at the same time to acknowledge your letters by Captain Watson of the *Louisa*, dated on board the *St George* at Spithead the 26th August, and that near St Helens the 31st of the same month, as well as those by Captain Fox and Captain Mostyn of the 22nd and 24th of last August, as also that of the 8th September with all the intelligence.

I am sincerely concerned to find that you still have that troublesome disorder and that your health won't permit you to come out. It would have been a very great pleasure to me to have had the honour of paying my respects to you here; but as I can't have that satisfaction, I shall endeavour to do everything in my power to forward the service, only wishing I may be so fortunate as to have your approbation of my actions, as I can say very truly there is not anything I have more at heart than your good opinion.

I have considered well all the intelligence you have sent me and, by what I can learn from thence, I think our only views at present must be to lay in the way of the French convoy outward bound. In order thereto, I propose cruising between the latitudes of 45.00 and 47.00 N. in the meridian of Cape Ortegal, and am making the best of my way thither as fast as the winds will permit me. This appears to me to be the most likely track for them and everybody here is of the same opinion. I hope we shall have the good fortune to meet with them, if they should come out, while we are in a condition to keep the sea.

With respect to the intelligence you sent me relating to the galleons, as it's uncertain when they will come home, and likewise impossible for me to divide my force in the present necessitous condition of the ships under my command, I must lay aside all thoughts of them during this cruise which cannot be of long continuance. And indeed, if I may presume to give my opinion, I should think sixty or seventy leagues to the westward of Cadiz would be the best station to look out for them, in which case a squadron must go out from England directly thither, well watered and victualled. For, by the uncertainty of weather and the negligence of the Agent Victualler, I find the ships that join me, so far from being in a condition to go on distant or different expeditions, that it is with difficulty I can keep them any reasonable time with me. For the same reason, I cannot send my frigates to look into Cartagena; and I flatter myself, when you weigh this case maturely, you'll find it necessary to send two well stored and furnished from England on this service. Besides, had I had positive orders from you for that purpose, I could not have put them in execution till yesterday when I was joined by the *Rainbow*, *Weasel*, and *Viper*. If your opinion shall agree with mine, I hope you'll find two frigates in port to dispatch on that duty.

You'll perceive by the state and condition of the ships, I shall not be able to stay out past the month of October, for which reason, if you would please to give directions at Plymouth for having a supply ready of stores and provisions of all kinds, against the ships that are only to boot-top get thither, by this means they will soon be ready for the sea. Captain Fox acquainted me when I joined him, he had received certain intelligence from a Portuguese that came from Ferrol the day before, that there were no vessels of any kind in that port but a large old eighty-gun ship, which he said was repairing very slowly, and that there had not been any ships there during some months. Notwithstanding this intelligence, I have detached the *Viper* to cruise off that port. I observe the *Glorioso*[1] arrived in Galicia before I sailed from Plymouth.

I have received a letter from Mr Clevland[2] dated the 28th August wherein he tells me it is their Lordships' directions that for the future I send them constant accounts of my proceedings without referring them to you, for which reason I have sent them by this opportunity an account of all my proceedings since my last to you for their satisfaction, a copy of which I send you enclosed.

I am in great hopes the station I am going to will throw us in the way of the enemy, either outward or homeward bound. With regard to lying in wait for them, all that any man can do is to put the most reasonable supposition in practice, and that I hope you will think I have done.

I wish with all my heart this may find you perfectly recovered and in a good state of health, and that I may be so happy as to obey all your commands in the manner you would have me. I don't know

[1] The *Glorioso* (74) was taken two days later, on 8 Oct., having resisted a remarkable series of attacks by the privateer George Walker. (W.L. Clowes, *The Royal Navy* (London: Sampson Low, 1897–1903, 7 vols) iii, pp. 285–6—this volume being invaluable for compiling these footnotes. See also Part I, p. 11, n. 6.

[2] John Clevland: a clerk at the Navy Office 1722–31; Clerk of the Cheque at Plymouth 1731–43; Clerk of the Acts (and thus a member of the Navy Board) 1743–6; 2nd Secretary of the Ady 1746–51; Secretary of the Ady 1751–63 (died in office).

anything would give me more pleasure, as I am, always with the utmost truth and respect etc.

36.   *Hawke to Warren*

Devonshire at sea
11 October 1747

Sir,

The *Oxford* and the *Grand Turk* parted company with me the 7th instant in the morning. The winds coming to the southward soon after gives me room to hope that they had but a short passage ...

In my last, I mentioned to you the difficulties I labour under with regard to provisions and water for the ships of the squadron. The beer proving so very bad on board of almost every one of them has been the means of shortening the water greatly ...[1]

I was in hopes, when I had the honour of writing to you last, that I should have been able to have kept out the *Monmouth, Windsor, Falkland, Gloucester,* and *Portland* some time longer. But water being so scarce I am afraid it won't be in my power to detain them so long as I could wish. Therefore, to make the best of it, I have resolved to let them go in by one or two at a time, that the enemy may not get intelligence of a number being returned into port at once; and by taking this step I hope we shall be able to stay out some time longer than we could otherwise have done ...

I have now with me two frigates only, the *Hector* and *Shoreham*, neither fit to be sent anywhere, the first being very weak, leaky, and going badly (the time of her contract being just expired) and the latter so very foul that she hardly goes through the water at all. If you shall send any clean ships out, I believe you will find it proper to send a number together and to assign them such a station as you shall think best. For, as it's the middle of October, blowing weather is naturally to be expected which will render their joining me, if I shall be out, or any other, during their cruise very uncertain. The winds having been set in westerly for some days past, I am apt to think the French fleet will not attempt sailing now, if they have not passed us; and that I believe they could not have done, unless they pushed out well to the northward.

The 8th of this month Captain Haddock of the [venerable fourth-rate] *Advice* happened to fall in with our squadron from seeing the

---

[1] Hawke's complaint about the beer led the Lords to raise the matter with the Board of Victualling who blamed the warm weather (Baugh, *Naval Administration* (N.R.S.) pp. 448–9). For Hawke's similar complaint in 1759 evoking much the same answer, see Documents 234 (with n. 1), 235 and 249 (Clevland's minute) below.

West India fleet into the Channel. He told me that six days ago he had spoke with a privateer which had met a Dutch vessel four days from Rochelle, who informed him that, when he came from thence, there were eight sail of ships of war and near two hundred sail of merchant ships and vessels, but knew nothing of when they were to sail. Captain Haddock likewise spoke with the *Tigress* privateer, belonging to Bristol, who had a French Martinicoman in company with him. The captain of the *Tigress* told him that he took that ship in the latitude of 47.00 N. and West longitude from London 9.00, and that she came out in company with three more and had left two hundred sail with two frigates behind who he said were not to sail till March. I am in hopes the latter part of this is not true and that these will prove to be the forerunners of the rest, as they may have lost company with them. Our present situation, if fortune will stand our friend, seems to be very well calculated for intercepting both the outward and homeward bound trade of the enemy ...

I shall contribute everything in my power to keep the ships out with me as long as possible and will stay out myself while I can keep any number together, and when I do go in shall take care to leave some out under the command of Captain Mostyn, if he joins me, or Cotes, if we can find enough water for them. I have only to add that I hope this will find you growing better every day. It will give me infinite pleasure to hear that you have recovered your health again ...

37. *Hawke to Corbett* (holograph)

Devonshire at sea
12 October 1747

Sir,

I wrote you an account of all my proceedings by the *Oxford*, Captain Callis, whom I sent into Plymouth agreeable to their Lordships' orders.

I have only now to acquaint you that I have sent the *Falkland* into Plymouth Sound to clean and refit as she is foul and in want of water, etc. I find it will be impossible for me to keep out the five following ships long: the *Monmouth, Windsor, Gloucester, Portland,* and [*Shoreham*] being all in want both of water and everything else.

Captain Barradall [of the *Falkland*] having acquainted me by letter that he is extremely ill and not capable of doing his duty is the reason of my sending his ship in now, that he may have an opportunity of recovering his health while his ship is cleaning.

Before the *Viper* could depart for her station off Ferrol, I reflected that she might meet with some of the enemy's privateers, which would frustrate her putting her orders in execution. For this reason I sent the *Rainbow*, Captain Baird, and the *Viper* under his command with orders to cruise there as long as their water and provisions should last, provided they should procure no material intelligence in the meantime.

The 8th of this month Captain Haddock of the *Advice* fell in with us and from him I received the enclosed intelligence. We have had winds to the southward and westward for these few days past, which makes me believe the French fleet will not attempt sailing now, if they have not already passed us, and that I think they could not have done unless they pushed out well to the northward. The situation we are now in seems to me very well calculated for intercepting both the outward and homeward bound trade of the enemy.

I shall do everything in my power to keep the ships out with me as long as possible and intend staying out myself while I can keep any number together; and when I go in, shall leave some out, if we can find water enough for them. I am etc.

[On 14 October, the Second Battle of Cape Finisterre was fought. There is a general account of it in Hawke's dispatch of 17 October [39]; and much additional detail will be found in the record of Fox's trial [49].]

38. *Instructions from Hawke to the Squadron*

Devonshire at sea
15 October 1747

[Captain Scott belatedly produced the under-mentioned authority (see 31 above) and the following order was distributed to all ships in the squadron on 16 October. Meantime, lacking a commander-in-chief's commission, Hawke had held a council of war on the 15th. See 39a below.]

Pursuant to an order from the Rt Honourable the Lords Commissioners of the Admiralty, dated 8 September 1747; you are hereby required and directed to put yourself under my command and follow such directions as you shall, from time to time, receive from me for your further proceedings, sending me weekly, by proper opportunities, the state and condition of your ship; for which this shall be your order. Given etc.

39. *Hawke to Corbett*

Devonshire at sea
17 October 1747

Sir,

At 7 in the morning of the 14th of October, being in the latitude of 47.49 N. longitude from Cape Finisterre 1.2 W., the *Edinburgh* made the signal for seven sail in the SE quarter. I immediately made the signal for all the fleet to chase. About 8, saw a great number of ships, but so crowded together that we could not count them. At 10, made the signal for a line of battle ahead. The *Louisa*, being the headmost and weathermost ship, made the signal for discovering eleven sail of the enemy's line of battle ships. Half an hour after, Captain Fox in the *Kent* hailed us and said they counted twelve very large ships.

Soon after, I perceived the enemy's convoy to crowd away with all the sail they could set, while their ships of war were endeavouring to form in a line astern of them, and hauled near the wind under their topsails and foresails, and some with topgallant sails set. Finding we lost time in forming our line while the enemy was standing from us, at 11 made the signal for the whole squadron to chase. Half an hour after, observing our headmost ships to be within a proper distance, I made the signal to engage which was immediately obeyed. The *Lion* and *Princess Louisa* began the engagement and were followed by the rest of the squadron as they could come up, and went from rear to van.

The enemy having the weather gauge of us and a smart and constant fire being kept on both sides, the smoke prevented my seeing the number of the enemy or what happened on either side for some time. In passing on to the front ship we could get near, we received many fires at a distance till we came close to the *Severne* of fifty guns, whom we soon silenced and left to be taken by the frigates astern. Then, perceiving the *Eagle* and *Edinburgh* (who had lost her fore topmast) engaged, we kept our wind as close as possible in order to assist them. This attempt of ours was frustrated by the *Eagle* falling twice on board us, having had her wheel shot to pieces and all the men at it killed, and all her braces and bowlines gone. This drove us to leeward and prevented our attacking the *Monarque* of seventy-four and the *Tonnant* of eighty guns within any distance to do execution. However, we attempted both, especially the latter. While we engaged with her, the breechings of all our lower deck guns broke and the guns flew fore and aft, which obliged us to shoot ahead, for our upper and quarterdeck guns could not reach her. Captain Har-

1   11 am: The British close on the French escort,
                while the convoy escapes

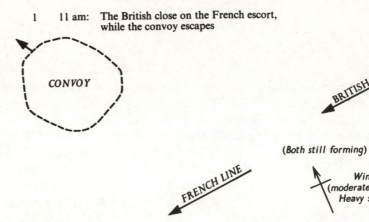

2   Noon: First phase of action developing

The Second Battle of Cape Finisterre

3   2 pm: French rear being eliminated

Shoreham ◐ *Severne* (*Prize*)

Hector ◐ *Fougueux* (*Prize*)
Kent ◌

Devonshire ◌ Eagle ◌
Yarmouth ◌   ● *Neptune*
Nottingham ◌
Edinburgh ◌   ● *Monarque*

*French van and rest of British
squadron sailing ahead*

Wind

4   4.15 pm: Final phase. Intrépide heading back towards Tonnant.

◌ Tilbury

Tonnant ● ◌ Kent

Windsor ◌ ◌ Devonshire

Lyon ◌

Portland ◌ ● *Trident*

◌ Defiance

◌ Gloucester

◌ P. Louisa
Terrible ●

● *Intrépide*
◌ Monmouth

land in the *Tilbury*, observing that she fired single guns at us in order to dismast us, stood on the other tack between her and the *Devonshire* and gave her a very smart fire.

By the time the new breechings were all seized, I was got almost alongside the *Trident* of sixty-four guns, whom I engaged as soon as possible and silenced by as brisk a fire as I could make.

Just before I attacked her, observing the *Kent*, which seemed to have little or no damage, at some distance astern of the *Tonnant*, I flung out Captain Fox's pendant to make sail ahead to engage her, as I saw it was within his power to get up close with her, she being somewhat disabled, having lost her main topmast. Seeing some of our ships at that time not so closely engaged as I could have wished and not being well able to distinguish who they were, I flung out the signal for coming to a closer engagement. Soon after I got alongside within musket shot of the *Terrible* of seventy-four guns and seven hundred men. Near 7, she called out for quarter.

Thus far, I have been particular with regard to the share the *Devonshire* bore in the action of that day. As to the other ships, as far as fell within my notice, their commanders and companies behaved with the very greatest spirit and resolution, in every respect like Englishmen. Only I am sorry to acquaint their Lordships that I must except Captain Fox whose conduct on that day I beg they would give directions for inquiring into at a court martial.

Having observed that six of the enemy's ships had struck, and it being very dark and our own ships dispersed, I thought it best to bring to for that night; and, seeing a great firing a long way astern of me, I was in hopes to have seen more of the enemy's ships taken in the morning. But instead of that I received the melancholy account of Captain Saumarez being killed, and that the *Tonnant* had escaped in the night by the assistance of the *Intrépide* [74] who, by having the wind of our ships, had received no damage that I could perceive. Immediately I called a council of war, a copy of the result of which I send you enclosed.

As to the French convoy's escape, it was not possible for me to detach any ships after them at first or during the action, except the frigates; and that I thought would have been imprudent, as I observed several large ships among them; and to confirm me in this opinion, I have since learned that they had the *Content* of sixty-four guns and many frigates from thirty-six guns downwards. However, I took a step which seemed to me the most probable to intercept them, for as soon as I could man and victual the *Weasel* sloop, I detached her with an express to Commodore Legge.[1]

As the enemy's ships were large, except the *Severne*, they took a great deal of drubbing and lost all their masts, excepting two who had their foremasts left. This has obliged me to lie by these two days past in order to put them in a condition to be brought into port, as well as our own, which have suffered greatly.

I have sent this express by Captain Moore of the *Devonshire* in the *Hector*, and it would be doing a great injustice to merit not to say that he signalized himself greatly in the action.

Their Lordships I hope will excuse me for not sending them by this opportunity the state and condition of our ships, as I have not yet been able to collect them, every ship being so much employed.

I propose sending as many ships into Plymouth as I can spare, exclusive of a sufficient number to carry the prizes to Portsmouth. We have taken

Le Monarque	74 guns
Le Terrible	74
Neptune	70
Le Trident	64
Le Fougueux	64
Severne	50

Captain Stanhope[2] [of the *Hector*] sent his boat and took up numbers of packets thrown into the sea from the *Severne* and *Fougueux*. I could not spare time to get them translated; besides they were too wet to be handled. I hope you'll get some important intelligence from them, as I have, that six ships of war are fitting at Brest for the East Indies.

Since writing the above, I have received certain intelligence that the *Terrible, Neptune, Fougueux*, and *Severne* were destined for Martinico to bring home a fleet from thence.

I did not receive till the 15th instant their Lordships' commission of the [8]th September, by which they were pleased to honour me with the command of the Western Squadron, Captain Scott having mislaid it. I am etc.

---

[1] The Hon. Edward Legge, commodore and c.-in-c. Leeward Is, had died there on 9 Sept. 1747. He was replaced by George Pocock, the future Admiral and captor of Havana in 1762. The French convoy's escort, apart from the *Content* (an E. India-man), consisted only of the frigate *Castor*; and a number of the merchantmen were taken by the British in the W. Indies.

[2] Stanhope: L 1740, C 1745. Knighted after Battle of Lagos 1759 and commanded the *Swiftsure* (70) at Quiberon Bay.

Enclosure:

39a. AT A COUNCIL OF WAR HELD ON BOARD HIS MAJESTY'S SHIP DEVONSHIRE AT SEA, 15 OCTOBER 1747

Present:

> Edward Hawke, Esq., Rear-Admiral of the White Squadron of His Majesty's Fleet, President.

Captain Thomas Fox	Captain Charles Watson
Captain Thomas Cotes	Captain Charles Saunders
Captain Charles Steevens	Captain George Bridges Rodney
Captain John Moore	Captain Thomas Hanway
Captain Thomas Stanhope	

The council being assembled, Captain Watson objected to ranking with Captain Fox till his character should be cleared up with regard to the aspersions cast on it for his behaviour in an action with the enemy on the 14th instant and being seconded by all the other members, Captain Fox was accordingly excluded from the council.

They then came to the following resolution:

1. That four ships, the least of them of sixty guns, could only be sufficient to go in quest of two French ships, the *Tonnant* of eighty guns and the *Intrépide* of seventy-four, which had escaped from the action in the evening of the 14th.

2. That none of the ships under their command were at present in a condition to be sent on this service.

3. That by the time a sufficient number of them could be got ready, it would be impracticable to come up with the enemy's ships.

[Copied signatures follow:] ED. HAWKE
etc.

A copy JOHN HAY.

40. *Hawke to Anson*

Devonshire at sea
17 October 1747

My Lord,

I take this opportunity of paying my regards to your Lordship by Captain Moore of the *Devonshire*, whom I have sent express in the *Hector* to the Lords of the Admiralty with the account of the action we had with the French on the 14th instant, for the particulars of which I must beg leave to refer you to them and him. The many obligations that I lie under to your Lordship will always make me glad of every occasion to acknowledge them. I esteem myself very lucky in having had so gallant and active an officer with me as Captain Moore, who merits everything that is handsome to be said of him. I entreat your Lordship to believe that I am etc.

41.   *Hawke to Warren*

Devonshire at sea
17 October 1747

Sir,

If I had not met with the misfortune of having my right hand and side of my face burnt with powder, I should not have made use of an amanuensis, but given you myself a full detail of our action on the 14th. For though your bad state of health has obliged you to resign the command of the squadron, yet the many and great obligations I lie under induce me to send you enclosed the material part of my letter to the Lords of the Admiralty. Wishing you a speedy recovery, I am etc.

42.   *Hawke to Corbett*

Devonshire at sea
[28 October 1747]

Sir,

Since my last I have been joined by Captain Mostyn in the *Hampton Court*. After considering the state and condition of all the ships in the squadron, I find there is an absolute necessity for all of them to go into port, as they are in want of provisions and water and many other things to refit them for sea. For this reason, I have ordered Captain Mostyn to Plymouth to boot-hose-top his ship and hold himself in constant readiness for the sea, in case their Lordships should be inclined to send him to cruise off Ushant, with any other ships, till the squadron shall be refitted. I have sent His Majesty's ships *Monmouth, Edinburgh, Princess Louisa, Eagle, Windsor, Gloucester, Portland*, and *Shoreham* to clean and refit at Plymouth with all possible dispatch. The remainder I take to Portsmouth together with their prizes, viz. the *Devonshire, Yarmouth, Kent, Lion, Nottingham, Tilbury, Defiance*, and the two fireships.

The Count du Guay, who commanded the *Terrible* and is now a prisoner on board the *Devonshire* with the major part of her officers, has desired me to intercede with their Lordships for permission to return as soon as possible to France on his parole. He is an old man and very infirm and weakly, so afflicted with asthma that he can hardly breathe ...

43.   *Corbett to Hawke*

Admiralty Office
30 October 1747

Sir,

I have received by Captain Moore and laid before the Lords Commissioners of the Admiralty your letter of the 17th with an account of the action between you and a French squadron commanded by Monsieur de L'Etanduère and the great victory gained by His Majesty's squadron under your command.

Their Lordships direct me to congratulate you in their name for the great service you have done your country in defeating so great a force of the enemy and taking so many of their capital ships, wherein you have shown a conduct that has very much distinguished your character and fully answered the expectations of their Lordships who entrusted you with the command of the squadron.

You will know from other hands what great satisfaction you have given, not only to the King and his ministry, but to the trading interest in the City, and indeed to all His Majesty's good subjects.

I have great pleasure in communicating their Lordships' sentiments to you, who have ever been with great regard etc.

44.   *Rear-Admiral William Chambers[1] to Hawke*

Plymouth Dock
30 October 1747

Sir,

Yesterday was delivered to me by Captain Mostyn your letter of the 20th instant and I most heartily congratulate you on your late good success against the enemy in taking six of their ships which, in the situation of affairs at present, must render it of singular good service for the good of our country, and I hope you will meet with a reward suitable to your merit ...

[1] Chambers: L 1726, C 1736, RA 1747 when he succeeded Hawke in the command at Plymouth.

Pray give my compliments to Mrs Hawke whom I wish all joy on this occasion. I am with great truth,

Your most obedient humble servant,
WILLIAM CHAMBERS

45. *Lieutenant James Hobbs to Hawke*

Plymouth
[30 October 1747?]

Sir,
I heartily congratulate you on your late success over the French and am glad to hear you are in good health and, I hope, safe arrived at Spithead with all your prizes. I am very sorry I had not the honour of being with you, notwithstanding which, Sir, I hope you'll please to think of me having no friends to rely on but yourself; and if this glorious affair has given you an opportunity of providing for the few friends which was out with you, I hope you'll be kind enough to apply to their Lordships for me in time before they shall put any more upon you, for Lord Anson has a great many hanging on him.

My Yorkshire friends are still in the country. They have never applied to the Admiralty or anybody else in my behalf, or when they will, the Lord knows. My dependence was always little on them, for I entirely relied on your favour.

If you want your chest or anything else that you left here to be sent to you, please to let me know and I shall take care to forward them. I am sorry the maid carried away the key of your chest. Otherwise I could have got your clothes aired.

My best respects wait on you and Mrs Hawke. I am etc.

46. *Corbett to Hawke*

31 October 1747

Sir,
Admiral Steuart[1] being directed to assemble a court martial for enquiring into the conduct of Captain Fox in the late engagement ... I am commanded by the Lords Commissioners of the Admiralty to signify their directions to you to get matters ready for the trial as soon as possible. I am etc.

---

[1] Steuart: C 1709, RA 1742, VA 1743, A 1747, Adm. of the Fleet 1751. He commanded at Portsmouth in the later part of the war.

47.   *Corbett to Hawke*

2 November 1747

Sir,

I have received and communicated to my Lords Commissioners of
the Admiralty your letter of yesterday's date representing that it is
your opinion that all the officers who refused to rank with Captain
Fox should be summoned to attend as evidences ... but at the same
time their Lordships order me to observe to you the inconvenience
of calling more captains from Plymouth than are absolutely necessary, which puts them to great expense and trouble, as well as delays
the trial. But the Lords leave it to your discretion ...

48.   *Hawke to Corbett*

Devonshire at Spithead
4 November 1747

Sir,

Late last night, being to pay my respects to Lord Anson, I
received both your letters of 2nd November by express. In answer to
the first I send you enclosed an account of the officers and men killed
and wounded on board each ship now at Portsmouth, which I
should have sent before but could not collect at sea, the weather
being so bad and every person so much employed ...

With regard to the captains and other officers whom I have
desired to be summoned from Plymouth to attend Captain Fox's
court martial, I could not avoid desiring their attendance in order to
give their reasons for refusing to rank with him. It is doing justice
both to His Majesty and to Mr Fox ...

The *Prince Frederick* and *Bellona* will be ready in a few days to
proceed to sea. As soon as they are, either Sir Peter Warren or
myself will endeavour to station them where they will be most likely
to fall in with the French privateers mentioned in the intelligence ...
Enclosure:

48a.   *Casualties suffered on 14 October 1747: partial return of 4*
November 1747

	Killed	Wounded
Devonshire	12	52
Kent	1	10
Yarmouth	22	70
Defiance	11	42
Lion	20	79
Tilbury	6	13
Hector	1	1
	73	267

[The *Nottingham* (whose captain had been killed) also went into Portsmouth. She seems to have lost:

	13	39

With the figures varying from one source to another, the following may be cited for the ships sent into Plymouth:

Monmouth	22	68
Edinburgh	5	19
Princess Louisa	18	60
Eagle	16	52
Windsor	8	41
Gloucester	8	17
Portland	7	14
	84	271]

49.   *Court martial of Captain Thomas Fox*

November–December 1747

At a court martial held on board His Majesty's ship the *Duke* in Portsmouth Harbour by several adjournments on the 25, 26, 27 and 30 November; 1, 2, 3, 4, 7, 10, 11, 12, 14, 16, 17, 18, and 21 December 1747.

Present

Sir Peter Warren, Knight of the Bath and Vice-Admiral of the

White Squadron of His Majesty's Fleet (President), Henry Osborn, Esq., Rear-Admiral of the Red[1] William Chambers, Esq., Rear-Admiral of the White, Hon. John Forbes, Esq., Rear-Admiral of the Blue[2]

Captains Merrick de l'Angle[3]   Temple West[4]
         Peircy Brett[5]   Edward Pratten[6]
         Hon. Augustus Keppel[7]   William Parry[8]
         Andrew Jelfe[9]   Peter Denis[10]

All duly sworn according to Act of Parliament.

The court proceeded to inquire into a charge exhibited by Sir Edward Hawke, Knight of the Bath and Rear-Admiral of the White, against Captain Fox of His Majesty's ship *Kent* for misconduct and misbehaviour in the action of the 14th of October last between a squadron of His Majesty's ships under Rear-Admiral Hawke's command and a squadron of French ships of war, and having heard the evidence for the King and the defence made by Captain Fox and

---

[1] Osborn: L 1717, C 1728, RA 1747, VA 1748, A 1757. C.-in-c. Mediterranean 1757–8, when he ably impeded La Clue's squadron; but he suffered a stroke and retired from active service.

[2] Forbes: L 1731, C 1737, RA 1747, VA 1755, A 1758. A Ld of the Ady 13.12.56–6.4.57; refused to sign Byng's death warrant. Again a Ld of Ady 2.7.57–20.4.63.

[3] De l'Angle: L 1734, C 1742.

[4] Peircy Brett: son of a naval Master. L 1734. Circumnavigated with Anson, at whose instance he was posted 29.12.44. Fought and turned back the *Elisabeth* (having 58 guns against the *Elisabeth*'s 64) which was carrying munitions for the Young Pretender 1745. Served at First Finisterre 1747. Knighted 1753. Commodore in the Downs 1758–61. Second-in-command, Mediterranean and RA 1762. A Ld of Ady 1766–70. VA 1770.

[5] Keppel: circumnavigated with Anson: L 1742, C 1744. Aged 24, commanded a squadron sent to treat with the piratical Dey of Algiers 1749–51. Thereafter he acted as a commodore and c.-in-c. on several occasions, taking Gorée in 1758 and, in a major combined operation, Belle Isle in 1761. Meanwhile he was to the fore under Hawke in 1759. Second-in-command to Pocock at Havana 1762; RA and c.-in-c. Jamaica 1762–4. In politics, joined the Rockinghams; a Ld of Ady 1765–6. During Falklands crisis became VA of the Blue (25.10.70) and prospective c.-in-c. in the Channel. Despite his political links, was made c.-in-c. of the 'grand fleet' 1778. Fought drawn battle at Ushant in July. Court-martialled 1779. Triumphantly acquitted but did not again serve at sea. First Ld of the Ady Apr. 1782–Jan. 1783 and Apr. 1783–Dec. 1783; created viscount 1782.

[6] Jelfe: L 1735, CR 1744, C 1746.

[7] West: L 1734, C 1738. Cashiered after Battle of Toulon but soon restored. Warren's flag captain at First Finisterre. RA 1755. Commanded Byng's van at Minorca 1756. A Ld of Ady 17.11.56–6.4.57 and 2.7.57–9.8.57 (died in office).

[8] Pratten: L 1739, C 1743.

[9] Parry: L 1738, C 1744, RA 1763, VA 1770, A 1778.

[10] Denis: son of a Huguenot refugee. L 1739. Circumnavigated with Anson. CR 1744, C 1745. Served at First Finisterre and Quiberon Bay. RA 1770, VA 1775 (died 1778).

maturely considered the same, were of opinion that part of the charge had been proved against him, the said Captain Fox, that he had been guilty of misconduct in backing his mizen topsail, in leaving the *Tonnant*, and in waiting for his boat and not going down immediately to the assistance of the ships to leeward upon the Admiral's message. All of which the court do attribute to misconduct and not to cowardice, because his courage has been so fully proved to them as not to leave the least room for suspecting it, and part of that misconduct seems to them to proceed from his listening to the persuasions of the First Lieutenant and Master and giving way to them. Therefore the court are of the opinion that he, the said Captain Thomas Fox, falls under part of the 11th and 12th articles of the Articles of War, established in the thirteenth year of King Charles the Second ... and do adjudge him, the said Captain Fox, to be dismissed from command of the *Kent*; and he is hereby dismissed from that command accordingly.

P. WARREN

GEO. ADKINS   HEN. OSBORN
Deputy Judge Advocate   etc

The court being opened, the President addressed himself first to the court and then to the Prisoner as follows:

To the court
Gentlemen, the command of my superiors rather than my own choice has made me president of this court martial. I am not ashamed to own my want of experience in proceedings of this nature, nor am I desirous of acquiring more than what the present occasion of our being called together may give me. I shall depend on your candour in excusing my mistakes and in setting me right when I err; and all and every of the members of this court may be assured that it will be my endeavour to pay them a proper and becoming attention.

To the Prisoner, Captain Fox
The King, our most gracious master, who during the whole course of his reign has given the most convincing proofs of the mildness of his government and of his princely clemency towards all his subjects, has on the present occasion, for the sake of doing public justice to you, authorized us here met to bring you to your trial in this court martial for a misbehaviour and breach of duty charged upon you in the action of the 14th of October last, when a squadron of His Majesty's ships under the command of Rear-Admiral Hawke

engaged, and were eminently victorious, over a squadron of the
French King's ships of war.

How disagreeable so ever the present service enjoined [upon] us
may be to men of compassionate dispositions—for it is my ardent
wish that this trial may be the last of the kind known in the British
Navy—yet what we owe to our King and to our country calls upon
us to discharge this our duty with the utmost faithfulness and
impartiality; and you may be assured from the honour and candour
of the gentlemen who compose this court that, towards you, we will
acquit ourselves with a becoming humanity and tenderness.

Whatever help or assistance, therefore, you shall yet want to be
added to such as you may have already provided, this court will
cheerfully grant, with every indulgence that the laws of the land and
the rules and usages of such courts will permit. Innocence has
nothing to fear; guilt everything to apprehend. That you may be able
to make it clearly appear that the first of these is your case is the
charitable wish, I dare say, of all your judges. May God direct you in
your defence and us in our judgement.

Wednesday the 25th November 1747
Admiralty's warrant, the 17th July 1747, empowering Admiral
Steuart, Admiral of the White Squadron of His Majesty's Fleet to
call and assemble courts martial. Read.

Admiral Steuart's order to Sir Peter Warren...dated November
1747 to preside at this present court martial. Read.

Mr Secretary Corbett's letter of the 13th instant to Admiral
Steuart enclosing a copy of His Majesty's Advocate General,
Attorney General and Solicitor General, their opinion that no depositions ought to be taken previous to any court martial; and signifying their Lordships' directions that no more depositions be taken
hereafter, and that all witnesses be summoned by the Judge Advocate. Both read.[1]

Mr Secretary Corbett's letter of the 18th instant to the Deputy
Judge Advocate enclosing a copy of His Majesty's Advocate
General, Attorney General and Solicitor General, their opinion in
relation to the Judge Advocate's asking questions of witnesses when
under examination upon a trial. Both read.[2]

Admiral Steuart's letter to the Deputy Judge Advocate enclosing

[1] This ruling set an important precedent for the future conduct of naval courts
martial. See J. K. Laughton's *D.N.B.* article on Keppel.

[2] It will be seen that the Deputy Judge Advocate did not interrogate the witnesses
during this trial.

a copy of Mr Secretary Corbett's letter to him, dated the 19th November, with regard to the manner of taking minutes at future courts martial. Read.[1]

Deputy Judge Advocate's letter to Mr Secretary Corbett thereupon, dated the 21st November 1747. Read.

Mr Secretary Corbett's letter dated 23rd November 1747 in answer. Read.

The Deputy Judge Advocate desires the directions of the court thereupon. The court are of the opinion that if the Deputy Judge Advocate takes the narration of the facts from the witnesses *viva voce* and, after taking it, reads it over to the witnesses in open court and then inserts it in the body of his minutes, those being signed by himself agreeable to the general practice in suchlike cases, will be sufficient.

The court sworn
The Prisoner, Captain Fox of His Majesty's ship *Kent*, brought into court.

The witnesses all called in to hear the charge read...The court proceeded to examine the witnesses for the King.

Captain Watson of His Majesty's ship the *Princess Louisa* called in and sworn.

Q. President Captain Watson, you have heard the charge exhibited by Sir Edward Hawke against Captain Fox...Please inform the court, upon the oath you have taken, as far as fell under your observation, Captain Fox's behaviour on that day's action.

A. In regard to my situation, I was in the van of our ships. After I engaged the sternmost ship, I passed the enemy's other ships till I got to their van; and, in regard to the *Kent*'s behaviour, it was impossible for me, at the distance we were asunder, to say whether the *Kent* did do her duty or not. I own I made objections in ranking with Captain Fox. The day after the action, the signal for all captains being made, I went on board the Admiral about 12 o'clock. It was the general murmur of the gentlemen aboard that Captain Fox had not done his duty, that he had not engaged the enemy in such a manner as might be expected from a ship of his force; and, hearing these things and several other matters from Captains Cotes, Hanway, Rodney, Moore, and others, I objected to rank with him, or to sit at a council of war, till such time as he had cleared his character.

[1] Corbett's letter to Steuart is in Adm.2/506, pp. 118–19.

Q. Was the line of battle formed?

A. No, but the signal was made.

Q. Where was the *Kent* stationed?

A. She was to have led with her starboard tacks on board.

Q. What number of ships were there of the enemy?

A. Nine.

A. Was the *Kent* in her station astern before the signal for the line of battle was hauled down?

A. Yes.

A. Was the enemy in a line?

A. Yes, in an extensive line, ahead of one the other.

Q. Where was the *Tonnant*?

A. I think pretty near centre.

Q. When the signal for the line was hauled down, did you see the *Kent* make sail?

A. I am not certain.

Q. After you began to engage, did the enemy preserve their line?

A. Yes, such a line as it was. A very extended one. Until the *Neptune* struck.

Q. What was the distance between your engaging and the signal for the line being hauled down.

A. Very little.

Q. Did you see at any time that day any of the ships of the enemy unengaged who might have been engaged by any of ours?

A. Yes, sometimes for a little space, as ships passed to and fro.

Q. Was there any ships of our line who by tacking could have fetched the wake of the sternmost ship of the enemy line?

A. I don't believe the leewardmost of ours could. Perhaps three or four might.

Q. Was the enemy's line close hauled upon a wind?

A. Upon a wind.

Q. Were the *Tonnant* or *Intrépide* to leeward of you when you saw them?

A. Right ahead, as near as possible, was the *Tonnant*. I can't say how the *Intrépide* was, but several of our ships were about her both to windward and to leeward of her.

Q. Could any of our ships have weathered the *Tonnant*?

A. I believe some of the sternmost might.

Q. *(President)* to the *Prisoner* Have you any questions to ask of Captain Watson?

A. Nothing.

Withdraw.

Captain Cotes of His Majesty's ship *Edinburgh* called in and sworn.

Q.   (President) Captain Cotes, you have heard the charge exhibited by Sir Edward Hawke...Please to inform the court...as far as falls under your observation, Captain Fox's behaviour on that day's action.

A.   On the 14th October last, in the latitude 47.45N. or thereabouts, the wind at S.S.E., at daybreak in the morning we saw seven sail to the S.W. for which we made the signal to the Admiral. He answered it and made the signal for a general chase. At 8, discovered them to be a large fleet of ships. At 10, the Admiral made the signal for the line of battle ahead. Before the line was quite formed, near 11 o'clock, the signal for the line was hauled down, and a general signal for all the fleet to chase to the S.W. was made. Soon after 11, the signal was made to engage the enemy who were then in an irregular line of battle. The signal was obeyed by our headmost ships. The enemy soon after got on board their foretacks and made sail. After we had passed four of the enemy's ships and engaged them, two to windward and two to leeward, and were steering for the enemy's ship in the centre which appeared to me to be their Commodore, I observed one of our large ships laying astern of the enemy under her topsails, with her mizen topsail aback, which ship I verily believe to be the *Kent*; and as I thought it very extraordinary to see a ship of her consequence keeping out of the action, I sent for my First Lieutenant John Hinksman to take notice of her bad behaviour. Soon after, coming to action with the centre ships of the enemy, I ordered the lieutenant to his quarters. After engaging some time, was disabled by my fore topmast being shot away and falling on my guns the side next the enemy. Whilst I lay in that condition, the *Kent* neither came up to my assistance nor to engage the ship that disabled me, but still lay astern with her mizen topsail backed. This includes till a little past 2 o'clock, after which I never observed her...

Q.   How long did you engage?

A.   At different times till near 4 o'the clock.

Q.   What time do you judge it might be when you first saw the *Kent*, as you apprehend, with her mizen topsail aback?

A.   Near 1 o'clock, as well as I can recollect...

Q.   Were there any of the enemy's ships astern of you?

A.   There were four, who I passed before I engaged the centre ship.

Q.   Were there any of our own ships astern of you engaged with the enemy at the time you saw the *Kent* in that position?

A.   The Admiral and several of our ships were engaged astern of me at that time...

Captain Saunders of His Majesty's ship *Yarmouth* called in and sworn...

Q. (President) ...please to inform the court [of] Captain Fox's behaviour in that day's action.

A. I only saw Captain Fox at one time of the day, as near as I can judge about 2 o'clock, and then to leeward of me and not in any position at all to engage the enemy, he being too far to leeward.

Q. How long had you been engaged when you saw the *Kent* in that position?

A. Upwards of two hours.

Q. Can you tell if the *Kent* had before that time been at all engaged?

A. She fired at the enemy over me, which was the reason of my observing her.

Q. Did her shot, do you apprehend, reach the enemy?

A. I cannot say. Her shot could not very well endamage the enemy because I lay directly between them...

Q. Did she appear to you to be disabled in her masts, rigging, or sails?

A. Not at all.

Q. Were there, do you apprehend, any ships of the enemy in such position that the *Kent* could have engaged them closer than she did that with whom you were engaged?

A. After the *Kent* had fired a little over me, she fell astern and fired at one of the enemy's ships who had a quarter of an hour before called to me for quarters. There was no ship after that to engage in the rear...

Q. What time did you begin to engage the *Neptune*?

A. About 12...

Q. Were the nearest ships to you ahead, both the enemy's and ours, at a greater distance from you at that time the ship surrendered to you than at the beginning of the engagement?

A. A great deal farther from me...

Q. How long did the enemy's and our ships ahead engage after the enemy's ships in the rear had surrendered?

A. A great while after dark.

Q. Did you see the flashings or hear the guns after dark?

A. Yes, I was engaged myself after it was dark.

Q. Did you make sail after the ship had struck to you to the ships ahead.

A.   Yes, as soon as I could get clear of the enemy's ship I fell aboard of.

Q.   How long might that be?

A.   More than half an hour.

Q.   Pray what sail could you make?

A.   No more than what I had when I left off engaging, which was foresail down, fore topsail on the cap, main topsail hoisted but half of it shot away, and the rest much shattered.

Q.   Can you inform the court how far the nearest of the enemy's ships might be to you when you first pursued them?

A.   About four miles.

Q.   At what time did you come up to engage them ships ahead after the ship had called for quarters?

A.   After dark a good while.

Q.   Did you before it was dark distinguish the French ship aboard which the Commodore was?

A.   Yes, and it was her I followed and engaged.

Q.   Were there any ships of ours engaged with others of the French ships at the same time?

A.   No, all the enemy's ships but her and another [the *Intrépide*] had ceased firing some time before that.

Q.   At what time did your engaging the ships cease?

A.   About 10, as near as I can tell.

Q.   Was there any firing after you gave over?

A.   No...

Q.   What ships of ours were engaged with you at the time you engaged the two French ships, the *Tonnant* and *Intrépide*?

A.   The *Nottingham* and *Eagle* only.

Q.   Did the ships of the enemy alter their position or go away large at or after the time of your engaging them?

A.   They went away large.

Q.   Did they go from you?

A.   Yes.

Q.   What sail could you perceive they had out then?

A.   The *Tonnant* went away with her mainsail, foresail, and fore topsail.

Q.   At what time of night did you lose sight of the enemy's ships?

A.   I believe about 12...

THE COURT ADJOURNED TILL THE MORROW MORNING, 8 O'CLOCK.

Second day
Thursday the 26th November 1747
Captain Steevens of His Majesty's ship *Portland* called in and sworn.
[He stated:]

Between 11 and 12 the morning of the 14th October, after the signal for the line was hauled down and the general signal for chasing was made, I observed from my own ship that the *Kent* was under her three topsails and foresail, with her mizen topsail aback, which I was greatly surprised and concerned at, thinking it the duty of every ship at that time, when the general signal was out for chasing, to carry all the sail they could till they had got up with the enemy in the station they intended to engage. According to the best of my judgement, between 4 and 6 in the afternoon I observed Admiral Hawke in the *Devonshire* with the signal out for coming to a closer engagement with the enemy, and had at the same time the *Kent*'s signal out, a white pendant at the main topmast head. I then observed the *Kent* standing after the Rear-Admiral, and observed the *Tonnant* and *Intrépide* bearing away out of their line, standing to the westward...

Q. [President]   In what part of the engagement was you, in the rear or van of the enemy?

A.   About half after 12, I received and gave fire to the *Monarque*. After that, I passed Rear-Admiral Hawke as close as I possibly could to leeward and received and gave fire to the *Tonnant*, the French *chef d'escadre*, and by my shot carried away his mizen topmast head with his flag upon it. I then passed and received and gave fire to the *Terrible*; and, coming up with the *Trident*, I shortened sail and engaged her for about two hours and a half, and remained in that station the whole action till the *Terrible* struck to the Admiral about 7 o'clock...

Q.   When you saw the *Kent*'s signal out, did you take notice of what the *Kent* did on that occasion?

A.   She stood after the Admiral with her three topsails and courses.

Q.   How near do you imagine she came to the Admiral?

A.   At the time I saw her, she was a good distance from him and I did not observe her afterwards.

Q.   Was the Admiral's ship at that time between the *Kent* and the enemy?

A.   Yes.

Q.   Had the Admiral engaged then?

A.   Yes, some time before, for above four hours, and was then stretching to go on ahead, first to the *Trident* and after that to the

Terrible...

Q. Pray, Sir, did you object [to] ranking with Captain Fox at a council of war held on board the Admiral's ship the day after the action?

A. Yes, Sir, I did.

Q. Give the court an account of your reasons for so doing.

A. From my observing his having shortened sail and laying with his mizen topsail aback when Admiral Hawke had the general signal out for chasing, as before mentioned, and from what I heard the other captains who were at the council of war say.

Q. You will be so good as to name those captains.

A. Captains Watson, Cotes, Moore, Rodney, Stanhope, and others whose names I can't recollect...

Q. What was the signal for a closer engagement?

A. A flag at the main topmast head, half red, half white...

Captain Steevens withdraw.

Captain Rodney of his Majesty's ship *Eagle* called in and sworn. [He stated:]

On the 14th October last, early in the morning, a signal was made by some of our ships discovering strange ships in the S.W. quarter. Some time after, the Admiral made the signal for a general chase. About 9 we saw a great number of ships which proved to be the enemy. About 10, the Admiral made a signal for the line of battle ahead with larboard tacks aboard. As the *Eagle*'s station was the sternmost ship of the line, except the *Kent*, we soon got into it. About 11, before the line was quite formed, a signal was made for a general chase. About half past 11 the Admiral made the signal to engage the enemy, which was presently obeyed by the ships of our van. Some little time after, the *Kent* and *Eagle* being the only ships of our line of battle astern of the enemy's rear, I took notice to my First Lieutenant [John Harrison] that I intended to attack the sternmost of the enemy's ships and thought it would be prudent if both *Kent* and *Eagle* stuck close to the said ship till she struck. With that intent, we steered directly for her. The *Kent*, who was then before our weather beam, backed her mizen topsail and let us shoot ahead of her. Shortly after, we began the engagement [with] the enemy's said rear ship which proved to be the *Neptune*; though the *Kent* might have attacked the said ship first, had she not backed her mizen topsail, she being to windward and sailing better than the *Eagle*. After being engaged some time with the *Neptune* on our larboard side, we were attacked by another of the enemy's ships [the *Fou-*

gueux] on the starboard side, which put us between two fires and obliged us to divide our men in order to fight both sides at the same time. During our being thus hard pressed, the *Kent* did not come between the *Eagle* and either of the enemy's ships in order to save us from a double fire.

After exchanging a few broadsides with the ship on my starboard side she, being much disabled, dropped astern and left us engaged with the *Neptune* only. A short time after, one of my officers on the poop told me that the *Hector* was engaged with the said ship that fell astern of me, which I plainly saw from my stern windows. Some short time after that, I was informed the said enemy's ship had struck to the *Hector*. I immediately looked through the stern and perceived the firing had ceased. Our engagement with the *Neptune* still continued; but, about 2 in the afternoon, an unlucky shot carrying away the steering wheel—our masts, rigging, and sails being very much shattered—so as to render the ship ungovernable, we unfortunately fell twice aboard the *Devonshire* who was on our lee quarter coming up to our assistance. This accident prevented my observing anything more of the action for a considerable time, as I was employed in putting the ship again in a proper condition for battle. However, to the best of my memory, between 3 and 4 in the afternoon, I observed the *Kent*, who did not seem damaged, steering for the French Admiral's ship. I then remarked to some of my officers that I hoped the *Kent* would stick close by her and regain the honour I thought she had lost at the beginning of the battle; but, to my great surprise, I saw the *Kent* bear round up, discharge some of her guns, then [sheer] to leeward and ahead withall, till quite clear of that ship's fire.

Q. *[President]* How far do you think the *Kent* was from the *Neptune* when you began to attack her?

A.   Upon my word, I can't tell, for I minded only the *Neptune* for a little while...

Q.   Can you tell us what sail the *Kent* had out when she backed her mizen topsail?

A.   I cannot recollect.

Q.   Can you tell where the *Kent* was when you was attacked both sides?

A.   I frequently saw her through my stern...

Q.   How long after the *Devonshire* came up to your assistance did the *Neptune* strike, do you imagine?

A.   I don't know...

Q.   Who did the *Neptune* strike to?

A. I don't know. Not to me...

Then the court adjourned till the morrow morning, 8 o'clock.

Third day

Friday the 27th November 1747...

Lieutenant John Harrison[1] of His Majesty's ship *Eagle* sworn [and he stated:]

...About the same time [as the *Eagle* closed on the *Neptune*] the *Kent* backed her mizen topsail, let us shoot past her, run up with the *Neptune* and engage, which we did at the distance of pistol shot and continued engaging her upwards of two hours, during which I often looked on our weather quarter but did not observe the *Kent* engaged, though I always saw her...I encouraged our people by showing her to them, saying here was a sixty-four gun ship would soon come to our assistance. At last an unfortunate ball shot our wheel away which occasioned our falling twice aboard the Admiral... I then imagined the *Kent* would have taken our place, as she lay in a position capable of so doing; but I observed she edged away... Some time after, she steered as I judged for the French Admiral and I imagined intended to have engaged her close, but found when she came pretty nigh, she bore away round, fired some guns at her, then ran to leeward and ahead withall till quite clear of her fire...

[The interrogation of this witness went on for some time. Then the *President* asked:]

Q. Was there any other ship but the *Kent* near to the French Admiral and the ship [the *Nottingham*] that bore down to him?

A. By the time that ship bore down, the *Kent* was a good way ahead, and I believe the *Yarmouth* and *Eagle* were the two nearest ships to the French Admiral.

Q. Did the *Yarmouth* and *Eagle* bear down to the French Admiral and that ship?

A. The *Eagle* did. The *Yarmouth* was right astern of her.

Q. And did you both engage the French Admiral?

A. Not directly.

Q. Did you after?

A. Yes.

Q. Did you at the time you began the attack see the *Kent*?

A. When the *Yarmouth, Eagle*, and *Nottingham* bore down to attack, it was the close of the evening; but when we began the attack

---

[1] John Harrison: L 1741, CR 1755, C 1755. Superannuated RA 1779.

it was too dark to see any distance, so I did not see the *Kent*...

(*President* to Prisoner)   Have you any questions to ask?...

Q. *[Prisoner]*   When you observed the *Kent* to have shot ahead of the *Tonnant*, did you observe her main topmast gone?

A.   I believe it was.

Q.   Do you think it was probable the *Kent* carried it away?

A.   I can't tell.

[President]   Withdraw.

Captain Hanway of His Majesty's ship the *Windsor* called in and sworn. [He stated:]

Some time after I had come up with and engaged several of the enemy's ships, agreeable to the signal for chasing and engaging, and was passing on to engage the other ships in the enemy's line, I observed (it being first pointed out to me by several of my officers and people) the *Kent* under her foresail and topsails, and mizen topsail aback, though the sternmost ship of the enemy appeared at that time to be some distance ahead of the *Kent* and had loosed her topgallant sails (as I apprehended) to have closed with the next ship. As I came to action myself immediately after, I saw nothing more of the *Kent*'s behaviour till between 3 and 5, this being between 1 and 2, as I apprehend. After I had engaged every ship in the enemy's line, except the headmost, and was standing on to her to assist the *Monmouth*, that ship [the *Intrépide*] tacked and kept her wind towards the English fireships, which obliged me to wear to return the action. I could not tack, my rigging and masts being so much shot.

After repassing the two ships I have since heard called the *Terrible* and *Trident*, [and] perceiving the Admiral ahead of the French Admiral, I was standing on the starboard tack with what sail I could make towards the French Admiral to give him battle, which I imagined the *Kent* was going to do, who appeared at that time the nearest ship to her. But as I was passing the *Devonshire*, I was called to follow the Admiral, and therefore I immediately wore; at which time, or near it, I perceived the captain of the *Kent*'s signal out, which I ordered to be repeated as I was astern of the *Devonshire*. Soon after, that signal was hauled down and the *Kent* exchanged some shot with the French Admiral. A very short time after, I had wore and was on the starboard tack. I was called to from the poop to observe that the *Kent* had quitted the French Admiral and was making sail from her, which I then saw.

About that time, whether a little before or a little after I can't say, I saw the *Intrépide* bearing down to the French Admiral and, I believe, passed so near as to hail her, as the French Admiral immediately wore after her and kept before the wind under her foresail and a part of her mainsail—the only sail she appeared to me to have to set.

After I had wore the second time I observed the signal out for closer engaging, but know not when it was thrown out. Some time after, I observed the *Kent* to have quitted the French Admiral. Admiral Hawke made her signal to tack, which I again ordered to be repeated; but can not say positively whether it was or not, as I was every moment expecting to come to action. My reason for ordering it to be repeated was that I understood that signal to be a direction to follow the French Admiral...

...a considerable time after it was dark...I was satisfied that the *Terrible* had struck by her ceasing to fire and calling for quarters.

As soon as my yards could be secured and tackles fixed, I ordered a boat to be hoisted out and, soon after I had put off to go aboard the Admiral, seeing a ship at some distance on my lee quarter, I hailed the *Windsor* to know what ship that was and was assured by my Third Lieutenant (the only one I had left) it was the *Kent*.

When I came on board the *Devonshire*, I found Admiral Hawke in the gunroom dressing by the Surgeon. He had been very severely blown up by gunpowder. I acquainted him with the circumstances of my own ship and the position of several ships that were nearest to him, and informed the Admiral that just as I was coming aboard I had heard several guns fired to leeward, which I believed to be from some of our ships who had renewed the action with the French Admiral. Admiral Hawke seemed surprised that the *Kent* was not one of those ships and directed me to send immediately to Captain Fox to let him know that he should take any ships he could find in a condition to proceed with him, and go immediately to the assistance of His Majesty's ships then engaged, but if he found those ships had struck, then to give assistance to any of our disabled ships, or of the enemy's that had struck and might want it, and directed me to lay by the *Terrible*.

I put off from the *Devonshire* and soon after met the *Kent*'s boat with her First Lieutenant, who was going aboard the Admiral. I acquainted the lieutenant with the Admiral's directions and repeated them a second time to avoid any mistake, which I thought the quickest way of executing the Admiral's commands...I saw the ship I was informed was the *Kent* some considerable time after—above an hour and a half...

[Interrogation ensued. Then the court adjourned.]

Fourth day

Monday the 30th November 1747...

Captain Moore of His Majesty's ship *Devonshire* called in and sworn. [He stated:]

...But the time I took most notice of the *Kent* was a little before the *Devonshire* engaged the second ship of the enemy's van, which I believe was the *Trident*. A little before that, I saw the *Kent* laying astern of one of the enemy's ships which we took for the *Tonnant*...I stood for nearly a quarter of an hour in the balcony, expecting to see the *Kent* make sail and engage the *Tonnant*; but his not doing so made me take the liberty of calling Admiral Hawke to me and I asked whether he thought the *Kent* was doing the duty of a man of war. He gave his opinion she was not, which occasioned Captain Fox's pendant being thrown out. Captain Fox immediately observed this signal and set his foresail...but instead of engaging as I expected he would have done, he fired some shot at, and received some few shot from the *Tonnant*'s quarter and kept lasking away ... Soon after this, we in the *Devonshire* were engaged with the ship I took for the *Trident*. After she surrendered and we were going with what sail we could make up to the *Terrible*, I saw the *Kent* coming towards us, for what reason I could not conceive, for the object he could have engaged was then astern of him. The Admiral then ordered his, Captain Fox's, signal to be made to come to a closer engagement. The flag being ready bent to the halyards and the pendant not immediately ready, I bid the signalman hoist the flag, observing to the Admiral that it could not affect any of the rest of the gentlemen as they were all, except the *Kent*, either closely engaged or in such a disabled condition they could not make sail...The *Kent* took no notice of this signal but continued sailing after us...

The *Kent* might now plainly see we wanted no more assistance and might have tacked or wore and gone back to the *Tonnant*, but he did not do so. There was no other method left than to make his signal for tacking [but] I was very doubtful whether Captain Fox could [see the signal]. It was not observed by him. [Then] we began to engage the *Terrible*, which continued till after dark...

Q. President to Captain Moore ... As the *Tonnant* was joined by the *Intrépide*, was there any of our ships at liberty, and in a condition, to have assisted and supported the *Kent* against the *Tonnant* and *Intrépide* when they so joined?

A. Our ships were all greatly disabled, but if I can judge by their behaviour in the day, they would have used such means as to have come to the *Kent's* assistance...

Q. Then I apprehend the Admiral thought three ships necessary for that service?

A. I believe he thought the three ships [*Kent, Tilbury,* and *Lion*] not sufficient force, but he could get no more...

Q. (Sir Edward Hawke) When the *Kent* lay alongside the *Trident*, you say she was but indifferently employed. Pray how was she employed?

A. The reason I said so was because I know there could be no other duty performed alongside a ship who had struck but sending his boat aboard, which I thought not proper employment for a ship of that force...

[The evidence given on the following six days of the trial added little of substance about the course of the battle or the behaviour of the *Kent*.]

The eleventh day

Thursday 10th December 1747...

Prisoner upon his defence produces his defence contained in four sheets of paper which he prays the Deputy Judge Advocate may be permitted by the court to read for him...

> Gentlemen. It is with the utmost concern that I appear before this court in character of an offender; and though the course of near forty years service, twenty of which as a commissioned officer, without blame or censure, is a matter of great satisfaction to me, yet it is by no means equal to the anxiety of mind I feel on this present occasion. The heavy charge of which I stand accused has in the compass of a dozen lines, to the remembrance of the world, blotted out all the little claim I ever had to merit, either as a zealous officer or an honest man, and branded me at once with infamy and shame; and how innocent soever I may appear of the facts charged against me in the judgement of this court, after the evidence I have to produce shall have been heard and examined with that candour and impartiality wherewith the evidence against me [has] been treated in the course of this trial, yet 'tis hardly probable that I shall ever be able to stem that torrent of popular prejudice wherewith my reputation has been born down and which has rendered me the common subject of every coffee house and public paper...
>
> ...as 'tis as natural for English seamen not to be fond of a coward for a commander, as 'tis for English captains to refuse to rank with a coward, I hope the testimony of my officers and ship's company will by no means be suspected of partiality, as

'tis on the truth and plainness of their evidence that I am to
make my defence...

...I still made sail ahead to the *Tonnant*, which ship I engaged
as properly and as zealously as was within my power, for I first
raked her and then shot along her side, where I engaged for
near or quite three quarters of an hour...we both fought under
sail, and that was the reason of my bringing down her main and
mizen topmasts, except the flag-stave which was gone before,
[so] that I shot so suddenly ahead; which, as soon as I found, I
did my utmost to lay aback and come on her again, my rigging
being greatly shattered, till my officers, seeing my signal on
board the Admiral, advised me that he wanted help, and that
'twas better to follow him than be accused of disobedience.
They, and everybody that stood near me, know with what
reluctance and concern I left this ship and it will fully show itself
in evidence...So I most solemnly assert that if I had seen or
known of any signal made for me to tack, I should most gladly
have obeyed it. But I can by no means think myself in fault (and
hope my judges will not think so) for my not construing a
general signal for closer engagement to relate to me in particular...

Lieutenant George Ryall, First Lieutenant of His Majesty's ship
Kent, called in and sworn. [He stated:]

[After dark, having hoisted out a boat from the *Kent*,] I ordered
the coxwain to pull aboard the Admiral, as we were not far from
him, and there I should know what the orders were. When I got
aboard the *Devonshire* I met Lieutenant Hammond[1] of the *Louisa*
who said, 'Ryall, I am glad I have seen you, for you have saved me
the trouble of going aboard the *Kent*, for it is the Admiral's order
that you, with us, wear and go astern to take care of the same ships.'
I repeated these orders to Lieutenant Smelt[2] [of the *Devonshire*]
and asked him if he had any further commands for me. He answered
'No'. I then returned aboard the *Kent* and we wore and went astern
in obedience to those orders.

Q.(Prisoner) ...Did I endeavour, or not, after I shot ahead of
the *Tonnant*, to lay all aback to endeavour to come on her again?

---

[1] This name is incorrect. The officer concerned was, in fact, Stephen Hammick (L
1745, CR 1761).
[2] Smelt: L 1741, CR 1748. Hawke tried without success to get him posted after
Second Finisterre, but he reappeared as a Regulating Captain in 1755 (Mackay,
Hawke, pp. 90, 95, 203–4).

A.   I was not on deck just at that time, but when I did come up, saw every sail aback that I understood could be backed, because the braces forward were shot.

Q.   How did I behave immediately before and during this time of action...?

A.   I think that in the whole course of that day's action Captain Fox behaved, in my opinion, like a good officer. He took pains in encouraging the people, did his utmost to destroy the enemy and made all haste that ever he could to the assistance [of whoever] he thought wanted it...

Q.   Do you know of any person hurt with musket balls, or was the *Kent* too far distant from the several ships she engaged with to receive any hurt from their musketry?

A.   There were two or three wounded with musket balls, one of whom was shot in his throat between decks when I was talking with the lieutenant about the breechings; and, as to distance, I think we were never without musket shot while engaged and what more confirms me in that opinion is a musket ball came through a quarter gallery wainscot door.

Q.   Pray describe to the court the position of the *Kent* and *Yarmouth* with regard to the *Neptune*.

A.   When we raked the *Neptune*, the *Yarmouth* was a little before our beam, and when we lay upon her quarter the *Yarmouth* was on our starboard bow.

Prisoner has no more questions.

Q.(President)   Pray Mr Ryall, when you backed the mizen topsail to let the *Eagle* shoot ahead of you that her guns might bear upon the enemy, was the signal to engage the enemy out on board the Admiral?

A.   I believe it was.

Q.   Was not the *Kent* nearer the enemy's ship [the *Neptune*] that the *Eagle* engaged than the *Eagle* was at the time you backed your mizen topsail?

A.   The difference of the distance is so small that I think we were near about equally distant from the enemy.

Q.   Could you have got to windward of the *Neptune* then?

A.   Yes.

Q.   Then is it not reasonable to think that the *Eagle* would have been as cautious of firing into you as you seemed to be of hurting her?

A.   Yes, Sir. But nobody aboard the *Kent* thought the *Eagle* would lay alongside that ship; and, by backing our mizen topsail, we were willing she should give the enemy her fire in passing him, which she could not have done had we continued abreast of them...

Q.(Sir Edward Hawke) I think you said you did not see the *Kent*'s signal till 20 minutes after 5 and that you made sail before 5. Pray, Sir, [what] was the reason of your making sail after me, before you saw your signal out?

A. Because it was seen, though I did not see it.

Q. Who was it did see it?

A. Particularly, I can not name anyone, but it was the general cry forward.

Q. I would beg leave to know, when you went aboard the *Devonshire*, whether Lieutenant Smelt told you himself that it was my orders for you only to take care of the crippled ships.

A. No. But I told him the orders I had, and showed Lieutenant Hammond to him and asked him if I could speak to the Admiral or Captain Moore; but he told me, no, the Admiral was blown up and in the wardroom, and Captain Moore was busy with him, but that there were no other commands for me.

Q. Court Did you not see the *Kent*'s signal to tack?

A. No.

Q. Did you hear it was out?

A. No, never, till I came into Portsmouth harbour.

Q. When you last saw your signal out, in what position was your ship from the Admiral?

A. He was about a mile ahead of us, a little to our lee bow.

The court adjourned till the morrow morning, 8 o'th'clock...

The fourteenth day

Monday the 14th December 1747...

President Captain Fox, who would you have brought in?

A. Captain Wilkinson, Captain of Marines, if the court please.

[*Captain Wilkinson* stated:]

The 14th October last, between 6 and 7 in the morning, being told that a large fleet were seen ahead, I went on the quarterdeck where I heard Captain Fox giving orders to make more sail and clear ship. I likewise heard him order the Gunner to get everything ready for engagement. An hour and a half or thereabouts afterwards, I saw everything clear and the shot lockers filled on each side of the main deck, quarterdeck, and forecastle. There were some hen-coops in the soldiers' way on the poop, of which I acquainted the Captain. He immediately ordered them to be tossed overboard, which was done. About half past 9 I was told the Admiral had made the signal to form the line, at which time we tacked. Captain Fox hailed the Admiral as he passed by him but I did not hear the particulars. Some time afterwards, we tacked again. About 11, beat to arms. Went to my quarters on the poop. About 12, heard our headmost ships begin to engage. Half an hour afterwards, we came pretty nigh the sternmost of the enemy—the *Eagle* then near abreast of us to leeward. Our mizen topsail was then backed, the *Eagle* shot ahead and engaged. We then filled and went down to another of the enemy's ships [the *Fougueux*] and engaged her till she struck. The *Hector*, who was then near us, hoisted a boat out and took her in possession. We soon after came up with another of the enemy [the *Neptune*] who was then very closely engaged with the *Yarmouth*, and fired some guns at her. She struck to the *Yarmouth*.

[We] saw another of the French [the *Tonnant*] about a mile ahead, steered after her, and soon came within musket shot. [We] fired incessantly on her for at least half an hour and carried away her main topmast; shot ahead; backed our main topsail.

Our soldiers having expended all or most of their ammunition (most of them having fired twenty-six rounds) I went to Captain Fox to desire he would order us a fresh supply and asked him on which side we should next engage. He answered: 'We must stick by this ship [and] engage to leeward.'

The First Lieutenant came to him at this time and told him the Admiral had made his signal to follow him. Captain Fox said 'God dammit, it can't be. What can the Admiral want with me?' The lieutenant made some reply which I did not distinctly hear. I returned immediately to my quarters and soon after saw the main topsail filled. One of the French headmost ships tacked and stood towards the ship we had last engaged. We fired several shot at her as she passed by us. From this time, we ceased firing.

Q. (Prisoner) At what distance do you think we engaged the *Fougueux* and how long?

A. I believe about two hundred yards from her, that was the utmost; and we engaged her about three quarters of an hour.

Q. At what distance do you think we fired at the *Neptune*, after the *Fougueux* had struck?

A. About four hundred yards or more.

Q. At what distance do you think we engaged the *Tonnant*?

A. Within 150 yards, I think.

Q. How did I behave immediately before and during the time of action...?

A. Before the action, when the drum was beating to arms,

Captain Fox called his officers aft, shook them by the hand, and drank success to the day, and said: 'This is the day will do honour to the British Fleet', or words to that effect. He afterwards went round the ship and exhorted every private man to do his duty [and] told them he would regard them as they behaved that day. I saw Captain Fox frequently during the engagement, sometimes observing the enemy and at other times what was doing in the ship, all which times he seemed in the greatest spirits, and when he was told the Admiral had made his signal, appeared in the greatest uneasiness on leaving the *Tonnant*.

Q. Did you hear of the least murmur or dissatisfaction expressed by any of the officers or people of the *Kent* with respect to my conduct or behaviour in the action, intimating by any means that I had been remiss or negligent in my duty?

A. When we left the *Tonnant*, the soldiers and others on the poop looked very dissatisfied, but were far from laying it to Captain Fox's charge...I never heard any whisper that the Captain had not done his duty, but quite the reverse; they all thought he had.

Q. (President) ...Do you remember anything of a boat being sent from the *Kent* after the *Terrible* had struck or of the message she brought back?

A. I remember the First Lieutenant went in a boat aboard the *Devonshire*. When he came back, he told us in the wardroom he had got us off an ugly job.

Q. What did he mean by that?

A. He did not explain himself.

Q. Had he been aboard the Admiral then?

A. He said he came from the Admiral...

Q. Did you hear there were any preparations making or intention showed by the *Kent* for going down to assist the ships engaged to leeward after the *Tonnant* had struck?

A. I was told by some of the officers that we designed to go down, but that we were ordered then to go to assist the lame geese.

Q. Was it before or after the First Lieutenant said he had got you off an ugly job that you heard this?

A. It was after.

Q. Can you remember who the officers were that the First Lieutenant mentioned his having got you off an ugly job to?

A. There was Mr Maxwell, the Lieutenant of Marines, and the Surgeon, and more whom I can't recollect...

Q. When you heard that firing to leeward, did you not observe any anxiety in the officers and people of the *Kent* for the fate of those ships so engaged or any desire to go to their assistance?

A. I heard many of the private men, both soldiers and seamen, wish they were there...

Q. (Sir Edward Hawke) What time of day was it the *Kent* left the *Tonnant?*

A. I cannot be positive. I believe a little after 4...

Lieutenant Maxwell of Marines on board His Majesty's ship *Kent* called in and sworn...

Q. (President) Do you know anything of a boat's going from the *Kent* after the *Terrible* had struck?

A. No.

Q. Did not the First Lieutenant come into the wardroom after his return from the Admiral's ship?

A. Yes.

Q. Did he not mention something of a message he had brought from the Admiral's ship, and what was it?

A. I did not distinctly hear, being walking backwards and forwards. He said at first there were orders for our ship to go down and engage the two ships that got by us, but that them orders were countermanded, and said he had got rid of an ugly job; and, patting me on the breast, said: 'Little man, let everyone do as much as we have done today, for I think we have done very well.'

Q. Pray, what do you apprehend he meant by that ugly job?

A. Really, I can't say...

The fifteenth day

Wednesday, 16th December 1747...The Deputy Judge Advocate acquainted the court that he had received an answer from Mr Secretary Corbett to his letter of the 11th instant which he read...

> Admiralty Office, 14 December 1747...their Lordships do not think proper to interfere with the proceedings of courts martial. But, as you express a want of information, I will venture to tell you what I can gather from the sentiments of those I have conversed with, which are that the office of a court martial being to come at the knowledge of the truth of matters under their inquiry and examination, and they being a court of honour and not tied down to the strict forms of other courts, they are to follow their judgement in using proper methods for answering the ends of their meeting...

A debate arose whether or not Lieutenant Smelt should be called upon and asked if, on the 14th October, when Lieutenant Ryall

came aboard the *Devonshire*, he, Mr Ryall, told Mr Smelt that
Lieutenant Hammond had told him that it was the Admiral's orders
that the *Kent* should wear with the *Louisa* and *Defiance* and go
astern to take care of the same ships, and then asked Lieutenant
Smelt if he had any farther commands for him, to which Lieutenant
Smelt answered 'No'.
[The court voted 11–1 in favour of calling him.]

Lieutenant Smelt of His Majesty's ship the *Devonshire* called in and
sworn. The question [was] put to him... [and he replied:]
    I don't remember that when Mr Ryall came aboard ...he repeated
any orders to me at all regarding the *Kent* ... I never heard any
orders at all for the *Kent*...
    Q. (Mr Ryall)   Do you remember my bidding you a good night
and asking you if you had any farther orders for me?
    A.   I have some faint remembrance of Mr Ryall's bidding me
good night, but as to orders, I heard nothing of.
    Q. (Court)   Do you remember anybody with Mr Ryall?
    A.   No, I do not, nor did I ever tell Mr Ryall he could not, or
might not see or speak to the Admiral.
    Mr Smelt and Mr Ryall withdraw...

The seventeenth day
Friday 18th December 1747...
Prisoner   I will not trouble the court with any farther evidence in
my defence, but as I have a remark or two to offer, with which I
could not be prepared till my witnesses were all examined, I therefore hope that, at the opening of the court to consider of their
judgement, they will permit me to do it.
President   To be sure, by all means.

And then the court adjourned to Monday morning, 8 o'th'clock.

The eighteenth day
Monday, 21st December 1747...
President to Prisoner   Sir, whatever you have now to offer the
court, they are ready to receive it.
Prisoner offering a paper prays it may be read by the Judge Advo-
cate. The Deputy Judge Advocate reads it as follows:

> Gentlemen...My leaving the *Tonnant*, [as] I hope has fully
> appeared to the court, was in obedience to my signal...Wha-
> tever has been said by those two officers with respect to their
> being mistaken in the appearance of the signal by taking the fly

of the flag [as] a white pendant, I must...say that I never knew it...I saw my pendant, and my pendant only. It appears by the oaths of five other persons that they also saw it by itself. Why else should I make sail? Why should I express concern at being obliged to leave the ship?

...I believe it is an instance not to be produced that in the hurry and confusion of engagement every man can lay his hand upon his heart and say: 'There is nothing which I have left undone! There is no point in which I have erred!'...May God, who has directed me in my defence, direct you also in your judgement.

THOMAS FOX

That being finished, the court asked him if he had anything farther to offer.

Prisoner No.

The court ordered to be cleared and they began to debate upon the sentence, and came to the following resolutions:

Resolved that the following questions be put:

Q. Does it appear to this court that Captain Fox has been guilty of the whole or part of the charge exhibited against him?

A. Guilty of part, unanimously.

Q. Wherein has he been guilty of that part? Has it been in point of courage, conduct, or disaffection?

A. In point of conduct only, unanimously.

Q. In what particular does his misconduct appear?

A. In backing his mizen topsail: Yes 9, Noes 3.

In his leaving the *Tonnant*: Yes, unanimously.

In waiting for his boat and not going down immediately to the assistance of the ships to leeward upon the Admiral's message: Yes 10, Noes 2.

Q. Which or what part of the Articles of War does he fall under?

A. Part of the 11th: [Yes] 2; 11th and 12th: [Yes] 4; 11th and 14th: [Yes] 3; 11th, 12th, and 14th: [Yes] 3.

Q. What punishment do you award him?

A. To be dismissed from the command of His Majesty's ship the *Kent*.

GEO ADKINS
Dep. Jud. Adv.

PART III

JULY 1748–JANUARY 1754
ADMIRAL BETWEEN THE WARS

INTRODUCTION

The treaty of Aix-la-Chapelle was not concluded until October 1748. However, active hostilities had ceased by 30 July when Hawke was appointed in Warren's place to command at Portsmouth [Document 50]. During the years of peace which followed, Henry Pelham's ministry was intent on economy and the Navy was accordingly run down to the minimum level that was politically acceptable. The documents printed here relate to such subjects as manning [53–4], the valuation of the prizes taken at the Second Battle of Cape Finisterre (including two personal letters from Hawke to Anson on the subject) [54, 61–2], discipline [52, 55–8, 65–70, 75], quarantine [66], local politics impinging on Hawke as an MP for Portsmouth [67], the wearing of uniform [73], relations between naval officers and dockyard staff [71–3, 75], and the maintenance of the guardships (a prime component of the Navy's seagoing reserve, partly manned, and supposedly available for operational use at short notice) [64, 73, 78–9].

By 1751 the authorized establishment of enlisted seamen had been cut down from 40,000 during the last eight years of the recent war to a figure of 8,000. This low level had not been seen since 1733. In 1752, however, protests from William Pitt and the merchant interest induced the government to restore the more normal peacetime provision of 10,000. Indeed, between the Seven Years War and the end of the century the establishment of seamen would never fall below 16,000. Meanwhile the Pelhamite economies greatly diminished naval activity at Portsmouth. In consequence, documents relating to the admiral are scarce, especially between November 1752 and December 1754.

50. *Instructions from the Lords of the Admiralty to Hawke*

26 July 1748

By the Commissioners ... to Sir Edward Hawke, Vice-Admiral of the Blue Squadron of His Majesty's Fleet at Portsmouth.

Whereas we have ordered Sir Peter Warren to strike his flag and come ashore, you are hereby required and directed to take upon you the command of His Majesty's ships and vessels at Spithead and in Portsmouth Harbour, and to hoist your flag on board such one of them in Portsmouth Harbour as you think proper. Given etc.

VERE BEAUCLERK
BARRINGTON
J. STANHOPE[1]

51. *Hawke to Clevland (holograph)*

Portsmouth
31 July 1748

Sir,

Yesterday Sir Peter Warren gave me their Lordships' order for taking upon me the command of His Majesty's ships and vessels at Spithead and in Portsmouth Harbour. I have accordingly hoisted my flag on board the *Fougueux*[2] in the Harbour, she being the only ship fit for that purpose at present. I am etc.

52. *Hawke to Clevland*

Fougueux in Portsmouth Harbour
4 August 1748

Sir,

Upon comparing the warrant I received from their Lordships for calling and assembling courts martial, bearing date 21st July 1747, with the abstract of the late Act of Parliament, I find that I am not thereby sufficiently authorized to appoint such courts and must therefore beg that their Lordships would be pleased, by the return of this express, to send me a new commission. For if we do not begin on Saturday, I am afraid there will not be a sufficient number of captains to constitute a court, as some of the sloops may sail and

---

[1] On 26.2.48, when Lord Sandwich replaced the Duke of Bedford as 1st Ld, the Hon. John Stanhope was appointed to the Board of Ady. He died in office, 3.12.48.
[2] The *Fougueux* (64) was one of the prizes taken on 14.10.47. ·

some of the ships be paid off in the beginning of the week.[1] I am etc.

53. *Hawke to Clevland*

Fougueux in Portsmouth Harbour
7 August 1748

Sir,

I have your letter of the 4th signifying their Lordships' directions to me to endeavour to complete the *Prince Henry*'s complement. There are now in this harbour only the *Invincible* and *Dover*, which are to be paid off. While their companies were on board I directed the commanders of the *Baltimore* and *Porcupine* sloops, which were both in want of men, to go on board those ships and try if any would enter with them, but not a man offered his service, declaring in general that they would not enter for any ships till they should have received and spent their wages. If this was the case with regard to these sloops, there is but little probability of any entering on board a ship destined for a distant voyage.

Their Lordships will see by the enclosed return that there are now sick at the Hospital[2] one hundred and seventy-three men belonging to different ships. I should be glad to know if they would approve of my sending such of them as may be fit for service, upon their recovery, on board the *Prince Henry* [bound for the coast of Guinea]; and if I may promise that the wages for their respective ships shall be paid them before she proceeds to sea. I should likewise be glad to know if I may send the remainder of them on board the *Fougueux* as they shall be discharged from the Hospital till their proper ships shall arrive...

Minute: 8 August. Own receipt. Notwithstanding my letter of yesterday, to turn over as many men from the *Dover* as will make up the *Prince Henry*'s complement. Usual orders to pay. The sick men to be sent on board the *Fougueux* till their ships come into port when they are to be sent to their proper ships.

---

[1] A court martial required a president together with at least five post captains or, if these were lacking, commanders. See Rodger, *Wooden World*, for this and for discipline more generally.

[2] This refers to the hospital at Gosport. Work had begun on Haslar Hospital in 1745, but no patients were admitted there till 1754.

54. *Hawke to Clevland*

Fougueux in Portsmouth Harbour
13 August 1748

Sir,

Pursuant to their Lordships' directions of the 9th to complete the *Prince Henry*'s complement from the *Dover*, I gave Captain Knowler[1] orders to turn over one hundred and nine men into her. She had been before dismantled, and all her men ashore, so that I directed him to send his officers about and collect them on board, ordering at the same time Captain Jasper,[2] with his officers, to attend with boats to receive them. Last night, Captain Knowler reported to me that, in the morning, he had got all the men his officers could find on board and used every argument to persuade them to comply with their Lordships' orders; but that a number of them immediately jumped into the vessel that was to receive them and carried her off, with the lieutenant who endeavoured to prevent them, and only forty-nine remained, whom he turned over. By this, their Lordships will perceive the difficulty of turning over men from a ship after she is unrigged and cleared in order to be paid off. I should be glad to know if they would approve of my completing the *Prince Henry* from the first ship that shall arrive, before she shall receive her order to proceed into the Harbour.

I have directed Captain Jasper to proceed immediately to Spithead in order both to secure these men and to be in greater readiness to receive any others their Lordships shall order to be put on board the *Prince Henry*.

I have received both your letters of the 11th and shall give the *Kent*, on her arrival, orders to remain at Spithead during the time their Lordships have prescribed and no longer. As to the number of prizes taken by the ships under my command during the war, I have been so much at sea that I have not yet received any perfect account of them or of the names and abodes of the agents; but as soon as I do, they shall be transmitted to you by the first opportunity. I am etc.

Minute: 16 August. Own receipt. The *Princess Royal* storeship being ordered to [be] paid off, to complete the *Prince Henry*'s complement out of her...

[1] Knowler: L 1739, C 1746.
[2] Jasper: L 1739, C 1745. Cashiered in 1754 for misconduct at Havana.

55.   *Hawke to Clevland*

Fougueux in Portsmouth Harbour
16 August 1748

Sir,

Yesterday was held on board the *Fougueux* a court martial for the trial [for mutiny] of the persons late belonging to the *Old Noll* privateer.[1] After hearing the evidences against them, one was acquitted, ten ordered to be whipped and sent in any of His Majesty's ships on a foreign voyage, and the other seven sentenced to die. As the crime of the latter was chiefly owing to ignorance and thoughtlessness, I hope their Lordships will give me leave to beg that they would intercede for mercy to be shewn them. I am etc.

56.   *Instructions from the Lords of the Admiralty to Hawke*

26 August 1748

Whereas their Excellencies the Lords Justices have been pleased to signify to us their pleasure to grant a pardon to Timothy Bryan [and six others] condemned for mutiny on board the *Old Noll* privateer, we do therefore in pursuance of their Excellencies' pleasure require and direct you to release them from their confinement and to order them on board His Majesty's ships *Prince Henry* and *Siren* in such manner as you shall judge proper. Given etc.

57.   *Hawke to Clevland*

Fougueux in Portsmouth Harbour
28 August 1748

Sir,

Agreeable to their Lordships' directions of the 25th, I have ordered the captains of His Majesty's ships at this port to give their men leave to go ashore, provided they can be trusted.   Last night I received your letters of the 26th, enclosing their Lordships' orders for pardoning the mutineers lately belonging to the *Old Noll* privateer, and shall observe their Lordships' commands in appointing a day for putting the sentence of the court martial into execution, which shall be done with all the solemnity usually practised upon the

---

[1] It was even more difficult to man privateers than warships; and it is not surprising that murder and mutiny were also more common in privateers. (Rodger, op. cit., pp. 185, 238.)

like occasions and the men brought forth in order to be executed before their pardon shall be produced.

I have delivered their Lordships' order, with your letter of the same date, to Captain Keppel. Most of the seamen being very desirous of coming ashore to this place makes me apprehensive that he will not get a sufficient number of the *Anson*'s to enter voluntarily that will be able to carry the *Centurion* round to Sheerness. However, if he should not, I shall take care to follow their Lordships' directions on that head and do everything in my power to forward him ...

58.   *Hawke to Clevland*

Fougueux in Portsmouth Harbour
31 August 1748

Sir,

Pursuant to their Lordships' directions of the 26th instant, I have been aboard the *Prince Henry* and pardoned the mutineers lately belonging to the *Old Noll* privateer. The ceremony was carried through with the same solemnity as if they had really been to die. They were all very penitent, behaved with great decency and resignation, and seemed truly sensible of their Lordships' goodness when their pardon was read to them.

The *Siren* sailed on Sunday evening; and as the *Prince Henry* is the only ship here that is going a foreign voyage, I have directed Captain Jasper to enter these men as part of his complement and to discharge the same number lately turned over which he shall judge most unfit for the voyage. I am etc.

59.   *Clevland to Hawke*

8 September 1748

Sir,

Not having received a letter from you these two last posts, I am commanded by my Lords Commissioners of the Admiralty to observe to you that it hath been usual for the officers appointed to command in chief at any of the ports to correspond with their Lordships by every post. I am with great regard, Sir...

60.   *Hawke to Clevland*

Fougueux in Portsmouth Harbour
10 September 1748

Sir,

I have received your letter of the 8th instant, in answer to which I am to acquaint their Lordships that my not writing by the two posts you mention was entirely owing to my having nothing relative to the service to communicate to them.

Yesterday the *Viper* put into Spithead, the wind blowing fresh easterly, and as the weather is moderate today, though the wind is still in the same quarter, I have given orders for her, the *Southsea Castle*, and *Blandford* to sail immediately to the eastward...

Minute: 12 September. Own receipt. Approve [the second paragraph].

61.   *Hawke to Anson*

Portsmouth
15 September 1748

My Lord,

I beg leave to trouble your Lordship at the request, and on behalf of the captors of the six French men of war taken the 14th of October last.[1] I believe that after the repeated orders the Navy Board have given to the officers of this yard for surveying them with all the strictness possible to find out their defects, no one can make the least doubt of their having valued them at the lowest rate. Your Lordship, who is so well acquainted with things of this nature, I flatter myself will be an advocate of the agents when they shall make their remonstrance to the Lords of the Admiralty against making the farther deduction of £1664.3.4 ¾ from the value of the *Terrible, Monarque* and *Trident*, which is looked on as a great hardship after they have been so much undervalued.

I hope your Lordship will be so good as to pardon this freedom and to believe that I am, with all imaginable truth and respect...

[1] These prizes were the *Monarque* (74), *Terrible* (74), *Neptune* (70), *Trident* (64), *Fougueux* (64) and *Severne* (50). The rules about prize money—not a matter regulated by the Admiralty—are summarized in Baugh, *Administration* (Princeton), p. 112, n.72.

62. *Hawke to Anson (holograph)*

Portsmouth
28 September 1748

My Lord,

I have the honour of your letter for which I am infinitely obliged to you. I can only say in my own justification for giving your Lordship so much trouble about our affair with the Navy Board that I should not have presumed to have taken that freedom could myself or the captors have hoped for redress from any other hands than your Lordship's.

Though I am sensible Sir Jacob Acworth[1] has not dealt by us as he would wish to be dealt with himself, yet I am convinced your Lordship has done everything in your power to induce him to do us justice, so that, if the Navy Board should not think proper to act in the manner they ought to do, still we are nevertheless to return your Lordship a great many thanks for espousing our part with so much friendship...

My wife joins with me in desiring our compliments may be acceptable to your self and Lady Anson, and I am always, with the utmost truth and respect ...

63. *Hawke to Clevland*

23 October 1748

Sir,

... Some days ago, I received a letter from the Mayor and Aldermen of the town of Portsmouth praying that as they had heard of an order having been lately sent down here for only recalling all His Majesty's ships paid off at this port for seamen who appear for their own wages, or their wives and widows appearing for them, and then the books to be immediately returned to London, by which the inhabitants of this town, who have purchased tickets or otherwise credited seamen, will be put to great inconvenience and expense in getting their money, beside the great detriment it will be to the trade of the town and of Gosport, by preventing a very large sum of

---

[1] Jacob Acworth (knighted in 1722) was Surveyor of the Navy from 1715 to 1749 when he died in office. He had established himself as the leading figure on the Navy Board, predominating even over Captain Richard Haddock (the elder) who was Controller from 1734 to 1749—retiring a few days after Acworth died in March. (For details of such appointments, see J. M. Collinge, *Navy Board Officials 1660–1832* (London: Institute of Historical Research, 1978); and its indispensable companion J. C. Sainty, *Admiralty Officials 1660–1870* (London:I.H.R., 1975).

money from circulating in them, therefore [they hoped that] I would represent it to their Lordships of the Admiralty, and use my interest, that the ships which are paid off here may be thoroughly recalled before the books shall be sent away from this port.

As I am circumstanced with regard to this Corporation, I could not avoid giving attention to a case wherein their interest seems so much concerned. But if, in this, I should ask a thing without precedent or incompatible with the public good, I hope their Lordships will forgive me...

Minute: 25 October. Let him know I have mentioned to the Lords what he says with regard to the books being ordered up to Town and have the pleasure to acquaint him that order is in some measure countermanded, so that his friends at Portsmouth need be under no uneasiness on that account, and that I always with great pleasure receive his comments, being most truly

64.   *Instructions from the Lords of the Admiralty to Hawke*

22 November 1748

Whereas we have appointed the ships of war named in the margin [*Fougueux, Anson, Bristol,* of 64, 60 and 50 guns], and shall also soon appoint others to do the duty of guardships in Portsmouth Harbour, as well for the defence and preservation of the ships in ordinary and the storeships and magazines of that yard from danger, either by accident or design, as also that the said ships may be in forwardness and sooner got ready if there should be occasion to fit them out for the sea; you are hereby required and directed to hoist your own flag on board such of the said ships as you think fit, their captains being directed to orders, and you are to observe the following instructions:

1.   You are to apply to the Navy Board to cause the ship in which you hoist your flag to be placed at proper moorings as near to the middle of the Harbour as possible.
2.   Whereas you will receive in a paper hereunto annexed a state of the numbers and qualifications of officers, seamen, and servants allowed to a guardship, amounting in the whole to one hundred and forty for the third rate ships, and one hundred and twenty to those of the fourth rate, you are to take care that the captains do keep the same always complete...
3.   Every guardship is to be allowed her upper and quarter deck

guns only, and a third part of her small arms...

6. You are every night at eight of the clock to fire a gun to set the watch and to discharge the same at five in the morning...

7. You are to appoint two boats belonging to the said ships, well manned and armed, commanded by a lieutenant or master, to come to you every evening for your orders...

9. You are to order the lieutenant commanding the said boats to look into the creeks and other places where any boats or vessels may probably be harboured, as well as for preventing thievery or embezzlement, as the running of clandestine goods, as any attempt by a supposed enemy...

11. You are to order the captains of the guardships not to suffer any other ships, vessels, or boats to pass up and down the Harbour without being hailed from their ship...

13. You are to take care that the captains of the guardships do frequently exercise their ships' companies with small arms and also in the management of the great guns...

14. Whereas we have thought fit to allow each guardship forty able seamen more than in the last peace, not only for the speedier equipping of the said ships where occasion shall require, but that there may be a sufficient number at all times to assist in carrying on the working of the dock, ropeyard, and moorings in Portsmouth Harbour, whereby the expenses of keeping a considerable number of riggers and labourers will be lessened; you are, as often as the Commissioner of His Majesty's Navy at Portsmouth shall signify to you that there may be occasion for any number of men belonging to the guardships to carry on the aforesaid or other services, to cause them to attend accordingly...so long as there shall be a necessity for it...

65.   *Hawke to Corbett*

Fougueux in Portsmouth Harbour
22 June 1749

[On 10 October 1748, the *Chesterfield* (40) lay off Cape Coast Castle on the West African coast. Her captain, O'Brien Dudley, and others were ashore. The ship was then taken over by mutineers under the leadership of Lieutenant Samuel Couchman who was followed by Lieutenant John Morgan of the marines and some thirty other men. The boatswain, Mr Roger Gastril, dissented. Owing, at least in part, to Couchman's lack of resolution and ruthlessness, Gastril was able to arm a like-minded faction and retrieve the situation.]

Sir,

In compliance with their Lordships' directions on Tuesday morning, I set out for Portsmouth where I arrived yesterday before noon and hoisted my flag on board the *Fougueux*, the *Monarque* as yet not having men enough nor being in a proper condition for this purpose.

Last night I received yours of the 19th and 20th with their Lordships' orders enclosed for assembling a court martial for the trial of the persons therein mentioned, all which shall be put into execution with the utmost dispatch.

Notwithstanding Captain Campbell[1] of the *Chesterfield* had received from Captain Steevens orders to discharge such of the marines, belonging to the *Chesterfield*, whose names were not in the lists either of witnesses or prisoners, yet as it is uncertain which of them the lieutenant of marines may call upon to give evidence in his behalf, I have therefore directed him not to put it in execution till the lieutenant of marines shall have received his charge and given me a list of his evidences, which I hope will meet with their Lordships' approbation...

Minute: Approve.

66.   *Hawke to Corbett*

Invincible[2] in Portsmouth Harbour
5 July 1749

Sir,

... His Majesty's order, with regard to ships coming from West Barbary performing quarantine [against the plague], I have delivered to the captains of His Majesty's ships now at this port and shall to those of the two sloops as soon as they shall arrive from their present cruise.

I have intimated to Lieutenants Couchman and Morgan the orders I have received to cause the sentences of the court martial held for their trial to be put in execution on Friday the 14th instant...

---

[1] James Campbell: L 1742, CR 1744, C 1749. Cashiered for not obeying orders at Havana in 1762.
[2] The *Invincible* (74) was taken by Anson's squadron on 3.5.47. She was wrecked near St Helens 19.2.58. (In 1986, important recoveries of artifacts were reported.)

67. *Hawke to Corbett*

Invincible in Portsmouth Harbour
8 July 1749

Sir,

...Compassion excites me to address their Lordships in behalf of that unfortunate person, Lieutenant Morgan, now under sentence of death. He was but little acquainted with the sea service, is extremely weak and ignorant. Besides, he has a wife and several small children whose bread depends solely on him. It is true his crime was heinous, but I would fain hope that the above considerations might induce their Lordships to intercede with His Majesty graciously to spare his life...

Minute: Own receipt. No comments from the Lords about the lieutenant of marines...

68. *Hawke to Corbett*

Invincible in Portsmouth Harbour
11 July 1749

Sir,

Yesterday the court martial finished the trial of the prisoners from the *Chesterfield*...

Agreeable to their Lordships' directions of the 3rd July, I have this day ordered Roger Gastril, boatswain of the *Chesterfield*, to repair to the Admiralty Office, it having appeared in the course of the trials that he behaved with prudence and resolution in recovering His Majesty's ship from the mutineers and with great candour and honesty as an evidence.[1] At the same time, I cannot with justice pass over the behaviour of Thomas Gilliam, the mate, in silence, as it appeared to the court that the boatswain could not have succeeded without his aid and assistance. I am etc.

Minute: 13 July. Let him know I have communicated his letter to their Lordships who will pay due regard to Mr Gilliam's behaviour, and for that purpose they desire he will inquire into his time of service in the Navy, and if it be such as qualifies him for a lieutenant, send him hither that he may have an order to pass his examination.

[1] Gastril was appointed Master Attendant at Woolwich 13.7.49 (Adm. 6/17, p. 475).

69.   *Instructions from Hawke to the Captains of the Guardships*

Invincible in Portsmouth Harbour
13 July 1749

By Sir Edward Hawke, Knight of the Bath ...

Whereas I have, pursuant to warrants from the Right Honourable the Lords Commissioners for executing the office of Lord High Admiral of Great Britain, etc., dated the 3rd instant, given instructions for putting into execution on board His Majesty's ship *Chesterfield* tomorrow morning two sentences of courts martial held on board His Majesty's ship *Invincible* the 28th and 30th of June last, whereby Lieutenant Samuel Couchman and Lieutenant John Morgan were adjudged to be punished with death by being shot on board such ship as should be directed; you are hereby required and directed to send by 8 o'clock tomorrow morning an officer in one of your boats, with a file of musketeers, to attend and assist at putting the said sentences in execution on board the *Chesterfield*.

When I shall cause a gun to be fired and a flag, striped white and yellow, to be hoisted at the main topmasthead of the ship where my flag is flying, you are then to summon your ship's company upon deck and make known to them the punishment, together with the crime for which it is inflicted...

70.   *Hawke to Corbett*

Invincible in Portsmouth Harbour
15 July 1749

Sir,

Yesterday the sentences of the courts martial against the late Lieutenant Samuel Couchman and Lieutenant John Morgan were put in execution on board the *Chesterfield*...

Thomas Gilliam has been eighteen years at sea, some time of which he was master of a merchant vessel, but, being taken in her, entered on board the *Chesterfield*, where he acted as midshipman and mate near four years. This day I have directed him to go to Town and wait on their Lordships...[1]

71.   *Hawke to Richard Hughes, Esq.*[2]

Invincible in Portsmouth Harbour

---

[1] Gilliam was commissioned on 5.12.49, but seems not to have progressed further.
[2] Hughes: L 1693, C 1702. Commissioner at Portsmouth 1729–54.

24 July 1749

Sir,

I think myself obliged to trouble you with the enclosed letters, one from Captain Stanhope to me, the other from his first lieutenant to him, wherein you may perceive that officer has been treated very ill by John Brown, a quarterman caulker belonging to the dockyard. I know Mr Bennett[1] to be a prudent, discreet officer and a good kind of man, and am well assured he would no ways have interfered with the business of the said Brown had he not found there was an absolute necessity for it from the positive behaviour of the man, who insisted upon caulking the upper deck though it had rained for two days before and was very much swelled, besides being lumbered with hawsers in order for the transporting of the ship, when at the same time the gun deck was clear and fit for that purpose.

If this man is not taken proper notice of on this occasion, these people may go on insulting the officers and will consequently treat them with contempt whenever they shall meet them in the dockyard. Therefore, as I think it is in your power to do this gentleman justice, I thought it would be best to make you acquainted with it first and not trouble the Admiralty, unless there could be no other way of procuring that gentleman satisfaction for his ill treatment...

Enclosure 1:

71a.   *Captain Thomas Stanhope to Hawke*

Fougueux
21 July 1749

Sir,

I have this morning received a letter from Lieutenant Bennett, first lieutenant of His Majesty's ship *Fougueux* under my command, acquainting me that he has been insulted in his command on board the said ship by John Brown, a quarterman caulker belonging to His Majesty's dockyard at this port. As I look upon such behaviour to be showing great disrespect to the Lord High Admiral's authority and manifestly tending to the weakening of the service...I think it my duty to acquaint you therewith, enclosing the said lieutenant's letter, that the whole affair may be laid before the Right Honourable the Lords Commissioners of the Admiralty or such other notice taken of it as you shall please to direct. I am etc.

[1] Bennett: L 1741, CR 1759, C Jan. 1760. Hawke's flag captain in the *Royal George*, 1760–2. Attracted the King's displeasure in 1770 (Document 440).

Enclosure 2:

71b. *Lieutenant William Bennett to Stanhope*

21 July 1749

Sir,

I would willingly have avoided troubling you, had not I looked on my character as concerned if I had put up with the affront offered me by one John Brown, a quarterman caulker, yesterday whilst commanding officer [*sic*].

About two in the afternoon the caulkers came on board and, without asking any questions, were going to work on the upper deck. As that was entirely lumbered, I very civilly asked the quarterman if it would not be better to work between decks...His answer to me was abruptly that they had orders to work there and there they must work. I could not help taking notice of the manner this positive answer was delivered in and asked him how he dare attempt to work without acquainting me. He said sneeringly that he did not know he had any business to acquaint anybody and still persisted to work there.

I must own that this rude behaviour obliged me to call him an impudent scoundrel, a fool, or some words to that purpose—told him he should not work there and that I had no business to give such [a] rascal my reasons for not letting him.

He then said that if he must not work there that he would go on shore. He accordingly went, I know not to whom, but presently came back and took all the caulkers away with him; and in less than ten minutes they came back, he with them, took possession of the deck, and began to work.

I went to him and told him he should answer for his insolence, if he did not take them off from working on that deck. He still persisted in his former behaviour and, in open defiance, ordered them to work. I hereupon called to Mr Claus, second lieutenant, and Mr Simpson, the master, to take notice that he insisted on caulking, the planks being swelled on account of the rain that had been above twelve hours upon them. I might no doubt have prevented their working but, I question, not without using violence, which is the only thing, very likely, that they wanted.

I beg, Sir, that this abuse may be inquired into, that I may not be subject to be laughed at as I go through the yard by those people who were present and laughing at seeing their quarterman get the better of me by working against my will. I am etc.

72. *Hughes to Hawke*

Portsmouth Dock
25 July 1749

[Hawke appears to have gone sick on shore at about this time. The immediate outcome was that five items of this correspondence were sent up to the Admiralty without a covering letter and without even a copy of Hawke's letter to Hughes of 24 July [Document 71 above]. Of the five items received by Clevland, Documents 71a and 71b comprise the first two. The other three items now follow.]

Sir,

I have the favour of your letter of the day preceding, giving cover to one from Captain Stanhope to you and another from his first lieutenant to him, representing the ill treatment the latter has received from Thomas (not John) Brown, a quarterman to the caulkers in this yard, a man of unquestionable character which, as you are pleased to desire, I have inquired into, as is evident from the enclosed papers...and cannot help observing it appears to me from his own letter, as I presume it must to you, that Lieutenant Bennett was the aggressor—for which I am concerned, because I have heard he is a pretty gentleman.

I need not tell you, Sir Edward, because you are very sensible, everybody should be confined to, and act in, their proper sphere only...for unless that is done, His Majesty's service cannot be carried on with that harmony, expedition, and good order it naturally requires...That the artificers which have from time to time worked on board His Majesty's ships in commission are often abused and evil treated is (I am sorry to say it) demonstrable from the frequent complaints I have received on that head. This makes them extremely uneasy...

Therefore, as it is high time a stop should be put to such irregular proceedings for the future, I request you will be pleased...to lay this affair before the Right Honourable the Lords Commissioners of the Admiralty...

I am sorry to add that Mr Bennett has treated every person concerned with great contempt, which I could have wished otherwise...

Enclosure 1:

72a.   *J. Lock to Hughes*

Portsmouth Dock
25 July 1749

Sir,

... I pray leave to acquaint you that Thomas Brown followed the directions I gave to the foreman...to caulk the upper deck as soon as possible. My reason for the same was that, when the ship should be transported to her moorings, she might be soon ready to take in her guns without interfering with the workmen or interrupting the service; and had he disobeyed my commands, I should have thought him not fit to be continued in his employment. I must beg leave to observe that, if the gentlemen of the fleet take upon them to threaten the workmen with putting them in irons and use them ill, as hath been too frequently done, we shall not be able to get any of the workmen to go on board ships; and as to a commanding officer of a ship expecting to be acquainted when workmen are sent on board and to have his leave to go to work, and where he thinks fit to order them, is something extraordinary and what I never knew to be practised in the Navy...I have never had any complaint against [Thomas Brown] since he has been in his employment...

Enclosure 2:

72b.   *Statement by Thomas Brown*

[25 July 1749]

... The first lieutenant came out and told him to go down and work in the gunroom...The said lieutenant then asked him how he dared to come on that ship to work without first acquainting the commanding officer therewith. Brown told him it was not customary so to do on board ships in the Harbour—only those at Spithead... [He said] he would go on shore to his officer and ask him where he was to work ... Mr Johnson, his foreman,...bid him call his hands away that they might be put to work on some other ship; but...before he, Brown, had placed his hands on other work, Johnson returned and told him that it was the builder's order to go back and work on the *Fougueux* as before... The lieutenant came out very angry...

The said Thomas Brown farther observed that while he was on the said ship's gunwale, just before he left her, the other quarterman, William Stockman, directed his people to go to and attend to that part of the work allotted to them; whereupon the said lieutenant hastily approached Stockman with his fist clenched very near the said Stockman's face, telling him if he was a young man, as he was an old one, he would do something to him—but what, the said Brown did not perfectly hear. The said lieutenant [was] calling out very loud for the master at arms to come and put him in irons.

The lieutenant also said that the master caulker of His Majesty's yard was a scoundrel, the foreman a fool, and Brown himself not much better...

73. *Instructions from Hawke to the Captains of the Guardships*

Monarque in Portsmouth Harbour
14 November 1749

Pursuant to an order from the Right Honourable the Lords Commissioners for executing the office of Lord High Admiral of Great Britain and Ireland, etc., bearing date the 8th instant; you are hereby strictly required and directed to appear on all proper occasions in your proper uniform, [and] in particular never to sit at a court martial in any other habit. You are also to oblige the officers and gentlemen on the quarter-deck of His Majesty's ship under your command to appear in their uniform whenever they shall be on duty and on other proper occasions, and not to suffer any of the latter to walk the said quarter-deck unless they strictly comply with such your order.

And whereas complaint has been made that the officers of the dockyard have not that assistance of men from the guardships that might be expected, you are hereby strictly required and directed to send twelve men, or more if required, with a proper [officer] on shore every morning from the guardship under your command to assist in the works of the yard. Besides, I am directed by their Lordships to acquaint you that if you should make any difficulty in sending the number of men that shall be demanded, you may expect to have her complement reduced to its ancient proportion. Given etc.

74. *Admiralty Minute*

6 April 1750

[On this occasion the Earl of Sandwich, who was First Lord from 1748 to 1751, presided at the Board which, in tune with deepening naval economies, was now meeting only about once a week. The wording of the minute notwithstanding, Anson was among the four Lords present.]

Mr Smith, purser of the *Fly* sloop, complaining of ill treatment he has received from Captain Wyatt[1] her commander; resolved that the same be sent to Lord Anson with directions to inquire into the complaint and report what truth he shall find therein.

75. Instructions from the Lords of the Admiralty to Hawke

11 May 1750

Whereas James Hopkins Smith, purser of His Majesty's sloop, the *Fly*, has complained to us of being greatly oppressed in the execution of his duty by Captain Wyatt, commander of the said sloop, and Captain Wyatt having requested that this complaint may be inquired into at a court martial, we send you herewith Mr Smith's and Captain Wyatt's letters relating to this matter, together with a letter from Lord Anson, containing his report of an examination his Lordship made thereinto, and require and direct you to assemble a court martial for inquiring into the purser's complaint. Given etc.

SANDWICH
ANSON
BARRINGTON
DUNCANNON

Enclosure:

75a. Anson to Corbett

William and Mary yacht at Harwich
16 April 1750

Sir,

In obedience to their Lordships' instructions signified to me by your letter of the 10th instant, I have inquired into the complaint exhibited against Captain Wyatt by Mr Smith, purser of the *Fly* sloop, which seems principally to have been grounded upon the purser's not having leave to be on shore whenever he desired it and to have taken its rise from the dispute that happened about a monkey. For till that time the purser acknowledges to have met with

[1] Wyatt: L 1740, CR 1748, C 1756.

the civilest treatment imaginable from the captain and to have been generally invited to his table. I shall therefore set that affair in a clear light, since Mr Smith has but lightly touched upon it, before I enter into particulars of his complaint.

Captain Wyatt, on the 5th September (which is the era Mr Smith has assigned to his ill treatment), was in a very bad state of health and, hearing the chattering or noise of three monkeys[1] near his cabin, which were extremely offensive, he ordered them to be carried into the foretop and to be kept there, that he might not be disturbed with them in his illness. Notwithstanding these orders the purser, to whom one of these monkeys belonged, sent his servant to fetch it out of the top and, having received it from him, was carrying it aft with an intent, as he says, to convey it to his berth or cabin. But the sentry, who had orders not to suffer it to come abaft, endeavoured to prevent it, which seems to have frightened the monkey and caused it to make a great noise. Upon this, Captain Wyatt went upon the deck with some warmth and, in his passion, he believes he might ask what rascal, scoundrel or villain had dared to insult him in that manner after the orders he had so lately given, not knowing who it was, for it was in the dusk of the evening, nor suspecting it could be an officer so wanting in respect, especially the purser who had received so many marks of his favour. But he was not long in this uncertainty, for, to his great astonishment, Mr Smith faced him immediately with the monkey on his shoulder. This appeared such an aggravation of the insult that the captain ordered him to throw it overboard, which he refused to do, though the orders were repeated several times. At last one of the officers wrested it from him and threw it into the sea; and the captain returned to his cabin, after telling the purser he must not expect any further favours or indulgences from him, or words to that effect.

[Regarding his refusal of leave for the purser at Mahon in Minorca, Wyatt said] that he was induced to lay this restriction upon the purser for the abuse he had frequently made of the leave granted him by return on board at very indecent hours, and sometimes disguised with liquor...

---

[1] Animals were often taken to sea, sometimes as pets, though more often to provide food (Rodger, *Wooden World*, pp. 69–71).

76. *Admiralty Minute*

24 May 1750

The *Fly* sloop being sailed from Portsmouth [for the white herring fishery off Shetland]; resolved that Sir Edward Hawke be directed to return the order and papers for trying the purser of her, and Captain Wyatt is to be acquainted, if he applies on his return, a court martial will be ordered.

77. *Hawke to Clevland*

Portsmouth
28 April 1752

Sir,
I have lately been troubled with a violent cold and cough, by which I am reduced to a very weak and bad state of health and, as I have often been in this way, my physician tells me I have no chance to get thoroughly well of my present disorder, nor to my being liable to continual complaints of this kind for the future, unless I go to Bristol to drink the waters of that place.

I shall therefore be particularly obliged to their Lordships if they will please to grant me two months leave of absence, as I have not troubled them before on this head, and it being a case of absolute necessity that obliges me to do it now, induces me to hope their Lordships will excuse my requesting their favour...

Minute: 29th April. To have two months leave as he desires.

78. *Instructions from the Lords of the Admiralty to Hawke*

31 October 1752

[On that same day, the Lords informed the Navy Board that the guardships at Portsmouth and elsewhere were to be docked and that they might be recommissioned in about two months time.[1]]

Having ordered His Majesty's ships named in the margin [*Monarch* (74), *Invincible* (74), *Berwick* (70), *Kent* (70), *Fougueux* (64), *Anson* (60), *Tiger* (60)] to be paid off at Portsmouth, you are hereby required and directed to give orders to their captains forthwith to make out proper pay books and transmit them to the Navy Board for that purpose. You are also to direct them to put on shore

---

[1] See Adm. 2/216, pp. 485–6.

their guns, powder, and spare stores, but not to unrig them or break up their ground tier, but to strike their yards and topmasts and deliver them in that condition into the care of the officers of the yard.

When the said ships shall be ready for paying off, you are to strike your flag and repair on shore. Given etc.

ANSON[1]
DUNCANNON
W. ELLIS

79. *Hawke to Clevland*

Monarque in Portsmouth Harbour
3 November 1752

Sir,

This morning sailed for Plymouth His Majesty's ship *Success*.

In obedience to their Lordships' order of the 31st October, I have given the necessary directions for getting the guardships at this port ready for paying off and, as soon as they are, shall strike my flag. I am etc.

80. *Hawke to Clevland* (holograph)

21 January 1754

Sir,

I have received your letter of the 20th instant[2] and think myself extremely obliged to their Lordships for the honour they have done me in giving the offer of the command in the East Indies.

It is a sensible mortification to me that I am prevented from accepting it by my present state of health, which confines me to my house and renders me incapable of undertaking so great a voyage.

I hope that their Lordships will believe, when in my power, I am always ready to obey their commands...

Minute: 23 January. Let Sir Edward know I have communicated his letter to the Lords who are concerned for his want of health and have not the least doubt of his zeal or inclination to serve, was he in a condition to take him this command.[3]

---

[1] Sandwich having been dismissed as First Lord, Anson had succeeded him in June 1751.

[2] Clevland's letter is not in Adm. 2/512 or in Hawke's papers.

[3] The command had already on the 22nd been offered to Rear-Admiral Charles Watson (Adm. 2/512, p. 78) who accepted. See p. 16, n. 2.

PART IV(a)

FEBRUARY 1755–MAY 1756
PRELUDE TO THE SEVEN YEARS WAR

INTRODUCTION

By January 1755, intensified colonial competition between Britain and France, especially in North America, had led to a state of undeclared hostility between the two countries. On 5 February John Clevland, the Secretary of the Admiralty, wrote asking Hawke whether his health would permit him to serve and Hawke at once replied in the affirmative. On taking command at Portsmouth he supervised the preparation of a squadron, hastily dispatched under Boscawen to the Canadian approaches, as well as that of the Western Squadron with which he was himself to sail.

The documents touch on problems arising from hurried mobilization after a period of sharp naval contraction. Manning and health come to the fore [Documents 81–2, 86–95]; discipline and gunnery exercises, both crucial for British superiority over the French, are also featured [85, 92]. Hawke's secret instructions, issued by the Lords Justices during George II's absence in Hanover [99], are given in full, together with Anson's private letter thereon [100]. These instructions illustrate the complexity of a situation falling short of declared war. They also exemplify the crown's control over naval strategic policy, especially in its wider aspects. However, it should be remembered that Anson, as First Lord of the Admiralty, was not only a Lord Justice but also, in the more normal way, participated in the deliberations of the inner cabinet. In this way, he was able to ensure that national strategy took full account of the Admiralty's view.

A rare item in the form of a prize money agreement is printed here [101]. It was concluded on 23 August 1755 between Hawke and the captains (and commanders) of the Western Squadron at sea. Orders had just reached them to extend their seizure of French shipping to

113

the merchant category.

For Hawke's cruise between 24 July and the end of September it seemed—with his wartime operations yet to come—that the dispatch of 1 October [102] was sufficiently representative. As ever, the admiral is highly sensitive to Admiralty criticism of his efforts [102–4]. Of course, as their Lordships well knew, this defect was allied with an exceptional determination not to be found wanting on any day of battle that might present itself.

In February 1756 Hawke resumed command of the Western Squadron. During this wintry cruise, no major interception was effected. Among the relevant documents chosen, the Admiralty's orders of 27 February 1756 [105] may be compared with those issued earlier by the Lords Justices [99] from the viewpoint of scope and importance. The ill-fated Byng, having been appointed to the Mediterranean command on 11 March, passed Hawke's squadron on his voyage out to Minorca [108]. Hawke, for his part, having handed over command of the Western Squadron to Boscawen, returned in the *St George* to Spithead on 8 May.

81.　*Instructions from the Lords of the Admiralty to Hawke*

6 February 1755

You are hereby required and directed forthwith to repair down to Portsmouth and take upon you the command of His Majesty's ships there and at Spithead, hoisting your flag on board such ship as you shall think proper, and to cause the utmost diligence to be used in the equipment of the ships fitting out, and to forward the same by all means in your power, taking care to keep the officers and men strictly to their duty; and you are to send to our Secretary daily accounts of all proceedings relating to the above-mentioned service, and also accounts twice a week (so as to arrive at this office on Monday and Thursday) of the state and condition of every ship as to men and other particulars. Given etc.

ANSON
DUNCANNON
ED. BOSCAWEN[1]

---

[1] Boscawen was the 3rd son of the 1st Viscount Falmouth; L 1732, C 1737, RA 1747 and c.-in-c., India 1747–50. A Ld of Ady 1751–61 (died in office). VA 1756, A 1758. Naval c.-in-c. at Louisbourg 1758. Defeated La Clue at Lagos 1759. He was a keen but humane disciplinarian who, like Hawke, endeavoured to improve health at sea.

82.   *Hawke to Clevland*

Terrible at Spithead
21 February 1755

Sir,

...Five men sent by the Major of Sandwich on board the *Arundel* I find very unfit for service, besides having the itch and labouring under other distempers. To prevent the infection spreading, I have sent some of them to the hospital[1]...

83.   *Clevland to Hawke*

25 February 1755

Sir,

I am commanded by the Lords Commissioners of the Admiralty to send you herewith an account they have received from Portsmouth of a poor countryman, who entered on board the *Grafton*, being beat in such a manner by Lieutenant Prescott[2] as to jump overboard, only for doing some of the ship's business in an awkward manner, owing entirely to his inexperience; and that when he was taken up again by a boat that happened to be in the way and put on board the ship again, the same lieutenant repeated the same barbarity in a more severe manner than before. And as such inhumanity is very offensive to their Lordships and brings an odium on the service, whereby many useful men are deterred from entering into it, their Lordships desire you will examine very strictly into the affair and lay before them a true account of it...

84.   *Hawke to Clevland*

Terrible at Spithead
28 February 1755

Sir,

Enclosed is a copy of the report[3] made to me by the captains whom I directed to go on board the *Grafton* to inquire into the circumstances of the countryman's jumping overboard. I have only

---

[1] Haslar Hospital had opened some wards by 1754. When completed in 1761, it was the largest brick building in Europe (Rodger, *Wooden World*, p. 110). Boscawen would sail in April with typhus on board and lose 2,000 men.

[2] Prescott: L 1743, CR 1761.

[3] According to the three captains, the man was mad. He had been sent back to his home on the Isle of Wight. Prescott had not ill-treated him.

to add that on inquiry I find Lieutenant Prescott bears the character of a sober, diligent, discreet officer...

Minute: 1 March. Let him know I have communicated it to the Lords who are very well satisfied with the report.

85.   *Instructions from Hawke to All Captains at Spithead*

Terrible at Spithead
5 March 1755

You are hereby required and directed to keep as many men as can be spared from the necessary work of His Majesty's ship under your command, with petty officers, taking the whole's ship's company and supernumeraries in turns, employed in exercising great guns and small arms after the manner prescribed in the printed form. And this you are not to fail doing on all proper occasions, as you will answer to the contrary. For which this shall be your order.[1] Given etc.

86.   *Hawke to Clevland*

Terrible at Spithead
8 March 1755

Sir,
   ... I hope their Lordships will consider my situation with regard to fitting the ships at this port. It is but few men I can procure from the tenders under my orders, as most of the hands are pressed from merchant ships coming into the Channel by the cruisers and tenders to the westward, before they arrive within the limits of our tenders' stations; and those I have procured are not even sufficient for the duty and security of the ships at Spithead. All the volunteers belonging to those ships, too, are out in the tenders, so that I have but very few seamen to assist the landmen in fitting the ships in the Harbour. It would be some help to me if their Lordships would give directions for returning me the volunteers sent from this port in the *Speedwell*, since they have thought proper to order her to another station...

---

[1] In various actions of the Seven Years War, the French suffered disproportionate casualties compared with their British opponents. Dr Rodger concludes that the main cause was 'a much higher British rate of fire' and that this flowed from 'discipline and training' (*Wooden World*, pp. 55–9).

87. *Clevland to Hawke*

11 March 1755

Sir,

Herewith you will receive fifty proclamations for continuing the bounty to volunteer seamen, and the reward for persons who discover seamen that secrete themselves, and allowing a bounty to all ablebodied landmen entering the sea service, in order to your distributing the same to the captains of the ships under your command and causing them to be made as public as possible. I am etc.

88. *Clevland to Hawke*

11 March 1755

Sir,

Lieutenant Charles Middleton,[1] who is employed on board the *Princess Augusta* tender in procuring men in Bristol Channel, having informed my Lords Commissioners of the Admiralty that he should this day return to Portsmouth with the men he had got, being in all twenty-three, and their Lordships being of opinion that a vessel of her size should carry a hundred men, I am commanded to signify their direction to you to reprimand him for returning to Portsmouth with so small a number of men and that, for the future, you direct how many men each tender shall endeavour to procure before she returns to port. I am etc.

89. *Hawke to Clevland*

Terrible at Spithead
16 March 1755

Sir,

... Last night arrived at Spithead Lieutenant Middleton in the *Princess Augusta* tender with thirty-two men, twenty-nine of which are able seamen, and three ordinary. He has parted with only six men in lieu so that, the vessel being small, she could not well contain more people than he had on board her. Upon a strict examination I

---

[1] Middleton: L 1745. In Oct. 1748, he was one of those ashore (doing a survey) when the *Chesterfield* mutiny occurred (See Document 65). Was in the *Anson* (60) on Boscawen's cruise, 1755—the nearest he ever came to action at sea. Served in the Leeward Is 1756–61; CR 1757, C 1758. A successful Controller 1778–90. RA 1787, VA 1793, A 1795. A Ld of Ady 1794–5; and, at age of 80, 1st Ld 2 May 1805–10 Feb. 1806. Created Baron Barham 1805.

cannot find he has been negligent in his duty. I have ordered the tender to be completed for sea and shall dispatch her to her station again, as soon as the weather abates...

90.   *Hawke to Clevland*

St George at Spithead
29 March 1755

Sir,

The sick at the hospital daily increasing and the agent having represented to me that he had already all his cradles and bedding employed, I have given him directions without loss of time to supply the hospital with more of each...

Minute: 31 March. Let him know the Lords have ordered provision to be made for the reception of two hundred men more.

91.   *Hawke to Clevland*

St George at Spithead
30 March 1755

Sir,

... The sick in the ships at this port daily increasing, and several surgeons and surgeons' mates appointed for them not having yet appeared, occasion greater numbers being sent to the hospital than otherwise would be. I must therefore beg the favour of their Lordships to hasten the guard of soldiers for it. For till it arrives, the benefits expected to arise from that hospital are in great measure frustrated by the desertion and straggling of the men, and their having opportunities of selling their clothing for spirituous liquors which greatly retard their cures. This day I shall, in company with several captains of the squadron, visit it in order, as much as lies within my power, to remedy these and any other irregularities I may observe...

Minute: 1 April. Send an extract of [the first sentence above] to the Navy Board and [tell them] to hasten the surgeons and their mates to their duty. Let Sir Edward know it.

92. *Instructions from Hawke to the Captains of the Thirty Ships and Vessels at Spithead*

St George at Spithead
30 March 1755

The present exigency of affairs rendering it absolutely necessary that the greatest regard and attention should be paid to the fitting and keeping in constant readiness for sea the squadron of His Majesty's ships at present under my command; you are hereby required and directed every night to lie on board His Majesty's ship under your command and to be particularly careful that all the Lieutenants and inferior officers do the same, not suffering any of her company to straggle on shore in the daytime, or any boats to be absent from the ship after the watch shall be set at night.

You are also to be very constant, diligent and careful in exercising and otherwise disciplining your ship's company and to keep her at all times complete as to water, provisions and other stores. For which this shall be your order. Given etc.

By command of the Admiral
J. HAY

93. *Hawke to Clevland*

St George at Spithead
31 March 1755

Sir,

Yesterday, after post, I received the accompanying letter from the contractor for Haslar Hospital, not by way of complaint, but in compliance with my directions to lay a state of that hospital before me. I immediately went over, in company of several captains and two surgeons. As there is but one man to serve as porter at the gate, light the fires, and many other offices, I found the gates had not been properly attended, and idle people with liquor had thereby access, and the sick people free egress and regress; to remedy which, I ordered the porter to attend the gates only and do no other duty. If their Lordships approve of it, I think there is an absolute necessity for another porter, and two labourers to pump water, light fires, and clean and sweep about the rooms, even after the twelve invalids are placed there; for it would require at least nineteen sentries, constantly on duty, to guard the hospital properly. I found also thirty-two men fit to return to their ships, and several incurables, whom I ordered to be discharged to make room for others...

94.   *Hawke to Clevland*

St George at Spithead
1 April 1755

Sir,

...Having ordered a commission officer and surgeon to inspect the hospital three times a week, I find by Captain Storr's[1] report last night that the agent had rectified what I found amiss at my last visitation. The guard of twelve men is placed there; but a place of such extent would require a greater number, if their Lordships think proper...

95.   *Hawke to Clevland*

St George at Spithead
27 April 1755

Sir,

...It having been represented to me that the necessaries supplied to the ships for the use of the sick are as follows:

The sugar is extremely black, coarse and ready to run into molasses, and the fruit in general mouldy and so masked and clotted that it is scarce possible to determine the species it was of. The sago, or rather what was put up for it, full of dust and musty. The cinnamon very coarse and having neither spicy taste nor flavour. The sheets so patched and darned that it is impossible to make a roller of a yard long out of them, and several short of the number allowed. Instead of shallots and garlic, stipulated by contract, there is in each box a few ounces of chocolate, no way adequate, as to usefulness, to the articles it is given in lieu of.

I must therefore request that their Lordships would give directions to inquire into the same...

96.   *Clevland to Hawke*

28 April 1755

Sir,

I have received and read to my Lords Commissioners of the Admiralty your letter of yesterday's date, complaining of the bad-

---

[1] Storr: CR 1746, C 1748. He was Hawke's flag captain in the *St George*, 1755–6. RA 1779.

ness of several species of the necessaries supplied to the ships under your command for the use of the sick men; and in return I am ordered to acquaint you that the Navy Board are directed to attend their Lordships tomorrow, that an immediate stop may be put to such proceedings and such measures taken with the contractor as his infamous conduct deserves. In the meantime, it is their Lordships' direction that you order the surgeons' necessaries to be surveyed and all such to be returned as shall appear unfit for service. I am etc.

97.   *Instructions from the Lords of the Admiralty to Hawke*

6 May 1755

[On 24 April Boscawen had sailed with eleven barely manned ships of the line and many infectious men; and on 11 May a reinforcement of six of the line would sail from Portsmouth to join him. Not till then would Hawke be able to concentrate his attention on his own squadron.]

You are hereby required and directed to concert measures for making a general press at Portsmouth and the adjacent parts and then cause all seamen and seafaring men whatsoever to be pressed without regard to any protections excepting all masters of ships and vessels, and the first mates, boatswains, and carpenters of such as are of 100 tons or upwards, and also excepting the men belonging to outward bound ships and vessels, which shall either have broke ground or shall be cleared at the custom house, laden and ready to sail.

You are to cause this order to be executed as soon after the receipt of it as possible and in the meantime to take care that the utmost secrecy be observed...

98.   *Line of Battle*

St George at St Helens
21 July 1755

The *Monmouth* to lead with the starboard and the *Culloden* with the larboard tacks on board.

Frigates	Rates	Ships	Commanders	Guns	Men	Division
	3	*Monmouth*	Capt. Harrison	64	480	

	4	*Medway*	Denis	60	420	
	3	*Orford*	Steevens	70	520	
Savage sloop	2	*Prince*	Saunders	90	750	Sir. Ed. Hawke
	2	*St George*	Sir Ed. Hawke	90	770	Kt of the Bath
			Storr			Vice-Ad. of
	3	*Lancaster*	Hon. Capt.	70	520	the White
			Hamilton[1]			
	3	*Captain*	Capt.	64	480	
			Catford[2]			
	4	*Newcastle*	Lloyd[3]	50	350	
	3	*Nassau*	Cokburne[4]	64	480	
Ambuscade [40]	4	*York*	Pigot[5]	60	420	
	3	*Elizabeth*	Montagu[6]	64	480	
	2	*Prince George*	Rodney	80	700	Temple West Esq.
			Temple West Esq			Rear-Ad. of the Red
	3	*Buckingham*	Everitt[7]	70	535	
	2	*Barfleur*	Ld. Harry	80	700	
			Powlett[8]			
	4	*Weymouth*	Hanway	60	420	
	3	*Culloden*	Ward[9]	74	600	

Given etc.

99.   *Secret Instructions from the Lords Justices to Hawke*

22 July 1755

By the Lords Justices: Secret Instructions for Sir Edward Hawke, Knight of the Bath, Vice-Admiral of the White Squadron of His Majesty's Fleet. Given at Whitehall the 22nd day of July 1755 in the twenty-ninth year of His Majesty's reign.

Whereas divers encroachments have been made by France upon

[1] Hamilton: L 1736, C 1741. He died on 18.12.55.

[2] Catford: L 1727, CR 1742, C 1743.

[3] Lloyd: L 1734?, C 1746, RA 1775, VA 1778.

[4] Cokburne: C 1741. An Extra Commissioner 1756. Controller 1756–70.

[5] Pigot: L 1742, C 1746, RA 1775, VA 1776, A 1782. Replaced Rodney as c.-in-c., Leeward Is 1782–3.

[6] Montagu: L 1740, CR 1745, C 1746, RA 1770, VA 1776, A 1782.

[7] Michael Everitt: L 1744, C 1747.

[8] Powlett: L 1739, C 1740. Submitted highly dubious evidence at Lestock's court martial 1746. Secured the suspension of Vice-Adm. Griffin 1750. Was popularly dubbed 'Captain Sternpost' for leaving Hawke's squadron in August 1755 and seeking shelter from the gales on account of a mildly defective rudder. Never again actively employed but : RA 1756, VA 1759, A 1770.

[9] Ward: L 1737, C 1741.

His Majesty's rights and possessions in North America by building
forts and making settlements upon lands undoubtedly belonging by
treaty or otherwise to the Crown of Great Britain; and whereas
actual hostilities were committed by the French in the month of
April 1754, by their summoning a fort which was building on the
Ohio, under the command of an officer bearing His Majesty's commission, and the said officer was compelled to surrender the same; in
consequence whereof His Majesty found himself obliged, in order to
maintain the honour of his Crown and to defend his possessions in
North America, to give the necessary orders to repel force by force
and to prevent the French from landing additional troops in North
America, for which purpose they had sent a large squadron of men
of war and transports into those seas, which could only be intended
to make other encroachments or to support those already made; and
whereas it is the King's determined resolution not only to continue
the most effectual methods for the protection and defence of his
rights and possessions and the trade of his subjects in North America, but likewise to provide for the defence of his dominions and the
security and protection of the navigation and commerce of his
subjects in all parts, which is now become more immediately necessary, as all the means of negotiation have hitherto proved so ineffectual that there is reason to apprehend it is the intention of France to
pursue the hostilities they have already committed by an open rup-
ture; and whereas Monsieur de Mirepoix, Ambassador of the Most
Christian King, in consequence of orders he has received from his
Court, has actually left this kingdom without taking leave, we have
therefore thought proper, in the present circumstances, to give you
the following orders, and we do in His Majesty's name order and
direct you to take under your command Rear-Admiral West and
sixteen of His Majesty's ships of the line, with such frigates as shall
be directed by the Lords Commissioners of the Admiralty, and
proceed immediately to sea, and cruise between Ushant and Cape
Finisterre, in order to put in execution the following instructions;
taking care not to go to the southward of Cape Finisterre unless
from some intelligence you may receive you shall, without leaving
however the home service too much exposed, find it necessary to go
beyond the same Cape Finisterre.

1st.   You are to protect the trade and ships of His Majesty's
subjects; and in case you should meet with the French squadron, or
French men of war of the line of battle, you are to intercept them,
making use of the means in your power for that purpose, and to send
them under a proper convoy directly to Plymouth or Portsmouth,

taking care that every person belonging to all ships so intercepted be well treated, and that no plunder or embezzlement be made of any effects on board. But if you shall have certain intelligence that the French have committed hostilities by their men of war, or in consequence of any commissions granted to privateers, or any letters of marque, or reprisals against any of His Majesty's subjects, or their ships, or effects, you are then to commit all acts of hostility against the French, and endeavour to seize and take by every means their ships and vessels, as well those of war as merchants, that you shall meet, sending them into some convenient port in His Majesty's dominions to be there kept till His Majesty's pleasure shall be known concerning them.

2nd. You are to fix upon some proper place where the ships under your command shall rendezvous in case of separation, notice whereof you are to send, sealed up, to the Secretary of the Admiralty; and you are constantly to keep a ship or vessel passing between the fleet and the rendezvous, that you may the more readily receive such orders as it shall be necessary to send you.

3rd. You are to continue on this service till further order, or so long as the ships' provisions and water will admit, and then you are to return with them to such ports as the Lords Commissioners of the Admiralty may direct.

4th. You are to transmit to one of His Majesty's Secretaries of State and to the Lords Commissioners of the Admiralty every ten days (or oftener if anything material occurs) a particular account of your proceedings, the frigates and other vessels being appointed to attend you for that purpose, and to proceed with your dispatches to Plymouth from whence they are to be forwarded by express.

5th. You are to observe and follow such orders and instructions as you shall receive from His Majesty, under his royal sign manual, or from the Lords Justices during His Majesty's absence, or from one of His Majesty's principal Secretaries of State, or from the Lords Commissioners for executing the office of Lord High Admiral of Great Britain for the time being.

WILLIAM	HOLLES NEWCASTLE
THO. CANTUAR	DORSET
HARDWICKE C.	ROCHFORD
GRANVILLE P.	ANSON
MARLBOROUGH C.P.S.	T. ROBINSON
RUTLAND	H. FOX
ARGYLL	

100. *Anson to Hawke*

Admiralty
22 July 1755

My dear Sir,

By the messenger that brings you this letter you will have your orders which are only at present to take all French ships of war, but I make not the least doubt but the French will declare a war, and that you will hear of their having taken our ships, and that our Channel will be full of their privateers; but you will be very well satisfied that they have seized some of our ships before you fall upon their trade and you will take particular care to keep up such a correspondence with the place of your rendezvous that I may send you the earliest notice if we have any accounts at the Admiralty of the French having begun the war with us. The messenger waits to set off and I think there is nothing of consequence now to say. I heartily [wish] you all kinds of success, being

Your sincere friend and humble servant,
ANSON

Make my compliments to the captains of your squadron

101. *Prize Money Agreement*

23 August 1755

[On 23 August Hawke, with the Western Squadron in the Bay of Biscay, received additional secret instructions which had been signed by the Lords Justices on the 6th. These allowed him to divide his squadron with a view to seizing all French vessels entering the Channel or the Bay. He was being reinforced for this purpose. The new orders were occasioned by 'farther hostile preparations of the French, particularly against these kingdoms', but there was still no declaration of war. On the same day that Hawke received these orders, the following agreement was concluded.]

We the under written captains and commanders in His Majesty's Navy, now cruising under the command of Sir Edward Hawke, Knight of the Bath, Vice-Admiral of the White Squadron of His Majesty's Fleet, do mutually promise and agree that we will equally share amongst us the profits that shall arise to us, or to any of us, from capture on the French, or other His Majesty's enemies, during the term of our present cruise; and we do farther promise and agree that if any ship, or ships, shall be detached from the rest of the fleet by Sir Edward Hawke and sent to any port of England, either with dispatches, or for the security of any ships seized on for prize, or for disability, or to clean, the captain or captains of such ship or ships shall continue to share with the rest, during the term of a fortnight after his arrival into port, or (if he doth not continue into port a fortnight and is ordered to rejoin the fleet) during the whole term of the cruise. If his stay in port exceeds a fortnight, or if within that term he is ordered upon other service, this agreement to be then determined and continue no longer in force with respect to him. In witness hereof we have hereunto interchangeably [sic] set our hands and seals on board His Majesty's ship *St George* this 23rd August 1755.

H. HARRISON	G.B. RODNEY	R. HARLAND
H. POWLETT	CHAS. CATFORD	MICH[L]. EVERITT
JOHN HAMILTON	THOS. HANWAY	JN[O]. STORR
H. WARD	J. MONTAGU	JN[O]. LOCKHART[2]
GEO. COKBURNE	PETER DENIS	JOS. ROWLEY[3] 8th Sept.
CHAS. SAUNDERS	HUGH PIGOT	J. BYRON[4] 15 Sep.
CHAS. STEEVENS	JN[O] BOYD[1]	

[1] Boyd: L 1746, C 1761. He was a commander when he signed this prize money agreement.

[2] Lockhart (later Sir John Lockhart Ross, Bt.): L 1743, CR 1755, C 1756. He illustrates the tortuous evolution of the rank of commander. At Second Finisterre he commanded the *Vulcan* fireship but afterwards reverted to lieutenant. Here, however, his signature (when a commander) is found with those of the post captains. Subsequently, he fought brilliant frigate actions in 1757–8. On 24.11.59, having sent Campbell home with the Quiberon dispatches, Hawke appointed Lockhart captain of the *Royal George*. Lockhart assumed the name of Ross in 1760 on succeeding to the estate of Balnagowan and became reputedly 'the best farmer in Scotland' (*D.N.B.*). RA 1779, VA 1787.

[3] Joshua Rowley: L 1747, C 1753. In 1762, with an inferior force, he saved a convoy from Ternay. RA 1779; served under Byron at Grenada and under Rodney at Martinique (1780). Created baronet 1786. VA 1787. (See also p. 35, n. 1 and p. 251, n.1.)

[4] Byron: 2nd son of 4th Baron Byron, he sailed in Anson's storeship in 1740 and, as a midshipman of 18, was shipwrecked on the coast of Patagonia in 1741. Did not reach England till 1745; published famous *Narrative*, 1768. CR 1745, C 1745. Sailed round the world in the *Dolphin* (24), the Navy's second ship to be coppered, in 1764–6. RA 1775, VA 1778. Worsted at Battle of Grenada 1779. Renowned for his bad luck.

102. *Hawke to Clevland (holograph)*

St George at Spithead
1 October 1755

Sir,

I have received your letter of the 30th and am extremely sorry to find that their Lordships think any of the ships of my squadron could have stayed out longer. I hope they will be of another opinion when they reflect that most of the men had been pressed after long voyages, cooped up in tenders and ships at Spithead for many months, and the water in general long kept in new casks, which occasioned great sickness, beside the number of French prisoners and the men spared to navigate them into port. For my part, I should not have come in had it been possible for me to have continued longer out.

On receiving orders for reprisals on 23rd August and intelligence of Count du Guay's squadron having sailed from Cadiz the 1st of that month, I did not think it probable he would come in by Cape Finisterre when he must have heard I was cruising there. Therefore I changed my rendezvous to between 47.00 and 48.00 N., forty leagues to the westward of Ushant, with which I also acquainted you in my letter of the 30th August. Sometimes I stretched to the southward and sometimes to the northward of it, with which I also acquainted you in my next letters. I stationed the *Newcastle* off Finisterre, the *Medway* in the rendezvous between 47.00 and 45.00 N., and the *Monmouth* and *York* between Rochefort and Belle Isle, sending the *Savage* to the ships stationed to the northward, that I might be acquainted with any intelligence they might receive. The only accession of ships I received was the *Essex* and *Vanguard*. The first was not so well appointed in any respect as the ships I carried out with me and brought in with her only 20 ton of water. The *Vanguard* joined me only the 15th September, and then I was obliged to send her in as her fireplace was down, and she had above an hundred French prisoners, and number of men in her prizes.

Reckoning on tolerable fair weather, I imagined the ships I sent in might have been ready to come out against I came in, which would have formed a squadron, with the *Captain*, *Culloden*, and *Barfleur*, of seven sail...

Upon the whole, I am conscious of having used my utmost endeavours to answer the end of my being sent out and of never having once lost sight of the principal object of my cruise. If their Lordships should be of another opinion, I am ready and willing to resign my command to anyone else in whose abilities they may have more confidence...

103. *Clevland to Hawke*

7 October 1755

Sir,

Upon Friday the 3rd instant and not before, I received your letter of the 1st which I had no opportunity of communicating to my Lords Commissioners of the Admiralty till this day, being the first time they have met since its receipt, and am commanded by them to acquaint you that, on the further perusal of my letter to you of the 30th past, they cannot conceive any part of it which conveys an idea of their being dissatisfied with your conduct, nor was it their intention; but they lamented the situation of His Majesty's ships under your command was such as to make it necessary to send the greatest part of them into port at a time when there was a prospect of intercepting so many French ships, and particularly Monsieur Motte's squadron, who got into Brest the 23rd of last month. Wherefore they are sorry to see that part of your letter wherein you express that you are ready and willing to resign your command to any other in whose abilities they may have more confidence than yours, which they are persuaded you can have no more reason to suspect. I am etc.

[Copies of these two letters (Documents 102 and 103) do not appear in Hawke's letter books.]

104. *Hawke to Clevland*

St George in Portsmouth Harbour
9 October 1755

Sir,

I have received your letters of the 7th instant and beg leave to return my hearty thanks to their Lordships for the trouble they have taken to explain themselves. Let me assure them farther that my not meeting success was not owing to want of inclination or hearty endeavours to act, could I have found the opportunity I sought for, and I am morally certain that, had I stayed out longer, the ships' companies had been totally ruined... On Saturday, I shall strike my flag and I thank their Lordships for the leave of absence with which they have indulged me. I am etc.

105. *Secret Instructions from the Lords of the Admiralty to Hawke*

27 February 1756

Whereas we have received intelligence from Captain Rawling,[1] commander of His Majesty's ship the *Seaford* of his seeing six sail of French men of war put to sea from Brest, we send you herewith a copy of the said intelligence, and require and direct you to take the ships named in the margin [*St George, Northumberland, Captain, Edinburgh, Medway, Newcastle, Hampshire, Swan* sloop], now at Spithead, under your command, and the three East India ships, and any other trade ready and desirous of accompanying you, under your convoy and proceed without a moment's loss of time down the Channel, calling off Plymouth for Rear-Admiral Mostyn and the ships named in the margin [*Culloden, Monarch, Orford, Dunkirk, York*], and taking them under your command, you are to accompany the aforesaid East India ships 150 leagues to the westward of Ushant, when you are to leave them to the care of the *Hampshire*, unless any well grounded intelligence that you receive shall render it necessary for their safety that you should see them as much farther as such intelligence shall render absolutely necessary. When you part with the *Hampshire* and the East India ships, you are without loss of time to make Cape Ortegal, where a frigate is ordered to join you to give you such intelligence as she may be able to gain off Brest and Rochefort, and you are then to proceed off either of those places, or cruise in such other manner as may be most likely to prevent any French ships putting to sea from thence, or to intercept the French squadron, if at sea, which is to be the principal object of your attention, or any others that may get out, sending us frequent accounts of your proceedings and your rendezvous.

If you gain no intelligence of the French squadron being at sea, in or near the Bay, and shall find they are not returned into one of the said French ports, you are to leave such cruisers off those ports as you shall find necessary and return to England with the rest, repairing to Spithead with such as you carry from thence, and send the others into Plymouth.

If you don't meet with any frigates off Cape Ortegal, you are to stretch across the Bay off Brest and inform yourself of the state of matters there, detaching at the same time one of your squadron off Rochefort to bring you intelligence of the state of affairs at that port and, according to the situation of things, you are to regulate your

[1] Rawling: CR 1753, C 1755. Died in 1757.

conduct in the manner before mentioned.

In case you should, in your way down the Channel, be certainly informed that the French squadron are in the Bay of Biscay, you are to see the *Hampshire* and East India ships no farther than you shall judge necessary for their safety, and then, leaving them to pursue their voyage, you are to repair and cruise in such manner as you shall judge most likely to meet with the French ships, which you are to use your best endeavours to seize, agreeable to the orders you have already received. Given etc.

ANSON
W. ROWLEY
R. EDGCUMBE[1]

106. *Line of Battle*

St George at sea
14 March 1756

The *Chichester* to lead with the starboard and the *Orford* with the larboard tacks on board.

Frigates	Rates	Ships	Commanders	Guns	Men	Division
	3	Chichester	Capt. Brett[2]	70	520	
Lyme	4	Medway	Denis	60	420	
	4	Rochester	Duff[3]	50	350	
	3	Edinburgh	Stanhope	64	480	Sir Edward Hawke
Sheerness to repeat signals	2	St George	Sir Edward Hawke Kt	90	770	Kt of the Bath Vice-Ad. of the Blue
	3	Somerset	Capt. Storr Geary[4]	64	480	

[1] The Hon. Richard Edgcumbe was an MP from 1747 till he succeeded as the 2nd Baron Edgcumbe in 1758. An occasional soldier (rising to major-general) and a Ld of Ady 1755–6.

[2] William Brett: brother of Peircy; L 1740, C 1747.

[3] Duff: CR 1744, C 1746. Howe's second-in-command for the landings at Cherbourg and St Malo 1758. Served Hawke with distinction 1759. Was with Rodney at Martinique 1762, but would not serve as his flag captain (Spinney, *Rodney*, pp. 202–5). RA 1775, c.-in-c., Newfoundland 1775–7. VA 1778.

[4] Geary: L 1734, C 1742. Took several Spanish and French prizes 1743–5. RA 1759 under Hawke off Brest. VA 1762. C.-in.c., Portsmouth 1769–70 (including the Falklands crisis). Adm. 1775. Commanded the Channel Fleet 1780. Baronet 1782.

	4	*Dunkirk*	Hon. Capt. Howe[1]	60	420	
Hunter dogger	3	*Vanguard*	Hon. Capt. Byron	70	520	
	4	*York*	Capt. Pigot	60	420	
	3	*Northumberland*	Rt. Hon. Ld Colville	70	520	
Seaford	3	*Monarque*	Savage Mostyn Esq.	74	715	Savage Mostyn Esq
			Capt. Taylor[2]			Rear-Ad. of the Blue
	3	*Ipswich*	Tyrrell[3]	64	480	
	4	*Newcastle*	Lloyd	50	350	
Swan sloop	3	*Orford*	Steevens	70	520	

Given etc.

107. Instructions from Hawke to Captain Robert Duff

St George at sea
19 April 1756

You are hereby required and directed to make the best of your way with His Majesty's ship under your command and the *Eagle* (the captain of which has my direction to follow your orders) to cruise for eight days between the latitudes of 47.20 N. and 45.10 N., keeping, in order to intercept French ships of war or merchant vessels, fifteen leagues W. of Belle Isle. But if you should sooner procure any intelligence proper to be communicated to me or meet with a greater number of ships of war outward bound than you are able to cope with, you are to make the best observations in your power, before you leave them, of their number, strength and the course they steer, and then make the utmost dispatch to join me from the latitude of 45.50 N. to the latitude of 48.30 N., fifteen leagues to the westward of Ushant, being very attentive to the winds till you shall join me. And in case of not meeting with any such intelligence or number of ships of war, you are, at the expiration of the time above specified, to make the best of your way to join me in the station last prescribed. For which this shall be your order.

Given etc.

[1] Howe: L 1744, CR 1745, C 1746. Took the *Alcide* 1755. Under Hawke in 1757, he closely bombarded Aix (Document 155). Commanded landings on the French coast 1758; succeeded as 4th Viscount Howe. Prominent under Hawke in 1759. A Ld of Ady 1762–5. Treasurer of the Navy 1765–70, but apparently refused to profit by it. RA 1770 and appointed c.-in-c., Mediterranean. VA 1775, A 1782. 1st Ld of Ady 1783–8. Created Earl Howe 1788. Perfected signals. Commanded Channel Fleet 1793–5; won Battle of 1 June 1794. Popular with the sailors who called him 'Black Dick'.
[2] Witteronge Taylor: L 1741, CR 1748, C 1755. Hawke's flag captain in the *Ramillies* 1758–9. He went down with her on 15.2.60.
[3] Tyrrell: L 1740, CR 1743, C 1743, RA 1762. Died in 1766.

108.   *Hawke to Clevland*

St George at sea, Ushant in sight
18 April 1756

Sir,

...After being as far to the southward as 44.55 N., and as deep in the Bay as Cape Penas, I returned to my rendezvous on the 16th. That night I was joined by the *York* and the *Rochester,* who had fallen in with Admiral Byng and his squadron off Cape Ortegal. But it blowed so hard that boats could not go on board him...

109.   *Secret Instructions from the Lords of the Admiralty to Hawke*

22 April 1756

Whereas it is necessary for the health and refreshment of the officers and seamen that the ships cruising to the westward should be relieved as frequently as may be, and we having directed Vice-Admiral Boscawen to proceed out to you with the [nine] ships named in the margin, you are hereby required and directed to add to them the five ships which sailed lately from Plymouth with Rear-Admiral Holburne[1] and also five or six of the other ships of the line under your command that are in the best condition, together with all the frigates, and leaving them with Mr Boscawen, you are to repair with the rest into port, sending to Plymouth such as sailed from thence, and proceeding with the rest to Spithead, in order to their being cleaned and refitted.

If the French should be so strong at Brest and the ports in the Bay as to require the whole force you will have, when joined by Mr Boscawen, to look after them, you are at liberty to continue out therewith, transmitting an account of it immediately to our Secretary. Given etc.

ANSON
DUNCANNON
W. ROWLEY
BATEMAN

Sent to Mr Boscawen.

---

[1] Francis Holburne: L 1727, C 1739, RA 1755, VA 1757. In the Western Squadron or on N. American coast 1755–7. C.-in-c., Portsmouth 1758–68. A Ld of Ady 28.2.70–2.2.71. Governor of Greenwich Hospital till he died in July.

110. *Hawke to Clevland*

St George at sea, Ushant EBN 17 leagues
27 April 1756

Sir,

On the 19th I dispatched the *Rochester* and *Eagle* to cruise for eight days between the latitudes of 47.20 and 45.10 N., keeping fifteen leagues W. of Belle Isle, leaving the *Seaford* to cruise on my rendezvous while I made a stretch to the southward. On the 20th, I sent the *Sheerness* to cruise for intelligence from the Isle of Yeu to the latitude of 45.50 N., keeping eight leagues W. from the Isle of Ré, off Rochefort.

In the morning of the 21st, I was joined again by the *Dunkirk*, and last night by the *Seaford*.

Enclosed is the state and condition of His Majesty's ships under my command. I am etc.

111. *Hawke to Clevland*

St George at Spithead
8 May 1756

Sir,

On the 6th instant in the morning I was joined in latitude 48.42 N., Ushant bearing S. 70 E., distant thirteen leagues, by Vice-Admiral Boscawen with the squadron under his command[1] ...

For the intelligence procured by the cutter, I must refer their Lordships to Mr Boscawen's dispatches; and I hope they will believe, during my cruise I neglected no means in my power to prevent any ships of war getting out either from Brest or Rochefort, though I could have but a very imperfect knowledge of the state of these ports for want of a cutter.

By Vice-Admiral Boscawen I received their Lordships' order of the 22nd and your letters of the 20th and 23rd ultimo. After maturely deliberating with Vice-Admiral Boscawen on the intelligence he had procured, I thought in the present state of the ships under my command my staying out in person of little consequence. In addition, therefore, to the ships he brought out with him, I left the *Terrible, Monmouth, Chichester, Somerset, Essex, York, Eagle, Newcastle,* and *Lyme*. This force, in my opinion, will be sufficient for the present object of this cruise...

[1] Boscawen arrived with eleven sail. Although he was a Ld of the Ady, he was junior in rank to Hawke (Boscawen being a Vice-Adm. of the Blue and Hawke a Vice-Adm. of the White) and therefore came under Hawke's orders till he left the station.

PART IV(b)

JUNE 1756–JANUARY 1757
MINORCA

INTRODUCTION

On 8 June 1756 Hawke was urgently summoned back to Portsmouth. During his month of recuperation ashore, the government had learned of the French landing in Minorca; and on 18 May, Britain had declared war on France. By early June it was known in England that Byng, having fought an indecisive action off Minorca, had retired to Gibraltar, thereby abandoning the British garrison at Mahon.

Although Hawke's instructions of 8 June are printed in full on pp. 213–17 of H. W. Richmond's N.R.S. volume *The Loss of Minorca* (1913), the case for reprinting most of these instructions here seemed very strong. Without them [Document 112] Hawke's role in this notable episode could not be readily understood. In particular, his exchange of letters with the unfortunate Byng at Gibraltar on 4 July [113–14] could not be omitted and these letters relate explicitly to the aforesaid instructions.

For Hawke's subsequent operations in the vicinity of Minorca, documentation has been limited to his dispatch of 12 September [116] with its uncomplimentary reference to part of his instructions dated 8 June. In a single volume of *Hawke Papers* it seemed better here, as elsewhere, to restrict the inclusion of operational material which was largely unremarkable in character and offered little in the way of incidental enlightenment. In the latter regard, the entertaining, and often highly informative, account of this campaign to be found in *Augustus Harvey's Journal*, edited in 1953 by David Erskine, comes especially to mind.

The course of events was that Hawke, having assumed command at Gibraltar of the Mediterranean fleet, duly sent Byng and Temple West, his second-in-command, together with Lieutenant-General

Thomas Fowke, the Governor of Gibraltar, back to England under
arrest. As soon as the winds permitted, Hawke sailed with the fleet
and, finding that the garrison at Mahon had surrendered, he duly
blockaded Minorca. However, the French had prudently reduced
their garrison to a size better able to feed itself during the coming
months than could a British fleet so remote from its sources of
supply. By 2 October, Hawke had been forced to return to Gibraltar
with a squadron that was sickly and exhausted. The Admiralty
agreed with his submission that the larger ships should not be left to
winter at Gibraltar and, on 14 January 1757, the admiral returned to
Spithead with most of the squadron [118]. It was probably not till
then that Hawke learned that his wife had died at Lymington on 29
October. The inscription on her tombstone is printed here [117].
Hawke probably laid the stone in the spring of 1757. As the inscription mentions he had by then been advanced to Admiral of the Blue.
This was by a promotion of February 1757. The church in question
stands about a mile north of Swaythling, Southampton, where Sir
Edward and Lady Hawke had lived for several years.

112.   *Instructions from the Lords of the Admiralty to Hawke*

8 June 1756

By the Commissioners for executing the Office of Lord High
Admiral of Great Britain and Ireland etc.

Instructions for Sir Edward Hawke, Knight of the Bath, Vice-
Admiral of the White, hereby appointed Commander-in-Chief of
His Majesty's ships and vessels employed in and about the Mediter-
ranean.

Whereas the King's pleasure has been signified to us that we
should give you directions to repair without loss of time to the
Mediterranean to supercede Admiral Byng in the command of His
Majesty's ships there, and that we should appoint some proper flag
officer to serve under you in the room of Rear-Admiral West; you
are hereby required and directed forthwith to repair to Portsmouth
and embark on board His Majesty's ship the *Antelope*, together with
Rear-Admiral Saunders, whom we have directed to proceed with
you and serve under your command; and it being intended that Lord
Tyrawley, whom the King has appointed Governor of Gibraltar in
the room of Lieutenant-General Fowke, together with the Earl of
Panmure, who is going thither in the room of Major-General Stuart,
who is ordered to be recalled, shall proceed in the same ship;

you are, so soon as those officers are on board, not to lose a moment's time in proceeding to Gibraltar (the captain of the *Antelope* being directed to follow your orders) and upon your arrival there, you are to deliver the enclosed packets to Admiral Byng and Rear-Admiral West, and immediately take upon you the command of all His Majesty's ships which you shall find at Gibraltar and any others that may be in the Mediterranean, all their officers and companies being hereby enjoined to a strict obedience to your orders, and hoisting your flag on board such ship as you shall, from time to time, find convenient, you are to assign any other which you shall judge most fitting for Rear-Admiral Saunders and take him also under your command.

You are to make an immediate and expeditious inquiry into the conduct and behaviour of the captains of the ships hereby put under your command; and if you find any reason to believe any of them to have been tardy and not to have acted with due spirit and vigour for the honour and service of the King and nation, you are forthwith to suspend such captains and appoint others in their stead in whom you can confide for properly executing their duty. You are to order the captain of the *Antelope* to receive Admiral Byng and Rear-Admiral West on board and return with them to Spithead; and if you shall suspend any of the captains, you are to send them also home in her.

Having done this, if you shall not be well assured that Fort St Philip upon the island of Minorca is in possession of the enemy, you are to use the utmost dispatch in repairing thither with your squadron and to exert yourself in doing everything that is possible to be done by you for its relief; and to attack and use your utmost endeavours to take, sink, burn, or otherwise destroy any squadron of the enemy's ships that may be employed to favour and assist in the attack upon that fort.

If you shall find the enemy have succeeded and are in full possession of Minorca, you are, however, to endeavour by all means to destroy the French fleet in the Mediterranean, and for that purpose to employ the ships under your command in the most effectual manner you shall be able, and constantly to keep sufficient cruisers round the island of Minorca, and take care they exert all possible diligence to prevent the enemy landing any troops, ammunition, stores or provisions upon that island, and to annoy and distress them there as much as possible; and, in general, you are to employ the utmost vigilance and vigour to annoy and distress the enemy everywhere within the extent of your command and by every method and means in your power; to protect Gibraltar from any hostile attempt and also Minorca, should the present attack upon it miscarry; and you are likewise to give all possible attention to the security of the trade of the King's subjects in and about the Mediterranean, and to the taking or destroying any privateers belonging to the enemy.

If any French ships of war should escape your squadron and proceed out of the Mediterranean, you are forthwith to send to England a proportionable part of the ships under your command, observing that you are never to keep more ships in the Mediterranean than shall be necessary for the performance of what is before recommended to you. And that you may be the better enabled to execute the services expected of you, you are to take care to keep the ships or vessels under your command in constant and good condition, and to have them cleaned as often as shall be necessary for that purpose, causing the same to be done (if Minorca shall be in possession of the French) either in some port in the King of Sardinia's dominions or at Gibraltar, as you shall find to be most convenient.

And whereas the King's pleasure is signified to Lord Tyrawley to cause the troops under his command to be disposed of as he shall see best for His Majesty's service and the preservation of his possessions in the Mediterranean...; you are to consult with Lord Tyrawley...and to co-operate with him in everything that may tend to the good of the King's service...

In case of your disability by sickness or otherwise, you are to leave these instructions, and any others which you may receive from us, with Rear-Admiral Saunders, who is hereby required to put the same in execution... Given etc.

ANSON
WILL ROWLEY
BATEMAN
R. EDGCUMBE

113.   *Hawke to Byng*

Ramillies in Gibraltar Bay
4 July 1756

Sir,

Upon looking over my orders this morning, I find myself obliged, in obedience to their Lordships' directions, to send home all the commissioned officers that were on board the *Ramillies* and *Buckingham* during the late action. I have accordingly by this morning's post acquainted their Lordships that I have complied with it and I shall this afternoon order them on board the *Antelope*. I hope you will believe that nothing but a peremptory order could have induced me to do this, as you was desirous of the contrary, as I should always be extremely glad to have it in my power to oblige you, being very sincerely, Sir,

Your most obedient and humble servant,
EDWARD HAWKE

114.   *Byng to Hawke (holograph)*

Hampton Court, Gibraltar
4 July 1756

Sir,

I have received your letter of this day's date and can have no objection to your putting their Lordships' orders in execution, for after their treatment of me I cannot be surprised at anything.

I am obliged to you for the excuse you make about it and I shall always be ready to believe your attention and friendship for me and hope you will be assured of my being most sincerely, Sir,

Your most obedient humble servant
J. BYNG

115.   *Line of Battle*

Ramillies in Gibraltar Bay
10 July 1756

The *Intrepid* is to lead with the starboard and the *Captain* with the larboard tacks on board. The *Experiment* is to repeat signals and the *Fortune* sloop to go ahead in the night carrying a light on her ensign staff.

Frigates	Rates	Ships	Commanders	Guns	Men	Division
Fortune	3	*Intrepid*	Capt. Young	64	480	
sloop	4	*Deptford*	Amherst[1]	50	280	
	3	*Hampton Court*	Hon. Capt. Hervey[2]	64	480	
Dolphin	2	*Prince George*	Chas. Saunders Esq	80	715	Chas. Saunders Esq
			Capt. Wheeler[3]			Rear-Ad. of the Blue
	3	*Buckingham*	Pratten	70	520	
	3	*Defiance*	Baird	60	400	
	3	*Nassau*	Sayer[4]	64	480	
	3	*Lancaster*	Hon. Capt. Edgcumbe[5]	70	520	
Experiment	2	*Ramillies*	Sir Edwd. Hawke Kt	90	770	Sir Edwd. Hawke Kt
			Capt. Hobbs			of the Bath
	3	*Ipswich*	Tyrell	64	480	Vice-Ad. of the White
	4	*Princess Louisa*	Lloyd	60	400	
	4	*Kingston*	Parry	60	400	
	3	*Culloden*	Taylor	74	600	
Chesterfield	3	*Trident*	Phil Durell Esq	64	500	Phil Durell Esq
	3	*Revenge*	Cornwall[6]	64	480	
	4	*Isis*	Tinker[7]	50	350	
	3	*Captain*	Catford	64	480	

Given etc.

[1] John Amherst was the younger brother of General Jeffrey Amherst. L 1739, C 1758, RA 1765, VA 1770, A 1778. C.-in-c. Plymouth 1776–8.

[2] The Hon. Augustus Hervey succeeded his brother as Earl of Bristol in 1775. L 1740, C 1747. Very active and prominent during the Seven Years War, including the blockade of Brest (see Part IV(e)). MP 1754–75; a Ld of Ady 1771–5. RA 1775, VA 1778. See David Erskine (ed.), *Augustus Hervey's Journal* (London: Kimber, 1953).

[3] Wheeler: L 1742, C 1748. A spirited, outspoken officer who, in June 1761, was killed on his quarterdeck while taking a French privateer of 50 guns (Rodger, *Wooden World*, pp. 75, 246, etc.).

[4] Sayer: L 1743, C 1746, RA 1770, VA 1776.

[5] The Hon. George Edgcumbe was the younger brother of Richard (p. 130, n. 1) whom he succeeded as Lord Edgcumbe in 1761. L 1739, CR 1742, C 1744. MP 1746–61. Served off Brest and at Quiberon Bay 1759. RA 1762, VA 1770, A 1778; c.-in-c. Plymouth 1766–70 and 1773. Created Earl of Mount-Edgcumbe 1789.

[6] Cornwall: L 1734, C 1744.

[7] Tinker: L 1748, C 1756.

116. *Hawke to Clevland*

Ramillies at sea
12 September 1756

Sir,

My last was dated 25th August in Altea Bay which I left the 1st of this month, having been prevented watering sooner by strong easterly winds which occasioned a great swell tumbling in upon the shore.

On the 29th ultimo, as I lay there, the *Isis*, whom I had detached to cruise off Benidorm, chased in a ship under English colours, firing at her as she stood in for the midst of the squadron. When she approached us, I fired to bring her to, which was followed by several other ships in the squadron. Upon this she hauled down her English colours, hoisted French, and struck. Some of our boats took possession of her but I ordered them to leave her to avoid giving offence to the Spanish court.

Since my leaving Altea, we have had light breezes and, for the most part, contrary. On the 6th instant, between Formentara and Majorca, in a sudden squall in which all the ships of the squadron were taken aback, the *Intrepid* and the *Buckingham* fell on board each other. The latter lost her bowsprit and everything belonging to it... This accident obliged me to lie by four days before I could get the *Buckingham* in a condition to proceed.

On the 11th I was joined by the *Dolphin*, whom I had detached from Altea to Barcelona, expecting orders from their Lordships might have been lodged there for me. I only received an answer from Sir Benjamin Keene to the letter mentioned in mine of the 29th July. As far as has been in my power, I have distressed the French on Minorca in obedience to my orders. I hoped the Toulon squadron, as I have constantly been advised by every vessel I stopped, would have come to their relief.[1] I am of opinion they wanted it. But in this also I have the mortification to be disappointed. The time is now come that the squadron must go into port on many accounts beside the most principal one, want of provisions. My orders of the 8th of June say I am 'to clean them as often as necessary either in some port of the King of Sardinia's dominions or at Gibraltar, as I shall find to be most convenient.' What port in Sardinia can be convenient?

---

[1] In fact, because Minorca had been successfully occupied, the French lost no time in demobilizing the squadron at Toulon. They were thus repeating the policy of 1745–8 (p. 13, n. 1) but were regretting it by 1757. The British never, for the rest of the war, released their stranglehold on the Mediterranean. When La Clue at last got through the Strait of Gibraltar, his squadron was crushed off Lagos (1759).

What port there can furnish us with a sufficient quantity of provisions, or what certainty have I of even being received there at all? At the time I received these orders, I foresaw all these difficulties, but on account of the exigency of the times made no objection, flattering myself that their Lordships would soon send me more explicit orders on these heads. I have now been near ten weeks out and own I am sensibly mortified at not having heard from England.

'Tis true I can go to Gibraltar, and must. But I cannot clean or repair any above a fifty or sixty gun ship there; neither should above a sixty be left in a bay so open and exposed to wind and weather during the winter. Besides, their Lordships must be sensible there are several of the ships of the squadron that will not be fit to stay abroad the winter. We have had an excessive bad season ever since we left Gibraltar...we are still greatly distressed with the fever and flux which have proved very mortal...

117. *Inscription on Lady Hawke's Tombstone in the Church of St Nicholas, North Stoneham, Hampshire*

[1757]

To the memory of Catharine, Lady Hawke, the best wife, the best mother and the best of friends, for engaging tenderness and good nature the delight of all that knew her, who died 29th October 1756, this stone was placed by Sir Edward Hawke, Knight of the Bath and Admiral of the Blue.

Likewise under this stone lies William, the son of Sir Edward and Lady Hawke, who died Sep. 14th 1753, aged 4 days.

118. *Hawke to Clevland*

Ramillies at Spithead
14 January 1757

Sir,

The winds would not permit my sailing from Gibraltar before the 9th ultimo. I left there under the command of Rear-Admiral Saunders the *Culloden* and *Guernsey* in the mole, the *Hampton Court, Revenge, Princess Louisa,* and poleacre. On 29th November I dispatched the *Trident* to carry home the trade from Cadiz...

In the night between the 19th and 20th, in hard gales, squally weather and a great sea, I bore down to several ships which had made signals of distress. In the morning [I] found the *Prince* and

Lancaster with their main yards gone...

When I was ordered to the Mediterranean, I had just returned from a long cruise to the westward. Since my embarking at Portsmouth, I have never slept one night out of the ship, or scarce set my foot on shore, all which have so impaired my health that I must beg the favour of their Lordships to indulge me with leave to be on shore some time for the re-establishment of it.

The *Lancaster* only is come in with me. I wish the rest may arrive in safety, as for these two nights past signals of distress have been made from several ships when it was not in my power to help them. The weather was so hazy, with very hard gales and a high sea. I am etc.

Minute: Read and answered.

PART IV(c)

JULY–DECEMBER 1757
ROCHEFORT AND AFTER

INTRODUCTION

In June 1757 William Pitt became for the second time Secretary of State and *de facto* leader of a reconstructed ministry nominally led by the Duke of Newcastle. Pitt's ideas about British national strategy now took decisive shape. It was of the essence to secure Frederick of Prussia's survival against the armies ranged against him, namely those of France, Austria and Russia. If the potential of the French nation could be absorbed in the continental struggle, Britain would continue to dominate the seas, sweep up French shipping, and win the competition for empire in North America and India. Now that Frederick and Cumberland, who commanded the allied force on Frederick's western flank, were coming under pressure especially from the French, Pitt wished to use British sea power to create a useful diversion. As George II was Elector of Hanover, Pitt had come to accept that Frederick could be supported from that continental enclave which had previously seemed merely a source of weakness. Pitt also saw that British landings might pin down enemy forces on the French coast. He therefore obtained the support of the inner cabinet and the King for an attack on Rochefort.

The original of George II's instructions to Hawke of 5 August 1757 [Document 122] is to be found at the National Maritime Museum. Such examples of instructions issued directly by the crown to the naval commanders of amphibious expeditions during the war are not easy to trace. For instance, an Admiralty document printed here [124] refers to Hawke's aforesaid instructions, but no copy of them seems to be held among the Admiralty records at the Public Record Office. Likewise, no copy appears there of the instructions issued to Saunders for the attack on Quebec in 1759. The King's instructions to Hawke were, of course, the work of Pitt. They express forcefully enough the strategic objects in view. Ensuing documents [125–36, 138–40, 142–4] touch on various aspects of such a combined expedition: supplies, accommodation and equipment for the troops, pilots, signals, organization of the landing, coastal surveys, intelligence of the defences and strength of the enemy, interservice relations, and—at least by implication—the exploitation of surprise.

As Hawke later explains, he had no option but to permit a council of war to be assembled [161]. Pitt had provided for this in the King's aforesaid instructions [122]. However, although the council endorsed the soldiers' refusal to land on the mainland at all, the mere appearance of the expedition off Rochefort was sufficient to divert numbers of French troops in that direction, even if this threat came too late in the campaigning season to help Frederick or Cumberland. Pitt had understandably been impatient for the expedition to depart [145], but he had doubtless, at inception, underestimated the time required for preparation.

Document 141 is not connected with the Rochefort expedition as such. It is included because it dramatically emphasizes the low status of warrant as compared with commissioned officers, or even 'young gentlemen', at that time.

The expedition itself, from its sailing in September to its ignominious return a month later, is covered in a fair amount of detail [147–57].

No sooner had Hawke arrived back at Spithead with the fleet on 8 October than he received orders to provision and water his ships for a cruise to last for four months [169]. He was to look out especially for a French squadron commanded by Du Bois de la Motte. The latter, who had replenished the Louisbourg garrison and escaped back to France in 1756, was expected to break out a second time from Louisbourg during the autumn of 1757. On 21 October, just before sailing, Hawke rushed off to Pitt a self-justification of his part in the Rochefort expedition [161]. This adds interesting detail to the admiral's previous accounts [155–7].

Hawke then found himself engaged on another frustrating cruise in trying, wintry conditions [162]. On 14 December he reached Spithead with half a dozen battered ships. Others had failed to make contact and were still struggling with the elements [163].

119. *Anson to Hawke (holograph)*

11 July 1757

Dear Sir,

I was very sorry you was gone out of town, as I should have wished to have had an hour's conversation with you this evening, and indeed it appears to me so material that, though I am very sorry to give you the trouble, yet I must beg the favour to see you in town; and I should be very glad [if] you would make Portsmouth in your way hither, without raising curiosity or alarm; but it is absolutely necessary that all the ships ordered to clean this spring should without a moment's [loss of] time be got to Spithead, as there may be immediate service for them. I am most sincerely

Your most obliged humble servant

ANSON

120. *Instructions from the Lords of the Admiralty to Hawke*

4 August 1757

By the Commissioners...to Sir Edward Hawke, Knight of the Bath and Admiral of the Blue Squadron in His Majesty's Fleet.

You are hereby required and directed to repair down to Portsmouth and hoist your flag on board His Majesty's ship the *Ramillies* and cause all possible dispatch to be used in getting ready such of His Majesty's ships as shall be fitting and refitting there. Given etc.

ANSON
GEO. HAY[1]
GILBERT ELLIOT[2]
J. FORBES

121. *Pitt to Hawke*

5 August 1757

Sir,

I send you herewith the secret instructions the King has been pleased to sign for your guidance and direction in the important

---

[1] George Hay was a lawyer and politician; MP 1754–78. Except for the months April to July 1757, he was a Ld of the Ady 1756–65. Knighted 1773.

[2] Gilbert Elliot was a man of parts: politician, philosopher and poet. MP 1753–77; held a variety of posts, including a seat on the Ady Board 1756–61. Succeeded as 3rd baronet Elliot of Minto 1766. Spoke persuasively in the Commons for George III's policies.

command with which His Majesty has honoured you. I have only to add my most sincere wishes for your success on this occasion and to observe that I am, with great truth and regard, Sir,

Your most obedient humble servant

W. PITT

122. *Secret Instructions from the King to Hawke*

5 August 1757

GEORGE R

[Seal]   Secret instructions for our trusty and wellbeloved Sir Edward Hawke, Knight of the Bath, Admiral of the Blue Squadron of our fleet, and commander-in-chief of our ships to be employed on a secret expedition for our service, or for such other officer on whom the command in chief of our said ships may devolve. Given at our court at Kensington the fifth day of August 1757 in the thirty-first year of our reign.

Whereas we have thought fit to employ a considerable body of our land forces on a secret expedition under the command of our trusty and wellbeloved Sir John Mordaunt, Knight of the Bath, Lieutenant-General of our forces, and whereas we have appointed you to be commander-in-chief of a squadron of our ships of war to act in conjunction and to co-operate with the said Sir John Mordaunt in the execution of the services prescribed to him, for your better discharge of the great and important trust thereby reposed in you we have judged it proper to give you the following instructions:

1st   You shall immediately upon the receipt of these our instructions repair to Spithead where we have ordered a squadron consisting of at least sixteen ships of the line and a proportionate number of frigates to rendezvous, together with transport vessels for our troops (who are to embark from the Isle of Wight) and also the vessels with the artillery and stores, which squadron and transports you are to take under your command; and so soon as the troops shall be embarked, you are to proceed without loss of time to the coasts of France.

2nd   Whereas we have determined, with the blessing of God, to prosecute the just war in which we are engaged against the French king with the utmost vigour, and it being highly expedient and of urgent necessity to make some expedition that may cause a diversion and engage the enemy to employ in their own defence a considerable part of their forces destined to invade and oppress the liberties of the Empire and to subvert the independency of Europe, and, if possible, to make some effectual impression on the enemy which, by disturbing and shaking the credit of their public loans, impairing the resources of their navy, as well as disconcerting and in part frustrating their dangerous and extensive operations of war, may reflect lustre on our arms and add life and strength to the common cause; and we being persuaded that nothing in the present situation of affairs can so speedily and essentially annoy and distress France as a successful enterprise against Rochefort, our will and pleasure is that you do co-operate in attempting, as far as will be found practicable, a descent on the French coast at or near Rochefort in order to attack, if practicable, and by a vigorous impression force that place, and to burn and destroy, to the utmost of your power, all docks, magazines, arsenals and shipping that shall be found there, and exert such other efforts as shall be judged most proper for annoying the enemy. After this attempt on Rochefort shall either have succeeded or failed, and in case the circumstances of our fleet and forces shall, with prospect of success, still admit of further operations, Port L'Orient and Bordeaux are to be considered next as the most important objects of our arms on the coast of France; and our will and pleasure accordingly is that you do proceed successively to an attempt on both or either of those places, as shall be judged practicable, or any other place that shall be thought most advisable from Bordeaux homewards to Havre in order to carry and spread, with as much rapidity as may be, a warm alarm along the maritime provinces of France; and you are, as far as you shall be able with the fleet under your command, to be aiding and assisting to Sir John Mordaunt in the performance of the several services aforesaid.

3rd   In case, by the blessing of God upon our arms, our forces should become masters of any places on the coast of France, our will and pleasure is that they do not keep possession thereof, but that, after demolishing and destroying as far as may be all works, defences, magazines, arsenals, shipping, and naval stores, you do proceed successively on the ulterior operations of this expedition, according as any of them shall be judged advisable and may be performed within such time as shall be consistent with your return, with the fleet under your command, so as to be in England at or about, as near as may be, the end of September, unless the circumstances of our ships and forces shall urgently require their return sooner; and our troops are to be landed at Portsmouth or such other of our ports as the exigency of the case may suggest.

4th　Whereas it is necessary that, upon certain occasions, councils of war should be held, we have thought fit to appoint, and do hereby appoint, such a council, which shall consist of four of our principal sea commanders and of an equal number of our principal land officers, including the commanders-in-chief of our sea and land forces (except in cases happening at [sic] land, relating to the carrying on any military operations to be performed by our land forces only; and, in like manner, except in cases happening at sea with regard to operations to be performed by the fleet only); and all such sea and land officers are hereby respectively directed from time to time to be aiding and assisting with their advice, as often they shall be called together by you or the officer commanding our land forces for that purpose; and in all such councils of war, when assembled, the majority of voices shall determine the resolutions thereof; and in case the voices shall happen to be equal, the president shall have the casting vote.

5th　Whereas the success of this expedition will very much depend upon an entire good understanding between our sea and land officers, we do hereby strictly enjoin and require you, on your part, to maintain and cultivate such a good understanding and agreement, and to order the sailors and marines, and also the soldiers serving as part of the complements of our ships, to assist our land forces, if judged expedient, by taking post on shore, manning batteries, covering the boats, sercuring the safe re-embarkation of the troops, and such other services at [sic] land as may be considered consistent with the safety of our fleet; and as we have instructed our general and commander-in-chief of our land forces, on his part, to entertain and cultivate the same good understanding and agreement, and to order that the soldiers under his command shall man the ships when there shall be occasion for them and when they can be spared from the land service; and in order to establish the strictest union that may be between you and our said general and commander-in-chief of our land forces, you are hereby required to communicate these instructions to him, as he is directed to communicate those he has received from us to you.

6th　As our service may require you or the commander-in-chief of our land forces should, on particular occasions, dispatch a sloop or small frigate to England with intelligence, you shall always take care to have with you one or more sloops or small frigates for that purpose.

7th　You are to transmit constant and particular accounts of your proceedings to one of our principal Secretaries of State and to our Commissioners for executing the office of our Lord High Admiral of Great Britain; and you shall observe and follow such instructions as you shall receive from us under our sign manual, or from one of our principal Secretaries of State, or from our Commissioners for executing the office of our High Admiral of Great Britain for the time being.

G.R.

123. *Instructions from the Lords of the Admiralty to Hawke*

5 August 1757

Having ordered the commanders of the King's ships and vessels named in the annexed list to follow your orders for their further proceedings, you are hereby required and directed to take under your command such sixteen of those of the line as can soonest be got ready to proceed on service, together with the frigates and small vessels, and use the utmost expedition in getting these manned and ready in all respects for the sea. In case you take the *Royal William*, you are to cause Vice-Admiral Mostyn's retinue and servants to be removed into the *Royal Ann* or *Barfleur*, whichever of them you shall leave behind. And having ordered Vice-Admiral Knowles and Rear-Admiral Brodrick[1] to put themselves under your command, you are also hereby required to take them under your command accordingly. Given etc.

List of the ships and vessels whose commanders are directed to follow Sir Edward Hawke's orders:
[Here follow the names of the nineteen ships of the line and twelve others—frigates, fireships, bomb vessels, busses, and a cutter. For those that went to Rochefort, see Document 147.]

124. *Instructions from the Lords of the Admiralty to Hawke*

6 August 1757

In pursuance of His Majesty's pleasure signified to us by Mr Pitt, one of his principal Secretaries of State, you are hereby required and directed, in addition to our order of yesterday's date, to proceed with the squadron put under your command and the transport

[1] Brodrick: L 1728, CR 1741, C 1741, serving with credit under Vernon 1739–43. RA 1756, VA 1759; Boscawen's second-in-command at Lagos 1759, and continued as c.-in-c. blockading the French remnant in Cadiz.

vessels named in the enclosed list (which are ordered to join you and follow your orders) to Spithead where you will receive His Majesty's pleasure for your future conduct; and you are strictly to follow such orders and instructions as you shall receive from His Majesty or one of his principal Secretaries of State. Given etc.

125. Clevland to Hawke

6 August 1757

Sir,

The Commissioners for Sick and Wounded being ordered to send down to Portsmouth eight bushels and a half of dried apples to be disposed of as you shall direct, I am commanded by my Lords Commissioners of the Admiralty to recommend it to you to cause them to be put on board any ship of your squadron with directions to her captain to inform their Lordships what effects they are found to have upon the health of the seamen. I am etc.

126. Instructions from the Lords of the Admiralty to Hawke

6 August 1757

Whereas it has been judged that the use of portable broth in the Navy will tend very greatly to the recovery of the health of sick seamen, particularly in scorbutic cases, and a large quantity, which hath been prepared in consequence thereof and put on board the hospital ship, having been taken on shore and ordered to be distributed on board the ships under your command, you are hereby required and directed to cause application to be made to the agent to the Commissioners for Sick and Wounded Seamen at Portsmouth for it and cause it to be distributed in equal proportions on board the ships of your squadron, directing the captains to put the same under the charge of the pursers as a store, who are to keep it in a place which we have ordered to be made in the breadroom for that purpose, and to issue it to the sick by demands to be made from time to time by the surgeons (verified by their attestation) and to account with the above-mentioned Commissioners for the expense thereof, producing such demands from the pursers as vouchers thereto and making affidavit that they only issued the broth in that manner, and the surgeons making oath that they never made such demands but for the use of the sick. You are likewise to direct them to make very nice and particular observations on the effects of it upon the sick and report to us their opinion of its utility. Given etc.

127.   *Hawke to Clevland*

Ramillies at Spithead
7 August 1757

Sir,

I have received their Lordships' order of the 4th instant for hoisting my flag and using all possible dispatch in getting such of His Majesty's ships as are fitting and refitting ready for sea, in obedience to which I this morning hoisted my flag on board the *Ramillies* and shall forward the ship to the utmost of my power.

My secret instructions have also been transmitted to me by Mr Pitt, one of His Majesty's principal Secretaries of State.

I have likewise received their Lordships' order of the 6th with the list of transports which shall be punctually complied with. None of the transports are yet arrived.

Rear-Admiral Brodrick will for this day transmit you the state and condition of His Majesty's ships at Spithead and in the Harbour.

I have also received their Lordships' order of the 5th with a list annexed of the King's ships and vessels whose commanders they have ordered to follow my directions for their farther proceedings. As soon as I shall have maturely considered the state and condition of the ships, I shall acquaint their Lordships with the names of the sixteen of the line which I shall take under my command for service...

128.   *Hawke to Pitt*

7 August 1757

Sir,

I have received your letter of the 5th instant, enclosing the secret instructions His Majesty has been pleased to sign for my guidance and direction in the command with which he has honoured me. I beg you will do me the justice to believe that I shall exert my utmost abilities for his honour and the service of my country. I am etc.

129. *Hawke to Clevland*

Ramillies at Spithead
8 August 1757

Sir,

I have received their Lordships' several orders of the 6th instant and given directions for discharging from the *Barfleur* the nine men belonging to the *Rising Sun*. I shall also give the necessary directions concerning the portable broth and dried apples.

As soon as the horse ships and baggage ship shall arrive, I shall order them to proceed to Southampton.

I have also received your and Mr Milne's[1] several letters. While the troops continue on the Isle of Wight, one of the cutters shall be employed to carry Mr Taylor and the money thither. I shall also carefully observe their Lordships' directions with regard to the money destined for Plymouth.

As there is a want of men, I shall continue the marines on board the *Achilles*...

I have ordered the *Royal William* out to Spithead where she is to receive her guns on board as soon as they arrive, which I hope will happen in company with the transports, as I have been informed that they have been shipped some time. Vice-Admiral Mostyn's retinue and servants shall be removed into the *Royal Sovereign*, which ship I think unfit for the service I am going upon. The sixteen ships of the line I purpose taking with me are the *Ramillies, Royal George, Royal Ann, Namur, Royal William, Neptune, Princess Amelia, Barfleur, Magnanime, Torbay, Dublin, Burford, America, Alcide, Dunkirk* and *Achilles*. Their Lordships will perceive by the state and condition of such of them as are at this port (transmitted to them yesterday) that there is great want of men. I therefore beg that directions may be immediately given that their several rendezvous be broke up and the tenders belonging to them to repair hither. Also the men lent from the *Royal Ann* to the *Union* to be returned. In the meantime I have directed Vice-Admiral Knowles and Rear-Admiral Brodrick to muster all the ships' companies in order to make an equal distribution of the seamen. Their Lordships will also observe the great want of surgeon's mates.

I purpose making up the company of the *Royal Ann* from the *Royal Sovereign*.

I should be glad if their Lordships would order two more busses to

---

[1] Milnes: a clerk at the Ady 1725–51; Chief Clerk 1751–6; Deputy Secretary 15.6.56–16.10.59, when he retired.

join me.

This morning arrived the *Experiment* tender from St Malo with
ninety-nine prisoners, mostly Palatines of the American and Shirley's regiments. They were taken at Oswego. As they are afflicted
with the jail distemper, I have sent them to the hospital. There are
beside, three women and two children belonging to them for whom
no provision is made. I am etc.

130.   *Hawke to Lieutenant-General Sir John Mordaunt*[1]

Portsmouth
8 August 1757

Sir,

I have the favour of your letter of this day's date and have
communicated it to Admiral Knowles.[2] We would with great pleasure do ourselves the honour of waiting upon you at the camp, but
the service is so pressing that it is out of our power to stir from
hence. Yet I hope we shall soon have an opportunity of meeting to
consult the properest manner of embarking the troops. The moment
the baggage and horse ships arrive, I shall order them to proceed to
Southampton.

I shall be obliged to you if you will direct a list of troops to be
embarked, distinguished by battalions according to their seniority,
particularly specifying the number of commission and non-commissioned officers of each class, to be sent to me, that I may be the better
able to form the three divisions of the transports.

Admiral Knowles desires me to make his compliments with mine
to yourself and Major-General Conway,[3] and I beg you will believe
that I am etc.

[1] Mordaunt: he was active in his early career, serving at Culloden 1746, and in the
Low Countries. MP 1754–67. Lt.-general 1754. Court martialled after the Rochefort
expedition, but acquitted. General 1770.
[2] Knowles: L 1730, CR 1731, C 1737. Versed in French language, mathematics and
mechanics. Acted as surveyor and engineer of the fleet at Cartagena 1741, and well
regarded by Vernon. Governor of Louisbourg 1746–7; RA 1747. While undoubtedly
able, he was touchy and temperamental; and, in 1748, he became involved in various
duels and courts martial after an action off Havana (he being c.-in-c. Jamaica 1747–
9). Briefly in command of Western Squadron 1756, when VA. Defended Mordaunt
after the Rochefort expedition and was not again employed at sea. Adm. 1758. He
served in the Russian navy as an administrator during the Turkish war (1770–4).
[3] Conway: served at Dettingen 1743, and then at Fontenoy, Culloden and Lauffeld.
Major-general 1756; Lt-general 1759. Served under Ferdinand of Brunswick 1761–3.
MP 1741–84 (except for ten months in 1774–5); a troubled Sec. of State 1765–8.
General 1772. He opposed prolongation of the American War and, in 1784, he joined
Fox. Field marshal 1793.

P.S. I have given directions to my captain to receive your things on board the *Ramillies* and to order them to be put into my apartments.

131. *Instructions from Hawke to All Captains at Spithead*

11 August 1757

Pursuant to an order from the Lords Commissioners of the Admiralty, you are hereby required and directed, whenever any British prisoners shall be sent on board His Majesty's ship under your command, immediately to enter them as part of your complement, at the same time putting them on your bounty and two months advance lists, in order to their being paid as customary before the ship proceeds to sea. You are also to demand of the Storekeeper and Clerk of the Cheque the several slops mentioned:

One hat or cap, one handkerchief, two shirts, one jacket, one waistcoat, one pair breeches, one pair shoes, one pair stockings, a bed.

Given etc.

132. *Hawke to Clevland*

Ramillies at Spithead
13 August 1757

Sir,

I have received your letter of the 10th with the accompanying copies of His Majesty's order in council for extending the bounty to seamen and landmen who secrete themselves. I have distributed them to the captains of His Majesty's ships at this port.

I have received and delivered their Lordships' order of the 11th to Captain Innes[1] of the *Mermaid* [to take charge of a convoy]... I have stopped the *Medway* from docking and directed her to be fitted with the utmost expedition...

Several people have been from Shoreham, Newhaven, and Arundel to acquaint me that their coast is greatly infested by two French dogger privateers. On Thursday, they run two vessels ashore at Arundel and chased another into Shoreham...

This morning arrived a Lieutenant of the *Alcide* in the *Eltham* tender from Weymouth with twenty-three impressed men.

Enclosed I send you a letter from the released prisoners lately

[1] Innes: L 1739, CR 1752, C 1756, RA 1780.

arrived in the *Experiment* tender whom I have sent to the hospital. I am etc.

Minute: 15 August. Own receipt. Approve [orders given to the *Medway*]. Send this letter [from the Oswego prisoners] to Lord Barrington and acquaint him the Lords desire he will order these men to be taken care of, as the Lords apprehend they are still in His Majesty's land service. Let Sir Edward know it.

133.   *Clevland to Hawke*

16 August 1757

Sir,

The Portsmouth mail having been robbed this morning, I send you herewith duplicates of my letters of yesterday...

Enclosure:

133a.   *Clevland to Hawke*

15 August 1757

Sir,

I have received and read to my Lords Commissioners of the Admiralty your letter of yesterday's date, with the enclosed from Captain Howe with the list of pilots procured from the islands of Guernsey and Jersey, and in return I am ordered by their Lordships to acquaint you that they will make good all engagements entered into on that account; but they desire you will let them know when the service they are wanted for is over that they may order them to be discharged...

134.   *Hawke to Clevland*

Ramillies at Spithead
19 August 1757

Sir,

Yesterday, after post, arrived His Majesty's sloop *Albany* from Ireland and a tender with one hundred and fifty-four impressed men, out of whom I have completed the complement of the *Alcide* and put the remainder on board the *Royal Sovereign*, purposing from these supernumeraries to supply the sick and lent from the squadron just before it shall sail.

I have received your three letters of the 17th and directed Vice-Admiral Knowles and Rear-Admiral Brodrick to inquire into the complaint of the company of the *Medway* against Captain Proby...[1]

To save time, I yesterday exchanged sixty men from the best-manned ships here, viz. twenty [from] the *Jersey*, twenty [from] the *Chesterfield* and twenty [from] the *Peregrine* sloop, to strengthen the company of the *Princess Amelia*...

Enclosed I send you a second petition from the poor men taken prisoner at Oswego. Their case is really deplorable and required a speedy attention. I am etc.

Enclosure:

134a. *Second Petition of Returned Oswego Prisoners*
(unmodernized)

To the Rt. Honourable Sir Edward Hawke
Most Sheweth The Pressent Distressed Condition of the Remaining Few of his Majestys 50th & 51st Regiments of Foot Taken Prisoners of War at Fort Oswego In North America Who After Doing Duty In ye Aforesaid Garrison for Almost the Space of 2 Years Being Scituated In the Desserts Upwards of 300 Miles Beyond any of our Inhabitants Without any Coming to our Releif Being Over Powered by the Great Inequality of the Enimy Forces We were Obleidged to Surrender on the 14th of August Last We here Present Being the Only Misfortunate of all the Rest of Our Campanions Being Carryed Naked into Old France Where Our Sufferings has been Unexpressable Confined in a Dungeon In Bresst untill the 17th of Decr. and Then Marched of To Dinan Being Eleven Days Marching In the Most Miserable Weather that Ever poor Creatures Marched, our Entertainment on the Road Being no Other than What their Horse Stables Afforded us and the wett Litter with our own Wett Rags for our Bedding, With a Little Bulliong and Bullocks Liver once A Day with a Pound of Bread as Black as Our Hatt and now After Almost Three Years Confinement are Destitute of Officers, Having 2 Suits of Cloathing Due unto us and Some 21 Months Butt the Leeast 14 Months Pay having None of Our Own Officers here to Befriend us Most Humbly Rely on Your Excellencys Goodness In Displyaing To Your Distressed Memoralists that Most Benevolent Acct of Charity In Righting the Wronged to Justice

---

[1] Proby: C 1746. Appointed commodore and c.-in-c. Mediterranean 1769.

Minute: 20 August. Own receipt and acquaint him the Lords hope he will take no more than are absolutely necessary, there being other ships that must be manned.

22 August. Send Lord Barrington [new Secretary at War] a copy of the enclosed [petition].

135. *Hawke to Clevland (holograph)*

19 August 1757

Sir,

Last night I held another consultation with Vice-Admiral Knowles and the director of the embarkations, where we were unanimously of opinion that there will still be wanting at least four thousand ton of transports more. I directed Mr Thames to send an account of this to the Navy Board by express last night. I am etc.

136. *Clevland to Hawke*

20 August 1757

Sir,

I have communicated to my Lords Commissioners of the Admiralty your letter of yesterday's date, informing them that upon a consultation with Vice-Admiral Knowles and the director of the embarkation you were unanimously of opinion that at least four thousand tons of transports are still wanting, and I am commanded by their Lordships to acquaint you that they have reason to believe this person whom the Navy Board have sent to Portsmouth is ignorant in what manner the transports are fitted, otherwise he could not mistake so much in his calculation, for these ships have all of them two flush platforms between the decks for the men to lay their bedding upon, by which means many more may be conveniently stowed than in cabins, the usual method of fitting transports, wherefore their Lordships are of opinion that there will be sufficient room, agreeable to what I wrote to you in my letter of yesterday. However, to remove the difficulties and uneasiness which Mr Thames has raised, Mr Cokburne, the Controller of the Navy, is sent down to Portsmouth with directions to do everything possible to furnish such other ships as shall be ready, if necessary. I am etc.

137. *Hawke to Clevland*

Ramillies at Spithead
20 August 1757

Sir,

...As I am only senior and have no commission to command at this port, I do not apprehend I have authority to order the sentence of any court martial to be put in execution. I therefore beg their Lordships' directions with regard to the execution of the sentence passed on the boatswain of the *Peregrine* sloop. I am etc.

Minute: 22nd August. Own receipt... There is no doubt of his powers to carry the sentence into execution being by virtue of his commission as commander-in-chief, whilst he is senior officer from the Lords having ordered a commission appointing [him] commander-in-chief of the squadron to be employed on a particular service.

138. *Hawke to Clevland*

Ramillies at Spithead
21 August 1757

Sir,

...Just as I was dispatching an express in answer to yours with regard to the tonnage of the transports, the Controller of the Navy arrived. He having undertaken to settle the matter, I shall not trouble their Lordships farther upon it...

Last night arrived the *Triton* tender from Studland Bay where she was forcibly carried and the two hundred and ten prisoners she brought over made their escape...

Minute: 22 August. Own receipt... The Lords hope everything [relating to the transports] will be to his satisfaction.

139. *Hawke to Clevland*

Ramillies at Spithead
22 August 1757

Sir,

I have received...your several letters [of 20 August].

I never proposed taking more men than what would equal the complement of each ship. Where there was but a few wanting in any particular ship, I should not regard it. But at present, as two battalions of soldiers, raw and undisciplined, are included in the complements, I think it necessary that we should be complete...

With respect to Mr Thames, I beg leave to refer their Lordships to the enclosed copy of a letter he sent me on Saturday. Mr Knowles and I had several conferences with him on the subject of it, not with any intention of starting difficulties or retarding the service, but on the contrary to obviate them before it should be too late. We are still of opinion that the tonnage of the transports first provided was deficient... In transporting troops to and from Holland, with a fortnight's water and provisions, and a short passage, one ton a man might be shifted with. But where troops are to be many weeks at sea, men must have room to sit and lie under cover. In this case, can it be imagined that a ship of four hundred tons burthen could be capable of receiving four hundred men? Let there be deducted from her tonnage the room necessary for her proper crew, ballast, cables, and other stores; room for several months provisions and water for the soldiers; for their arms, tent poles and other baggage. What remains can only be allowed for the reception of men. It was my duty to direct Mr Thames to remonstrate on this subject to the Navy Board. Notwithstanding, I was from the first determined, and am so still, to embark the troops in the best manner possible on board whatever number of transports shall be ordered...

Minute: 23rd August. Let him know I have communicated his letter to the Lords and they hope from the account received this day from Mr Cokburne that everything they judge necessary is now done.

Enclosure:

139a. *Henry Thames to Hawke*

Portsmouth
21 August 1757

Sir, By a letter I received from the Honourable Navy Board, date the 8th instant, they directed me to allow two tons per man... When I had made a disposition, I found they could not receive on board but six regiments at that allowance...and your honour ordered me to acquaint the Navy Board thereof. I sent an express accordingly and received their answer, date the 12th instant, that I was to allow one ton to each man...

Your honour then asked my opinion whether I thought one ton

sufficient for a man. I answered I was convinced to the contrary, for that the ship's hold would be taken up with the provisions, tents and tent-poles, arms chests, baggage, etc.... and that there was only between decks for the men; and, the weather being so hot, would impair the men's health, if allowed no more room...

140.   *Hawke to Clevland (holograph)*

Ramillies
24 August 1757

Sir,

I have now by me His Majesty's commission appointing me commander-in-chief of the squadron to be employed on a particular service. I hope my meaning has not been so far misunderstood as to imagine I wanted a commission of the same nature to corroborate that of His Majesty. Supposing I had such a commission, which I think entirely unnecessary, I should still be under the same doubt with respect to my having authority to order the sentence of a court martial to be carried into execution. I think it would be an illegal act without their Lordships' orders for that purpose. As senior on a foreign service, I should have no doubt; but, without a positive commission in Great Britain, I look on every officer as so immediately under the direction of the Lords Commissioners for executing the office of Lord High Admiral as not to have any executive power himself.

...An expression at the end of your letter I own greatly astonishes me, viz. 'The Lords hope everything relating to the transports will be done to your satisfaction.' I never was dissatisfied with any number appointed and only thought it my duty for the public credit, as well as the private reputation of the Boards concerned, to give my opinion in a matter wherein some difficulty might have arisen when too late to be remedied. I meant it well and, as conviction is the best argument, I hope that discharge of my duty will not be construed to my disadvantage, since the Controller has thought fit to make so great an addition to the first tonnage. If such addition had not been, upon mature deliberation, thought absolutely necessary by his superiors, or even by himself alone, I cannot think it would have been done in complaisance to any private person's opinion. Besides, I beg it may be considered that the difficulty arose from a quarter here I have no immediate concern of my own. For, upon my honour, had the first transports arrived in time, the troops should have been embarked on board them in the best manner they could without the least objections being made by me...

Yesterday sailed out of harbour to Spithead His Majesty's sloop *Peregrine*...

141. *Instructions from the Lords of the Admiralty to Hawke*

25 August 1757

Whereas a court martial held at Spithead the 16th instant, at which Rear-Admiral Brodrick was president, for the trial of Richard Willis, boatswain of His Majesty's sloop the *Peregrine* for neglect of duty and other offences, it was adjudged that the said Richard Willis should be immediately dismissed from his employment as boatswain and rendered incapable of ever serving again as an officer in His Majesty's sea service, and also to be punished for his said offences with three hundred lashes on his bare back with a cat of nine tails on board of such ships at such times and in such proportions as the commander-in-chief shall think proper to direct, and afterwards to serve before the mast on board of such of His Majesty's ships as the said commanding officer shall choose to order him on board of. You are hereby required and directed to cause the said sentence to be carried into immediate execution. Given etc.

[Hawke's consequential order stated that Willis, having been found guilty 'of neglect of duty, of abusive and reproachful language to his captain, and behaving with contempt to the other officers', was to receive fifteen lashes aboard each of twenty named ships— the *Ramillies* not being one of them.]

142. *Holograph Notes by Hawke: 'Memo. for the Fleet'*

[September 1757]

To consider for a very proper place for a rendezvous which must be near upon (after we are past Plymouth and Torbay) off the place where we design to go.

To get a number of printed signals for the merchantmen.

To see that all the men of war have the Sailing and Fighting Signals and Instructions, as likewise the private additional signals.

To get a number of the Sailing and Fighting Instructions from the Admiralty.

To consider with the flag and general officers which will be the properest place to attempt. To settle this in going along and to fix upon the ships and troops that are to make the attack which, if done at all, must absolutely be done upon the first going in or otherwise they will be prepared to make head against you. No time to be lost upon these occasions.

To see that all the ships are manned that goes with me, and victualled and watered for Channel service.

To see likewise that they have their stores on board for the same service.

Not to undertake anything without good pilots ...

To endeavour to cover the landing of the men by sending in two, three, or more, frigates inshore to fire grape and partridge, to scour the country while the men are disembarking.

To be particularly careful to do this upon their embarking ...

To make out lines of battle.

To make out signals for the ships and the transports.

To order all the fleet to sail in divisions, taking it in seniority after their admirals, and the transports to bring up the rear.

To inquire of Phill. Durell at Portsmouth how Mr Vernon regulated the transports [at Cartagena in 1741].

Mr Vernon's letters relating to Portobello, Cartagena, and Panama. Lediard's Naval History ...

When the troops are landed, to send out ships and vessels to cruise between the main squadron and the Isle of Oléron or Bordeaux, and between the [squadron] and the Isle of Ushant or the Penmarks.

To consider well what force is, or may be, at Brest before I part with any of my ships.

Annex:

142a. *Draft 'Memorandum for the Service'* (holograph)

The transports that carry the soldiers must be distinguished by the seniority of the regiments or battalions by a long, broad vane at their different mast heads. For instance, the first regiment a long red vane at the main topgallant mast head; the second, the same vane at the fore topmast head ... the 16th, a long broad vane, half red, half blue, and so on for the different mast heads. The six tenders that carry the six Lieut. Cols. to distinguish them by putting a ball in their long vane ... To divide the whole number of tenders into three divisions and to appoint a man of war of the line and a frigate to each ...

In case of going in with a design to anchor upon the enemy's shore, to give positive directions for the divisions of the fleet to lead in, in order of the line of battle, and for each division to follow ... In case of going in upon the enemy's shore, to be careful that you go in with the beginning of the flood, lest any of your ships happen to touch ...

143. *Hawke to Clevland*

Ramillies at Spithead
4 September 1757 per express 10 a.m.

Sir,

... The transports are in sight. This morning I sent the cutters out to meet them with orders not to come to at Spithead but proceed directly for Cowes to take the troops on board. I am etc.

144. *Hawke to Mordaunt*

Portsmouth
4 September 1757

Sir,

The transports are arrived and I have ordered them down to Cowes to receive the troops on board as soon as you shall be ready. If you could by the bearer let me know the precise time that I may send proper vessels to assist in the embarkation, it would greatly oblige, Sir,

Your most obedient servant ...

145. *Pitt to Hawke*

Whitehall
5 September 1757, 4 o'clock in
in the afternoon

Sir,

The wind having been fair for the transports going to Spithead ever since Friday morning, I am to acquaint you that His Majesty expects with impatience to hear that the troops are embarked; but if, by any delay, the embarkation should not be completed when this letter reaches you, I am to signify the King's pleasure that the most particular diligence be employed in getting the troops on board and proceeding without the loss of a moment to the execution of your orders and instructions with regard to the expedition under your care.

His Majesty having been informed that ten battalions under the orders of Sir John Ligonier were all completely embarked at Williamstadt within the course of the twenty-four hours in which they arrived at that place, the King expects to hear by the return of the messenger that the fleet under your command, with the troops on board, have proceeded to sea, in case the wind permits, agreeable to your orders and instructions.

I am with great truth and regard, Sir,

Your most obedient humble servant

W. PITT

P.S.   The messenger that carries this has my orders to stay to bring an account of the fleet's sailing.

146.   *Hawke to Clevland*

Ramillies at Spithead
6 September 1757, ¾ past 12 at noon

Sir,

I have just received your letter of yesterday's date with the extract of Captain Wheeler's. I proposed sending the *Southampton* and *Hunter* cutter a day before me to look into Brest for intelligence and then join me on my rendezvous. I shall detach her tonight with directions to keep a very good lookout for the frigates mentioned in that letter.

The squadron is unmooring, all the troops by this time embarked, and as soon as they come up I shall proceed to sea, if the winds and weather will permit.

The *Jersey* and *Mermaid* are sailed with their convoy to the westward. I am etc.

147.   *Line of Battle*

Ramillies at Spithead
7 September 1757

The *Magnanime* to lead with the starboard and the *America* with the larboard tacks on board.

Frigates [etc.]	Rate	Ships	Commanders	No. of Guns	Men	Division
[*Jason* (50)]						
Firedrake	3	*Magnanime*	Hon. Capt. Howe	74	700	

Escort	2	Barfleur	Capt. Graves[1]	80	700	
Hunter cutter	2	Neptune	Chas. Knowles Esq.	90	770	Chas. Knowles Esq.
			Capt. Galbraith[2]			Vice-Ad. of
Infernal	3	Torbay	Hon. Capt. Keppel	74	700	the Red
Bomb tenders	2	Royal William	Capt. Taylor	84	770	
Pluto	4	Achilles	Hon. Capt. Barr-			
			ington[3]	60	420	
Beaver	2	Namur	Capt. Denis	90	750	
Chesterfield	2	Ramillies	Sir Edwd. Hawke Kt	90	780	Sir Edwd. Hawke
to repeat signals			Capt. Hobbs			Kt of the Bath,
						Ad. of the Blue
Southampton	1	Royal George	Capt. Buckle[4]	100	870	
Postilion	4	Medway	Proby	60	420	
Proserpine	3	Burford	Young	70	520	
Canterbury bus	4	Dunkirk	Digby[5]	60	420	
Cormorant	3	Dublin	Rodney	74	600	
Coventry	3	Princess Amelia	Tho. Brodrick Esq.	80	665	Tho. Brodrick Esq.
			Capt. Colby[6]			Rear-Ad. of
Pelican	3	Alcide	Douglas	64	500	the White
Medway bus	4	America	Hon. Capt. Byron	60	420	

Given etc.

148. *Hawke to Clevland*

Ramillies at St Helens
[Thursday] 8 September 1757

Sir,

... On Tuesday the squadron was unmoored in order to drop
down to St Helens to wait for the transports, but the wind dying

[1] Samuel Graves: L 1739, C 1744, RA 1762, VA 1770, A 1778. He was some twelve years older than his cousin, Thomas Graves, who commanded at the Chesapeake in 1781.

[2] Galbraith: L, CR 1745, C 1756. Superannuated RA 1780.

[3] The Hon. Samuel Barrington was a younger brother of the 2nd Viscount Barrington (p. 23, n. 2). L 1745, CR 1747, C 1747; served with Rodney and Hawke 1759. RA 1778, VA 1779; c.-in-c. West Indies from 1778 and took St Lucia in 1779. Adm. 1787.

[4] Buckle: L 1739, CR 1744, C 1745. Despite his seniority, served as Boscawen's flag captain at Lagos. Commanded a strong squadron off Brest in 1761. RA 1770, VA 1775, A 1780.

[5] Digby: L 1752, C 1755. Served at Quiberon Bay; also at Ushant (1778). RA 1779; Rodney's second-in-command at relief of Gibraltar. C.-in-c. N. America 1781–3.

[6] Colby: L 1742, CR 1746, C 1756.

away obliged me to moor again. Yesterday at 4 o'clock in the morning I made the signal to unmoor and sent an officer to Cowes to see them all from thence. The last of them arrived about noon when I made the signal to weigh, and about 3 p.m. got this length, where I was obliged to come to, as they could not get out. I immediately sent Lieutenant McKinley with the cutters, with repeated orders for them to join me.

Finding the *Chesterfield* could not be got ready to accompany me and, by the tenders not arriving with the lent and new-raised men, the squadron in want of men, I directed Captain Legge to discharge one hundred and thirty-one men into different ships. He will be supplied when the tenders arrive ...

149.   *Hawke to Clevland*

Ramillies at sea
10 September 1757

Sir,

On Thursday last after I wrote to you the wind died away, which obliged me to come to again till half an hour past 5. Then a moderate breeze about W.N.W. springing up, I made the signal to weigh and at 7 made sail with all the transports. On Friday we had contrary winds till evening and this morning I was joined by His Majesty's ship *Essex*, by whom I send you a copy of my rendezvous. We have now a fresh gale with wind at N.N.E. Portland bears N.E. 11 leagues. I am etc.

Minute: 14 September. Own receipt by the first opportunity.

150.   *Pitt to Hawke*

Whitehall
15 September 1757

Sir,

His Majesty, by his secret instructions dated the 5th day of August last, having directed the return of the fleet under your command together with the land forces on board, 'so as to be in England at, or about, as near as may be, the end of September, unless the circumstances of the ships and forces shall necessarily require their return sooner'; I am now to signify to you the King's pleasure that you do not consider the above-mentioned time limited for your return as intended in any manner to affect, or interfere, with the full execution of the first and principal object of the expedition, namely 'attempting, as far as shall be found practicable, a descent on the French coast, at or near Rochefort, in order to attack and, by a vigorous impression, force that place and to burn and destroy, to the utmost of your power, all shipping, docks, magazines and arsenals that shall be found there and exert such other efforts as shall be judged most proper for annoying the enemy.' And with regard to any other particular attempt, which agreably to your orders you shall have commenced and in the execution whereof you shall be actually engaged, it is also His Majesty's pleasure that you do not desist from or break up the same, merely and solely on account of the time limited for your return by the instructions above-mentioned, but that, notwithstanding the same, you do continue with the fleet during such a farther number of days as may afford a competent time for the completion of any operation under the above circumstances, after which you are to take care to return with the fleet under your command and the forces on board in the manner directed in your former instructions. I am etc.

151. *Memorandum by Hawke*

Ramillies
20 September 1757

The Admiral earnestly recommends it to the captain of each ship having marines or soldiers on board to see that their arms are in very great order and all the firelocks good.

That each man have two good flints and thirty-six rounds of ammunition, except the Grenadiers, who are to have a double proportion.

That each soldier and marine have but one shirt and one pair of stockings and one pair of shoes in his knapsack.

To direct the lieutenants commanding the boats for the disembarkation to be very careful to range the boats in divisions and in such manner that every regiment may be all together.

As it is more than probable that the disembarkation will only be opposed by militia which may be easily dispersed, it is earnestly recommended to all the marines and soldiers, when directed to attack, to march up vigorously, preserving their fire till they come very near, so as to do certain execution and, whenever their General orders, that they run in with their bayonets.

As soon as the troops shall be possessed of a post on shore and the chief engineer marked out an entrenchment to secure the provisions, heavy artillery, powder and other necessaries for the army, that then all the tents, blankets, watchcoats, knapsacks, remainder of the entrenching tools, spare ammunition, provisions, scaling ladders and petards, be immediately brought on shore. Also the fascines and gabions from the *Tyloe* tender.

Six days allowance of provisions, consisting only of bread, cheese, beef and pork, to be sent on shore after the troops are landed. And as the duty of the disembarkation will be hard upon the boats' crews, it is recommended that they may be relieved as often as possible.

No marines to be landed that have been in the French service.

ED. HAWKE

Delivered to the captains of
His Majesty's ships...

152.   *Instructions from Hawke to Knowles*

Ramillies at sea
20 September 1757

If in standing between the Isles of Ré and Oléron I shall find the winds and weather will admit of proceeding to Basque Road and attacking the Isle of Aix, I will hoist a red flag on the flagstaff at the fore topgallant mast head and fire three guns. Then you are hereby required and directed without loss of time to stand in as near to the said Isle of Aix as the pilots will carry you with all or as many of the ships of your division as you shall think sufficient for that service, and batter it till such time as the garrison shall either surrender or abandon it. In either case, you are to land a number of men sufficient to demolish it with all possible dispatch, sending me the earliest intelligence of your proceedings. For which this shall be your order. Given etc.

153.   *Instructions from Hawke to Brodrick*

Ramillies in Basque Road
23 September 1757

You are hereby required and directed without loss of time to take to your assistance Captain Douglas, Captain Denis and Captain Buckle, such other officers and pilots, with such cutters and boats as you shall judge proper, and proceed to reconnoitre the French shore

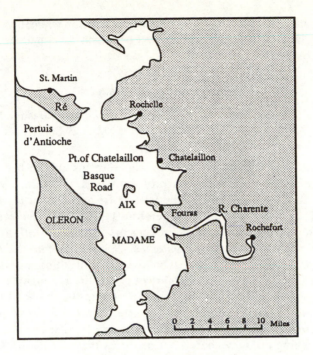

The Coast near Rochefort

from Rochelle to Fort Fouras, sounding all along, in order to discover the most convenient place for landing the King's troops, particularly noticing what fortifications may be upon it; of all which you are to make a report to me as soon as possible in writing, signed by you and the three captains and whom else you may think fit. Given etc.

154. *Instructions from Hawke to Brodrick*

Ramilies in Basque Road
24 September 1757

You are hereby required and directed, without a moment's loss of time, to cause His Majesty's ship *Barfleur* to be lightened two foot, sending such stores, with proper directions for the care of them, on board such ships of your division as you shall think fit. In the evening you are to send boats to lay warps for warping her in, early in the morning, as near as possible to Fort Fouras, which you are to attack with her and the two bomb vessels [*Firedrake* and *Infernal*] with the utmost vigour, in order to make a diversion while the troops shall be landing near the said fort. For which this shall be your order. Given etc.

155.   *Hawke to Clevland*

Ramillies in Basque Road
29 September 1757

Sir,

From the time I wrote you last on the 13th instant we had light breezes, for the most part contrary with fogs and calms, which prevented our getting sight of the Isles of Ré and Oléron till about noon of the 20th. I attempted to get into Basque Road that evening and made the disposition for attacking the Isle of Aix with the red division composed of the *Magnanime, Barfleur, Neptune, Torbay* and *Royal William*, with frigates, bomb vessels, fireships and cutters. Between 4 and 5, and no probability of getting in that night, I made the *Magnanime*'s signal, being the nearest ship, to chase a French ship of war of two decks in the S.E. quarter. She was followed by the *Torbay, Royal William, Escort* [sloop], *Coventry* [28] and a cutter. Night coming on, they chased her as far as they could with safety into Bordeaux River, where it is reported she is aground. As these ships could not join the squadron that night, not to lose sight of my principal object, I supplied their rooms in the red division with the *Dublin, Burford*, and *Achilles* and at 7 in the morning of the 21st made the signal for the vice-admiral to stand in, in order to attack the Isle of Aix. As he approached the entrance between the islands, the weather being a little hazy, his pilot refused to carry his ship in, as did all the rest of the pilots of his division, which obliged him to tack and join me.

About 11 the *Torbay, Magnanime, Royal William* and *Escort* joined company. At 3 p.m. the vice-admiral made sail with his division in a line ahead; but the wind blowing right out with a tide of ebb, we were obliged to come to an anchor at 6.

At 7 in the morning of the 22nd we weighed but, having little wind, came to again at 12. At ¼ after 3, weighed again and, spreading in a line ahead, got into Basque Road at ½ after 9. About an hour before I was joined by the *Viper* sloop with His Majesty's orders signified by Mr Pitt, one of his principal Secretaries of State, to finish any operation [which] might have been begun after the principal object of his instructions.

With the tide of flood at 10 in the morning of the 23rd, the vice-admiral weighed with his division in pursuance of my former order and stood towards the Isle of Aix, it being the general opinion that the troops could not be landed with safety till it had been reduced. The *Magnanime* led.

About 12, the fire began from the fort with shells and great guns and continued while our ships approached till about ten minutes after 1, when the *Magnanime* brought up within less than forty yards of the fort, where she kept an incessant fire for about thirty-five minutes, as did the *Barfleur* which brought up about five minutes after her abreast of the fort.

About ¾ after 1 the firing ceased, the garrison having struck their colours and surrendered. They had in the fort eight mortars of about 14 inches diameter and thirty guns, sixteen of which were 18 and the remainder 14 pounders. The *Magnanime*, though damaged in her rigging, yards, and masts, yet had only two soldiers killed and eleven wounded. Of the garrison, which consisted of near six hundred seamen and soldiers, only one was killed and seven or eight wounded.

On the morning of the 23rd I observed a French man of war over the land to the S.E. of the Isle of Aix. Being desirous of destroying her, I directed Captain Byron of the *America* to take with him the *Achilles* and *Pluto* fireship and, as soon as the red division should begin to batter, go and destroy her. But the French flung their guns overboard, cut their cables and, otherwise lightening her, run up the Charente. It is said she was the *Prudent* of 74 guns, bound for Louisbourg.

Enclosed I send you a plan of what the fort was, and what it soon would have been by the additions they were making.

It having been thought necessary, in order to secure a safe landing for the troops, to sound and reconnoitre the shore of the main as soon as the fort had surrendered, I directed Rear-Admiral Brodrick, with Captains Denis, Douglas and Buckle, to perform that service and make their report to me. 'Twas the afternoon of the 24th before they returned. A copy of that report accompanies this. After maturely considering it, I was of opinion they might land, on which Sir John Mordaunt desired a council of war might be assembled to consider of it. There it was granted by everybody that a landing could be effected. In confidence of their judgement and knowledge of their own profession, we assented to their reasons for not proceeding to attempt taking Rochefort by escalade. A copy of the result of that council of war is here enclosed. He desired a second, which was assembled early on the morning of the 28th. Herewith I send you the result of it. Immediately the disposition was made for the landing under the direction of Rear-Admiral Brodrick and all the captains of the squadron. Part of the troops were actually in the boats when I received a letter from Mr Brodrick, a copy whereof I herewith transmit.

Last night I applied to him to know whether the general officers of the land forces had any farther military operation to propose, that I might not unnecessarily detain the squadron here. This morning I received Sir John's answer, a copy of which is here enclosed. It was the daily expectation of their undertaking something which induced me to stay here so long. As I have now got their final resolution, I shall sail for England tomorrow morning.

Though before I came here this place was represented as very difficult of access, and so narrow that ships could not lie in safety from the forts—nay, the pilots made many baulks before we came in—yet I find it a safe, spacious road in which all the Navy of England, merchant ships included, may ride without the least annoyance; and that a squadron may at any time by laying here prevent any armament from Rochefort and ruin all the French trade to Ré, Oléron, or the continent within these islands.

I have ordered the *Burford, Alcide, America, Dunkirk, Coventry, Postilion, Beaver, Pelican, Cormorant, Escort,* and *Hawke* cutter to Plymouth to wait their Lordships' orders. The rest I shall bring to Spithead with me.

Their Lordships may be assured I have discharged my duty to my King and country with truth, diligence, and integrity, and wish more could have been done for the good of the service.

The pilot of the *Magnanime* has behaved like a man of bravery and skill, and as such I beg leave to recommend him to their Lordships. I am etc.

156. *Hawke to Anson*

Ramillies in Basque Road off Rochelle
30 September 1757

My Lord,

The *Viper* sloop joined me within the entrance of this place just before we came to an anchor, Mr Knowles' division having brought to some little time before. I have kept her all this time, flattering myself with the daily hopes that the land officers would come to a determination to land the troops to try what was possible to be done for their country, notwithstanding they were of opinion it was impracticable to take the town of Rochefort by escalade. If there is faith in man, my Lord, you may believe that I have urged this to them continually, painting the absolute necessity of it in the strongest terms that I could possibly think of. But I am infinitely concerned to tell your Lordship that you will see by their result that all this has availed nothing. I made no hesitation in attempting to remove every obstacle out of the way that was in my power, in which I happily succeeded, and wanted no council of war, nor would have had any if they had not been demanded, to confirm me in opinion that it was right I should use my utmost endeavours for my King and country.

I have wrote the Admiralty as full an account of our proceedings as I can, but it is impossible to give your Lordship a thorough detail of the whole unless I had the honour of seeing you in person, and therefore shall be glad you will please to order me to have leave to go to town when I shall arrive at Spithead.

This is a much finer road than what the chart describes it to be, being much larger and more spacious, and where the whole fleet of England might lie upon occasion with great safety; and now that we are acquainted with it, it is in our power, with a superior force, to prevent the enemy from making up their fleets here, which will lay them under infinite difficulties and subject them to great hazard, [it] being always in our power, now that we know the place, to prevent any squadron fitted at this port to join that of Brest.

I gave directions to Mr Knowles, immediately upon the reduction of the fort of Aix, to demolish it; and as he will have finished tonight, I shall sail tomorrow morning early and hope, if we should have favourable winds, that we shall not be long after the *Viper*.

The *Prudent* threw all her guns overboard and many other stores, and run up the River Charente. We cut the buoy away where they lay and, as the ground is very muddy at that place, probably they may never be able to get them up. I have only to add that I beg your Lordship will believe me to be, with the highest and sincerest truth and regard...

157. *Hawke to Clevland*

Ramillies at St Helens
6 October 1757

Sir,
Early in the morning of the 1st instant, I sailed from Basque Road with the squadron of His Majesty's ships under my command and all

the transports. After writing to you on the 30th ultimo, I received intelligence of a number of French merchantmen hourly expected at Rochefort and Bordeaux under the convoy of three men o'war of the line and some frigates. In order to intercept them I left the *Torbay, America, Achilles, Dunkirk, Coventry, Escort* and *Tartar* to cruise for a fortnight in the tract of these two ports. At the expiration of that time, I directed the *Torbay* to repair to Spithead and the rest to Plymouth. The *Tartar* [(20)] joined me off the Isle of Ré at noon of the 1st instant. Off the Start we met with a hard gale of wind which separated us in such a manner that I cannot exactly tell what number of ships and transports are arrived. I am etc.

P.S. The debates at the council of war of the 25th ultimo were so various, tedious, and uncorrected that it was impossible to take minutes. When I wrote you last, I forgot to send you the minutes of that of the 28th which are here enclosed.

Enclosure:

157a. *'Minutes of a council of war assembled on board His Majesty's ship RAMILLIES in Basque Road this 28th of September 1757'*

PRESENT:
Sir Edward Hawke, Knight of the Bath, etc., President
Sir John Mordaunt, Knight of the Bath, etc.
Rt. Hon. Henry Seymour Conway, Major-General
Hon. Edward Cornwallis, Major-General
Colonel George Howard[1]
Charles Knowles, Esq., Vice-Admiral of the Red
Thomas Brodrick, Esq., Rear-Admiral of the White
Captain George Bridges Rodney

The council, in order to determine whether the forts leading to, and upon the mouth of the River Charente were open and capable of being attacked by land, proceeded to examine:

1. Lieutenant-Colonel Wolfe[2] who declares it is not a strong place, seeming to be principally fortified towards the sea. Yet he saw

---

[1] Howard rose ultimately to field marshal (1793). He commanded the 3rd Buffs at Fontenoy, Falkirk, Culloden and Rochefort. KB 1763.

[2] Wolfe: In 1743, at the age of 16, he acted as adjutant at Dettingen and was promoted to Lieutenant. Brigade-major 1745. Served at Culloden 1746. In 1749, when aged 22, became lt.-colonel (20th Foot). He was quarter-master general at Rochefort; a brigadier at Louisbourg (1758). As a major-general, died in 1759 at the taking of Quebec.

people at work on the land side. That if our troops could come at the barbette battery by it, it might be of great use in taking the fort, provided there was proper ammunition for that purpose. He further gives it as his opinion that Fort Fouras cannot be taken but by artillery or escalade.

2.   Lieutenant-Colonel Clerk[1] who says he could make no kind of judgement of Fort Fouras on the land side by the help of a telescope, the only method he has ever had of observing it.

3.   A French prisoner, who says Fort Fouras is a circular fort. Upon the back of it towards the land there was no ditch when he saw it three years ago. That it had 24 pieces of cannon mounted towards the sea and embrasures for guns towards the land. That Fort la Pointe is, like Fouras, circular, and has 22 pieces of cannon. On the east side, towards the land, it has a wall like that of Fouras. That the landing in the Bay of Chatelaillon is the best landing of any place here; and that, when landed, and you get upon the Rochefort Road, it is a fine open country. That on Friday morning of the 23rd instant, he was in Fort Fouras. That there were but 22 or 24 guns in it, and not above 50 men of all kinds. That there are much about the same number of guns in Fort la Pointe and that both forts are enclosed by a wall in much the same manner on the back towards the land.

The council having maturely considered the evidence, Sir John Mordaunt declared he was of opinion that something further should be attempted and that he would give his orders accordingly that moment, if any—meaning the general officers of the troops—would say it was advisable.

Vice-Admiral Knowles declared he had received great light from the persons examined and therefore thought something should be attempted.

Major-General Conway declared for the attempt merely from his own opinion without regard to the evidence.

Sir Edward Hawke, appealing to every member of the council for the truth of what he said, declared that he was now of the same opinion which he had given both before and at the council of war of the 25th that the landing could be effected, that the troops ought to be landed for some farther attempt, which was alone matter of consideration with the general officers of the troops, he not taking

[1] Clerk: in 1754, when a lt., he examined the fortifications of Rochefort on his own initiative; suggested the expedition of 1757. Appointed lt.-colonel and chief engineer of the expedition. Rose to major-general while serving in Portugal under Count Lippe-Bückeburg 1762. General 1793.

upon him to be a judge of land operations, but would from his confidence in their abilities and skill in their own profession readily assent to any resolution they should come to and assist them to the utmost of his power. This being settled after some debate, Sir Edward Hawke, Vice-Admiral Knowles, Rear-Admiral Brodrick and Captain Rodney withdrew.

The council of war being reassembled and the question put: whether it is advisable to land the troops to attack the forts leading to and upon the mouth of the River Charente.

YES	NO
Colonel George Howard	Hon. General Edward
Capt. George Bridges Rodney	Cornwallis but afterwards
Rear-Admiral Brodrick	acquiesced with the majority.
Rt. Hon. H. Seymour Conway	
Vice-Admiral Knowles	
Sir John Mordaunt	
Sir Edward Hawke	

A copy, J. HAY.

158. *Hawke to Anson*

Ramillies
8 October 1757

My Lord,

This moment I have the honour of your Lordship's favour of yesterday, just as I was setting out for my house in the country, from whence I purposed going to town tomorrow. I now intend to come up directly and shall not trouble your Lordship with anything about the expedition till I can do it in person. I am etc.

159. *Hawke to Clevland*

Ramillies
8 October 1757

Sir,

Yesterday morning I received your letter of the 6th instant and immediately gave direction for the stores, provisions and water of His Majesty's ships which arrived with me to be completed to four months with the utmost dispatch...

160. *Anson to Hawke (holograph)*

Admiralty
19 October 1757

Dear Sir,

Vice-Admiral Boscawen's great uneasiness at not being employed at this time when there is an object in view has determined the sending him out under your command. I know the delay this must occasion, which must be disagreeable to you, but he determines to be down with you at Portsmouth soon enough for you to sail on Friday morning. I could say to you much if I had you here *tête à tête*, but Knowles' imprudence always hurts him and he has enemies enough to seize every occasion that offers. I have always wished him well with all his indiscretion.[1] His busy spirit constantly draws him into difficulties. I think Admiral Boscawen comes to you with a disposition to be agreeable to you and I can only say, for my own part, that no man can wish you more success, nor is more your friend than

Your obliged and affectionate humble servant

ANSON

161. *Hawke to Pitt* (holograph)

Spithead
21 October 1757

Sir,

My being ordered to sea in a hurry and the possibility of an inquiry's being made into the reasons of the miscarriage of the late secret expedition before my return induce me to take the liberty of laying before you this sketch of my conduct in this affair.

The King my master's commands were to me ever sacred and in the execution of them I never pretend to have or use any judgement or will of my own, my whole duty consisting in a literal performance of what directions he or his ministers in his name please to give me. On this principle I sailed with the squadron entrusted to my command, with the transports, from off St Helens on the 8th September, resolutely determined to execute my part in the destined enterprise. Being by His Majesty's instructions of 5th August ordered to return at or about the last of September and contrary winds having detained us so long in England, and even a little while upon our

---

[1] After the Rochefort fiasco, Knowles was second only to Mordaunt as a target of public criticism. He published a pamphlet defending his conduct. (See also p. 159, n. 2 above.)

passage, the Generals Mordaunt and Conway before we reached the place of our destination began to think it too late to undertake anything. The consideration of our detention in England, the warning the enemy had to prepare for our reception, and our almost total ignorance of the coast we were to attack, confirmed them in their opinion that it was most advisable to return to Britain without risking any attempt and in consequence they urged me to assemble a council of war for that purpose. In my opinion a council of war can neither excuse nor exculpate a commanding officer in breaking his master's orders and therefore I refused their request till I was urged on the article to co-operate in all things with the generals of his troops. On this I declared to them that if I did consent to assemble the council, I would steadily adhere to my resolution of not returning till we had seen and tried our object. The *Viper* sloop arriving in the meantime, this matter dropped, to my great satisfaction.

The opinion of rank and service entrusted with so respectable a command always weighed greatly with me. Therefore, as great stress was laid in all our conversations about landing on the probability of the troops being annoyed from the vicinity of the Isle of Aix to the place of disembarkation, in order to remove that objection, on the 20th September I gave Vice-Admiral Knowles orders to stand first into Basque Road with his division and attack that island. On the 23rd at noon that service was happily performed and the objection totally removed. In the same conversations great difficulty seemed to rise about the landing place pointed out being a proper and secure one. To obviate this, on the 15th I had given the same officer directions to reconnoitre the French shore from the Pointe du Che to Fort de la Pointe as soon as he got in. But the instant the fort on Aix surrendered, that no delay might arise from Mr Knowles's engagements there I dispatched Rear-Admiral Brodrick with the Captains Douglas, Denis and Buckle to reconnoitre the coast from Rochelle to Fort Fouras. On the 30th I sent you a copy of their report. From that report it plainly appears the landing could be effected, and I imagined would have been the instant I acquainted Sir John Mordaunt with the result of the reconnoitring. But a council of war was demanded and assembled on the 25th to deliberate on it. Here it was unanimously granted that we could land the troops and were ready to do it. I urged at the same time the necessity of making an attempt; but of the nature of it I could not be a judge, being unacquainted with land operations; that it was entirely the business of the commanding officers of the troops.

Early in the morning of the 25th, we were doubting but the

council of war would come to a resolution to land. I ordered the transports inshore that no time might be lost. Instead of landing, it took a very different and to me unexpected turn. As to the first precarious reason of winds and weather, I could not, as a seaman, when the question was urged, say I could bring them off in a storm and a great surf. As to the intelligence from neutral reports, they neither were produced by me, nor did I ever lay stress upon them, having never been at pains to collect them. That Rochefort could not be taken by escalade I assented to, not to appear singular and from an opinion of their being the proper judges. For though, by the examination of the evidence with regard to the wet ditch and the opinion of the generals thereupon, I was induced to think in the same manner as themselves, and that in such a case it could not be carried by escalade, and therefore impracticable in that method; yet I never did pretend to judge in regard of land operations so as to decide upon the enterprise in general, and whether or not a general might not find several resources to surmount difficulties which were unknown to me. There may be many ways of succeeding against a place of indifferent strength beside that of an escalade, without considering it on the foot of a general attack as against a well fortified town in Flanders, which would require great quantities of artillery and stores, and also more time than an enterprise of this nature could admit. Though I gave myself little trouble at this time in forming my opinion upon a subject out of my own province, yet it has since been remembered by others, and may be recollected, Sir, by you, who was present with Sir John Ligonier, Lord Anson and the Earl of Holderness, at the house of the latter, when Lieutenant-Colonel Clerk gave his opinion of the certain method of taking Rochefort by escalade and at the same time attacking the part which is unfortified, and might perhaps be only barricaded or weakly entrenched in a hurry, the generals, being asked their opinion (by you, Sir) said that in their opinion the escalade was improper, but that they thought the enterprise easy and that, by one method or other, they could take the place. When therefore the resolution was taken on the 25th that it could not be taken by escalade and therefore impracticable in that respect, there could be no reason for the generals not attempting Rochefort by some method or other, as they mentioned to you and which were entirely unknown to me, being in a profession of which I do not pretend to have any knowledge. Though I say I did not at that time recollect this circumstance, yet to convince you, Sir, that it was my opinion some attempt ought still to be made, I appeal to Sir John Mordaunt and General Conway if I

did not use many arguments to induce them to come to a resolution
to land, till I at last prevailed that a council of war might be
assembled on 28th. I easily foresaw what the result of that day's
council would be, and therefore to lose no time proposed in the
morning to send the transports, which then lay above a league from
the shore, close in. I hoped the debarkation would have been made
in the day to prevent mistakes and surprise, while at the same time it
would strike more terror. But, as it was resolved that the landing
should be in the night, I took every precaution in my power to have
it speedily and successfully effected by sending many of the captains
and above thirty lieutenants, giving orders to Lieutenant Price,
agent of the transports, to get them all under way as soon as the
boats should put off with the first detachments and run them close
inshore. As to what succeeded, I beg leave to refer you to the copies
of Rear-Admiral Brodrick's and Sir John Mordaunt's letters. A
proposal having been made on the evening of the 26th or 27th to
land on the island of Oléron, I frankly own I opposed it with all my
might. For I could perceive that nothing could derive from landing
against defenceless peasants and their salt pits, while the enemy must
be on the continent.

Thus, Sir, have I taken the liberty to lay my own conduct in this
unfortunate affair before you, and I submit it to your examination
and, if you think fit, to the world. All through the whole I am certain
of the integrity of my heart and the strong desire I had to serve my
King and country. I beg that you will believe that I am etc.

162. *Hawke to Clevland*

Ramillies at sea
16 November 1757

Sir,

In the morning of the 22nd October I sailed from Spithead with
the *Ramillies, Royal George, Namur, Princess Amelia, Barfleur,
Royal William, Neptune, Dublin, Alcide, Prince of Orange* and three
cutters. About noon the next day I got off Plymouth from whence I
was joined by the *Burford, Rochester, Lizard, Bideford* and *Speedwell*
sloop...

At noon of the 9th I was joined by the King's ships *Medway,
Dolphin, Pallas* and *Shannon*. In their way they had lost company
with the *Unicorn* and *Hussar*. By them I received your letter with the
melancholy news of the plague's having broke out at Lisbon; also an
account of the Brest squadron's being at sea. By the best intelligence

they received on their way to me, which was the first I had procured, seven or eight of them had got into Basque Road, having sailed about the time I did. If the weather had been in the least encouraging, I had a strong inclination to have followed them. But it has been so very stormy since that it is as much as we can do to take care of ourselves by being under a mainsail and mizen. By the best intelligence, which accompanies this, they must have got there by the 26th ultimo. If their destination was for sea, they must by this time be gone. If to be laid up for the winter, e'er now they must be up at Rochefort so that, should the weather in a few days permit, I see no purpose it could serve to look in there.

When I made the signal to weigh at Spithead, Vice-Admiral Knowles's flag was flying. He would not meddle with the business of the port, and Rear-Admiral Brodrick could not till the former's flag should be struck, so that I left orders for the *Pallas* and *Shannon* with Captain Gilchrist[1] and have enclosed a copy of my order to him.

As soon as I shall be joined by the ships from England, I purpose altering my rendezvous from 46.00 to 48.30 N., 100 leagues to the westward of Cape Finisterre, in order to look out for the Louisbourg squadron.

The weather has continued so bad since the 9th as to oblige us to lie under a mainsail without a possibility of a boat's passing, so that I could not send the *Speedwell* away earlier with my letters...

Minute: Received 20th. Read ditto.

163.   *Hawke to Clevland*

Ramillies at Spithead
15 December 1757

Sir,

Since my last by the *Speedwell* sloop, a copy of which I herein transmit to you, till the 8th instant, we had nothing but very hard gales about S.W., which drove and kept us to the northward of my rendezvous. On the morning of the 17th ultimo we missed the *Intrepid, Tartar* and *Dolphin*. Captain Duff in the *Rochester* acquainted me since that he saw the *Tartar* make a signal of distress and the *Dolphin* make sail towards her and stay by her. I have not

---

[1] Gilchrist: L 1741, C 1755. He was an outstanding frigate commander, but was severely wounded in 1759. (Maternal grandfather of Thomas Cochrane, 10th Earl of Dundonald.)

heard of any of the three since, except once of the *Intrepid* whose signal was made by the *Dublin* to bear down to her.

On the 23rd the *Dublin* made a signal of distress, as did the *Alcide* on the 25th, and bore away. Boats could not pass to know the reason, so I made the *Dublin*'s signal to follow her into port, as the latter's tiller had been twice broke. On the 23rd also lost sight of the *Rochester* in chase and, next day, missed the *Bideford* [frigate, Captain Samuel Hood[1]]. On the 1st instant the *Burford* chased out of sight and on the 6th I made the signal for the *Prince of Orange* to go into port, as I knew her company was very sickly.

The weather was so bad and the squadron so much diminished that I thought it most advisable to come into port, leaving the *Medway* and *Southampton* to cruise on my rendezvous. The *Shannon* I have sent into Plymouth. There arrived with me the *Royal George*, *Namur*, *Barfleur*, *Princess Amelia* and *Neptune*. The *Royal William* is astern and the *Pallas* parted company in a fog within Scilly.

I shall be obliged to their Lordships for leave to come to town.

Enclosed is the state and condition of His Majesty's ships under my command. I am etc.

Minute: 16 December. Let Sir Edward know I have communicated his letter to the Lords and that he has their leave to come to town.

---

[1] Samuel Hood: L 1746, CR 1756, C 1756. Cruised with Hawke, Nov.-Dec. 1757, and in April 1758 was with him at the Basque Roads (commanding the *Vestal* frigate). Took French frigate *Bellona* Feb. 1759. Unwell 1760–3 and served in the Mediterranean at his own request. Commodore and c.-in-c. N. America 1767–70. Created baronet 1778. RA 1780; served under Rodney in W. Indies 1780–2 (also under Graves at the Chesapeake 1781). Created baron in Irish peerage 1782. VA 1787. A Ld of Ady 1788–93. C.-in-c. Mediterranean 1793–4; occupied Toulon. Created viscount 1797.

PART IV(d)

MARCH–MAY 1758
THE BASQUE ROADS AND A RASH STEP

INTRODUCTION

On 5 March 1758 the Admiralty ordered Hawke to put to sea with 'the utmost dispatch' [Document 164]. He was to take such ships as were ready and intercept French convoys preparing to sail from the Biscay ports for North America and India.

Pending the arrival of these instructions at Portsmouth, Hawke was, on 7 March, writing to Anson of his fears that the Admiralty would not send him a commission as commander-in-chief of the Western Squadron. He clearly expected Anson to agree that it was a commander-in-chief's share of wartime prize money that had 'ever made the command of the Western Squadron valuable and desired' [165]. However the aforementioned instructions, duly embodying the commission, reached him that day [166]. While prize money—a matter not subject to the Admiralty's direct regulation—loomed large in naval officers' minds throughout the French wars, Hawke's well established sense of public duty will also have been noticed in the documents printed above, for instance in Part IV(c). In that respect he is representative of the growing professionalism of the naval service.

However, his commander-in-chief's commission did not prevent Hawke's subsequent irritation at being sent to sea in such haste at first without any of the frigates which loomed importantly in his instructions. Nor did any fireships or bomb vessels appear when they were needed [174]. Although the Basque Roads incursion of April 1758 marked a sharp reverse for French maritime policy, cordiality and even basic communication between Hawke and the Admiralty seem, by early May, to have ebbed away. Having received from Anson no prior intimations of the kind noticed earlier in this volume, Hawke was suddenly confronted by Howe, armed with orders to conduct a landing on the French coast. Misled by various straws in the wind, he concluded that Howe had been chosen to land where he, Hawke, was deemed to have failed, namely at Rochefort; and, egged on doubtless by his mischievous secretary, John Hay, Hawke proceeded to explode with vexation against their Lordships [177]. His subsequent submission to the Board is duly represented here [178]. The disorderly draft minute taken on 12 May by Cleveland, the Secretary of the Admiralty, effectively conveys the fluster engendered by this remarkable incident.

After serving for a month in the Channel fleet under Anson's command a thoroughly dispirited Hawke went sick ashore in mid-June and did not go to sea again until 1759—the 'year of victories'.

164. *Instructions from the Lords of the Admiralty to Hawke*

5 March 1758

Instructions for Sir Edward Hawke, Admiral of the Blue and commander-in-chief of a squadron employed and to be employed in the Channel, Soundings, or wherever else His Majesty's service shall require.

Whereas we intend that you shall command a squadron of the King's ships named in the annexed list [comprising the *Ramillies* and thirteen other ships of the line, some frigates and a sloop] designed to be employed to the westward, you are hereby required and directed to take the said ships under your command accordingly, their captains being directed to follow your orders.

You are to use the utmost dispatch in proceeding to sea with such of the ships of the line named in the margin [*Ramillies* (90), *Union* (90), *Newark* (80), *Torbay* (74), *Alcide* (64), *Intrepid* (60), and *Medway* (60)], as are at Spithead and Portsmouth [which they all were except the *Medway*], calling off Plymouth for the *Medway* and such of the frigates as shall be there ready to proceed with you, leaving orders with the captains of the rest of the ships and frigates to follow you as soon as possible; and you are to employ them either jointly or separately upon such stations as you shall judge most proper for protecting the trade of His Majesty's subjects coming into and going out of the Channel and for taking or destroying the enemy's ships of war, privateers, or trade going into or out of the Bay of Biscay, or navigating to or from any of the ports of France.

We having received intelligence that several ships are fitting at Brest, Rochefort, and other ports in West France, loaded with provisions and warlike stores, to proceed under convoy for North America, which are expected to sail every day; likewise that ten of the East India Company's ships are about to depart from Lorient under convoy and, having observed that most of the outward bound ships take their departure from Cape Finisterre, you are to make such disposition of your squadron as may be most likely to defeat the views of the enemy, and to annoy and distress them in the most effectual manner you shall be able.

You are to employ frigates to look frequently into Basque Road and off the island of Groix; and if a number of the enemy's ships shall at any time be collected there, you are to make an attempt upon them, if it shall be advisable, and endeavour to take or destroy them.

You are to continue at sea for one month from the time of your sailing and then repair to Plymouth Sound for farther orders, leaving such of the frigates as you shall judge necessary for protection of the trade upon proper stations for that purpose for a fortnight or three weeks longer.

Before you sail, you are to send a rendezvous sealed to our Secretary, and whenever you make any alteration therein to let us know as soon as possible; and you are to be very punctual in giving us frequent and particular accounts of your proceedings and of all the intelligence proper for our knowledge.

You are to complete the complements of the ships you take with you from the 2nd battalions of Lord Effingham's and General Stewart's Regiments, which are quartered in the neighbourhood of Portsmouth, sending to their commanding officers for such numbers as you shall want, both officers and men. But as a practice, greatly to the prejudice of His Majesty's service, has frequently been pursued of ships going to sea with more men than their complements, you are strictly enjoined to take particular care not to suffer any ship which proceeds to sea with you to carry a man more than her complement. Given etc.

ANSON
GEO. HAY
J. FORBES

165.   *Hawke to Anson (holograph—a draft)*

Portsmouth
7 March 1758

My Lord,

Ever since I have been here the weather has been extremely bad,
which has very much retarded the equipment of the ships which are
to be under my command, and where we shall get the men for them I
don't know, without your Lordship shall think it proper to lend
them some from the ships in the Harbour...We have a great number
of men at the hospital, in the hospital ship, and at town quarters, but
I am afraid we shall get but few from them, as the men recover but
slowly. The second battalions of Effingham's and Stewart's were so
very bad, sickly and ill-clothed that they have brought all kinds of
diseases into the ships... We should have their sound, healthy men,
and well sized, who will be of real use in case of coming to action.

I hope your Lordship will excuse my taking the freedom to remind
you of the commission for the command of the Western Squadron
which you was so kind as to say should be sent down to me. Forgive
me, my Lord, if I tell you that I shall not have it unless your
Lordship will be so good as to order it to be done in time for me and
to take the trouble to see that it is right. I am persuaded if your
Lordship will but consider the propriety of it, you will easily discern
that my request is founded on reason and justice, as it could never be
His Majesty's nor the Privy Council's intention that the flag officers
at home should be deprived of the same benefits from serving as
those who serve abroad, and this advantage no officer can have by
commanding a few great ships who are soon discovered and
avoided. It is the extensiveness of his command, and from the ships
who are stationed at a distance from him, that he can have any
hopes to better his fortune by, as he may run about till he is grey
headed with a body of large ships and it will be a very great chance
indeed if he is anything the better for it. It is this, my Lord, that has
ever made the command of the Western Squadron valuable and
desired. Pardon me, my Lord, for telling you my sentiments thus
freely. As a flag officer, I have only myself to plead my cause to your
Lordship. The captains have not only themselves but great numbers
besides, and unless your Lordship will please to consider the case of
flag officers under these circumstances, their rank and service will
avail them but little, as I am convinced it is the intentions of many of
the captains to dispute everything with the commanding officer, as
this will always be the case with a person like myself who has it not in

his power to do them favours. I entreat your Lordship to pardon this freedom and to believe that I am etc.

166. *Hawke to Clevland*

Ramillies at Spithead
7 March 1758

Sir,

Yesterday in the afternoon I received their Lordships' commission and instructions of the 5th instant with which I shall punctually comply.

I have had returns of the four companies of the 2nd battalions of Lord Effingham's and General Stewart's regiments. Of the first are fit for duty (commissioned and non-commissioned officers included) 313; of the second 368; in all, 681, a number scarce sufficient to supply the short of complement, sick and lent, of the *Ramillies, Union, Newark, Torbay, Alcide* and *Intrepid*, which I hope to have ready for sea by Thursday night [the 9th]. The bad weather has greatly retarded our fitting.

I have also received your letters of the same date. I shall transmit to you a copy of my rendezvous before I sail and take care to return by the time limited. I am etc.

167. *Hawke to Clevland*

Ramillies at Spithead
8 March 1758

Sir,

I have received their Lordships' order of the 6th and shall deliver it to Captain Legge as soon as the *Chesterfield* shall arrive...

Minute: 9 March. Own receipt and acquaint him the Lords hope he will make use of this fair wind...

168. *Instructions from Hawke to Captain Pratten of the INTREPID*

Ramillies at Spithead
8 March 1758

You are hereby required and directed to receive on board His Majesty's ship under your command one ensign, two sergeants, two corporals, one drum and forty-five private men of General Stewart's regiment, out of whom you are to complete your complement and enter the remainder in lieu of your sick and lent, bearing them on a separate list for victuals only; and on no account whatever to carry a single man to sea exceeding your complement. For which this shall be your order. Given etc.

By command of the Admiral,   E.H.
J. H[AY]

169. *Hawke to Clevland*

Ramillies at Spithead
9 March 1758

Sir,
    I have received and complied with their Lordships' directions signified in your letters of the 6th and 7th instant...
    The *Intrepid* sails out of harbour to Spithead this day. I am obliged to stay for sails for the *Ramillies* and *Union*, which will not be finished before Saturday morning [the 11th]. Had it not been for the *Invincible*'s sails,[1] we could not have got to sea [for] a considerable time. I am etc.

Minute: 10th March. Own the receipt and let him know the Lords do not doubt his using the utmost expedition in proceeding to sea, as his doing so may be of great consequence.

170. *Line of Battle*

Ramillies at Spithead
11 March 1758

    The *Torbay* to lead with the starboard and the *Newark* with the larboard tacks on board.

Frigates	Rate	Ships	Commanders	Guns	Men	Division
Vestal [32]	3	*Torbay*	Hon. Capt. Keppel	74	700	
Actaeon [28]	4	*Intrepid*	Capt. Pratten	60	420	
Tartar [28]	2	*Union*	Everitt	90	750	
Tamar [sloop] to	2	*Ramillies*	Sir Edward Hawke	90	780	Sir Edwd Hawke, Kt
repeat signals			Kt			of the Bath, Ad. of the
			Capt. Taylor			Blue

[1] The *Invincible* had been wrecked in February. See p. 99, n. 2.

Hussar [28]	3	*Alcide*	Douglas	64	500
Speedwell sloop	4	*Medway*	Proby	60	420
Lizard [28]	3	*Newark*	Holburne[1]	80	670

Given etc.

171. *Hawke to Clevland*

Ramillies at Spithead
12 March 1758, 6 a.m.

Sir,

Yesterday morning I received your letter of the 9th with the inclosed intelligence.

Last night I received and sent on shore to be put in execution by Vice-Admiral Holburne their Lordships' orders and directions of the 10th, as I was unmoored and lying at single anchor.   I am now under way in the *Ramillies* with the *Union, Newark, Torbay, Alcide,* and *Intrepid.* I take with me the *Otter* sloop with the convoy to Plymouth, where I shall leave her. I have left orders and sealed rendezvous for the *Chichester, Essex* and *Dunkirk* to follow me.

Enclosed is a sealed copy of my rendezvous. I am etc.

172. *Instructions from Hawke to Ships at Plymouth*

Ramillies off Plymouth Sound
13 March 1758

You are required and directed to use the utmost dispatch in getting His Majesty's ship under your command fit for sea in every respect. As soon as she shall be ready, you are to make the best of your way down Channel and, when you are got the length of Ushant, open the sealed rendezvous you receive herewith and strictly follow my directions therein for your farther proceedings. For which this shall be your order. Given etc.

Delivered to the *Magnanime, Stirling Castle, Achilles, Medway, Windsor, Vestal, Hussar, Actaeon, Lizard, Coventry, Tartar, Tamar* and *Speedwell.*

[1] William Holburne: L 1739, CR 1747, C 1748.

173. *Instructions from Hawke to Captains Pratten and Proby of the INTREPID and MEDWAY*

Ramillies in Basque Road
5 April 1758

You are hereby required and directed to receive on board His Majesty's ship under your command a pilot from the *Newark* or *Ramillies* and without a moment's loss of time proceed as near the French ships as the pilot will carry you, and batter them to pieces. For which this shall be your order. Given etc.

174. *Hawke to Clevland*

Ramillies in Plymouth Sound
11 April 1758

Sir,

In the afternoon of the 13th ultimo, I made sail from lying to off Plymouth in company with the *Union, Newark, Torbay, Alcide* and *Intrepid*.

As I had no frigates, on the 19th I detached the *Alcide* to go between Belle Isle, Groix and the main, and in case of not seeing or getting any intelligence of the enemy there to proceed and look into Basque Road, and then to join me on the rendezvous, of which I sent you a copy. As we soon after chased a long way to the westward so as to leave little probability of meeting with her, I determined to go directly for Basque Road, having received intelligence from several neutral vessels and British privateers that a convoy was making up there. On the 25th the *Coventry* [(28)] joined company. Her I detached to look into that road before me, make the best observations possible of the enemy and then to join me in the offing. But by flattering winds she was prevented from performing that service and she did not fall in with us again till the 6th when we were standing out from Pertuis d'Antioche.

In my way to Basque Road, on the 1st instant, I was joined by the *Chichester* [(70)], *Medway* [(60)], *Vestal, Hussar,* and *Actaeon*. The squadron was now composed of seven sail of the line and three frigates. About 9 at night of the 3rd, we made the light of Baleines on the Isle of Ré distant four or five leagues, the weather fair, and a moderate breeze at N.N.W. At 11 tacked and stood off till ½ past 2 in the morning of the 4th when we tacked again with the wind at N.E., brought to, hoisted our boats out, finished clearing our ship and prepared for action. At 3 made sail towards Basque Road. At daybreak we discovered a numerous convoy a few leagues to wind-ward of us and gave chase. But, the wind baffling us, it, with the three frigates that escorted it, got into St Martin's, except one brig which was run on shore and set on fire by the *Hussar*.

At noon [we] wore, bore away for Basque Road in a line ahead at two cables length asunder, with a moderate gale at N.N.W. As we learned afterwards they consisted of the *Florissante* 74, *Sphinx* 64, *Hardi* 64, *Dragon* 64, *Warwick* 60, and six or seven frigates, with about forty merchant ships. At ½ past 4, made the signal for a general chase to the S.E. but took care to preserve the line by verbal orders to the ships astern of me. At 5, the enemy began to cut or slip and soon to run in great confusion. At 6, their commodore, who remained last, made off when we were within about gunshot and a half. Many of those that fled first were by this time aground on the mud. As I knew for certain there was not sufficient depth of water for us to follow them, at ½ past 6 after sunset I came to an anchor with our best bower in 8 fathom water abreast of Aix, and kept under arms all night with guard boats rowing about.

At 5 next morning, saw them all aground, almost dry, about five or six miles distant from us. They had a whole tide of flood which would have carried them up under shelter of the guns of Fouras, if it had been possible for any ships of burthen either to get up or down from thence, except when they are light and on top of a spring tide. Many of the merchant and several of the ships of war were on their broadsides, and then I could not help regretting the want of fireships and bomb vessels.

As soon as the flood made, I put the best pilots on board the *Intrepid* and *Medway* and made the signal for weighing. They got about a gun shot farther in, come to an anchor and, sounding a little ahead of them at high water found but five fathom, of which the tide rises eighteen foot.

By this time all the boats from Rochefort and the adjacent places were employed in carrying out warps to drag them through the soft mud, as soon as they should be waterborn. In the meantime they threw overboard their guns, stores, ballast, and were even heaving water out at their ports, all of which we could plainly discern. By that means some of them got that day as far up as the mouth of the Charente; but the *Florissante* was not got above Fouras on the Thursday afternoon [the 6th], and the greatest part of their merchant ships left aground in towards the Isle Madame when we fell down to Basque Road. The frigates' boats cut away about eighty buoys laid on their anchors and what they had thrown overboard.

Had there been a channel for line of battle ships from Aix to Fouras, with a whole tide of flood in their favour it is more than probable they would have made use of it to have saved their guns and stores under the canon of that fort. Beside it was observed from where we lay, and at the same time from a better point of view [at] the east end of the Island of Aix, that in going up the Charente none of the enemy's ships were within random shot of Fouras. Nay, on the top of high water and a neap tide, the shore was dry near a quarter of a mile from that fort.

On the 5th in the morning, I sent Captain Ewer of the marines ashore to Aix with a flag of truce to assure the villagers they should not be annoyed in the least and to see if the enemy had been at work on the fort of Aix since our being there. He reported that they had raised on the ramparts of the old fortification on the land side, which they had widened for that purpose, a very strong, well made parapet of earth, twigs and sod, canon proof, parallel to and at about the distance of ten yards from the flanks and faces of the old works. The embrasures opened entirely towards the sea, with platforms of 2½ inch oak plank strongly spiked down to the joists of the same wood. To the outward joists of each platform were framed two pieces of timber, well kneed and let into the breastwork on each side of the embrasure, with ringbolts for working the guns as on board ships. It may be conjectured from this new disposition of their works that they intended to make only a glacis of the whole space between the new parapet and the sea and, by thus removing their guns about 120 yards further than before from the water's edge, prevent any annoyance from small arms of ships. I therefore sent him on shore again with twenty marines from each of the line of battle ships to destroy these new works, which he by night effectually did, both what was finished and unfinished, besides a great quantity of large oak beams, 2½ inch plank, pickets, fascines, gun carriages, mortar beds, working tools, bridges, and the only well in the fort. Where the old tower gate stood, there were no new works raised; but I am of opinion when the whole had been finished, they might have mounted twenty-four guns towards the sea. The number of embrasures finished were ten, and thirteen platforms.

When we got out of the road [on] the 7th I learned from a neutral ship which left St Martin that morning that the large convoy we left in there on the 4th was loaded with provisions and stores for America and the French islands, with fifteen more ready at Bordeaux to have been escorted by the ships of war which lay at the Isle of Aix. And as they may not have other King's ships ready, and the present circumstances of their settlements may oblige them to sail without convoy, I have left out the *Torbay, Medway, Coventry, Vestal, Hussar* and *Actaeon* to cruise upon them, which I hope their Lordships will approve of. I have brought into this port with me the *Ramillies, Union, Newark, Chichester* and *Intrepid*.

I have sent this express by Mr Johnston, my first lieutenant. I am etc.

P.S.   I had prepared the above against my arrival in Plymouth Sound, but to the westward of the Lizard fell in with the *Pluto* fireship. On Friday night the 7th instant, in company with the *Essex* and *Proserpine*, she fell in with twelve sail of merchant ships, escorted by a frigate of 22 guns, from Bordeaux bound to Quebec in latitude 46.00 N. They took the frigate, a letter of marque of 20 guns, and one other merchant ship. The *Pluto* unfortunately lost her captain whose place I have taken the liberty to supply with my first lieutenant Mr Johnston,[1] and farther recommend him to their Lordships' favour as he brings this express from Portsmouth, whither I have ordered the fireship as the wind is westerly.

175.   *Hawke to Clevland*

Neptune at Spithead
26 April 1758

Sir,
    ...Enclosed is a copy of the order I gave to Captain Keppel. I am etc.

Enclosure:

175a.   *Instructions from Hawke to Keppel*

Ramillies at sea
8 April 1758

Whereas I have received intelligence that there is at St Martin and Bordeaux a great number of ships and vessels of the enemy, ready to proceed to Louisbourg and their islands with stores and provisions; you are hereby required and directed to take under your command the King's ships named on the margin [*Medway, Coventry, Vestal,*

---

[1] Johnston (L 1744) was confirmed as commander of the *Pluto* from 19.4.58. Apparently never posted.

Actaeon, Hussar], their captains having my directions to follow your orders, and use your utmost endeavours to keep the said ships of the enemy in, or intercept them, should they venture out of those ports.

On this service you are to continue a month or five weeks and then make the best of your way to Plymouth Sound, acquainting the Secretary of the Admiralty with your arrival and proceedings. For which this shall be your order. Given etc.

E.H.

To the Hon. Capt. Keppel of
His Majesty's ship *Torbay*
By command of the Admiral
J.H.

176.   *Hawke to Clevland*

Neptune at Spithead
30 April 1758

Sir,
I have received their Lordships' orders of the 28th with which I shall take care punctually to comply...

Having some private affairs to settle, I shall be very obliged to their Lordships for three or four days leave, if they think I can be spared...

Minute: 1 May... The Lords would be very glad to indulge him on every occasion, but at this time they wish him to be on the spot, as not only the ships at Spithead but those cruising are under his command...

177.   *Hawke to Clevland*

Portsmouth
10 May 1758, 7 o'clock p.m.

Sir,
About four o'clock arrived here Captain Howe and delivered me their Lordships' order of the 9th.

In last September I was sent out to command an expedition under all the disadvantages one could possibly labour under, arising chiefly from my being left under the influence of land officers in council of war at sea. Last cruise, I went out on a particular service almost without the least means of performing it. Now every means to ensure success is provided, another is to reap the credit, while it is probable I, with the capital ships, might be ordered to cruise in such manner as to prevent his failing in this attempt. To fit out his ships for this service I have been kept here and even now have their Lordships' directions, at least in terms, to obey him. He is to judge of what he wants for his expedition. He is to make his demands and I am to comply with them! I have therefore directed my flag immediately to be struck and left their Lordships' orders with Vice-Admiral Holburne. For no consequence that can attend my striking it without orders shall ever outbalance with me wearing it one moment with discredit. I am etc.

178(1).   *Clevland's Draft Minute on Hawke's Submission to the Board (unmodernized)*

12 May 1758

Sir Edwd. Hawke being called in was ~~asked~~ acquainted That the Lords having recd his letter of the 10, sent for him to ~~give an opportunity of explaining~~ ~~know if he had anything to offer upon~~ ~~to know what he could have to say on so extr~~ which being of so extraordinary a nature sent for him to know what he had to say for taking such step.

His reason for it was he apprehended Mr How [*sic*] was going upon a service where he had the honor to command upon two expeditions which he thought a slur upon his reputation and that he thought he might have been represented to the King as an unfit person for such command, which affecting his credit he hastily determined to strike his flag, but being since informed that he was mistaken and that his Character and Honour was not so much touched as he apprehended, that the suspicion he had of Mr Howe's going to Basque road arose from the Lords asking him some days since for a draft of that road.

Did not strike his flag out of any resentment to any particular persons but merely because he thought his honor was affected.

178(2).   *Formal Admiralty Minute on Hawke's Submission to the Board*

12 May 1758

Sir Edward Hawke attending was called in and told that the Board looked upon his proceeding in striking his flag (of which he had informed them by his letter received yesterday) to be a very extraordinary step and desired to hear what he had to say in excuse of it.

Sir Edward said he thought Captain Howe to be intended to proceed with the troops and conduct an expedition to the place where he had lately been; and that it appeared so to him from a draft being desired, two days before, of the parts about Rochefort; that if it was so, he thought he must have been misrepresented to the King and therefore that his honour required his doing as he had done; but he since, upon reflection, finds himself mistaken and that he proceeded too much in a hurry, and acknowledges he has done an irregular thing; but that he did not do it with any view of disregard or disrespect to the Board but merely from thinking it would appear a slur upon him to the world, and that they would say that he, a flag officer, though he had been twice to those parts, was not thought fit to be entrusted with 16,000 of the King's troops or to carry on a service of consequence, and he thought he had better not serve at all if he could not serve with honour.

The above minute being read to Sir Edward, he acknowledged the same to be the purport of what he had said and then withdrew.

The Lords then proceeded to take the said letter and minute into consideration and came to the following resolution:

That Sir Edward Hawke's striking of his flag without order is a high breach of discipline. Therefore notwithstanding the acknowledgement contained in the said minute, the Lords do not think proper to restore him to the command of the ships in the Channel, although in consideration of that acknowledgement and of his past services they have not proceeded to any further censure.

Whereupon, as the most proper measure upon this occasion, the Lords have ordered Lord Anson [to] take upon himself that command.

PART IV(e)

MAY 1759–FEBRUARY 1760
THE BLOCKADE OF BREST AND BATTLE OF QUIBERON BAY

INTRODUCTION

Despite his clash with the Admiralty in 1758, the spring of 1759 saw Hawke restored *de facto* to the chief seagoing command. He was to cruise with a strong squadron off Brest where the French seemed to be preparing an expedition to invade some part of the British Isles. His instructions of 18 May show that, after a fortnight on his station, he was to return to Torbay, unless a definite invasion threat had emerged [Document 186]. The Admiralty may therefore not have planned a continuous close blockade of Brest, but the possibility of it was left open. By 27 May, Hawke was proposing to adopt this strategy [193].

The main impediments to such a policy were westerly winds which could be expected, from time to time, to drive the blockading ships towards the rocky coast of Brittany and the problem of health which would grow once the ships had been out for a few months. Scurvy, typhus, and other ills could be expected to afflict the ships' companies. The attrition suffered by the ships, also, was sure to be considerable. The way in which the squadron and its supporting services triumphed over these difficulties and the great extent to which the French fleet was kept bottled up to the detriment of its morale and seamanship can be followed through the succession of documents in this Part. If read as a narrative, they convey the gradually mounting tension, reaching its height in a climax scarcely parallelled in the days of sail.

There was nothing inevitable about the awe-inspiring *dénouement* of the campaign on a tempestuous and darkening 20 November. As may be seen by his dispatch of the 24th [327], Hawke could not be sure, on sighting the enemy fleet, that it would not opt to fight in a line of battle outside Quiberon Bay. Once Conflans had run for the bay, Hawke made his crucial decision to risk all on a close pursuit, using the French commanders as pilots among rocks and shoals with which the British were wholly unfamiliar.

Among the various questions to which the documents supply an answer is one concerning the control of naval strategy at that time. How was this shared between the Admiralty and the commander-in-chief? Hawke's campaign was crucial to British national strategy in 1759 and, as can be seen from the cases where dates are given both for writing and receiving the dispatches, the possibility existed through much of the year of fairly continuous control being exercised by the Board of Admiralty. This control was, of course, demonstrated at the outset [186]. However, once the campaign was under way Hawke communicated the way in which he proposed to conduct it [193, etc.]. In nearly every case his proposals were accepted; but the interesting exchange about the force posted, initially at the Board's suggestion, off Rochefort in September shows how the Admiralty, with its unrivalled supply of information from overseas, maintained control over the broad distribution of Hawke's ships in the light of developments [275, 289, 295, 296, 298, 302, 311, 314, 321].

The conclusive victory won at Quiberon Bay called, within the limits imposed by the onset of winter, for the establishment of a yet-tighter system of blockade [328, 330, 334]. But such was the severance of communications by wintry weather that it was not till the night of 7 January that Hawke received acknowledgement of his victory and permission to return home [338].

Finally, two items subsidiary to the main themes may be mentioned here: (*a*) the court martial of Alexander Hood (later Admiral Lord Bridport) [271–4, 276, 278, 280] and (*b*) the consultation held in September by the captains in a detached squadron as to whether an attack on French ships in the River Vannes was feasible [282d]. This touches on perennial aspects of amphibious operations.

179.   *Instructions from the Lords of the Admiralty to Hawke*

9 May 1759

By the Lords Commissioners...to the Honourable Sir Edward Hawke, Knight of the Bath, Admiral of the Blue, etc.

Whereas we have ordered the commanders of His Majesty's ships and vessels named in the annexed list [of fourteen, including frigates, at Portsmouth and eleven at Plymouth], to put themselves under your orders, you are hereby required and directed to take them under your command accordingly and employ them as shall be hereafter directed; and you are to repair without loss of time to Portsmouth and hoist your flag on board such of them as may be there as you shall choose.

And having ordered Vice-Admiral Sir Charles Hardy,[1] who is now at Plymouth, to put himself under your command, you are to take him also under your command accordingly. Given etc.

By [command] etc.   ANSON
J. C[LEVLAND]   GEORGE HAY
                                                        J. FORBES

180. *Instructions from the Lords of the Admiralty to Hawke*

9 May 1759

In addition to our order of this date, you are hereby required and directed to lose no time in proceeding to Torbay with such of the ships thereby put under your command as you shall find at Spithead ready for service and remain there until further order, directing such ships as shall not be ready to accompany you to follow you as soon as possible to Torbay, where we have directed Sir Charles Hardy to join you with the ships from Plymouth. Given etc.

181. *Instructions from the Lords of the Admiralty to the Victualling Board*

11 May 1759

Whereas a considerable number of His Majesty's ships are ordered to rendezvous immediately in Torbay, you are hereby required and directed forthwith to make provision for their being supplied *there* with fresh meat, in like manner as at *Spithead*.

And whereas we think fit that the said ships should have a small proportion of wine instead of beer, you are to cause a proportion thereof for ten thousand men for a month to be sent from Guernsey to Torbay to be distributed amongst them.

And as it will be necessary to keep the proportion of beer as complete as may be, you are to provide both at Portsmouth and Plymouth about three hundred tons of shipping to be ready to carry

---

[1] Hardy: L 1737, C 1741. Governor of New York 1755–7; knighted 1756; RA 1756. VA 1759; Hawke's second-in-command off Brest and at Quiberon Bay. Adm. 1770. Commanded the Channel Fleet 1779.

beer or other provisions to such places as may be ordered. Given etc.

182. *Hawke to Clevland*

Ramillies at Spithead
13 May 1759

Sir,

Last night I arrived here and this morning hoisted my flag on board His Majesty ship the *Ramillies*. Enclosed is the state and condition of the ships at Spithead and in this harbour. Those under my command I shall get ready for sea with the utmost dispatch. As the *Kingston* is at the back of the Island and will be in today, I hope I shall have no occasion for the *Bideford*'s men, unless the *Jason* should not return. What men are here I shall distribute today, and tomorrow transmit their Lordships another state of the squadron.

There are two lieutenants wanting on board the *Ramillies*, whose room I hope their Lordships will be kind enough to supply with Lieutenant Lee[1] of the *Royal Ann*, to be fifth, and Lieutenant Archibald Darroch, who is in town, to be sixth, and move Lieutenant Chaloner Ogle[2] to be fourth. I am etc.

Minute: 14 May. To be appointed. Own receipt and let him know it. Send immediately to Lt. Darroch.

183. *Hawke to Clevland*

Ramillies at Spithead
14 May 1759

Sir,

Yesterday in the afternoon arrived His Majesty's ships *Kingston* and *Dunkirk*, the first with two hundred and the latter with one hundred supernumeraries. From the *Kingston* I completed the *Royal George, Union, Resolution, Fame* and *Ramillies*, adding to the latter the men belonging to other ships on board the *Royal Ann*. The hundred and one from the *Dunkirk* I put on board the *Bienfaisant*, which completes her within twenty-seven men. If the *Jason* arrives I propose completing the *Temple* from her. If the *Nottingham* arrives, she must have her fifty men lent to the *Fame* and their place be

---

[1] Lee: L 1755, CR 1760, C 1763. He was one of the commanders who transferred to the Portuguese service in 1762 and were posted on their return. He died in 1770.
[2] A cousin of the late Adm. of the Fleet Sir Chaloner Ogle: L 1748, CR 1759, C 1762 and served at Havana.

supplied also from the *Jason*.

These ships arrived too late to distribute the men last night. It was done this morning by six o'clock. I shall be ready to sail on Thursday morning [the 17th] with the *Royal George, Ramillies, Union, Torbay, Magnanime, Chichester, Resolution, Fame, Kingston, Pallas, South-ampton, Melampe[1]* and *Dunkirk*.

Enclosed is the state and condition of His Majesty's ships under my command at Spithead and in Portsmouth Harbour. I am etc.

Minute: 15 May. Let him know I have communicated his letter to the Lords who approve of his proceedings.

184. *Hawke to Clevland*

Ramillies at Spithead
17 May 1759, 2 p.m.

Sir,

I received your letter of the 15th but not the orders mentioned therein. But from the hint in it I have taken upon me to order the *Temple* and *Bienfaisant*, which were in all respects ready, to accompany me to Torbay. I am now under way with the *Royal George, Ramillies, Union, Magnanime, Torbay, Resolution, Fame, Chichester, Kingston, Temple, Bienfaisant, Dunkirk, Pallas* and *Southampton*, and have left orders for the *Rochester, Melampe* and *Minerva* to follow me the instant they shall be ready. The latter will sail tonight or tomorrow morning. I have also left orders for the *Nottingham*. Enclosed is the state and condition of His Majesty's ships under my command. I am etc.

Minute: 18 May. Let him know I have communicated his letter to the Lords who very much approve of what he has done. And acquaint him that the Lords desire he will send a copy of his signals for knowing the ships under his command.

185. *Hawke to Clevland*

Ramillies in Torbay
18 May 1759

---

[1] The French frigate *Mélampe* had been taken in a brilliant action of Nov. 1757 by John Lockhart, later Vice-Adm. Sir John Lockhart Ross. (See p. 126, n. 2.) Armed with 36 guns, she was deemed one of the best frigates in the British service. During the campaign of 1759, she was commanded by William Hotham, the future Admiral. (See p. 282, n. 2 below.)

Sir,

At 8 p.m. this evening I anchored here with His Majesty's ships which sailed with me from Spithead yesterday. I found riding here Sir Charles Hardy in the *Hero* with the *Devonshire, Monmouth, Essex, Revenge* and *Montagu.* I have sent an express with orders for the *Colchester* and *Sapphire* to join me here without loss of time. I am etc.

Minute: Read.

186. *Secret Instructions from the Lords of the Admiralty to Hawke*

18 May 1759

Whereas we have received undoubted intelligence that the French are pressing their armament at Brest, L'Orient, Rochefort, and the other ports on the coast of France; that on the 7th instant there were nine sail of ships of war in the inner road of Brest, five of them of the line; that others were ready to proceed out of the harbour and that four of the line were expected there from L'Orient; that provisions and stores are collecting to Brest from several parts of the Bay; and it's given out that the enemy propose to attempt an invasion either upon Great Britain or Ireland; and whereas it is of the greatest consequence to prevent any such design of the enemy taking effect, you are hereby required and directed, so soon as you shall be joined by Sir Charles Hardy with the ships from Plymouth, to proceed with the squadron under your command off Ushant and cause as accurate an observation as possible to be immediately made of the enemy's force in Brest Road and forthwith send us an account thereof; and you are to continue cruising with the squadron near Ushant and Brest (taking all possible care not to be drove to the westward) and to defeat any designs the enemy may have conceived of invading these kingdoms, and to protect the trade of His Majesty's subjects, and also to annoy and distress the enemy by every means in your power; and you are to return with the squadron to Torbay, so as to be there by the expiration of fourteen days from the time of your sailing from thence, unless the attempts or operations of the enemy against this kingdom should make it necessary for the defence and security thereof to prolong your cruise or take any other station near the coast of Great Britain, in which case you are to send us an immediate account thereof; and upon your return to Torbay, you are to cause the provisions and water of the ships to be forthwith completed and to hold them in constant readiness for putting again to sea, taking care that none of the ships have ever less than two months provisions on board.

And whereas the intercepting the convoys which convey provisions and stores to Brest and Rochefort must tend greatly to disconcert the enemy's measures, you are to appoint such of the smaller ships of the line and frigates as you shall think sufficient to cruise on the most likely stations for intercepting the said convoys, ordering their commanders, in case they shall observe any number of ships of war and transports to sail from the French ports and they shall be too weak to attack them, to send one of the frigates immediately to give notice of it, either off Ushant or in Torbay, and another frigate to follow and observe their course till her commander shall be able to form a judgement whether they shall be bound to Ireland or not, and then to return and acquaint you therewith that you may detach such force after them as you shall judge necessary, in case it shall appear to you from their course that they are intended for Ireland; and you are immediately to forward to us by express an account of any information you receive relating thereto and of what you do thereupon. Given etc.

ANSON
GEORGE HAY
J. FORBES
H. STANLEY[1]

Sent to Torbay by Hutchenson,
the messenger, the same evening
at 20 minutes past 8 p.m.

187. '*A List of the French Navy at Brest, Rochefort, and Port Louis to rendezvous at Brest and to be commanded by Messieurs Conflans[2], Du Bois de la Motte, and Bauffremont.*'

[c. 18 May 1759]

At what port	Ships	No. of guns	In what condition

In Brest harbour:

---

[1] Stanley, a politician and diplomat, was a Ld of the Ady 1757–65. Gifted, and much admired in Parisian society; but he never laughed.

[2] Hubert de Brienne, Comte de Conflans, had joined the French navy in 1706 and had become *vice-amiral ès mers du Levant* in 1756 (a very high grade of admiral). In 1758 he was made a marshal of France.

	Royal Louis	116	Built as high as the middle deck
	Duc de Bourbon	84	Wants a thorough repair.
	Palmier	70	Wants to be repaired
Ad. Bauffremont [chef d'escadre]	Le Tonnant	80	
La Motte [lieutenant général]	Le Formidable	80	
Conflans [maréchal]	Soleil [Royal]	80	Carpenters' work completed and
Prince de Montbazon	Bizarre	64	rigging with all expedition the 3rd
	Thésée	64	May 1759
	Héros	74	
	Superbe	74	
	Magnifique	74	
	Juste	70	
	Intrépide	74	
In Brest road:			
	Eveillé	64	
	Northumberland	64	
	Sphinx	64	Fitted for sea. The last four ships
	Dauphin Royal	70	came from Rochefort the 24th
	Dragon	64	April last
	Glorieux	74	
	Inflexible	64	
In Port Louis (16th May 1759):			
Ad. Guébriant [chef d'escadre]	L'Orient	80	Fitted for sea
	Robuste	74	
	Solitaire	64	Fitting for sea
	Brillant	74	
At Rochefort:			
	Hardi	64	Repairing
	St Michel	64	

---

188.   *Hawke to Anson (holograph—a draft)*

[19 or 20 May 1759]

My Lord,

I am greatly obliged to your Lordship for the honour of your letter of the 18th which I received a little before one this morning by the messenger. The *Hercules, Nottingham*, and *Anson* have not joined me; but as the wind continues easterly, I make no doubt they will be with me tomorrow or by Tuesday [the 22nd] at farthest.

When I am joined by the above ships, we shall certainly be a very strong squadron, not ill manned as times are, and full sufficient, I hope, to frustrate any designs the enemy may have on this country. I have given out your Lordship's signals which, as I did not know how soon you might come to the fleet, I thought would be best, as most of the captains were already acquainted with them. In regard to my rendezvous, I shall be careful to keep between the extent of it and the land, and so near in at all times, when the weather will permit, that I flatter myself nothing of any consequence will be able to escape us.

I entreat your Lordship to believe that I shall use my utmost endeavours to execute my orders in the strictest, faithfullest manner possible. I am etc.

189. *Hawke to Clevland*

Ramillies in Torbay
20 May 1759, a.m.
'Recd. 21 May'

Sir,

By the *Minerva* which left Portsmouth the day after me, I received their Lordships' orders of the 15th and 16th, likewise your letter of the latter date. In consequence I dispatched orders to Plymouth for the *Achilles, Coventry, Venus, Thames* and *Actaeon*. At ½ before 1 this morning I received their Lordships' order of the 18th for taking under my command His Majesty's ships *Mars, Anson* and *Firm*, with their directions signified in your letter of the same date relating to the *Belliqueux, Achilles, Colchester, Rochester, Isis* and *Chatham*, and have sent by express the necessary orders to Plymouth.

At the same time I received their instructions for my sailing with which I shall strictly comply. I am now unmooring and shall lodge orders, with some proper person here, for such ships as may arrive after my departure which will be about noon.

Enclosed is the state and condition of His Majesty's ships and frigates under my command now with me, also a copy of my rendezvous and the signal for knowing each other. I am etc.

Minute: 21 May. Own receipt and let him know the Lords are pleased with the expedition he has made.

190.   *Hawke to Clevland*

Ramillies in Torbay
20 May 1759, 3 p.m.
'Recd. 25'

Sir,

At 1 p.m. His Majesty's ship *Gosport* sailed from hence with the convoy for Newfoundland.

We are now getting under way. As it blowed fresh at E.S.E. with a swell, several of the ships in unmooring parted their cables and leave them and an anchor behind, for recovery of which in our absence I have given directions.

Thinking it necessary for the better carrying on the King's service that the ships of the line should be put in three divisions, I have ordered Captain Geary to hoist a distinguishing pendant and command one, which I hope their Lordships will approve of. I am etc.

Minute: Own receipt. Approved, His Majesty having been pleased to appoint him Rear-Admiral of the White.

191.   *Line of Battle*

Ramillies in Torbay
20 May 1759

The *Mars* to lead with the starboard and the *Hero* with the larboard tacks on board.

Frigates	Rates	Ships	Commanders	Guns	Men	Division
Colchester [50]	3	*Mars*	Capt. Young	74	600	
	4	*Kingston*	Parry	60	400	
Thames [32]	3	*Revenge*	Storr	70	520	
	3	*Temple*	Shirley[1]	70	520	
Sapphire [32]	2	*Union*	Sir Chas. Hardy Kt	90	770	Sir Charles Hardy,
			Capt. Evans[2]			Vice-Ad. of the Blue,
						etc.

[1] Washington Shirley succeeded as the 5th Earl Ferrers when his brother was hanged for murder in 1760 (hanging by the drop being, it is thought, introduced on that occasion). Shirley (L 1742, C 1746) was elected an F.R.S. in 1761 for contributions to astronomy and mathematics. RA 1775, VA 1776. He died in 1778.
[2] Evans: L 1740, CR 1746, C 1748, RA 1779, VA 1780, A 1793.

	3	*Hercules*	Porter[1]	74	600	
Pallas [36]	4	*Dunkirk*	Digby	60	420	
	3	*Monmouth*	Hon. Capt. Hervey	64	480	
Pluto [fireship]	3	*Dorsetshire*	Capt. Denis	70	520	
Venus [36]	4	*Montagu*	Lendrick	60	420	
	3	*Belliqueux*	Saumarez	64	500	
Minerva [32]	3	*Torbay*	Hon. Capt. Keppel	74	700	
Southampton [36] to repeat signals	2	*Ramillies*	Sir Edwd. Hawke K.B. Capt. Taylor	90	780	Sir Edward Hawke, Kt of the Bath, Ad. of the Blue, etc.
	3	*Magnanime*	Rt. Hon. Lord Viscount Howe	74	700	
Isis [50]	4	*Achilles*	Hon. Capt. Barrington	60	420	
	3	*Fame*	Hon. Capt. Byron	74	600	
Melampe [36]	3	*Essex*	Capt. [John] Campbell	64	480	
Chatham [50]	4	*Nottingham*	Marshall[2]	60	400	
Proserpine [fireship]	4	*Firm*	Fergussone[3]	60	420	
	1	*Royal George*	Dorrill[4]	100	880	
Actaeon [28]	3	*Resolution*	Fras. Geary Esq.	74	600	Francis Geary Esq.
	3	*Chichester*	Capt. Willett[5]	70	520	Commordore
Coventry [28]	4	*Anson*	Whitwell[6]	60	420	
	3	*Bienfaisant*	Balfour[7]	64	500	
Rochester [50]	3	*Hero*	Hon. Capt. Edgcumbe	74	600	

Given etc.

[1] Porter: L 1739, CR 1744, C 1746. He was severely wounded on 10.10.59 (see Document 310b); and he died in 1763.

[2] Marshall: L 1732, CR 1743, C 1747. Commanded the *Nottingham* from 1754 to Aug. 1759. Returned to her later and served in the West Indies 1761–2.

[3] Fergussone: L 1739, C 1746. However, it was not Fergussone but John Reynolds who sailed as captain of the *Firm*. See p. 228, n. 1.

[4] Dorrill: L 1739, CR 1747, C 1755. He gave up command of the *Royal George* in June on account of ill health and was succeeded by John Campbell. (See Document 201.) He died in 1762.

[5] Willett: L 1741. In 1767 he was commodore at Chatham.

[6] Whitwell: L 1741, CR 1747, C 1748. Superannuated RA 1779.

[7] Balfour: L 1745, CR 1756, C 1758. On 25.6.58, he boarded and took the *Bienfaisant* in Louisbourg Harbour. Superannuated RA 1787.

192.   *Captain Lockhart to Hawke*

Chatham, Ushant Sound
21 May 1759

Sir,

This morning having met the *Coventry* and her captain [Francis Burslem] informing me that he is under orders to join you off Brest, I thought it proper to send you a copy of the observations and intelligence I have received during my cruise. Last night I sent the *Thames* in with the same account to be sent by express to the Secretary of the Admiralty...and hope soon to have the honour to be under your command, and, heartily wishing you success, I am etc.

193.   *Hawke to Clevland*

Ramillies off Ushant
27 May 1759
'Recd. 31 at night'

Sir,

On the 20th I got under way in Torbay with great part of the squadron. Only a few got out, the rest being obliged to come to again, there being but little wind and a great swell. At 5 next morning I made the signal to weigh and got out with all except the *Hero, Temple, Kingston, Bienfaisant* and *Southampton*, who followed in the evening. That morning I was joined by His Majesty's ships *Hercules* and *Nottingham* from the eastward and *Sapphire* frigate from Plymouth.

On the 22nd I detached the *Pallas* with orders to see the *Prince Edward* cutter safe into Plymouth with a man in the small pox from the *Royal George*, to prevent that fatal infection's spreading amongst her company.

Having only calms and light breezes, I did not arrive at my station till early in the morning of the 24th. At noon I was joined by the *Coventry*, to whom I had sent orders by express early on the morning of the 20th to proceed immediately to my rendezvous. Captain Burslem, who had fallen in with the *Chatham, Venus* and *Arethusa* delivered me a letter from Captain Lockhart, enclosing a copy of the intelligence sent to their Lordships by the *Thames*.

In the afternoon I sent the *Minerva*, supported by the *Nottingham*, to look into Brest water. Next morning they returned and acquainted me that they saw very distinctly eleven sail in the Road, all of which they judged to be large ships of war, with their colours

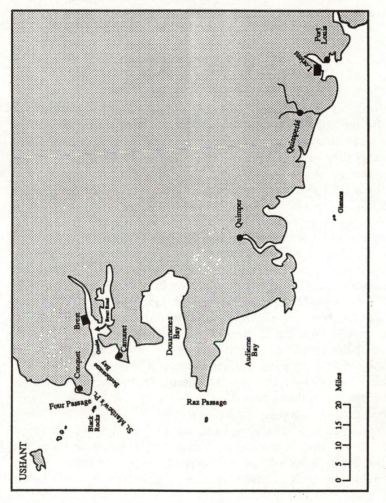

The coast near Brest

hoisted, yards and topmasts up, and topgallant yards across. One of them carried a flag on her mizen topmast head and another a broad pendant on her main topmast head. They all seemed ready for sailing. There were only two or three small vessels within the great ships in the Road.

The same afternoon I was joined by the *Colchester* (50) [Captain Robert Roddam] from Plymouth. Her, with the *Sapphire* and *Coventry*, I dispatched immediately to cruise off Port Louis, sending one of the frigates to look into Basque Road.

Having maturely considered the intelligence, I will venture to give my opinion that the enemy's intentions are not against Great Britain or Ireland but aimed at the relief of their islands. If their carpenters are sent to the eastward, I apprehend it is to repair the great loss of frigates they have lately sustained, as they have been for the most part built in these ports, where they have the timber and other materials for that purpose more at hand. This is mere matter of opinion.

But observing the four ships in such forwardness at Port Louis, I judged it to be of the greatest consequence to prevent their joining those at Brest. Therefore at noon of the 25th, I detached the *Torbay, Magnanime, Fame, Monmouth* and *Southampton* to cruise off Audierne Bay. They are to be joined by the *Colchester* the moment she shall perceive the enemy move, so that I think them sufficient match for them, while I keep a strict watch over the seventeen sail that may be fitted out at Brest.

At 9 this morning I was joined by His Majesty's ships *Anson, Rochester* (50) [Captain Robert Duff] and *Melampe*, by whom I received your letter of the 21st instant. It gives me the greatest pleasure to find that I have done my duty to their Lordships' satisfaction.

Yesterday in the afternoon I sent the *Essex* and *Montagu* to look into Brest Road. A thick fog prevented their seeing anything last night, but at 3 this afternoon Captain Campbell [of the *Essex*], on his return to me at ½ past 5, reported that he saw distinctly eleven sail riding in the Brest water, nine of which appeared to be ships of the line. All of them had jacks and ensigns hoisted. One of them had a white flag with a swallow tail at the mizen topmast head, and two of them pendants. The outermost large ship had a very bright side.

Upon the whole I do not think it prudent, as they may soon be joined by more from Brest Harbour, to leave them at liberty to come out by returning to Torbay till I shall receive farther instructions from their Lordships or the wind shall appear to be set in strong westerly. When I do leave the station, I shall leave orders for Mr. Keppel [of the *Torbay*] to follow me immediately with the ships under his command.

I have detached the *Rochester* and *Melampe* [Captain William Hotham] to keep a constant watch over their motions and the *Prince Edward* cutter to run between us with intelligence and constantly keep them in sight.

Enclosed is the state and condition of His Majesty's ships under my command. I am etc.

194. *Secret Instructions from the Lords of the Admiralty to Hawke*

1 June 1759

Whereas in your letter of the 27th past to our Secretary you have informed us of your proceedings and intentions, upon considering the state of the enemy at Brest and L'Orient, not to return to Torbay till you receive farther instructions; we do hereby signify to you our approval of your proceedings and direct you to continue with a sufficient force off Brest and L'Orient to prevent the French putting to sea, taking care to send from time to time such of your squadron as you shall find necessary to Plymouth or Torbay to recruit their provisions and water, and to refresh their companies, and dispatching to us constant accounts of the intelligence you shall procure of the enemy and of your proceedings.

And whereas we have ordered the *Defiance* [(60)] to proceed from Plymouth to join you and be under your command, and you may expect to be very shortly joined by her, as well as by the *Belliqueux* and *Achilles*, and the frigates *Thames* and *Actaeon* [for all four of which see 191], you are hereby required and directed, as soon as you shall be joined by two of the line of battle ships, to dispatch away to Spithead any two of the 50-gun ships under your command which shall be nearest at hand in case you shall have been joined by the *Isis*; but if she shall not have joined you, you are to send only one 50-gun ship away to Spithead.

We also recommend it to you, if other services will admit of it, to send a ship of the line with a frigate or two, from time to time, to cruise off Cape Ortegal and then round the Bay and join you, in order to intercept the enemy's ships that may escape the other divisions of your squadron. Given etc.

ANSON
GILB. ELLIOT

J. FORBES

Sent the same day to Plymouth to go by the first ship of his squadron. An attested copy sent to Torbay the 8th June 1759 at 11 p.m.

195. *Instructions from Hawke to Duff of the ROCHESTER*

Ramillies at sea
3 June 1759

By Sir Edward Hawke, Knight of the Bath, etc.

You are hereby required and directed to take under your command His Majesty's frigate *Minerva* [Captain Alexander Hood], the commander of which has my order to follow your directions, and with her and the *Melampe* continue to cruise off Ushant and, as wind and weather will permit, make as frequent and accurate observations as possible of the number, strength and motions of the enemy in Brest Road. And in case you shall observe any of their ships of war and transports to sail either to the eastward or westward, whom you shall be too weak to attack, you are immediately to detach one of the frigates to Torbay to give me notice of it, you with the other frigate following and observing their course till you shall be able to form a judgement whether they shall be bound up Channel, or to Ireland, and then detach the other frigate to acquaint me therewith, directing her commander to steer the most proper course according to the winds for meeting me at sea, in case I should have sailed on the first intelligence, from the nature of which you shall be able to regulate such order. In the meantime, you are to keep the enemy company till you are absolutely certain whether their designs shall be against Great Britain, Ireland, or on a foreign voyage, and then endeavour to join me, or put into the first port in England and by express acquaint the Secretary of the Admiralty with your proceedings. While on this service, you are to use your best endeavours to take, sink, or by every means in your power destroy such ships or vessels as you shall be able to cope with, aiding and assisting those of His Majesty's subjects and allies. For which this shall be your order.

To Captain Duff of His Majesty's ship   Given etc.
Rochester. By command   E.H.
of the Admiral,
J[ohn] H[ay].

196. *Hawke to Clevland*

Ramillies off Ushant
4 June 1759
'Recd. 7th'

Sir,

Since my last by express 27th of May, I have been joined by His Majesty's ships *Mars, Firm* and *Chatham* with the *Actaeon* and *Venus* frigates, by the two former on the 31st ultimo and by the three latter on the 2nd instant.

The intelligence I have since received only serves to strengthen me in the opinion of its being best for the service that I should continue on this station till I shall receive their Lordships' farther instructions, which I am in daily expectation of, as the winds hang to the northward. On the 29th of May, the *Rochester* and *Melampe* looked into Brest Road. Captain Duff acquainted me next day by letter that he saw there seventeen ships, sixteen of which were rigged and had their sails bent. Only one of them had topgallant yards aloft. About 3 in the afternoon of the day he looked in, that ship shifted her berth from the north to the south side of the harbour. The seventeenth ship had no main topmast up. Thirteen of the number appeared to be large, the other four frigates. There was neither ship or vessel in Berthaume or Camaret Roads.

The wind shifting from the eastward, I considered that no ships could sail from Port Louis for Brest and consequently that Mr Keppel's remaining off Audierne Bay could be of no service. In the evening of the 2nd, therefore, I called him off from that station and at 3 o'clock yesterday in the afternoon he rejoined me in the *Torbay* with the *Monmouth, Magnanime, Fame* and *Southampton*. Pursuant to my directions, on Sunday the 27th he sent the *Southampton* into Port Louis. Captain Fraine[1] stood so near as to be within two cannon shot of that port and, after a most accurate observation, could not discover any ship that had the appearance of a ship of war, except one, which lay above the point of Port Navalo, and she seemed only to be a frigate.

By the best information I have ever received, their ships of war are generally fitted up at L'Orient and seldom drop down to Port Louis till they are on the point of sailing, so that it is probable that the four

[1] Fraine: L 1745, CR 13.1.58. Posted 11.12.59.

ships of the line seen by the *Venus* and *Chatham*, 11th and 12th May, had sailed from thence before I reached my station and may be numbered with those in Brest Road. The object of my stationing ships there when the wind shall be easterly being thus removed, I shall keep the line of battle ships together, having directed Captain Duff in the *Rochester*, with the *Melampe* and *Minerva*, to keep a strict watch for convoys coming through the Passage du Raz, in case they should escape the *Colchester* and the two frigates stationed off Port Louis.

Captain Keppel also acquainted me that he had received intelligence of a French frigate, the *Félicité*, going into Bordeaux in order to proceed from thence with an outward bound convoy. I have this day detached the *Venus* [Captain Thomas Harrison] and *Southampton* to cruise for a fortnight off that port in order to intercept them or any other bound to Brest.

Yesterday in the afternoon I also called in the *Rochester* and *Melampe*. On the 31st of May, at 8 a.m., Captain Duff stood close into the entrance off Brest Road and distinctly saw twenty sail. Fifteen of the line were rigged with their topgallant yards aloft. The sixteenth, a large ship, had her topmasts struck. Three frigates and a snow made up the number twenty. Only ten of the large ships had their sails bent. Ever since, thick weather and westerly winds have prevented his looking in; but I detached him again last night with the *Melampe* and *Actaeon* to make another observation, which I am afraid he will not be able to make today.

When I first arrived on my station, I sent the *Minerva* out to chase. She spoke with a Danish ship of 350 tons, loaded with provisions, who had a sign out for a pilot from Ushant. His clearances, bills of lading, etc., for the Island of St Thomas, appeared all fair and signed, as I suppose by the customs in Denmark, by their King. She pretended to have been long out and therefore under a necessity of putting into Conquet Bay for water. Under such circumstances Captain Hood had no authority for stopping her. That night she anchored in the said road, but next morning was seen by the *Rochester* to get under way, set all the sail she could, and run into Brest Harbour. She said she waited for a consort which I am since informed lay loaded at Morlaix with provisions for the French fleet at Brest. A French frigate was expected there to take her under convoy, or take her provisions out and carry them to Brest.

The *Pallas* being very foul, I have sent her with this express into Portsmouth to clean with the utmost expedition and then to repair to Torbay for farther orders.

Enclosed is the state and condition of His Majesty's ships now with me. I am etc.

197. *Instructions from the Lords of the Admiralty to Hawke*

5 June 1759

By virtue of the power and authority to us given by Act of Parliament made in the first year of King William and Queen Mary, instituted an Act for abrogating the oaths of Supremacy and Allegiance and appointing other oaths, we do empower, direct and depute you to administer the oaths and tests appointed by Act of Parliament unto Francis Geary Esquire, appointed Rear-Admiral of the White, and to all other officers whose commissions and warrants shall be hereafter sent to you. And you are to return to this Board their subscriptions of the said test, together with certificates under your hand of their having taken the said oaths. For which this shall be your warrant. Given under our hands and the Seal of the Office of Admiralty this fifth day of June 1759.

ANSON etc.

198. *Hawke to Clevland*

Ramillies in Torbay
6 June 1759

Sir,

For several days preceding my last, by express of the 4th instant, we had had very fresh gales with a great sea. Yesterday it increased so much at south-west, with a thick fog, as to make several of the ships complain, more particularly the new ships. As in this weather it was impossible for the enemy to stir and our own ships stood in need of a day or two to get themselves to rights, in the evening I bore away for this place. I shall use the utmost dispatch in getting them ready for sea, which I hope will be by the time, or before, I can receive an answer to this. In that case, I shall sail again with any moderate wind, as, from the last accounts of the enemy, it appears to me to be of the greatest consequence that we should be on our station again before they can get a fair wind to bring them out.

There are come in with me the *Royal George, Union, Resolution, Mars, Hero, Torbay, Hercules, Magnanime, Fame, Temple, Dorsetshire, Chichester, Revenge, Monmouth, Essex, Bienfaisant, Kingston, Nottingham, Firm, Anson, Dunkirk, Chatham, Actaeon, Pluto* and

Proserpine.

I have left the *Rochester, Melampe, Minerva* and *Prince Edward* cutter off Brest. I am etc.

Minute: Own receipt.

199. *Hawke to Richard Cross of Exeter*[1]

Ramillies in Torbay
6 June 1759

Sir,

I desire you will with the utmost expedition supply the squadron of the King's ships now under my command in Torbay with 46926 lbs. of fresh beef, agreeable to the contract made by you with the Commissioners for Victualling His Majesty's Navy on the 21st May last; also that you get the like quantity ready to be shipped on Saturday next [the 9th]. I am etc.

200. *Hawke to Commissioner Rogers at Plymouth*[2]

Ramillies in Torbay
6 June 1759, 9 p.m.

Sir,

Being disappointed in my expectation of finding victuallers ready here to supply the squadron under my command, I am under a necessity of desiring that immediately on receipt of this you will order all the vessels you can procure round to me, loaded with beer, under convoy of the ship or frigate in greatest readiness at your port. No time must be lost in this, as I purpose going to sea on Saturday.

As the *Firm* and *Fame* are in great want, I have sent them to be supplied in the Sound. I hope their beer and water will be ready to put on board by the time they shall come to an anchor.

The topmasts in the accompanying demand, if not ready to be sent immediately, [are] to be put on board the *Firm, Fame* and *Belliqueux.*

Bread is likewise wanted, though not so much as beer. I am etc.

[1] Richard Cross, a butcher of Exeter, had undertaken to supply any quantity of 'well fed ox beef' at forty-eight hours' notice. It would be delivered in quarters into boats at Torbay. (See N.A.M. Rodger, 'The Victualling of the British Navy in the Seven Years War', *Bulletin du Centre d'Histoire des Espaces Atlantiques* (Bordeaux, 1985, No. 2, p. 8.)
[2] Rogers: CR 1741, C 1741. Commissioner at Plymouth 1753–74; created baronet 1773.

201. *Hawke to Clevland*

Ramillies in Torbay
8 June 1759

Sir,

Yesterday at noon I received their Lordships' order of the 1st June [194], with which I shall use my best endeavours to comply. At the same time I received your two letters of the 27th May and 2nd June with the extract of intelligence. With regard to the Danish ship, I wrote you the 4th instant. For the future I shall stop any of her consorts I may meet with.

Yesterday morning arrived here His Majesty's sloop *Tamar* with five victualling sloops, with 260 tons of beer without which, if the gale had not happened, at least ten of the ships must have come in, in a week's time. I have ordered the sloops back to Plymouth to be loaded again, in case their Lordships shall think proper to send them under convoy to my rendezvous. At present we have as much as will enable me to keep the squadron out a month or five weeks, if the wine should not come through from Guernsey. If the ships are to be supplied with wine, we shall need more water. As the *Firm* in particular had but four days' beer, I sent her to Plymouth, not being able to supply her quantity here; also the *Fame* in order to bring some anchors, with topmasts, for the *Magnanime, Chichester, Temple* and *Bienfaisant*. Many more had their topmasts sprung, but we have got pretty well to rights again and I am now unmooring, if the weather will permit. The ships from Plymouth have my express orders to join me off the Sound.

In obedience to their Lordships' order, I have dispatched the *Chatham* to Spithead. She sailed hence last night.

I shall be greatly honoured in having His Highness, Prince Edward,[1] on board the *Ramillies* and can only regret that I have not had an opportunity of being better provided for his reception than I am at present.

Captain Dorrill's ill state of health increasing daily has obliged him to apply to me for leave to stay behind, which I have granted. I have appointed Captain Campbell of the *Essex* to act as Captain of the *Royal George*, Captain Johnston of the *Pluto* to command the *Essex*, and Lieutenant Robert Taylor,[2] first of the *Ramillies*, to

[1] Edward Augustus, Duke of York (1739–67), was entered as a midshipman in Howe's care for the coastal landings of 1758. Thereafter C 14.6.59, RA 1761, VA 1762, A 1763.

[2] Having been first commissioned in 1740, Robert Taylor was finally appointed to a command on 21.9.59 (see Documents 269 and 275). He was never posted.

command the *Pluto* till farther order. Lieutenant Taylor, if I am not mistaken, is the oldest lieutenant now employed, a sober, diligent, good officer, and as such I beg leave to recommend him to their Lordships.

Enclosed is the state and condition of His Majesty's ships now with me. I am etc.

Minute: 15 June. Direct the Commissioners of the Victualling to provide beer and water at Plymouth for the squadron, and to ship the same aboard vessels they must hire for the purpose, and to have them ready in Plymouth Sound against Sir Edward Hawke sending for them.

Let Sir Edward know it, that he may send for it as he has occasion, and that the Lords have ordered the wine expected from Guernsey at Torbay to be brought to Plymouth Sound in case he should yet be at Torbay.

202.   *Hawke to Captain John Reynolds*[1] *of the FIRM*

Ramillies in Torbay
8 June 1759

Sir,

I desire that immediately on receipt of this you will give directions to the captains of the *Fame, Defiance* and *Belliqueux* positively to get out tomorrow and accompany them yourself to join me off Plymouth. You are to bring with you in those ships as many of the stores I wrote for to the Commissioner as you can conveniently get on board before you sail. I am etc.

203.   *Oaths sworn by Geary and Campbell*

[*Ramillies* at sea]
11 and 12 June 1759

Oath

We, Francis Geary and John Campbell [see 201], do sincerely promise and swear that we will be faithful and bear true alliance to His Majesty King George II. So help us God.

---

[1] Reynolds: L 1736, CR 1745, C 1746. Governor of Georgia 1754–9. As captain of the *Firm* in 1759, he played an important part in Hawke's system of blockade, but he missed the Battle of Quiberon Bay. RA 1775, VA 1778, A 1787.

FRANCIS GEARY
JOHN CAMPBELL

We, Francis Geary and John Campbell, do swear that we do from our hearts abhor, detest and abjure as impious and heretical that damnable doctrine and position that princes excommunicated or deprived by the pope, or any authority of the see of Rome, may be deposed or murthered by their subjects, or any other whatsoever. And we do declare that no foreign prince, person, prelate, state, or potentate hath, or ought to have, any jurisdiction, power, superiority, pre-eminence or authority, ecclesiastical or spiritual, within this realm. So help us God.

FRANCIS GEARY
JOHN CAMPBELL

Test
We, Francis Geary and John Campbell, do solemnly and sincerely in the presence of God profess, testify and declare that we believe that, in the sacrament of the Lord's supper, there is not any transubstantiation of the elements of bread and wine into the body and blood of Christ at, or after, the consecration thereof by any person whatsoever, and that the invocation of the Virgin Mary or any other saint, and the sacrifice of the mass, as they are now used in the church of Rome, are superstitious and idolatrous. And we do solemnly and in the presence of God profess, testify and declare that we do make this declaration, and every part thereof, in the plain and ordinary sense of the words now read to us as they are commonly understood by English protestants, without any evasion, equivocation or mental reservation whatsoever, or without hope of any such dispensation from any person or authority whatsoever, or without thinking that we are, or can be acquitted before God or men, or absolved of this declaration or any part thereof, although the pope, or any other person or persons, or any power whatsoever, should dispense with or annul the same, or declare that it was null and void from the beginning.
Sworn before me the 11th and 12th June 1759.

EDWARD HAWKE

204. *Hawke to Clevland*

Ramillies at sea
12 June 1759
8 a.m. the Start NE¾N. dist. 19 leagues
'Recd. 14'

Sir,

After the gale of wind we met with this day sennight, the pains we took to set the ships to rights in Torbay and the season of the year considered, I flattered myself we should have had nothing left but, in quiet and good order, to watch the motions of the enemy; and yesterday morning, I intended to have acquainted their Lordships of my having again got within reach of my rendezvous. But at 10 a.m. the Lizard bearing N.W. by N. eight leagues, we were surprised by a violent storm in which the *Hero* lost all her masts and the *Torbay* her main course and other sails. It did not abate till about the same time in the evening. I have sent the *Nottingham* to tow the *Hero* in safety into Plymouth and then return to me.

The cutter joined me from Captain Duff, who looked into Brest Road the 7th instant and then saw eighteen two-decked ships. I shall send from time to time to Plymouth for what may be wanting in the squadron and, except I shall be drove off by winds and weather, keep them constantly in view, so as either to prevent their coming out or doing my utmost, in case they should, to take or destroy them.

The sea is not quite down, so that I can not send you a more particular state of the squadron at present. I am etc.

Minute: Let him know I have communicated his letter to the Lords who are persuaded he will do everything in his power to answer the purposes for which he is employed.

205. *Hawke to Clevland*

Ramillies in Torbay
13 June 1759, 9 p.m.

Sir,

Yesterday I took advantage of the gales abating a little to dispatch the *Prince Edward* cutter with an account of the state of the squadron. Soon after the *Temple*, which was then to leeward, flung out a signal of distress. I sent the *Thames* [(32), Captain Stephen Colby] immediately to know the reason. She returned with an account from Captain Shirley that his foremast and bowsprit were very much sprung in two places, the foremast so unluckily in one place, just above the wedges, that he durst not move them to fish it; its other spring fourteen feet above the forecastle, which he was then endeavouring to fish. The bowsprit was sprung just within and just without the gammoning, so that an anchor stock would, in fishing, be almost cut through to make a groove for the gammoning.

I also found the rudder of the *Bienfaisant* in a very bad condition, owing to want of a careful inspection at Plymouth when complained of by the carpenter of that ship before she came out. I have set carpenters to work on it and hope soon to render it serviceable.[a]

By noon the gale came on again and continued very violent all night and this day, so that I was obliged to bear up for Torbay. Within the Start I perceived the *Hero*, who had lost company with the *Nottingham* at 1 this morning by the hawsers breaking. I dispatched the *Montagu* to take her in tow and, by favour of an ebb tide, got her safe moored here. The *Nottingham* is also come in.

On Monday morning [the 11th] I was joined by His Majesty's sloop *Albany* with the topmasts I mentioned in a former letter and the *Devonshire* tender with stores. They are both come in with me. The former is commanded by Mr Andrew Snape Hamond,[1] acting as lieutenant by order of the late Vice-Admiral Harrison since October 1758. He behaved remarkably well in the gale of wind by preserving the topmasts for the squadron at the utmost risk, and not withstanding the remonstrances of the whole company for cutting them away. He prudently considered, when the *Hero*'s masts went, she might want them. Lord Howe, who wants a lieutenant in place of one who never appeared, would be very well pleased to have him in the *Magnanime*.[b]

I sent orders yesterday to Plymouth to prepare masts for the *Hero*. We shall fit her in the best manner possible here for going round, for which purpose I have put a number of seamen and carpenters on board her.

I understand a packet from their Lordships by express to me is gone to Plymouth, whither I have sent for it. If it should bring no order to the contrary, I shall proceed to my station as soon as the weather will permit.[c]

Enclosed is the state and condition of His Majesty's ships now with me. I am etc.

[1] Hamond was duly appointed 5th lieutenant of the *Magnanime* 18.6.59. Subsequently CR 1765, C 1770, he was governor, c.-in-c. and commissioner at Halifax 1780–4 (having been knighted for services at Sandy Hook 1778). Controller (and Superannuated RA) 1794–1806.

Minute: 16 June. Own receipt of his letter and acquaint him the
Lords are concerned for the accidents that have happened to
the ships, but from the violence of the gale they were fearful it
might have been worse. They approved of what he has done and
have ordered the *Belliqueux, Defiance,* and *Windsor* to join
him...

[a]Send an extract to the Navy Board with directions to make the most
particular inquiry into it; and as the Lords have received frequent
complaints of this sort with regard to the ships fitted at Plymouth
Harbour, they are determined to dismiss whom they shall find to
blame.
[b]To be appointed. Let Sir Edward know it.
[c]The Lords recommend it to him to proceed the moment the weather
will permit.

206.   *Hawke to Clevland* (holograph)

[Personal]   *Ramillies* in Torbay
                                                          15 June 1759

Sir,

I am much obliged to you for your letter of the 5th instant which I
received last night, by an express from Plymouth, with the Admiralty packets of the 8th. Lord Anson is extremely kind in thinking of
the situation I am in with regard to my providing for Prince Edward,
for I came away in so great a hurry that I had scarce time to get even
common necessaries on board and therefore only gave directions for
sending me the plainest things I had, with the utmost dispatch.
Though this is the case, I am in hopes I shall do pretty well with
Lord Anson's assistance, as I shall take particular care that his
Highness wants for nothing that lies in my power to provide for him.
To be sure, he will not be so happy with me as if he was with his
Lordship, but I shall do my best to make everything as agreeable as
possible to him, from a just sense of the duty and gratitude I owe to
the King.

   You will have found that I took upon me to send Captain Clevland[1] to Portsmouth [196], because from a conversation I formerly
had with you relating to him I judged you did not much approve of

---

   [1] Archibald Clevland (L 1755) was the son of John Clevland and had been posted in
1756 when aged about 18. This letter testifies to the influence of the father — an MP,
as well as Secretary of the Ady (Rodger, *Wooden World,* p. 335).

his going to Plymouth; and as the *Pallas* [(36)] wanted cleaning, and he desirous of going into port for some particular reasons of his own, I suppose his expectation of commanding the *Windsor* [(60)], I thought it would be more for his benefit to let him go thither. If he serves with me, you may rest assured I shall take every opportunity to do him all the good offices in my power. He appears to me to be good natured and very alert in his duty, and I dare say will acquit himself as an officer upon all occasions as well as any young man in the service. There is an openness and frankness in him which please me much and have induced me, now and then, to give him some little hints that I thought might be useful to him.

I never saw so much bad weather in the summer since I have been at sea. We got in here very luckily, for it now blows extremely hard without and, had we laid to some hours longer, we should have drove past this bay. Very fortunately, we picked up the *Hero* off this place. The ship that I had ordered to take care of her and see her into Plymouth broke her tow in the night and, driving to leeward in the gale, could not work up again till I had got in to an anchor. I have sent people to assist in getting up her jury masts, which is done, and she is now in a very fit condition to proceed when the weather will permit.

May I entreat the favour of you to present my duty to Lord Anson and acquaint him how sensible I am of his obliging favour in this affair of Prince Edward. I beg you will believe that I am etc.

Minute: Read.

207.   *Hawke to Clevland*

Ramillies in Torbay
15 June 1759

Sir,
...The *Hero* is now fitted to go round to Plymouth, but I have heard nothing of the *Temple*. The rest of the squadron is in very good order and I wait for a fair wind and moderate weather, for it still blows hard between the W. and S.W.

The ship is ready for the reception of His Royal Highness Prince Edward. I am etc.

208.   *Hawke to Clevland*

Ramillies in Torbay
17 June 1759

Sir,

Yesterday His Majesty's ship *Pallas* arrived here from Portsmouth in her way to Plymouth. I ordered her to return here immediately... At the request of Captain Edgcumbe, I have appointed the carpenter of the *Nottingham* to the *Hero* in room of hers, who was killed in the storm; the carpenter of the *Thames* to the *Nottingham*; and Robert Pringle, carpenter's mate of the *Ramillies*, to be carpenter of the *Thames*; which I hope their Lordships will approve of. Both Lemington and Pringle are very good men in their several professions.

When I send any ships across the Bay, I shall direct them to call at Corunna.

I have just received your letter of the 13th by a cutter from Plymouth. While the weather permitted me to remain on my station, I had a particular eye on the Passage du Four and left it in charge with Captain Duff, as well as the Passage du Raz.

The bad weather has hitherto prevented my sailing. I am now unmooring and shall sail the instant the weather will permit. I am etc.

209.   *Hawke to Clevland*

Ramillies off Torbay
19 June 1759

Sir,

The weather becoming moderate on the 17th, I unmoored and lay all that night and yesterday at single anchor becalmed. A small breeze easterly springing up, at 6 this morning I got under way and by the help of our boats turned out, and am now making all the sail I can for my station.

At 8 this morning I was joined by His Majesty's sloop *Swallow* with the victuallers from Plymouth. I have ordered them to accompany me to my rendezvous.

Enclosed I send you three letters for courts martial, and am etc.

Minute: 21 June. A general power to Sir Edward Hawke to hold courts martial. Own receipt. Send him the power and return him the letters.

210. *Hawke to Clevland*

Ramillies off Ushant
21 June 1759
'Recd. 27th'

Sir,

I made the best advantage of the wind from Torbay and early yesterday morning reached my station with the whole squadron, except the two fireships whom we outsailed. I expect them every hour.

This morning I was joined by the *Swallow*, whose convoy bore away on Tuesday night as far to the westward as Falmouth. Next morning he chased them but was at too great a distance to come up with them, so he made the best of his way to acquaint me with what had happened. I have detached him again to look for them at Falmouth, Plymouth or Torbay and, if their masters should refuse to accompany him, to put careful persons from the sloop on board them and bring them to my rendezvous.[a]

This morning I was also joined by the *Rochester, Minerva* and *Melampe*. On the 18th, they took two French fishing boats off the Passage du Raz. The prisoners were all kept separate and, on examination, agreed to the ships named in the accompanying list[b] being ready in all respects, excepting a few men, and victualled for five months. They added that there were no troops more than usual at Brest. A Spaniard who came out on the 19th agreed in every tittle of the above intelligence except the last, affirming that troops were collecting there. At 8 last night, Captain Duff counted seventeen sail of the above and is of opinion they might all be there.

I am very happy, after all the bad weather, in having got safe on my station again before they stirred. The squadron will soon want butter and cheese which must be sent to the rendezvous.[c]

The enclosed letters from the *Montagu* will convince their Lordships of the necessity I am under to send her in to dock. The *Melampe*, who accompanies her, is in the same condition,[d] I am etc.

Minute: 27 June. Own receipt.

[a]They were expected into Plymouth and the Lords hope have joined him before this time.

[b]Observe that there was not the list mentioned to be enclosed, which is a disappointment to their Lordships.

[c]Acquaint the Commissioners of the Victualling herewith, direct them to get a supply of these species ready at Plymouth

and to let the Lords know what they do, that they may order a convoy to proceed with them.

Acquaint Sir Edward with it.

^dApprove.

[Addendum:] List came in his letter of the 22nd June 1759.

Enclosure 1:

210a. *'Memo. of Ships in Brest Road'*

18th June 1759

This, forgot to be sent yesterday
by the *Montagu*.

Le Tonnant	80	Monsieur Bauffremont. Flag.
Le Formidable	80	Monsieur de Verge St André [i.e. Saint-André du Verger]. Pendant.
L'Orient	80	
Le Magnifique	74	
Le Glorieux	74	
Le Superbe	74	
Le Brillant	74	
Le Héros	74	
L'Intrépide	74	
Le Dauphin	70	
[Le] Juste	70	
Le Bizarre	64	
Le Dragon	64	
Le Northumberland	64	
Le Thésée	64	
L'Eveillé	64	
Le Sphinx	64	
[L'] Inflexible	64	
[Le] Solitaire	64	
Le Soleil [Royal]	80	In the basin but ready to come into the Road.
Le Comète	30	} Frigates
Le Currelle [L'Ecureuil?]	12	

Enclosure 2:

210b.　*Captain John Lendrick to Hawke*

Montagu at sea
20 June 1759

Sir,　I am extremely sorry I should find myself under the necessity of enclosing you herewith a letter addressed to me from the carpenter of His Majesty's ship *Montagu* under my command, setting forth the quantity of water the ship constantly makes from a leak we discovered the 27th of May last, giving likewise his opinion of her being unfit to keep the sea from its increasing daily, which I humbly beg leave to refer to your consideration and likewise our inability to acquit ourselves properly should action ensue...

211.　*Hawke to Clevland*

Ramillies off Ushant
22 June 1759
'Recd. 29th'

Sir,

Last night at 9 p.m. the *Montagu*, after removing her provisions on board other ships, parted company for Plymouth with my letter to you of yesterday's date. The *Melampe* not being cleared of hers, as she only joined us yesterday, could not be sent in till this day.

Before the *Rochester* joined me, I had detached the *Magnanime* and *Thames* to look into Brest Road. Enclosed is a copy of Lord Howe's and Captain Colby's report. As it is necessary to keep a constant eye upon the enemy, I have sent the *Rochester* and *Pallas* to cruise in as close as winds and weather will permit, sending me constant account of the observations they shall make.

The *Pallas* joined me from Plymouth this morning. She left it on Wednesday [the 20th] and brought me their Lordships' order of the 16th instant for receiving and entering His Royal Highness Prince Edward and retinue, which shall be duly complied with on his arrival here. Also their order of the same date, to take the King's ships *Sandwich* [(90)] and *Windsor* [Captain Clevland] under my command.

By the same conveyance, I received your two letters of the 15th relating to the furniture and necessaries lodged with the storekeeper at Plymouth for His Royal Highness, and to the beer and wine for the squadron provided at Plymouth. I have sent orders to send all by the first ship that shall sail from thence to join me.

I have sent the *Minerva* to guard the east entry of [the] Four, while the *Rochester* and *Pallas* have an eye on the west. I am etc.

212. Hawke to Clevland

Ramillies at sea
3 July 1759
'Recd. and answered'

Sir,

...The operations of the enemy indicate a long cruise for the squadron. In order to preserve it in a condition to keep the sea, I purpose to send in two ships of the line to clean at Plymouth every spring. I have begun with the *Fame*, who has got a very malignant fever on board, and the *Bienfaisant*, whose rudder is not to be depended on. They are both above six months foul. I have also sent in the *Actaeon* as convoy to the victuallers and kept the *Swallow* [14] to repeat signals till her return. If their Lordships should not approve of this method of relieving the squadron, they will be so good as to acquaint me as soon as possible.

I have detached the *Kingston* to cross the Bay and call at Corunna.

Enclosed I send you ... Captain Duff's report of the appearance of the enemy ...

Enclosure:

212a. Copy of Report by Duff

1 July 1759

The appearance of the ships in Brest Road from the *Rochester*, July the 1st at 10 in the forenoon and at 7 in the evening, Fort de Leon bearing N.E., Camaret Castle S. by W. and the Fillette Rock E. by N.:

Twenty ships of two decks, one snow, one schooner, and one cutter, with French colours hoisted, a flag at the mizen topmast head on board one of the ships, and a broad pendant at the main topmast head on board another of the ships. The ships with their yards and topmasts struck and topgallant yards down; one of the ships without topgallant masts. About fifteen of the ships had their topsails bent but no courses.

One small ship with Danish colours hoisted.

213. *Instructions from Hawke to Captain Hervey of the MONMOUTH*

Ramillies at sea
3 July 1759

You are hereby required and directed to take under your command His Majesty's ship *Pallas* [Captain Michael Clements[1]], the commander of which has my orders to follow your directions, and proceed to cruise off Brest, making yourself and directing him to make the most accurate observations of the number and strength of the enemy. For this purpose you are to stand in, in company with him, as often as wind and weather will permit and as near as you shall judge you can go with safety. On this service you are to continue till farther order. Given etc.

To Hon. Capt. Hervey ...   E.H.

By command of the Admiral
J[OHN] H[AY][2]

214. *Hervey to Hawke*

Monmouth off Brest
4 July 1759

Sir,

... I think the ships in Brest in general seem but light and are certainly not yet ready for the sea; and though I could discern men in boats alongside of them, I could not see any number about the ships sufficient to think them anything like manned, as they would have appeared on the decks on our standing in, as they did everywhere on shore ...

215. *Hawke to Hervey*

Ramillies at sea
4 July 1759, 9 p.m.

[1]
  Clements: L 1756, C 1757. In June 1759 he succeeded Clevland in command of the *Pallas* (36). In Feb. 1760 he shared in the defeat of Thurot's squadron. See p. 356, n.1.
  [2] As usual, Hawke's orders were issued by his secretary, John Hay. Some of Hervey's feelings about Hay have been indicated above (p. 24, n. 1). Elsewhere he noted that 'we all knew Sir Edward was totally governed by a damned interested Scotch secretary, a fellow without a grain of understanding who had been bred up to business in a shop and had the impudence to show his ascendancy over the Admiral to the whole fleet.' (Erskine (ed.), *Hervey's Journal*, p.220.)

Sir,

I have received your letter with the account of the French fleet in Brest Road and am much obliged to you for your expedition and diligence in the execution of my orders. I would not have you risk the disabling of the *Monmouth* by attacking the Dutch vessels now under shelter of the batteries, but have sent you the two cutters and leave you at liberty to attempt cutting the doggers out by them and the boats, if you shall think it practicable; in which I am persuaded you will act with the greatest judgement and discretion.

Be so good as to send the *Hazard* cutter back as soon as possible. I am etc.

216. *Hervey to Hawke*

Monmouth off Brest Harbour
5 July 1759 at 3 p.m.

Sir,

About 11 this morning the cutters joined me, by which I had the honour of your very obliging letter. Your approbation will ever give me the greatest satisfaction. [He now thought that the Dutch doggers were too well covered by batteries, placed so high up as to be proof against gunfire from the ships.]

There is not the least alteration today in their fleet ... When you stood in about 11, they fired the alarm guns from several different signal places, a Dutch flag was hoisted at the mizen peak from the ship with the cornette, as also from the two with pendants ...

217. *Hervey to Hawke*

Monmouth off Brest
6 July 1759

Sir,

After I had sent the *Hazard* cutter to you yesterday, the wind came back fresh from the E.N.E. and gave me a very good opportunity of approaching again as near as I desired, and both the *Pallas* and myself opened the citadel of Brest, and stood within little more than three or four miles of the ships at our leisure. The batteries never offered to fire. There is not a frigate or merchant vessel to be seen but that Dane, and only two lateen yards vessels (seemingly) hauled up ashore by the citadel that appear like quarter-galleries but not bigger ...

[P.S.] ... I write no letters home now, nor suffer any person from my ship, [so] that whatever use you please to make of the intelligence we can get and send you may solely go from yourself first ...

218. *Hawke to Hervey*

Ramillies at sea
7 July 1759

Sir,

With the greatest satisfaction I received your letter of the 6th, as it so fully answered my purpose in sending the *Monmouth* on the service in which she is at present employed, more especially by your taking the boat. Though we must not absolutely depend upon intelligence received from an enemy, yet, as part of what you sent carries the marks of truth, it will quiet minds in England, which have lately been greatly alarmed; and you will, I hope, not only receive my heartiest thanks but those of the nation for the diligence and address you have shown on your present employment.

This will be delivered you by Captain Lendrick [of the *Montagu* (60)], who has my orders to put himself under your command. I have only further to desire that you will look narrowly to the Passage du Raz. I am etc.

219. *Duff to Hawke*

Rochester at sea
7 July 1759

Sir Edward,

Captain Clevland [of the *Windsor* (60)] has just now delivered me your orders to proceed and cruise off Audierne Bay for a convoy of the enemy's, to which station I shall proceed with all the dispatch possible. I am etc.

220. *Hawke to Clevland*

Ramillies
13 July 1759, 6 p.m.
St Matthew's Point bearing E.N.E. 6 miles

Sir,

Since my last of the 9th nothing material has occurred; but, as I had occasion to send in the *Prince Edward* cutter to clean and hasten the ships from Plymouth, I could not dispense with writing by her and sending an extract of a letter, of this day's date, from Captain Hervey in the *Monmouth* who is just within me ...

Enclosure:

220a. *'Extract of a Letter from Capt. Hervey off Brest'*

13 July 1759

I send you this with the master of the Danish ship, who is just come out of Brest. I can get nothing out of him more than that they are not half manned and that they have no troops at Brest. Their squadron to appearance remain exactly in the same situation. We are going to stand in again on board the *Pallas*.

221. *Instructions from Hawke to Geary, Rear-Admiral of the White, in the RESOLUTION*

Ramillies at sea
16 July 1759

In case of coming to action with the enemy, you are hereby required and directed, to avoid the inconveniences that may derive from colours similar to theirs, to hoist a red flag in place of a white on the flagstaff at the mizen topmast head and to direct all the commanders of ships in your division to hoist red ensigns. Given etc.

222. *Instructions from Hawke to Clements of the PALLAS (36)*

Ramillies at sea
16 July 1759

You are hereby required and directed to proceed forthwith with the four Swedish vessels cut out of Conquet Road to the port of Plymouth and there see them laid up in safety, either in Hamoaze or Catwater, till the determination of the Lords Commissioners of the Admiralty shall be known, leaving you all and singular concerned as captors to take what steps you shall think necessary for your own interest. You are not to continue in port more than four days...

223. *Hawke to Clevland*

Ramillies off Ushant
16 July 1759
'Recd. 23rd'

Sir,

This comes by the *Pallas* [Captain Clements], who this day joined me from Captain Hervey with four Swedish vessels he had cut out of Conquet Road. As I have cruisers off Brest Road [and] the Passages du Raz and du Four, I considered Brest as blocked up in the strictest sense; so that I gave Captain Hervey orders not to suffer a neutral vessel of any nation whatever to enter that port, but direct them to stand off the coast.[a] The four he has now sent to me are furnished with cargoes, according to their own account, which appear to be but too necessary to the enemy in their present equipment. Beside, from their manner of stowage and some other circumstances, there is ground to suspect they have guns and other contraband goods underneath all. As the weather will not permit me to search for them here, I have sent them into Plymouth under care of the *Pallas*, there to be detained till their Lordships' pleasure shall be known,[b] in terms of the latter part of the XI article of the treaty of alliance and commerce between Great Britain and Sweden 21st October 1661 and confirmed by subsequent treaties or otherwise.

Their Lordships will give me leave to send them the enclosed letter from a person sober, diligent, in every respect capable of his duty, struggling with the difficulties of supporting a numerous family.[c] I am etc.

Minute: 30 July. Own receipt.

[a]Approve of what he has done.

[b]Order the Commissioner at Plymouth to cause these ships to be thoroughly rummaged in the presence of the Customs House officers and some person on behalf of the captors [and] to send if there is any contraband goods on board and report what he finds to the Lords. Let Sir Edward Hawke know the Lords extremely approve of what he has done, and what directions they have given.

[c]The first rate is to be built in the room of the [old] *Royal Sovereign* and her officers removed into her before she is launched, this ship not being designed in addition to the Royal Navy.

Enclosure 1:

223a.   *Bradshaw Mann to Hawke* (unmodernized)

Ramillies
13 July 1759

Honourable Sir,

As nothing but your Goodness has emboldned me to trouble you, hope you will Pardon the Liberty I have taken, in noting to you the time of my Service in his Majestys Royl Navey, which is near thirty five years and as Follows.

First as an officers Servant on board one of his Majestys Ships, from thence apprenticed to Mr Anthony Bryant, then Builder Assistant at his Majestys Dockyard Deptford, whare I belonged Upwards of twelve Years, from thence warranted as Carpenter in one of his Majestys Ships, in which Station I have served near twenty Years, Upwards of fourteen of which, in the St George and Ramilies, have done my Duty with Approbation of my Commanders, as Sundry Certificates Testify, as well my Qualification as Diligence, humbly Conceive that if Your honour will be Pleased to recommend me to the Right Honble the Lords Commissioners of the Admiralty, I may be appointed Carpenter of a New Ship of the first rate ordered to be built at Chatham, which will not oneley be giting me a Regular remove, but will intitle me to a Servant in the Yard and will Grately ad to the Support of my Large familey all which will be in Duty bound to Pray etc etc and am Honble Sir with Utmost Respect Your Most Obt. humble Servt.

BRADSHAW MANN

Enclosure 2:

223b.   *'Extract of a Letter from the Hon. Captain Hervey off Brest, dated July 15th 1759'*

Yesterday, seeing four sail coming through the Passage du Four, to which the castle of Conquet hoisted a red flag—and they immediately hauled in for that road and anchored, the tide not letting them go into the harbour—I consulted the pilot and, finding that the wind, tide, and weather assured the safety of the ship and that he could place me, without anchoring, to cover the boats, I went immediately within the rocks up abreast of Conquet forts with the *Pallas* and all the boats, leaving the *Montagu* [Captain Lendrick], off St Matthew's convent to observe the motions of the French fleet, and in about two hours and a half the boats (being covered by the fire of our two ships) brought those four vessels out (who hoisted Swede's colours) from the fire of four forts and a battery and other detached pieces of cannon on points of rocks. I cannot help, Sir, commending to you the bravery of the officers and seamen on this occasion...

I stood off the harbour of Brest immediately after and found the enemy's position there exactly the same as by my last account to you, and was near enough to see boats alongside of many of them, their four flags still flying, and exercising their people at loosing and working their sails—which they do surprisingly bad indeed, and convinces me of the truth of that part of the intelligence in which we have agreed with regard to their want of men.

Yesterday morning I sent the *Hazard* cutter with the masters and master's mates of our three ships to sound in the Passage of Fontenoy and about the Race, and they have made themselves masters of the passage...

224. *Instructions from the Lords of the Admiralty to the Victualling Board*

19 July 1759

Whereas we judge it necessary that fresh provisions should be sent for the use of the sick on board the fleet under the command of Sir Edward Hawke; you are hereby required and directed to cause two vessels to be provided at Plymouth that one may be sent every week with live oxen and sheep for the use of the said squadron, the commanders of His Majesty's ships being directed to take them under convoy upon application from the Agent Victualler for that purpose. Given etc.

225. *Captain Edgcumbe to Hawke*

Hero in Hamoaze
20 July 1759

Sir,

Last post I received their Lordships' order to proceed to the fleet with His Royal Highness Prince Edward and yesterday the *Sapphire* [(32), Captain John Strachan] brought me your instructions to the same purpose; and I hope in a few days to be ready to sail with three or four of the frigates and will observe the signal you have directed me to make upon my approaching the fleet.

The victuallers that sailed with the *Colchester* are returned and the *Melampe*, who brings this, has orders to conduct them to you. The *Sapphire* has sprung her main trussel trees but I hope will be ready to sail with me. I am etc.

226.   *Hervey to Hawke*

Monmouth off Brest
20 July 1759

Sir,

... In order to get you some intelligence, I landed the boats on the Island of Benequet in order to intercept some boats which are generally there; and in the morning the officer returned to me with three men, one of whom rents the island of the convent of St Matthews and who gave me the intelligence enclosed ... confirming most of the rest I have had the honour to send you.

Finding there were twenty-one head of cattle on the island, I sent the boats (wind and weather favouring the descent) and in about four hours brought off twenty of them. I take the liberty of sending you one, Sir, as well as the other admirals, and have divided the others to the *Montagu*'s people and our own for a day's fresh meat for them tomorrow...

Enclosure:

226a.   *Information from Novel Arche*

Novel Arche, belonging and habitant of Conquet, taken by the boats of His Majesty's ship *Monmouth* off the Island of Benequet July 20th 1759:

Says he has not been of Brest of some time, that he rents the island of the convent of St Matthew and maintains his family by killing rabbits, etc.

That he heard the day before yesterday that the fleet with M. Conflans would be twenty-three sail in all of the line, but it was said would not sail till the 25th of August, but he did not believe it would at all. That the *Tonnant* had but 500 men on board, and few of them so many. That they pressed even farmers' boys of 16 and 17 years of age to go on board them. That what people they had, was made up of such; no troops of any kind on board, all doing duty on shore. He heard they wanted guns for two ships [and] the convoy much wanted, as four garvets went to Bordeaux and Nantes for wine and flour for the fleet.

This was all he knew and which was talked of publicly at Conquet; and that he heard we had bombarded Havre de Grâce. Two others with him that can only speak Brittany.

227. *Hervey to Hawke*

Monmouth off Conquet
21 July 1759, 9 a.m.

[Sir,]

About 8 in the morning, being off St Matthew's Point, we saw seven sail of ships coming towards the Passage du Four. They loomed large with the wind at east and had French colours out. Boats went out from Conquet to them. A red flag was hoisted in the fort and two guns fired for an alarm to them; and, in short, we soon perceived it was some convoy which they were giving directions to secure themselves from the same attempt we had made on the Swedes. One, which appeared the commanding frigate, came through the Passage du Four with two of the ships that kept close to Conquet Point and anchored in the mouth of the harbour, within the rocks of what they call Les Mulets, the tide not letting them go in. The other four hauled their wind and did not come through the Passage du Four, but plied in that bay which is called Whitesand Bay, just to the northernmost point of Conquet. This time it was the height of the flood tide, so that the pilot could not venture with the scanty wind it was. I dispatched a lieutenant to the admiral with this account in a Spanish vessel that came out of Brest, under pretence to the Spaniard that I was obliged to send all vessels to the fleet that went into or came out of Brest.

About 11, tide of flood beginning to slacken and the wind rather freshening, I persuaded the pilot to take charge of us to run up and let us at least see if it were possible to cut those ships away or destroy them. The *Montagu* I ordered to follow as close as possible. About noon we got abreast of the ships which were warping in the little harbour of Conquet. Finding there was no possibility of cutting them out where they lay, and the forts firing constantly at us, we began to fire at the frigate and two ships, as well as the forts, which we continued about half an hour, throwing several shot into them and the forts, when the wind dying away and veering to the southward of east obliged us to get out as fast as we could, this place being very narrow, tides very rapid, surrounded with rocks and shoals, and not above one mile and a half to work in. We got out about three quarters past 2, when the four ships to the northward of the passage got under way and plied still further into Whitesand Bay.

We received no other damage than one shot in our bends and some running rigging cut; the *Montagu* one in her foremast of no consequence, being already fished and well secured, and some through her sails.

I then plied up to Brest harbour against wind and tide and from about 7 had a view of the ships which go enclosed...

Enclosure:

227a. *Report by Hervey*

Appearance of the French fleet in Brest Road from the *Monmouth*'s quarterdeck, July 21st at 5, 6 and 7 p.m.; Camaret Point S. by E., Haystacks S.S.W, harbour's mouth E. by N. 4 miles:

There appeared twenty-two large ships—all their colours flying and four flags, as before.

One of these that lay the eastmost had only a small jack at the ensign staff and which I take to be the ship that last came out of their basin and I think appears to be not above a 50–gun ship at most. Beyond these were two smaller ships that appeared frigates of the smallest rate with colours flying also. The ships appeared to be in the same position and one was bending his mainsail. There were many boats about them.

228. *Hervey to Hawke*

Monmouth off Brest
22 July 1759 at ½ past 4 a.m.

Sir,

I have but just time to tell you by the cutter that four sail of the enemy's ships are now out of the Road laying to, which is to drive us off (the others not moving) and then get their convoy in from Conquet. The *Colchester* [(50), Captain Roddam] and a frigate is in sight; therefore we will not be drove off easily. I hope some ships will come in, and I think we shall be able to destroy these before they get within their batteries again.

I stood in last night at 7 o'clock and counted twenty-two of the line and two smaller ones—less, I think, than their usual frigates. I have not time, Sir, to send you the particulars of my yesterday's attempt upon those French ships which got within the inner rocks of

Conquet harbour before I could get up—wind and tide against us till near 12...

229. *Hervey to Hawke*

Monmouth off Brest
22 July 1759

Sir,

... We have been very unlucky this morning, Sir, the four ships never would come down further than Bertheaume Bay and, from [my] signal of the fleet, plied up again immediately. From the very first sight of them at 4 in the morning, the *Montagu* and I weighed and plied up towards them. I wish the frigate to leeward and *Colchester* had observed my signals to them at first. They being clean might have got up to me and possibly sailed better and diverted one of the enemy's 74–gun ships. They had a great advantage in returning, having not so far up to Brest as I had to work up to them. The strength of the tide they had by having Brest water open and more wind than we off St Matthews. However, we worked up to one of them pretty well, but not effectually; and when I found myself well within shot, despairing to be nearer we exchanged some few shot, some of which I am certain he felt. I pursued him till the three had got pretty near in, and he within the rock of the harbour's mouth. One went ashore upon the southernmost point and lay about a quarter of an hour. The pilot thought it would be little wind and, as I saw their whole fleet getting under sail, eight of which were moving out, I thought proper to bring to and watch their motions, as I could not at any rate go further in without risking the ship with a flood tide under the fire of all their batteries.

As soon as they perceived they had three ships in, they made a signal and came to again, on which I took in my signal for a fleet. They are now all at anchor again, but the one I was so near, who is within the rock of the harbour and under all the forts.

I never imagined they would make more than a show of coming out with the whole, as I am certain it took most of their people to man these. They worked very badly, and had we had but three leagues further, we should have worked alongside of the one we fired at. I am now returning off the convent and shall consult the pilot what is to be done about those store ships at Conquet, whose preservation occasioned these movements.

You may depend, Sir, on my taking all sorts of precautions. I was in great hopes I had drawn their fleet out—at best, some of their ships into your hands; but their situation is every way too favourable in this dangerous part of their coast...

P.S. I hoisted a broad pendant this morning when approaching them, by way of giving them a check; and, as soon as I perceived the *Magnanime* [Captain Lord Howe] standing in, took it in. I hope you will not disapprove that step on this occasion, when we every moment expected action.

230. *Hawke to Clevland*

Ramillies at anchor
23 July 1759
St Matthews Convent E.N.E. 6 miles
'Recd. 30th'

Sir,

On the 17th the *Sapphire* returned to me from Plymouth and brought me a letter from Colonel Brudnell, acquainting me that His Royal Highness Prince Edward was at Mount Edgcumbe and was very anxious to be with the squadron. As I had received no directions or information on that subject from their Lordships, and the then countenance of the enemy would by no means admit of my leaving my station, I sent orders to Captain Edgcumbe to receive him and his retinue on board the *Hero*, take under his command any ships of the squadron that should be ready, and proceed immediately to join me. I am also left to myself as to the manner of receiving him. As this is the case, I shall pay him all honour in the best of my judgement due to the grandson of my royal master...

On the 20th I was joined by the *Achilles, Colchester* and *Juno* [(36), Captain Henry Philips].

In the afternoon of the 21st I received the accompanying letter [227 and its enclosure 227a] from Captain Hervey. I immediately detached the *Achilles, Colchester, Juno* and *Pluto* fireship to his assistance. But as they could not work in close during the night, they did not join him sooner than the *Torbay, Dorsetshire, Magnanime,* and *Dunkirk*, whose signals I made early in the morning of the 22nd to chase in to the support of the *Monmouth* and *Montagu*, whom I suspected the enemy would attempt to drive away. I made all the sail I could with the squadron after them and soon discovered the two latter chasing three 74s and a 64–gun ship of the enemy. Never did officer show greater conduct and resolution than did Captain Hervey and was bravely seconded by Captain Lendrick. But the distance rendered all their efforts ineffectual. The whole squadron of the enemy had loosed their topsails at daybreak. About 11 a.m. they made a show of coming out. I had, full in their view and close to the entrance of the road, the squadron formed and lying to for their reception. On the enemy's furling their topsails, I came to an anchor a few miles without, where I purpose staying while the winds and weather will permit...

Their Lordships will perceive how difficult it is to guard the Passage du Four without cutters, of which I have only one. Though I have hitherto, to my utmost, prevented vessels getting into Brest, yet what get through du Four are sure of a sanctuary in Conquet harbour, which is daily more strongly fortified.

The *Hercules*'s company being very sickly, I sent her in to heel and refresh her men ten days in port. For the disappointment I met with by the two first I sent in not saving the spring has induced me to alter my plan and give orders for no more line of battle ships to clean. If the enemy should slip out and run, we must follow as fast as we can. I have not yet received the supplies of butter and cheese, beef, pork, etc., in so much that I can not help regretting the want of a commanding officer at Plymouth to see all orders executed with the expedition and punctuality necessary.

As I shall not now have it in my power to relieve the whole squadron and it must in all probability remain here a considerable time, will their Lordships give me leave to recommend to their consideration the sending out live cattle now and then, under such regulations as they shall think proper.

Captain Lendrick, who was last night superceded from the *Montagu* by Captain Rowley's returning [from captivity in France][1] to the command of her, comes to Plymouth by this opportunity and, if thought necessary, can give a very exact account of the enemy.

Enclosed is the state and condition of His Majesty's ships under my command. I am etc.

[Responding on 7 August, Clevland wrote that the Lords were considering the appointment of 'a commanding officer at Plymouth to quicken the dispatch'. From 15 August Thomas Hanway, who had commanded the *Windsor* at the Second Battle of Cape Finisterre, was in charge at Plymouth with the rank of commodore.]

---

[1] Rowley was one of the captains captured in Aug. 1758 while supervising the re-embarkation of the troops at St Cas Bay. He had recently been exchanged.

231. *Hawke to Hervey*

Ramillies off Brest
23 July 1759

Sir,

Your behaviour yesterday gave me the greatest satisfaction and merits the highest approbation. I had an additional pleasure, too, that of there being so many witnesses of it. I sincerely thank you, Sir, for your conduct and bravery and beg farther that you will, in a public manner in my name, thank your officers and company for their gallantly seconding your endeavour to destroy the enemy.

I have too just an opinion of your discretion, conduct, and resolution to doubt the utmost's being performed in every service on which you shall be employed. But I cannot think of running the risk of disabling three ships of the line for an object so inconsiderable as a privateer and four or five empty transports—for such they are. You will therefore send back to me the *Montagu, Juno* and *Pluto*, and continue with the *Achilles* and *Colchester* to watch the motions of the enemy in Brest Road. I am etc.

232. *Clevland to Hawke*

23 July 1759

Sir,

The present pressing call for frigates having put my Lords Commissioners of the Admiralty under a necessity of taking the *Coventry* [(28), Captain Burslem] from under your command to be employed on another service, I am commanded by their Lordships to acquaint you therewith, and am etc.

233. *Hawke to John Ommanney, Victualling Agent at Plymouth*

Ramillies off Brest
23 July 1759

Sir,

Several of the commanders of the King's ships under my command, whom I have sent in to refit at the port of Plymouth, having complained to me that they meet with great delays and neglect from the office under your direction, which have greatly obstructed the service and, if continued, will oblige me to break up the squadron watching the motions of the enemy, I desire you will use your best endeavours immediately on any ship's arrival in the Sound to get her empty casks on shore, and her water and provisions shipped.

The convoy is not arrived, but I observe from the bills of lading that the warranty of the cheese coming by it is near, if not already, expired, in which case the ships' companies must suffer greatly, as they do already by the beer brewed at your port, which is daily condemning. I beg these evils may be remedied and am etc.

234. *Hawke to Ommanney*

Ramillies at sea
24 July 1759

Sir,

This morning the victuallers arrived under convoy of the *Melampe*. The beer brewed at your port is so excessively bad that it employs the whole time of the squadron surveying it and throwing it overboard, so it is my direction that no more of it be sent, as I have dispatched an express to the Lords of the Admiralty to supply the squadron from the eastward.[1]

I likewise desire that the utmost dispatch may be used in sending out all the live bullocks and sheep ordered by the Board.

A quantity of bread from the *Ramillies* will be returned you by the *Elizabeth*. Though not altogether unfit for use, yet so full of weavils and maggots, it would have infected all the bread come on board this day. We had not time to pick it. It is my direction that you receive it into store for port expense, and am etc.

235. *Hawke to Clevland*

Ramillies off Ushant
24 July 1759

Sir,

After writing to you yesterday by the *Swallow* sloop, the western swell tumbled in, which rendered it unsafe for the squadron to remain at anchor off the Black Rock. I therefore weighed in the evening and stood off to my rendezvous, leaving the *Monmouth, Achilles, Colchester, Juno,* and *Hazard* cutter to watch the enemy's

---

[1] For Hawke's similar view in 1747 of the beer from Plymouth, see Documents 30 and 34 above. The victualling service at Plymouth is defended in Dr Rodger's paper on 'The Victualling of the British Navy' cited on p. 226, n. 1. For Clevland's minute on the subject, see Document 249 below.

motions. At sun rising this morning, I sent the *Temple* and *Firm* to repeat signals between me and them.

At the same time I was joined by the *Melampe* with twenty-one victuallers from Plymouth which we are clearing with the utmost dispatch. The beer brewed at Plymouth is in reality so little relief to the squadron that I have sent in orders to send me no more of it. Our daily employment is in condemning of it, which embarrasses us in many ways. I have therefore sent this express to entreat their Lordships will send us beer from the eastwards as far as possible, and directly to the rendezvous without touching Plymouth. In case of not finding me there, [it should come to me] off St Matthews Point where I shall mostly be while the wind shall be easterly. I have sent in the two fireships to clean, for as they are, with their utmost efforts they cannot keep up with me.

The *Coventry* is just arrived and brought me your letter of the 19th. I am extremely glad to find their Lordships have ordered bullocks and sheep for the preservation of the sick [224]. I hope such numbers will be sent as the ships' companies may have a share to prevent their falling down in scorbutic disorders.[1]

In my former [letter] I sent their Lordships the disposition I had made of the squadron. I never desired or intended to keep more line of battle ships than equalled the number of the enemy, which is now augmented to twenty-two. I have at present twenty-three and seldom have had more than twenty-four, and that only during a day. If ships take up a month by cleaning from the time they leave me to their return, it will be impossible for me to keep up the squadron. The only practicable way is to heel, etc., and confine them to ten days in port for the refreshment of their companies, in case they should miss the spring.

I have detached the *Melampe* to join Captain Duff [in Audierne Bay] and the *Coventry* to Captain Hervey, intending to send the *Juno* in convoy to the victualler.

As soon as the wind shall be fair, I shall send in the *Mars* and *Hercules*. I am etc.

---

[1] Since Hawke's time, medical science has emphasized the role of vitamin C in preventing scurvy. However, the efficacy of *fresh* meat has recently been reasserted. See Rodger, *Wooden World*, pp.86–7 (and his paper on scurvy to which he there refers). Certainly, the health record of Hawke's squadron was remarkable. See also Document 242 below for Ady. orders in this regard.

236. *Hawke to Hervey*

Ramillies at sea
26 July 1759

Sir,

I have received your letter by the cutter. The *Temple* is off the Black Rocks, the *Firm* in sight of her, and the *Montagu* without her, to repeat signals from you. The victuallers have kept me off these two days, but I am now standing in again.

I desire you will dispatch the *Colchester* to Audierne Bay with directions to look for Captain Duff in the direct track between that and Port Louis. If you cannot take all the provisions and water sent to you, put the remainder on board the *Colchester* to carry to Captain Duff. Tomorrow I shall send the *Revenge* or *Dunkirk* under your command. I am etc.

237. *Ommanney to Hawke*

Plymouth Victualling Office
27 July 1759, ½ past 8 p.m.

Sir,

I have this minute received your commands of the 23rd instant and am greatly concerned that some of the commanders of the ships that came here to refit should complain of the detention of their ships by neglects of any duties under my direction. I flatter myself, Sir, if you knew the duty that have been done here, loading out twenty-two sail of victuallers, unlading them of their empty casks, staves, hoops, etc., and the unlading a number of victuallers here with stores and provisions for the Office, and victualling the sundry men of war that have been lately here, and with the interruption of winds and weather sometimes, you would think the complaint groundless. I beg leave to say that no part of duty was ever knowingly omitted by me, and I hope the date of the demands and the time of their being complied with, with the considerations above, would acquit me of the charge. It was ever my whole attention and ever shall be, to give the utmost dispatch to business as possible and to give satisfaction to every commander. The *Hero* being getting under way, beg you will please to excuse my saying more at present than that I am, with the greatest respect etc.

238.　Hawke to Clevland

Ramillies at sea
29 July 1759
Ushant E ½ N., 5 leagues

Sir,

Since my last of the 24th, nothing material has happened nor is the appearance of the enemy changed. On the morning of the 22nd they certainly were twenty-two sail of the line, including the small one of about fifty guns. Ever since the 24th they make only twenty-one, with her. So that it is probable the ship which ran aground and was engaged with the *Monmouth* was hauled into the basin the night after.

The master of a Dutch vessel from Morlaix acquaints me that there are in that port four transports waiting an opportunity to slip to Brest, for which place he saw 5,000 troops march through.

Two Dutchmen came out of Brest yesterday and say the French fleet is manned and all the soldiers on board; that the French man o'war had about twenty men killed and wounded; but they did not know her name, nor her commander's, for they would tell them nothing relating to them; that the enemy has twenty-one sail of the line ready for sea, with four frigates and two bomb vessels not ready.

The 27th in the afternoon, I sent the *Anson* in for ten days refreshment, with eighteen victuallers under her convoy. The *Juno* goes this day with the other three. I send this by the *Firm*, with orders to clean if she can save the next spring, so that there will be then in port the *Hero, Fame, Bienfaisant, Hercules, Anson* and *Firm.*

I have sent the *Colchester* to join Captain Duff and the *Dunkirk* to Captain Hervey. I am etc.

239.　Clevland to Hawke

30 July 1759

Sir,

I have received and read to my Lords Commissioners of the Admiralty your letters dated the 13th and 16th instant, giving an account of your proceedings, all which their Lordships very well approve.

Their Lordships are perfectly well satisfied at your having taken the four Swedish vessels out of Conquet Road and have sent directions to the Commissioner at Plymouth to cause them to be throughly rummaged, in the presence of the Customs House officers and some person on behalf of the captors, to see if there be any contraband goods on board and report what he finds to their Lordships...

240. *Hawke to Ommanney*

Ramillies at sea
2 August 1759

Sir,
... Immediately on receipt of this, I desire you will apply to the senior captain of the King's ships at your port for a convoy and without a moment's loss of time dispatch a vessel to me with twenty oxen, between 6 and 8 cwt apiece, and an hundred sheep, and to do so weekly till farther order.

Also, that you will supply every ship of my squadron on coming out of port with two or three live oxen and twenty live sheep, with a proportion of hay, provided the sheep shall not be grass sheep, for if they should [be] there is great probability of their dying before they will take to dry meat. I am etc.

241. *Hawke to Clevland*

Ramillies at sea
2 August 1759

Sir,
Yesterday I was joined by the *Hero, Sapphire, Venus, Pallas* and *Actaeon* from Plymouth. I have the pleasure to acquaint their Lordships that in the first arrived safe His Royal Highness Prince Edward who is now in very good health aboard the *Ramillies*.

On the 31st July I dispatched the *Nottingham* [Captain Marshall] to clean, if she could save the approaching spring. This comes by the *Mars* which is to boot-hosetop, etc., and continue in port ten days for the refreshment of her company, which I hope will stop the progress of the scurvy amongst them. There are now in port the *Fame, Bienfaisant, Hercules, Anson, Firm, Nottingham* and *Mars*.

I have detached the *Sapphire* to relieve the *Minerva* under Captain Duff's orders. I cannot help wishing for another 50–gun ship to relieve the *Rochester*. For the *Colchester* [(50)], *Windsor* [(60)], *Sapphire* [(32)], and *Melampe* [(36)] are hardly of strength sufficient for the convoy from Rochefort, the stopping of which is very material, and at present I cannot spare a line of battle ship from the principal object.

I hope their Lordships have ordered a large supply of beer from the eastward.

The *Ramillies* being in want of lower shrouds and collars, topmast shrouds, stays and backstays to all the masts, I beg, as this is probably the time of least hurry in Portsmouth yard, that their Lordships would give directions for having it fitted and ready stretched. I am etc.

Minute: [13 August.] Own receipt. Acquaint him the call for ships is so great off Havre, Dunkirk, and the northward, that the Lords have it not in their power to give him another 50–gun ship and were so pressed that they had ordered the *Rochester* from under his command; but in consideration of what he represents, the Lords direct me to acquaint him that he is at liberty to keep her.

The Lords have ordered him all the beer from the eastward that can be provided, which they are informed is a considerable quantity, also a considerable supply of wine from Guernsey to be sent to him forthwith, and more will be shipped. But as the Lords are concerned to find such quantities of beer condemned, which has been brewed in the King's own brewhouses, the Lords recommend it to him to order one of the flag officers under his command, with some of the captains, to examine the same and report how they find it, that such further measures may be taken as shall be necessary.

Order the Navy Board to provide [what he requires for the *Ramillies*] at Portsmouth and send it to Plymouth to be ready against the *Ramillies* comes in. Let him know it, as 'tis not intended any of the ships should come up to Portsmouth, but that they should occasionally all be refitted at Plymouth; and when there is a number of them together, their Lordships recommend it to him to send the rear-admiral with them.

242. *Instructions from the Lords of the Admiralty to the Victualling Board*

2 August 1759

Having directed the Navy Board to cause four of the transports at Spithead of between two and three hundred tons each to proceed, under such convoy as Vice-Admiral Holburne is ordered to appoint, to Plymouth, there to return their provisions to your office, and to be employed in your service in carrying live cattle to the fleet under the command of Sir Edward Hawke, and to cause the said transports to be properly fitted for carrying the said cattle; you are hereby required and directed to cause live bullocks and sheep to be sent in the said transports to Sir Edward Hawke accordingly, not only for the use of the sick, but for the well men to be served with it by turns.

You are also to provide cabbages, turnips, carrots, potatoes, and onions, and send them for the use of the men on board the said fleet, taking care the pursers account for the same in some of the species of provisions. Given etc.

ANSON
G. HAY
J. FORBES

243. *Instructions from Hawke to Captain James Young of the MARS, 'Senior Officer of the King's Ships at Plymouth'*

Ramillies at sea
2 August 1759

You are to look into the orders of all ships and frigates of the squadron under my command and take care that their respective commanders strictly comply with them, endeavouring by proper applications and directions to the yard, victualling office, etc., that no delays shall be made in their fitting; [also] that immediately on your arrival, you order any frigate that may be ready to proceed with the vessel with live oxen and sheep for the sick of the squadron and signify your order relating thereto to the Agent Victualler. If there should be no frigate at the port ready, you are to send her by first line of battle ship.

You are immediately to dispatch all the cutters at the port to me, giving sealed rendezvous, to be opened when without the Ramhead, to the masters or commanding officers of such as have not before been on my station, taking particular care when any return into port that they do not remain there unnecessarily.

And as I have directed the Agent Victualler, upon any ship of the squadron leaving port, to supply her with two or three live oxen and twenty live sheep for the use of the sick, you are to give directions accordingly and [also] that, when they shall be slaughtered, the weight of their carcasses and the number of pieces into which they may be cut be noted in each ship's log book, and that certificates thereof from the masters and other proper officers be given to the pursers to enable them to pass their accounts; that each person supplied with fresh meat be checked of his salt; that strict care be taken to return by the first victualler the hides and tallow to the Agent Victualler at Plymouth; that on your sailing you leave a copy of these instructions with the next senior officer, with directions for his leaving the like, at his departure, to the next to him, and so on. Given etc.

244. *Hawke to Clevland*

Ramillies off Ushant
4 August 1759

Sir,

The *Southampton* left Plymouth with the *Hero* and other frigates, but in a gale of wind sprung her main trussel trees, to repair which Captain Edgcumbe [of the *Hero*] ordered her into port. She bore up for Falmouth and [finally] joined me yesterday. By her I received your letters of the 23rd and 24th. The *Coventry* is at present within Captain Hervey's command, but I have detached the cutter with orders for her to return to me. When she arrives I shall send her immediately to Portsmouth. The *Fortune* sloop [of 18 guns] has never been with me. A frigate of her size and force would have been of great service.

This morning I was rejoined by the *Bienfaisant*, which now makes the number of line of battle ships in the squadron twenty-one. By her I received their Lordships' order without date for sending in five ships successively to clean, refit, and refresh their companies. In obedience to their Lordships' order of the 1st June, on the 4th ultimo I sent the *Kingston* off Cape Ortegal. The *Windsor* I sent with the two 50–gun ships [*Rochester* and *Colchester*] to cruise between Audierne and Port Louis. The *Fame, Hercules, Anson, Firm, Nottingham* and *Mars* are in port. Their Lordships will give me leave to observe that the relief of the squadron depends more on the refreshment of the ships' companies than in cleaning the ships. By the hurry the latter must be performed in (unless the ship continues a month or five weeks in port, which the present exigency will by no means admit of) the men would be so harrassed and fatigued that they would return to me in a worse condition than they left me. This made me prefer ordering some of them to heel and boot-hosetop only, remaining at rest for ten days in port, and at their departure bringing such a quantity of fresh meat as would keep sweet at this season, two or three live bullocks, and twenty live sheep. The present bottoms of the new ships in particular are better and will last longer than if they were, by cleaning, to be burnt off and get a pease-porridge one in their stead.

However, I shall endeavour to comply with all their Lordships' directions in such a manner as, to the best of my judgement, will answer their intentions of employing me here. For, as to myself, it is a matter of indifference whether I fight the enemy, if they should come out, with an equal number, one ship more or one less. 'Tis true, in obedience to my instructions I send their Lordships from time to time such intelligence as I can procure, which has in general hitherto been from men intercepted in French boats. But I depend not on it. What I see, I believe, and regulate my conduct accordingly.

By the *Bienfaisant*, I have also received your letter of the 18th June.

Our daily employment is condemning the beer from Plymouth, in so much as that article is become very scarce in the squadron. Give me leave therefore to repeat my entreaties for beer being sent with the utmost expedition from the eastward.

Since writing the above, I have fallen in with a small Guernsey privateer from cruising in the Bay. On Sunday sennight she fell in with the *Rochester* and *Windsor*, and gave them intelligence of thirty sail under convoy of two frigates of the enemy being in Quiberon Bay. The *Rochester* and *Windsor* immediately made for that bay, but on arrival found that they had taken shelter in a harbour in the bay. He also reports that there are at Port Louis an hundred sail loaded with stores and provisions destined for Brest, under convoy of seven frigates and armed vessels. I am etc.

[For the Admiralty's letters and reactions of 13 August, see Documents 252 and 259 below.]

245. *The Victualling Board to Hawke*

Victualling Office
6 August 1759

Sir,

We have received your letter of the 29th past, enclosing reports of several surveys on beer, etc., on board His Majesty's ships under your command and are sorry to find thereby that so much beer has been condemned. One of the members of the Board [Captain Robert Pett] is now on the way to Plymouth to inquire the cause of the defect of the said beer and to facilitate the sending out from that port such provisions as you may demand from time to time. We are taking all possible measures to send supplies of beer from hence, Portsmouth, and Dover for the squadron under your command and upwards of eight hundred tons of that specie are now on the way and we are shipping between four and five hundred tons more from hence and Portsmouth, which will be hastened into the Bay as soon as possible. We are etc.

246. *Hawke to Clevland*

Ramillies at sea
6 August 1759

Sir,

Enclosed is the last apparent state of the enemy.

Beer is very short in the squadron and [of] what there is I receive daily complaints.

This comes by the *Coventry* which joined me [from Audierne Bay] this morning. I am etc.

247. *Duff to Hawke*

Rochester at sea
6 August 1759

Sir Edward,

The 5th instant I had the honour to receive by the *Sapphire* your letter dated the 1st and have used all the dispatch possible in completing the ships cruising with me to three months of such species of provisions as came in the victuallers.

The 27th July I stood close in with Port Louis where I saw five frigates and a number of vessels. The 28th, the masters of two Jersey privateers informed me that on the 27th, in the evening, they saw thirty-eight sail, most of them ships at an anchor, in Quiberon Bay; and some fishermen, which the privateers took near the Isle of Hedic, told me it was a convoy from Rochelle bound to Port Louis and from thence to Brest, and that thirty of the convoy were transports with troops on board. The wind being westerly, I bore up for Quiberon, and on the 29th in the morning got sight of, and chased the abovementioned convoy into the River Vannes. These vessels were convoyed by four frigates.

The fishermen likewise told me there was twenty-five transports at Nantes ready to sail to Port Louis to take in troops; and the master of a French barque that came out of Port Louis the 28th in the evening, and was taken that night by the *Weazle*, privateer of Guernsey, told me there was six thousand troops at Port Louis to be embarked in transports expected from Nantes, and that there was a convoy of one hundred sail expected from Bordeaux and that some of the men of war was to come from Brest to convoy them thither.

The 2nd instant, the master of the *Husk*, privateer of Jersey, informed me that on the 29th July he saw a great number of vessels and one large ship at the Isle of Yeu.

Enclosed is the state of the ships under my orders. A great part of the beer they have on board is very bad. I am, with great respect, Sir Edward, etc.

248. *Hervey to Hawke*

Monmouth off Brest
11 August 1759

Sir,

... Captain Clements [of the *Pallas*] has this morning brought me the enclosed account of Douarnenez Bay and he tells me 'tis a very fine one. I will take the first opportunity to reconnoitre it all over...

I have the pleasure to send you under the *Dunkirk*'s care five coasting vessels laden with ammunition, which Captain Clements' vigilance intercepted and took as he was going into Douarnenez Bay. The Frenchmen all escaped ashore. Only one paper was left which Captain Digby will deliver to you and which proves they sailed the 9th from Brest and are intended for some expedition that is going on from the River Nantes. There was another vessel which could not be got off from the rocks. I hope we shall be able to pick up more if they persevere in supplying the deficiency these will make...

Enclosure:

248a. *Report by Clements on Douarnenez Bay*

Pallas
11 August 1759

... The whole bay seemed a very fair one and very good anchoring, with a westerly wind being landlocked at about two miles from the shore; but I could not stand further in to take a survey up, having taken the deep laden vessels which I thought of too much importance to leave by themselves and being little wind and foggy.

249. *Hawke to Clevland*

Ramillies at sea
12 August 1759

Sir,

By the *Fame*, which joined me the 7th instant, I received their Lordships' order of the 30th July to send the *Rochester* to Spithead. I should have complied with it immediately by sending a frigate to call him off from his present service if the weather would have permitted. But ever since, we have had very thick fogs. Their Lordships will see by the copy of Captain Duff's letters [notably 247 above] how importantly he is employed and, by the want of beer in the squadron, that I have it not in my power to send a line of battle ship or even a frigate to relieve him. For the *Bienfaisant*'s beer has been mostly condemned, sixty butts out of a hundred, though received on board the 27th, 28th July and 2nd August. I attempted to distribute it but it stunk so, that my endeavours to render it of use were frustrated. I am distributing that in the *Fame*, yet I am afraid it will prove useless too. I shall also supply the *Actaeon* with beer from the *Venus*. The *Actaeon*'s, received the 20th July, is all condemned.

The *Hercules* left the squadron the 20th July. By letter from Captain Porter of the 5th August, I learn their Lordships have ordered that ship to clean and that he is apprehensive he shall not be able to save the approaching spring. In that case I must not expect her in less than seven weeks from the time of her leaving me, which must prevent another ship's being relieved.

I have also received your two letters of the 30th July. There is some mistake with regard to the *Duke*'s wanting a captain of marines, for in all her returns Captain Ogilvie is named. [The *Duke* (90) had joined Hawke some six weeks before. For a line of battle (25 August) with details of the ships, see Document 258.]

By letter from Vice-Admiral Holburne, I understand the *Fortune* sloop is sailed for Guernsey to bring wine for the squadron. Being ignorant of this, as soon as the frigates joined me I sent the *Southampton* thither for it. Neither of them are yet arrived. Wine, in proportion to the allowed quantity, is not a bad article, but as stinking water must be drunk with it, it will not support a squadron for continuance. I therefore beg leave to repeat my entreaties for beer.

Enclosed is the state and condition of His Majesty's ships now with me. I am etc.

Minute: 22 August. Own receipt. The Lords are sorry to hear the beer is so bad. They have ordered all there is at London and Portsmouth to be sent to him and directed every means to be used to supply the ships under his command with what is good, but the Commissioners of the Victualling inform the Lords that the uncommon hot weather this summer has occasioned the beer to spoil upon moving; whereupon the Lords have ordered a very large quantity of extremely good wine to be sent to him which, mixed with water, they are persuaded will contribute to the health of the men, and is what has has been approved of in all voyages, particularly in the Mediterranean, where ships have made long cruises. But, he says, as stinking water must be drunk with the wine, it will not support a squadron for a conti-nuance—which their Lordships agree to. Therefore they desire to be informed if the water in the ships under his command is worse than the water generally is, and if it be the occasion.

The Lords have writ to the captain of the *Hercules* [Jervis Porter] to hasten him and are much displeased with his delay.

250. *Hawke to Clevland*

Ramillies at sea
12 August 1759, 5 p.m.

Sir,

Since writing this morning I have been joined by the *Dunkirk* [with Hervey's letter of the 11th (248 above) of which Hawke enclosed a copy].

The five coasting vessels I have sent in under convoy of the *Minerva* with orders to clean.

Want of beer and frigates ties up my hands from taking any step with regard to Nantes. I am etc.

251. *Instructions from the Lords of the Admiralty to the Victualling Board*

13 August 1759

Whereas we have received repeated complaints of the badness of the beer sent from Plymouth to the ships under the command of Admiral Sir Edward Hawke, and being apprehensive that the beer may be spoiled by moving of the cask and raising of the lees after it has subsided; you are hereby required and directed to cause a quantity of good beer to be racked clear from the lees and put into other casks and sent to the fleet, to see whether by that means the beer will not keep better; and you are to report to us how the same answers.

And whereas we have directed the Navy Board to cause the provisions to be taken out of two of the smallest transports at Spithead, in order to their proceeding to Guernsey under such convoy as we may appoint, to carry wine to Sir Edward Hawke's rendezvous; you are hereby required and directed to send directions to your correspondent at that island to cause as much wine as the said transports can receive on board over their water to be shipped in them on their arrival, and to hasten them away with it to Sir Edward's rendezvous with all possible dispatch. Given etc.

ANSON
G. HAY
J. FORBES

252. *Clevland to Hawke*

13 August 1759

Sir,

I have received and read to my Lords Commissioners of the Admiralty your letter of the 4th instant...

Their Lordships hope some of your cruisers will have the good fortune to fall in with some of the ships at Port Louis, bound to Brest, as they are persuaded you will cause them to be diligently looked out for. And as there is reason to believe that M. Bompar, with a squadron of seven or eight sail of the enemy's ships, may be on his return to France from Martinique, their Lordships command me to acquaint you therewith, that you may endeavour to intercept him.

I have also their Lordships' commands to acquaint you that His Majesty's ship *Foudroyant*[1] is now ready at Spithead and will proceed to join you immediately, which will make thirty-two sail of the line under your command, including the two 50–gun ships, which their Lordships hope will be a sufficient force for the services entrusted to your care.

---

[1] This powerful 80-gun ship of nearly 2,000 tons had been captured in a remarkable action off Cartagena (in Spain) on 28.2.58. (See Arthur Gardiner and Robert Carkett in the *D.N.B.*; also Rodger, *Wooden World*, pp.56–9.) She had just emerged from extensive refitting and repairs in dock at Portsmouth. It was a rebuilt version of the *Foudroyant* that was commanded by John Jervis in the American War.

I sincerely wish you all imaginable success in your undertakings and am with perfect regard etc.

253. *Hawke to Commissioner Pett of the Victualling Board*

Ramillies at sea
14 August 1759

[See also Documents 245 (Victualling Board to Hawke, 6 August) and 249 (the Admiralty minute dated 22 August).]
Sir,

By the *Anson*, which joined me in the evening of the 12th, I was favoured with yours of the 9th. I must observe that, as to myself, I have no farther concern in the complaints but by virtue of the command with which I am vested, issuing orders for surveys on decayed unserviceable provisions when regular complaints are made to me and transmitting the state of the squadron, pointing out the means by which the intentions of its being at sea are frustrated. You must know that complaints from ships' companies are through the channel of subordinate officers carried to the captain, so that every person in the ship is satisfied of the reasonableness of the complaint before it is transmitted to the commander-in-chief. I know not what has happened at Plymouth. But I shall never be induced to suppose that captains would complain or masters (who can have no interest in the matter, and whose faith and bread are materially concerned) would wantonly condemn beer without reason. No, Sir, on the contrary I may have leave to imagine that condemned beer returned to the brewhouse has been reboiled before your officers have surveyed it.

Let me appeal to the reports of the surveys submitted to the Victualling Board and to you. Will it not appear from them that none of the eastern beer has been condemned? Because the materials have been good and skilfully managed. And is not this a demonstration that the badness of the Plymouth beer is owing to materials, either unskilfully used, of bad qualities, or want of a sufficient quantity? Officers of the yard and victualling are not so good judges in these cases as professed skilful brewers.

The means, therefore, of coming at the truth, in my opinion, would be, whenever any quantity of beer should be condemned, to seal up the casks and leave them to the judgement of brewers sworn to do justice, and on oath examine all persons concerned in the brewing of it as to the quantity and quality of the malt and hops, and the manner of treating them. But of this, at greater leisure, I shall write to the Board of Admiralty...

Five vessels of the size of those which brought the bullocks and sheep, every week, will sufficiently supply the squadron...

254. *Hawke to Clevland*

Ramillies at sea
17 August 1759

Sir,

On the 15th, the *Southampton* returned from Guernsey with three sloops which had on board two hundred and thirty-seven pipes of wine, which I have distributed to the King's ships in the squadron.

Last night arrived the *Torrington* with seven victuallers with bread, flour—articles we are not in want of—and about two hundred tons of beer, seven live oxen and twelve live sheep.

I have dispatched the *Juno* with seven empty victuallers for Plymouth. The *Torrington* shall return with the rest.

The foremast of the *Hero* being so badly sprung as to be reported on survey quite unserviceable, I have sent her to Plymouth to refit.

This comes by the *Rochester* and encloses the state of the squadron, with the sentences of the three courts martial. I am etc.

Minute: 23 August... Own the receipt and acquaint him the Lords have ordered an inquiry to be made why such improper species of provisions had been sent to him.

255. *Clevland to Hawke*

18 August 1759

Sir,

My Lords Commissioners of the Admiralty having received intelligence that four of the enemy's ships of war at Brest are to endeavour to escape your squadron and to take under their convoy a great number of merchant ships that are collecting together at Vannes and Paimboeuf, and proceed with them on a particular service, their Lordships command me to send you an extract of the said intelligence, and also of *l'Outarde* being returned from the River St Lawrence to St Andero in Spain. They recommend it to you to send some of your cruisers to learn the state of the transports at the above places and, if they should be come down the rivers, to endeavour to destroy them, and to prevent the enemy from carrying their designs into execution. I most heartily wish you success and am etc.

256. *Pett to Hawke*

Plymouth
21 August 1759

Sir,

I have the honour of receiving your letter of the 14th instant and am apprehensive I have been misunderstood in my intentions in writing a plain matter of fact, in which I did not mean to apologize or excuse anything that may be wrong at this port, or to prevent every inquiry that possibly can be made to find out the cause of this general complaint; neither did I mean by my proposal to find fault with the present practice of hauling beer on deck, but only that what was sent from hence might be drank with the least disturbance during the hot weather, as much the greatest part of it has been brewed since the month of March, whereas I imagine that most, if not all, of that from the eastward was brewed in the winter; and I beg leave to observe that I think there never was such a practice in the King's brewhouse as reboiling beer condemned by survey, nor do I believe that all the reboiling in the world would make stinking beer sweet or sour sound.

I have given directions no more dry provisions be sent till you signify to the contrary, but with all the expedition possible we are shipping the water and live stock. They come in the four transports sent from Portsmouth and are fitted here for that service, and those vessels employed before are now obliged to be used for water.

Permit me, Sir, to assure you I shall omit nothing in my power to give immediate dispatch to the service, and if therein I can meet your approbation, I shall esteem myself happy, being on all occasions with great respect etc.

257. *Clevland to Hawke*

22 August 1759

Sir,

My Lords Commissioners of the Admiralty having received information of the preparations of the enemy at Port Louis, Vannes, Auray, where a considerable number of transports are collected together under convoy of several frigates of war, and that a large body of troops are actually embarked on board the said transports to be employed on a particular service against some part of His Majesty's dominions; their Lordships recommend it most earnestly to you to do everything in your power to defeat their designs by taking or destroying these ships. And it appearing by Captain Duff's letter [247] you have enclosed to their Lordships [see 249] that he has been very active on this station, they wish to have him continued thereon as long as possible, and that you will cause him to be supplied with provisions and water for that purpose, and that you consult him to see if it will not be practicable, with bombs or fireships or both, to destroy the enemy's ships and vessels in the before-mentioned harbours, or wherever they may be, and to give their Lordships your opinion thereon.

And the better to enable you to perform these services, they have ordered the four ships named in the margin [*Falkland* (50), Captain Francis Drake, *Adventure* (32), Captain Matthew Moore, *Maidstone* (28), Captain Dudley Digges, and *Coventry* (28), still commanded by Francis Burslem] to join you forthwith, which is all the force they can possibly spare consistent with the many other services that call daily for ships. I am etc.

258.   *Line of Battle*

Ramillies at sea
25 August 1759

The *Mars* to lead with starboard and the *Hero* with the larboard tacks on board.

Frigates	Rates	Ships	Commanders	Guns	Men	Division
Minerva [32]	3	*Mars*	Capt. Young	74	600	
	4	*Kingston*	Parry	60	400	
Coventry [28]	3	*Belliqueux*	Saumarez[1]	64	500	
	3	*Hercules*	Porter	74	600	
Pallas [36]	2	*Union*	Sir Charles Hardy	90	770	Sir Charles Hardy, Kt,
			Capt. Evans			Vice-Ad. of the Blue.
Proserpine [fire-	3	*Fame*	Hon. Capt. Byron	74	600	etc.
ship]	4	*Achilles*	Barrington	60	435	
	2	*Duke*	Graves	90	750	
Actaeon [28]	4	*Montagu*	Rowley	60	420	
	3	*Bienfaisant*	Balfour	64	500	
	4	*Firm*	Reynolds	60	420	
	2	*Foudroyant*	Tyrrell	80	700	

[1] Thomas Saumarez: L 1744, CR 1747, C 1748. Died 1766.

Sapphire [32]	3	Dorsetshire	Denis	70	520	
	3	Torbay	Hon. Capt. Keppel	74	700	
Venus [36] to repeat signals	2	Ramillies	Sir Edwd. Hawke Capt. Taylor	90	780	Sir Edwd. Hawke, Kt of the Bath, Ad. of the Blue, etc.
Pluto [fireship]	3	Magnanime	Rt. Hon. Ld Visct Howe	74	700	
	3	Monmouth	Hon. Capt. Hervey	64	480	
	1	Royal George	Capt. Campbell	100	880	
Melampe [36]	4	Anson	Whitwell	60	420	
	3	Revenge	Storr	64	480	
Swallow [14]	4	Dunkirk	Digby	60	420	
	3	Temple	Shirley	70	520	
Thames [32]	4	Defiance	Baird	60	420	
	3	Chichester	Willett	70	520	
Southampton [36]	2	Sandwich	Francis Geary Esq. Capt. Norbury[1]	90	765	Francis Geary Esq., Rear-Ad. of the White, etc.
	3	Resolution	Speke[2]	74	600	
	3	Essex	O'Bryen[3]	64	480	
Colchester [50]	4	Nottingham	Lendrick	60	400	
Juno [36]	3	Hero	Hon. Capt. Edgcumbe	74	600	

Given etc.

259.   Hawke to Clevland

Ramillies at sea
28 August 1759

Sir,

On the 25th I was joined by the *Foudroyant* and in the morning of the 26th by the *Mars* as I was standing in for St Matthews Point. By the latter I received their Lordships' order for making a *feu de joie* before the harbour of Brest, on account of the glorious victory gained the 1st instant by the King's troops under the command of

[1] Norbury: L 1742, CR 1757, C 4.6.59.
[2] Speke: L 1745, CR 1749, C 1754. Died on 17.11.60.
[3] O'Bryen: L 1738, CR 1744, C 1745. In May 1756 he fought a hard, ultimately drawn, action — the *Colchester* (50) versus the French *Aquilon* (50). For the loss of the *Essex* on 21.11.59 see Document 327. RA 1770 (being one of those initially passed over but afterwards back-dated to 24.10.70). But he died on 17.12.70. An 'excellent officer' (Rodger, *Wooden World*, p.337).

His Serene Highness Prince Ferdinand of Brunswick over the French King's army commanded by Marshal Contades on the plains of Minden. Though I went in, the weather was too hazy to put it in execution; but at 3 o'clock in the afternoon yesterday off St Matthews Point, in sight of the French squadron, I paid obedience to it; and beg leave heartily to congratulate their Lordships on this signal and glorious victory.

By these ships I also received your two letters dated the 13th instant. I am greatly obliged to their Lordships for leaving to my direction such ships of the squadron as shall be sent in to clean. I have nothing at heart but the good of the service. But, finding ships could not be spared so long as some which were ordered to clean remained in port, and that the new ships' bottoms were very good and their companies, which were raw unseasoned men, so harrassed by preparing for dock and fitting after it that they returned to me in a worse condition than that in which they went, I was thereby induced to alter my plan with regard to some of them, and in particular the large ships. There are now in port the *Hercules, Resolution, Hero, Dunkirk, Chichester* and *Duke*, with the *Minerva* and *Juno* frigates. The latter was so sickly of a mortal distemper that I was under a necessity of sending her in before her turn otherways. By the constant state of the squadron transmitted to their Lordships, they may perceive I never kept more with me than a number equal to the enemy. It may be they may not venture out, but it would not be prudent to leave it in their power. If M. Bompar's destination should be Brest, I shall do my utmost to intercept him. But should he be bound to Rochefort, I must not think of him for the above reason.

The greatest part of the beer from Plymouth brewhouse has been condemned already. As the Portsmouth, Dover and London beer held good to the last, I look on it as a demonstration that the badness of the Plymouth beer was owing entirely to a want of due proportion of malt and hops. However, on the next application for a survey on any of it, I shall obey their Lordships' directions by ordering a flag officer and some captains to examine it.

By the *Diligence* sloop, which joined me in the night between the 25th and 26th, I received their Lordships' order of the 20th to take under my command the *Falkland, Adventure, Maidstone* and *Coventry*, with your letters of the 18th and 22nd and an extract of intelligence.

With regard to Port Louis and Vannes, I was pretty easy, as I had directed Captain Roddam[1] in the *Colchester*, with the *Windsor, Sapphire, Melampe, Pallas* and *Actaeon*, to guard them. And as to Nantes, I imagined their Lordships had been satisfied from the *Brilliant, Deptford* and *Aeolus* which I found had been cruising there. However, on the 26th at noon, I detached Captain Reynolds in the *Firm* to take under his orders the *Colchester, Windsor, Sapphire, Melampe, Pallas* and *Actaeon*, and look carefully into Port Louis, Vannes and Nantes, and if he should not find the enemy there, to make the best of his way to the coast of Ireland in quest of them and, whenever he should meet with them, to make the destruction of the transports his principal object. In case he should find them still in port (which is most probable as their escort of four men of war has not yet slipped past me from Brest) he is directed carefully to examine, in conjunction with the other captains, whether the enemy can be destroyed by bombs, fireships, or both, in any or all of these ports and send his report to me by the *Diligence* [(16)], which I have ordered to return to me in either case, and the instant she shall arrive, I shall dispatch her express either to Portsmouth or Plymouth for their Lordships' satisfaction.

I can form no opinion of those ports but from the French charts. In the entrance to Port Louis, there is 3 ½ fathom water at low water in spring tides. In the entrance of the River Vannes, there is 3 or 4 fathom and room for two frigates to anchor. Farther up, all vessels lie aground. In the mouth of Nantes River is a bar with only 5 feet of water on it at low water in spring tides. The tides rise there about 12 or 13 feet.

Had I not before the receipt of your letter of the 22nd dispatched the *Rochester* to Spithead in obedience to their Lordships' orders, I am afraid I could not have continued her on that service without the

---

[1] Roddam: L 1741, CR 1746; commanding the *Viper* sloop, made a gallant and very successful attack on Cedeiro Bay (near C. Ortegal). Highly commended by Warren and posted July 1747. RA 1778, VA 1779, A 1793.

company's receiving some refreshment in port. It was with great regret that I parted with Captain Duff and hope, as soon as his ship shall be fit for service, their Lordships will send him back to me.

My letter about the wine and stinking beer [249] implied no more than that beer, if it could be furnished, was preferable for the preservation of the men's health. The little fresh meat we have had has already showed itself in very salutary effects.

This morning I was joined by the *Adventure* and the two fireships, with two and twenty sail of victuallers. I have dispatched the *Adventure* to Captain Reynolds.

Enclosed is the state and condition of His Majesty's ships now with me. I am etc.

260. *Hawke to Clevland*

Ramillies at sea
3 September 1759

Sir,

About noon of the 31st August I was joined by the *Success* from Plymouth and, in the evening, by the *Falkland* with seven victuallers from Portsmouth. That same evening I dispatched the *Sandwich*, whose company was very sickly, to Plymouth with nineteen sail of empty victuallers under her convoy. [Meantime, Geary had shifted his flag on board the *Royal George*.] Next morning I sent the *Falkland*, the *Pluto* fireship, and a vessel with bread and beer to Captain Reynolds off Port Louis, and the *Success* with a beer vessel to Captain Hervey. The latter is not yet returned.

Enclosed is the apparent state of the enemy's squadron the 30th ultimo; also a complaint from Captain Hervey against the master of the *Prince Edward* cutter, with the state and condition of His Majesty's ships now with me. I am etc.

Enclosure 1:

260a. *Copy of a Report by Hervey*

Appearance of the French Fleet from the *Monmouth*'s quarter-deck, August 30th, 1759, at noon:

Camaret Point S.E. by S. about four miles.

Twenty-two sail of the line and three or four frigates in the same position as before to appearance.

Their flags flying as usual.

The ship with a cornette scraping his topmast and his ship on the heel.

One ship his main topmast down unrigged.

Two with mizen yards down.

One with lower yards down.

All with topgallant yards down.

Enclosure 2:

260b. *Hervey to Hawke*

Monmouth
30 August 1759

Sir,

I hope you will do me the justice to believe I am ever sorry to trouble a commanding officer with complaints, but I have so long bore the want of diligence and the surliness of the master of the cutter, I think it will be neglecting my own duty not to acquaint you of his insolence as well as specie of mutiny (if he is in the service) and I therefore beg to send you the enclosed complaint of him, and hope you will make some example of him, or transmit my letter and complaint to the Admiralty, as I believe you will find in these circumstances a very proper and timely example to the rest who are much of the same style to every officer, unless immediately to your own person, where only they have some respect and are under some restraint. I am, Sir,

Your most obedient and most humble servant,[1]

A. HERVEY

August the 29th, 1759, about 5 o'clock p.m. The *Prince Edward* cutter, Thomas Gittens master, joined me with the fourth lieutenant who I had dispatched to the Admiral the day before.

The lieutenant came on board and told me that the cutter's boat had been much damaged that morning and that the master was come on board to speak to me about her. I sent for him to me—Captains Barrington, Balfour, Lendrick and Fraine [of the *Southampton*] being then with me. When the master, Thomas Gittens, came in I said:

'Master, I am sorry your boat is stove. Can we repair her for you?'

He replied: 'No. She's too bad.'

I said: 'Well, send her on board. We'll try what we can do in the

---

[1] While readers of Hervey's *Journal* appreciate his remarkable qualities, they are unlikely to accept his claim to extreme humility!

morning.' I then perceived he staggered and was very drunk.

He said: 'She is not fit to repair and I'm of no use without a boat.'

I said: 'Indeed, hitherto you have been of very little with one; for you will never keep near me, and the other afternoon I had a signal to speak to you above two hours and a half which the *Southampton* repeated, and you would not come near me.' Upon which Captain Fraine said to him; 'Yes, I repeated your signal a long time and you would not stir.'

'By God,' says he, 'our jib is not so easily handed and I think I am near enough always.'

I replied to him: 'Well, Sir, take care you keep nearer for the future. If you don't, I'll fire a shot at you with your signal which I'll oblige you to pay for.'

He said, pulling on his hat: 'Well, by God, if you fire shot, I'll directly run away from you as fast as I can.'

I then told him I should keep him on board this night to prevent his deserting and send him a prisoner to the Admiral. And this is what exactly passed, word for word, as well as I can recollect, which I am ready to make affidavit on.

Monmouth off Brest, August 29, 1759

A. HERVEY

261. *Clevland to Hawke*

4 September 1759

Sir,

I have received and communicated to my Lords Commissioners of the Admiralty your letter of the 28th past, giving an account ... of the steps you had taken to look into Port Louis, Vannes, and Nantes, and to endeavour to intercept any embarkations the enemy may endeavour to make from those places, which their Lordships command me to acquaint you they approve of.

Their Lordships having received intelligence that M. La Clue sailed with the squadron from Toulon the 5th of last month and that Admiral Boscawen sailed from Gibraltar two days before, they have great hopes that the former will not be able to effect a passage through the Straits; but nevertheless they think it necessary to apprise you thereof, lest he should unfortunately escape Mr Boscawen and attempt to get into Brest or Rochefort, which their Lordships recommend to you to endeavour by all means to prevent, particularly the latter.

The *Rochester* will be docked in a few days and Captain Duff shall be sent out to you again when the ship is ready, with all possible expedition, as you desire...

262. *Hawke to Clevland*

Ramillies at sea
7 September 1759
'Recd. 11th by express'

Sir,

I have received your three letters of the 24th ultimo...

Enclosed is the copy of a duplicate of a letter from the Earl of Bristol[1] at Madrid, sent to me last night by Captain Hervey. Captain Ourry[2] of the *Success* [(24)], who fell in with the packet boat which brought it from Corunna, has not yet joined me with the original. Though it is more than probable that you have, before this can reach you, received the same intelligence, yet I think it my duty to send it express by the *Belliqueux*, which I am obliged to send into port to have the knee of her head repaired.

There are now in port, beside her, the *Hercules, Hero, Resolution, Dunkirk, Chichester, Duke,* and *Sandwich.* I am etc.

Enclosure:

262a. *Copy of Lord Bristol's Report on La Clue*

Madrid
24 August 1759

Sir,

I have just been informed from authority that twelve French ships of the line and three frigates from Toulon, under the command of Monsieur de La Clue, passed through the Straits of Gibralter in the night between the 16th and 17th of this month August, that five ships of the line as well as three frigates have put into the Bay of Cadiz, and it is not known what course the other seven large ships have steered.

Admiral Boscawen, I hear, has weighed anchor from Gibraltar and is gone in pursuit of them.[3]

---

[1] George William Hervey, 2nd Earl of Bristol, was the elder brother of Augustus Hervey. He was Ambassador Extraordinary at Madrid 1758–61.

[2] Ourry: L 1742, CR 1756, C 1757. He had an active role under Howe 1758. Commissioner at Plymouth 1775–83.

[3] On 18.8.59, Boscawen caught La Clue with seven of the line near Lagos. He took three and forced the enemy to destroy two others.

I thought it for the King's service to dispatch one of the packet boats at the Groyn with this important news and, into whatever hands this falls, I desire the contents may be immediately conveyed to Sir Edward Hawke, commander-in-chief of His Majesty's fleet in the Bay of Biscay. I am etc.

BRISTOL

263. *Hawke to Commodore Hanway at Plymouth*

Ramillies at sea
8 September 1759

Sir,

By the *Hercules, Juno* and cutter, which joined me this morning, I have the favour of your letters of the 2nd and 4th instant. Our objects here increase every day and occasions my repeating my desire of an extraordinary dispatch in sending out the *Dunkirk* and *Chichester* and the vessels with beer. The constant condemning the beer from Plymouth in the refitted ships has proved a dreadful stroke upon the squadron, as they, as well as such as have been long out, have been supplied from the pittance sent from the eastward. If the Commissioner and Agent Victualler will answer for its keeping but six weeks or one month, I should be glad of a large supply from thence at once. For, lying to so often for the few victuallers which come at a time is a great obstruction to that narrow watch we are obliged to keep over the enemy. Beside, the weather in all probability will soon prove too bad for sending out the victuallers, and if we should not be supplied before that shall happen, what will be the consequence for the nation?

Except one or two ships, the squadron is very healthy and, for the sake of our country at this critical juncture, I hope will continue. The *Foudroyant* is the worst and I must desire you will, from your late supply, send me by the first ship fifty or sixty able seamen for her...

I have several neutrals on board the *Ramillies* who all behave well and are good and useful men.

I hope there will be no occasion to dock the *Belliqueux*. If there should, I rely on your diligence and activity, of which, without a compliment, I entertain the highest opinion. I am etc.

264. *Instructions from the Lords of the Admiralty to Hawke*

10 September 1759

Whereas the French ships named [below], part of Monsieur La Clue's squadron, have escaped Admiral Boscawen and, it is probable, may intend to get into Port Louis; and whereas we have sent orders to meet Admiral Boscawen to send as many of the ships coming home with him as may be in a condition to join you, or, if none of them are in proper condition, to send into Plymouth such as can be soon got ready and then to order them to join you immediately; and whereas we have moreover ordered the *Royal Ann* [an elderly first rate noticed in 129 above] to proceed to you directly from Spithead and also ordered Commodore Hanway to dispatch away forthwith all the ships of your squadron at Plymouth, except the *Sandwich*; you are hereby required and directed, so soon as you shall be joined by a sufficient number of the said ships, to keep a detachment of proper strength down in the Bay either for intercepting the abovementioned French ships or, if they should get in, to prevent their sailing with any embarkation from thence. Given etc.

ANSON
GILBERT ELLIOT
H. STANLEY

74	*Le Souverain*	50	*Le Fier*
	Le Guerrier		*L'Oriflamme*
64	*Le Fantasque*	26	*La Chimère*
	Le Lion	24	*La Minerve*
	Le Triton		*La Gracieuse*

265. *Hawke to Clevland*

Ramillies at sea
10 September 1759
'Recd. 13 at 8 p.m.'

Sir,

The most satisfactory account I can give their Lordships of the state of the enemy at Port Louis, Vannes and Nantes is contained in the accompanying copies of letters, intelligence, etc., from Captain Reynolds, which were brought me by the *Diligence* [sloop] late in the evening of yesterday.

At the same time joined me the *Windsor* which is so leaky as to have been in danger of foundering. I shall send her into port this day. I am etc.

Enclosure 1:

265a. *Reynolds to Hawke*

Firm at sea
7 September 1759

Sir,

According to your orders of the 26th past, having taken the ships under my command, I proceeded off Port Louis and sent the *Pallas* as near as possible to look in and, having stationed her to watch that port, proceeded with the rest off Vannes and Nantes and sent the *Melampe* to look into the former and the *Sapphire* into the latter. I have enclosed the accounts which the captains of those ships gave me in writing and likewise the intelligence which I received from a Dutch dogger, together with the opinions of all the captains present concerning the destroying the enemy's ships and vessels in the above ports, Captains Clements and Drake[1] being absent—the first gone within the Glenans to fish his bowsprit and the other lost company; but Captain Clements is of the same opinion as the rest in regard to the Ports Louis and Vannes.

I have your order by the *Coventry* for not suffering any vessels to enter the French ports within my station and beg you'll please to give me your farther orders in regard to what shall be done with such neutral vessels as may be going into those ports; for if it be intended to detain them, they will soon be very numerous, and to put hands on board them all will take many men from us, as these are places much frequented.

My station being limited between Port Louis and Nantes, I have fixed the rendezvous S.W. six leagues from Belle Isle; but, from the present circumstances, I think we could better intercept anything bound to Brest if we were to cruise off the Glenans [little islands S.S.E. of Quimper] or anchor within them occasionally, and shall be glad to receive your commands thereupon, and I think a cutter would be necessary upon this service.

Captain Strachan[1] is of opinion that we might take the Isle of Yeu [between Belle Isle and the Isle of Ré] which would certainly be

---

[1] Francis Samuel Drake: L 1749, CR 1756, C 1756. He commanded the *Falkland* (50) 1757–62. RA 1780. Created baronet 1782, for services during the American War. Died in 1789.

a place of great use to us, as it is now to the enemy. As the *Firm* is so very weakly manned, 381 being the whole number mustered, 34 of them sick aboard and an appearance of more falling sick every day, I hope you'll please to order such of her men as may be returned to the fleet from the hospital to be sent to me by the first opportunity.

I have at length distributed the provisions, but taking beer and water out of these small vessels, if the wind be westerly, takes up a vast deal of time and is not to be done if it blows fresh. I wish, therefore, we were to have wine in lieu of beer, especially as it is generally very bad.

The *Sapphire* not joining me till the evening of the 4th instant, when it was too late to assemble the captains for their opinion in regard to burning the enemy's ships, and the bad weather we have had since, has hindered my sending the *Diligence* back till now; and as it blew fresh at W.S.W. and cloudy weather, we were obliged to beat off before the beer vessel could be cleared, which has also kept the *Windsor* till now.

I have enclosed the accounts of the state and condition of the ships and of vessels spoke with. I am etc.

Enclosure 2:

265b. *Minute of a Consultation*

Firm at sea
7 September 1759

Present...:
Captains Reynolds, Roddam [*Colchester*], Moore [*Adventure*], Strachan [*Sapphire*], Clevland [*Windsor*], Hotham [*Melampe*], Jacobs [*Actaeon*], Burslem [*Coventry*], Eastwood [*Diligence* sloop], Johnston [*Pluto* fireship].

In regard to its being practicable or not to destroy the enemy's ships and vessels in the harbour of Nantes, Vannes or Port Louis with bombs or fireships or both, then, the question being put in regard to [Nantes], Captain Strachan's report of a number of ships

---

[1] Strachan: L 1747, CR July 1756 (appointed by Hawke at Gibraltar). Posted by Hawke, Sept. 1756. In 1757, when commanding the *Experiment* (20) he took the privateer *Télémaque* (20) in a celebrated action. Commanded the *Sapphire* (32), 1757–62 (including all of Hawke's campaign of 1759). Succeeded as 3rd baronet, 1765. Died in 1777.

laying in Pierre Percée Road on the 4th instant being laid before us, the pilots of the several ships were examined concerning the said road, and we are unanimously of opinion, from the examination of the pilot of the *Firm* who is the only one that knows the place, that if each ship had proper pilots, the said ships, if they remained in Pierre Percée Road, might be destroyed; and as to Port Louis or Vannes, we are likewise unanimously of opinion, from what knowledge we have of those places, it does not appear to be practicable.

J. REYNOLDS	W. HOTHAM[2]
R. RODDAM	MAX[N] JACOBS[3]
MATT MOORE[1]	FRANCIS BURSLEM[4]
JOHN STRACHAN	JOSEPH EASTWOOD[5]
ARCH[D] CLEVLAND	JAMES JOHNSTON

Enclosure 3:

265c. *Report by Hotham*

An account of vessels seen in Morbihan Harbour, 31st August 1759:

1 frigate, yards and topmasts struck
4 ships ⎫
2 snows ⎬ appeared to be merchant ships
2 doggers ⎭
1 polacre

10 sail in all

Enclosure 4:

---

[1] Matthew Moore: L 1743, CR 1748, C 1756, RA 1780.

[2] Hotham: L 1755 with Hawke in the *St George*; also with him in the *Ramillies* 1756. Hawke (1756) appointed Hotham to command the *Fortune* (14) in which he took a powerful French privateer and was posted 1757. He continued very active during the Seven Years War and also during the American War. RA 1787, VA 1790, A 1794. Rather ineffective as c.-in.c., Mediterranean 1794–5. Created baron in Irish peerage 1797.

[3] Jacobs: L 1752, CR 1757, C 1758. Died in 1780. (Captains lacking exceptionally influential patrons or connections often, even where meritorious, had to wait at least twenty-five years from first posting to flag. As various notes in this Part have already indicated, quite a number of Hawke's captains fell short on longevity.)

[4] Burslem: L 1743, CR 1757, C 1759.

[5] Eastwood: L 1743, CR 1757.

265d.   *Report by Reynolds*

Intelligence from Ietse Wouters, master of *The Two Brothers*, a Dutch dogger from Nantes bound to Hamburg with wine and brandy, spoke with 31st August between Belle Isle and Nantes:

In Nantes River, there is a King's frigate between 30 and 40 guns, and two privateers in the French King's service of about 20 guns each, with about 25 or 30 sail of transports, as he believes, and many soldiers—the number he cannot tell. But, from what they report ashore, there are between ten and fifteen thousand ready to embark; but he thinks they have no design to come out, nor does he believe there are so many soldiers as is reported.

Enclosure 5:

265e.   *Strachan to Reynolds*

Sapphire at sea
4 September 1759

Sir,

Agreeable to your order of the 31st of last month to stand into Nantes River, in order to discover the number of the enemy's frigates and transports that may be lying there, we stood in till half past 6 that evening and discovered a cluster of ships in Pierre Percée Road, some of which appeared to be frigates. Am prevented from giving you a more particular account as my pilot would stand no nearer in, the wind not being far enough to the northward, the tide of flood made, and night coming on. I am etc.

Enclosure 6:

265f.   *Roddam to Hawke*

Colchester off the Isle of Groix
29 August 1759

Sir,

I beg leave to inform you that since I was favoured with your orders to command here, I have done everything in my power strictly to put them into execution and fancy I may venture to assure you nothing has escaped towards Brest within my district. The French frigate *Félicité* of 36 guns and an armed snow, who had long waited an opportunity of pushing for that place, [on] August the

21st, early in the morning, both got under sail between the Glenans and the main, upon which I ordered a frigate round to the north-ward passages and, notwithstanding the pilots were unacquainted, we pushed on with all the ships. Upon seeing this, they both run into Conquernan, which place I hoped we might come at; but, upon examining the pilots and a French fishing boat we had taken, the entrance was found so very narrow and rocky that it was thought a thing not practicable. However, Sir, I have the pleasure to acquaint you that there is good and safe anchoring between the Glenans and the main for all the Navy...

P.S. ... The fishing boat I took gave us an account of seven frigates and one hundred and fifty sail at Port Louis, bound to Brest with wine and other things for the fleet there.

Enclosure 7:

265g. *Report by Clements*

An account of ships and vessels lying at Port Louis this 29th day of August 1759, seen by Captain Clements, commander of His Majesty's ship *Pallas*; the fort bearing at the entrance of the harbour N.N.E., distance three miles, and the castle upon the Isle of Groix W. three miles distant.

Five frigates, one of which had no topgallant yards up, lying abreast of Port Louis town. In every respect they appeared to be ready for sailing. Several small ships, snows, etc., to the number of eighteen, which to all appearance belong to merchants, lay near the frigates with their sails bent. Higher up the harbour lay seven dog-gers with their sails bent, but whether neutral or not I could not distinguish, as none of them had colours hoisted. Just at the entrance abreast of the fort, a tier of small ships, snows, brigs, etc., lay fastened one to another to the number of eighteen, seemingly loaded, and from appearance coasting vessels. I cannot ascertain exactly the whole number lying there ... but those mentioned I plainly distinguished and rather think there are more, though none of any size.

Enclosure 8:

265h. *Report by Clements*

Intelligence received of the enemy's ships, etc., at Port Louis by Jonas Lowe and William Lattalow, masters of two shallops, the former belonging to Ryentee and the latter to Port Louis, taken the

31st August 1759, near the Isle of Groix, viz.
Frigates: two of 30 guns each; one of 26; one of 24; one of 20; and two of 14. In all respects completed and ready for sailing.

They could not ascertain exactly the number of merchant ships, etc. (there being so many) but from appearance imagined there could not be less than one hundred and eighty large and small, but the largest not exceeding two hundred tons burthen, all loaded with provisions, wine, brandy, etc., and are ready for sea. They came from Bordeaux and Nantes and are destined for Brest. The greatest part of them has been lying in the harbour between two and three months and the rest about five weeks... Two Company's ships are building at Port L'Orient and will be launched in two months time, of 60 guns each.

I inquired particularly whether an embarkation was going on at Port Louis, but was assured for an answer that they had a less number of troops than formerly in and about that port, and not a transport there. But it was rumoured on shore that a number of soldiers had marched to Nantes, and by their acquaintances which are in coasting vessels [they] were told that there were a good number of ships lying in that river; but whether they are intended for an expedition, they could not tell.

266. *Hawke to Clevland*

Ramillies at sea
12 September 1759

Sir,

By the *Resolution*, which joined me this day at noon, I received your letter of the 6th instant with the enclosed from Admiral Boscawen [about the Battle of Lagos]. I heartily congratulate their Lordships on the signal success of His Majesty's arms.

Enclosed is a copy of a letter I yesterday wrote to Captain Reynolds.

In room of the *Resolution* I have sent the *Torbay* in to clean and am etc.

Enclosure:

266a.   *Hawke to Reynolds*

Ramillies at sea
11 September 1759

Sir,

By the *Diligence* which, with the *Windsor* and victuallers, joined me in the afternoon of the 9th, I received your letter of the 7th which gave me great satisfaction. Since you have found the enemy in the ports you was directed to look into, nothing now remains but to prevent their coming out, or escaping if they do. For this purpose I would have you station one of the 50-gun ships and at least three or four frigates to cruise N. and S. off the west end of the Isle of Groix to cover Port Louis, which is now become the principal object; two frigates off Nantes, which in bad weather may come to an anchor just within the Cardinals in the entrance of Quiberon Bay; whilst you in the *Firm*, with the *Pluto* and the other 50-gun ship [*Colchester* or *Falkland*], shall cruise off the north end of Belle Isle at the distance of four or five leagues, so as best to support your cruisers of each side, keeping frigates constantly running between you and them with proper signals to make on discovery of an enemy and [of] the course they shall steer.

The Isle of Yeu at present ceases to be an object, both as lying outside the limits of your cruise and as the taking it must draw off great part, if not the whole, of your force which can and must be more importantly employed.

My orders were not to suffer any neutral vessels to enter those ports. I did not mean that they should be stopped, unless found with contraband effects, only that they should be sent off that coast.

As soon as wine shall be sent me—and I expect it every day—I shall detach a supply for the ships under your orders. Whenever any ship is to leave you by my order, you are to distribute all her provisions of every species among those that remain with you.

Whenever any of the *Firm*'s men return from hospital, they shall be sent to her. I am etc.

P.S. You are to send the *Success* back with the first material intelligence.

267. *Milnes to Hawke*

Admiralty Office
14 September 1759

Sir,

Having received a letter from Vice-Admiral Brodrick dated 26th August, of which the enclosed is a copy, informing my Lords Commissioners of the Admiralty that he had an account of five ships of the line (three of 64 and two of 50) with three frigates, part of M. de la Clue's squadron which escaped from Admiral Boscawen, being got into Cadiz and that he was cruising between Cape St Vincent and Cape St Mary to watch their motions, by which it appears that only the two remaining ships of 74 guns of the said French squadron can be shortly expected at any of the ports in the Bay of Biscay; and as it therefore seems unnecessary for you to make any immediate considerable addition of strength upon that account to the ships down the Bay, I am commanded by their Lordships to acquaint you that they have directed the ships of Admiral Boscawen's squadron to be cleaned and refitted upon their arrival, instead of proceeding to join you as soon as possible. I am etc.

268. *Secret Instructions from the Lords of the Admiralty to Hawke*

14 September 1759

Whereas you have transmitted to us in your letter of the 10th instant copy of a letter dated the 7th, which you received from Captain Reynolds of the *Firm* who commands the ships you have stationed down the Bay, together with the copy of a consultation he held on that day with the captains of those ships in relation to the practicability of destroying the enemy's ships and vessels in Nantes, Vannes, or Port Louis [Document 265b]; and it appearing thereby that the captains were of opinion, grounded upon the examination of the pilot of the *Firm*, that if each of their ships had proper pilots, the enemy's ships in Pierre Percée Road might be destroyed; and whereas we have directed any pilots that may be at Portsmouth or Plymouth, acquainted with the French coast down the Bay, to be sent out to you by the first ships which go thence to join you; you are hereby required and directed, if you can collect a sufficient number of proper ones from them and from the ships of your squadron that are with you, to send them away as soon as possible to the ships which are down the Bay, with directions to their commanding

officer to endeavour to take or destroy the enemy's ships in Pierre
Percée Road, in case he continues to think the attempt practicable
without exposing the King's ships to greater hazard than shall be
proportionate to the importance of the object. Given etc.

ANSON
GEO. HAY
GILB. ELLIOT

269. *Hawke to Clevland*

Ramillies at sea
15 September 1759

Sir,

On the 13th I was joined by the *Resolution* and *Spy, Dorsetshire*,
and *Prince Edward* cutters...

By them I received their Lordships' order of the 5th directing not
to impress any men regularly protected, also your letters of the 4th
and 5th. In obedience to their Lordships' directions signified in the
first [Document 261], I have sent the *Dorsetshire* [Captain Peter
Denis], *Resolution* and *Coventry* to cruise east and west from the
entrance into the Pertuis d'Antioche seven or eight leagues, purposing that they shall be reinforced by the *Firm* when the *Rochester*
arrives, and the *Chichester, Dunkirk, Thames* and *Swallow* [for
details of which see 258], for whose immediate joining me I have sent
directions to Plymouth.

I could not detach any ship till I was joined yesterday by the
Penguin with two transports with 313 pipes of wine. I have sent one
of them under her convoy with 36 pipes to Captain Hervey, and 100
to Captain Reynolds, to be distributed to the ships under their
orders. Tomorrow morning I shall send the other to Plymouth under
convoy of the *Proserpine* [fireship], whose captain being promoted to
a post ship, I have a second time appointed to command her
Lieutenant Robert Taylor, first of the *Ramillies*, in hopes he may
some time or other fall into the channel of preferment...[1]

Yesterday I was joined by the *Hero* and this day by the *Duke* and
Maidstone. The latter I have sent to Captain Reynolds to replace the
Coventry.

Enclosed are seven opinions concerning cannon locks and tin
tubes. In mine, both of them will be very useful. I am etc.

[1] It was another fireship, the *Pluto*, which Taylor had commanded in June (Document 201 and p. 227, n. 2. For the outcome, see Document 275.

270. *Hawke to Clevland*

Ramillies at sea
18 September 1759

Sir,

By the *Swallow*, which joined me on Sunday evening last [the 16th] with twenty victuallers, I received their Lordships' order of the 10th. You will perceive by mine of the 15th that, to the utmost of my power, I had anticipated it. In my opinion Nantes, Vannes and Port Louis are sufficiently guarded, and the *Dorsetshire* and *Resolution* [suffice] before Basque [Road] till the ships arrive from Plymouth; so that, since it is certain that Mr Brodrick has blocked up the five sail and three frigates in Cadiz, Brest and Port Louis still remain my principal object.

By the same sloop, I have received and have delivered the nine commissions enclosed in your letter of the 11th.

Last night I was joined by the *Rochester* from Portsmouth and immediately dispatched Captain Duff to take the ships and frigates off L'Orient under his orders.

Enclosed is a copy of a letter I received last night from Captain Hervey with the state and condition of His Majesty's ships now with me. I am etc.

270a. *Hervey to Hawke*

Monmouth off St Matthews Point
17 September 1759

Sir,

I hope the *Southampton* has joined you ere this, by which you will have had the enemy's position and also the state of these ships...

The enemy got a very small ship in yesterday of about 10 or 12 guns that came through the Passage du Four; and though the *Nottingham* and *Bienfaisant* slipped when she appeared, 'twas in vain—a lee tide gives them that advantage. The enemy was yesterday in the very same position. I have spoke with two Spaniards come out of Brest who confirm the very number of ships I have sent you an account of, Sir. One of them indeed says there are thirty sail of ships in all, great and small, men of war and merchant ships—which you see, Sir, is much the same thing. He says they are much dejected at Mr Boscawen's success.

I yesterday had so very fine a day, and consequently so fine an opportunity, that I could not help stripping the small island of Molène of all their cattle, and I laid the great island of Molène under contribution for cattle, which was quickly complied with...

271. *Hawke to Captain Alexander Hood*[1]

Ramillies at sea
19 September 1759

Sir,

As I think it necessary till the issue of your trial to suspend you from the command of His Majesty's ship *Minerva*, you are to take notice that you are suspended accordingly and to remain in a state of confinement on board the said ship till called upon to attend the court martial on board the *Union*.[2]

As I intend, if possible, that your trial shall begin tomorrow, I desire you will prepare your evidence, being charged with not complying with the 12th Article of War, and not having done your utmost to take or destroy three of the enemy's ships and two smaller vessels on the 17th instant. I am etc.

272. *Hood to Hawke*

Minerva at sea
19 September 1759

Sir,

I have your letter acquainting me with my suspension. As I am prepared for my court martial, I hope you will bring on my trial tomorrow. Sir, I have etc.

---

[1] Alexander Hood was Samuel Hood's younger brother: L 1746, CR 1756. C 1756 (being sent out to Saunders in the Mediterranean as flag captain, at that RA's request, and was with him till mid-1758). Commanded the *Minerva* (32) 1759–62. Recaptured the *Warwick* (originally of 60 guns) from the French 1761. Served in Palliser's division at Ushant (1778) and gave controversial evidence against Keppel afterwards. RA 1780, VA 1787, A 1794. He was Howe's third-in-command on 1.6.94 and commanded in the Channel 1795–1800. Created Baron Bridport 1794; Viscount 1801.

[2] Hawke turned again to his 1st lieutenant, Robert Taylor, to fill the vacant command. It was Hood's own 1st lieutenant, Samuel Swinton (L 1748), who had brought the charge against him, so he was also disqualified.

273.   *Hood to Hawke*

Minerva
21 September 1759

Sir,

It is impossible for me to express my unhappiness on the prospect that my trial cannot be brought on. I am confident, Sir, my trial cannot take up half an hour, as there is not one officer or a single man in the ship that has not offered to appear in justification of my conduct and will prove that everything was done to take, burn, and destroy the enemy's ships and was effectively executed. For God's sake, Sir, bring on my trial tomorrow if possible and relieve me from the burthen I feel in being a prisoner here, when there is a prospect of the ships being in action. If my trial cannot be brought on here, I hope you will send the ship to England with me and transit my accusation to the Admiralty, as I cannot support my present situation. I am etc.

274.   *Hawke to Hood*

Ramillies
21 September 1759

Sir,

Being as impatient as you can be to release you from your disagreeable situation, I gave orders for your trial coming on yesterday. Three of the Brest squadron being out occasioned putting it off. As the enemy is in motion, I am afraid it must be delayed while the wind continues easterly, as I must prefer watching them to all other business. But should it appear to be set in for any time, I shall readily comply with your request and send the *Minerva* to England, as I have nothing more at heart than relieving you from your present unhappy situation. I am etc.

275.   *Milnes to Hawke*

Admiralty Office
21 September 1759

Sir,

I have received and read to my Lords Commissioners of the Admiralty your letter of the 15th instant, giving an account of your proceedings with the squadron under your command.

Their Lordships having received an account of Monsieur Bompar's sailing with his squadron (a list of which [see 288] comes enclosed) from Martinique for St Domingo and may probably be soon expected home, they command me to recommend it to you to keep a proper strength down the Bay to intercept them; to enable you to do which the *Sandwich, Belliqueux* and *Torbay* are ordered to join you from Plymouth as soon as possible and the ships that came home with Mr Boscawen, which are gone into Portsmouth Harbour to clean, will be sent to you as fast as they are ready. I am etc.

[P.S.]   Their Lordships have appointed Lieutenant Taylor to command the *Arthur* armed vessel on your recommendation.

276.   *Hawke to Hood*

Ramillies
22 September 1759

Sir,
    As the wind seems to be set in easterly, and while it shall continue so, the state of the enemy will not admit of bringing on your trial, if you will signify to me in writing your desire to be sent into port, in order to relieve you as soon as possible I will immediately recall the order from Sir Charles Hardy and transmit the complaint to the Board of Admiralty.
    I likewise desire you will send me, by this opportunity, an account in writing of your proceedings on the 17th instant. I am etc.

[Writing the next day, Hood thanked Hawke for his 'very friendly and feeling letter'. He said that, 'upon reflection', he had decided to remain on the station until his trial could be held.]

277.   *Duff to Hawke*

Rochester in Quiberon Bay
23 September 1759

Sir,
    I had the honour to write to you by the *Success*, acquainting you that the enemy's convoy from Nantes was got in the Vannes and Auray [Rivers]. Captain Philips [of the *Juno* (36)][1] who was within gun shot of them when they came out of Nantes says they consisted of sixty-eight sail, thirty-seven of which were ships from two to seven

---

[1] Philips (later Towry): L 1742, CR 1756, C 1757. Died 1762.

hundred tons, twenty of them large snows and brigs. The others appeared to be coasters.

Captains Reynolds, Philips, Johnston [of the *Pluto*], and myself have been on a small island, about one mile and a half from the harbour's mouth, to reconnoitre. The frigates that escorted the last convoy, with between thirty and forty ships and vessels, lie in the mouth of the River Auray. The others are dispersed in the different branches of the two rivers where it would be difficult to come at them. Should it be judged proper to attempt the destroying the enemy's ships in the Rivers of Vannes and Auray, some more ships of force, with bombs, fireships, and armed ships of a small draught of water will be necessary, and pilots that are acquainted with the rivers, as none of those now here are acquainted further than the mouth of the harbour of Morbihan. I am etc.

[This letter did not reach Hawke till 3 October. See Document 286 below.]

278. *Hawke to Clevland*

> *Ramillies* at sea
> 23 September 1759
> St Matthews Convent NbE., 3 miles
> 'Answered 3 Oct.' [Document 287]

Sir,

About 10 o'clock in the morning of the 20th, the *Southampton* [(36), Captain Fraine] brought to my rendezvous an account from Captain Hervey that, about 5 p.m. of the 17th, three large ships appeared, coming out of Brest under an easy sail. I immediately sent in the *Anson* and *Revenge* to support him and worked in with the squadron with a fresh gale at E.S.E. At ½ past 11 p.m., I received an account by the *Triton* cutter that they had got in again to an anchor in Brest water.

In the evening of the 17th, they came to an anchor in Camaret, a little bay at the mouth of Brest, which is commanded by all the cannon and mortars with which the entrance is lined. Captain Hervey that night ordered the *Montagu* and *Nottingham* to guard the passage between the Black Rocks and the Parquet and, weighing in the *Monmouth* with the *Achilles* and *Bienfaisant*, continued all that night within three miles of the Passage du Raz to prevent their getting through that way. This disposition was made early enough for the enemy to perceive it.

The morning of the 18th, he discovered them still at anchor and crowded towards them with the wind at E.S.E., but a great swell from the N.W. About noon it fell little wind and veered from the sea. The three French ships got under sail and plied under their topsails, but never stretched out beyond the forts of Mingon or reach of the grand battery of Cornouaille. The wind soon after veering to the northward, Captain Hervey made the signal for the *Achilles* to stay without him to cover the three victuallers which I had sent in to him, and for the *Montagu* and *Nottingham* to weigh and keep between the *Achilles* and him, while the *Monmouth* and *Bienfaisant* got within three miles of the enemy who were attended by above an hundred boats and other small craft. The enemy immediately tacked and crowded all their sail to get into harbour. When our ships, having followed them as far in as they could with safety, hauled out in the evening, the enemy returned from the Goulet to anchor in Camaret Bay.

The *Bienfaisant, Southampton* and *Triton* cutter lay all that night on the lookout, as near as possible. In the morning, after Captain Hervey went in the *Bienfaisant* to reconnoitre them, as he approached they got under sail, as did in the harbour the rear-admiral [Saint-André du Verger in the *Formidable* (80)] and six other ships. But in half an hour, finding their three ships safe in the narrows, the latter came to an anchor again. The three got in, in the utmost confusion, insomuch that the boats were employed in towing them clear of each other.

They returned into Camaret Bay in the evening, but so deep in that there was little probability of their attempting to escape that night; yet, in order to prevent it, Captain Hervey that night kept the *Bienfaisant* and cutter between Toulinguet and Fontenay.

The 20th, it blew very fresh at E.S.E. At 5 a.m. he [Hervey] weighed and plied up to them. The enemy weighed also, while their rear-admiral and four sail more attempted to come out. As the three ships were never above two miles from the Goulet, they got safe to an anchor in Brest water about noon.

During this whole transaction, not one person could be seen on either shore which, on like occasions, used to be crowded with spectators.

On the 19th I was joined by the *Minerva* from cruising to the eastward of Ushant to guard the Passage du Four. Captain Hood acquainted me that on the 17th he chased five sail into a bay by the Isle of Gaspis, one of which, about three hundred ton, he burnt, and drove two more ashore. He received some damage, as [shown] by the accompanying report of a survey, from some small batteries on shore. That the other two might not be got off again, in the morning of the 20th I dispatched the *Venus* [Captain Thomas Harrison] to try to destroy them. I could not send the *Minerva* back as Lieutenant Swinton [the first lieutenant of that frigate] had wrote for an inquiry at a court martial into the conduct of Captain Hood and all the other officers of the *Minerva* in the action of the 17th. Without evidence I would not pretend to judge the merits of the cause [*sic*], but as the complaint against Captain Hood was for a capital crime I suspended him till the issue of his trial, which I ordered should come on next morning. But it blowed so hard, and [the squadron was] working in to St Matthews Point with the wind at E.S.E., [so that] the court could not be assembled. Neither can it while the wind is easterly and while the enemy seems to be in motion. Great inconveniences attend courts martial at sea, more especially in the face of an enemy, and therefore I wish their Lordships would withdraw their order empowering me to hold them.

On Friday I was joined by the *Royal Ann* [(100), Captain Sir William Burnaby] from Portsmouth and the *Chichester, Dunkirk* and *Thames* from Plymouth. The first brought me three pilots whom I shall send to Captain Duff... We can spare none from the squadron in which there are very few, which renders the duty of masters (considering where it cruises) very hard—more particularly of such as conduct squadrons—and I cannot help thinking it reasonable that they should have pilotage allowed them.

If it was practicable to destroy the enemy's ships and vessels at Pierre Percée, I cannot doubt of Captain Reynolds having attempted it long before now.

Enclosed is a list of young gentlemen whom I appointed to act in room of absent lieutenants.

I have received your letter of the 17th and am etc.

279. *Extract from Minutes of Hood's Court Martial*

Union at sea
24 September 1759

PRESENT:
Sir Charles Hardy, Knight, Vice-Admiral of the Blue
Francis Geary Esq., Rear-Admiral of the White
Sir William Burnaby[1]

---

[1] Sir William Burnaby, Bart. (L 1732, CR 1741, C 1742) commanded the largely port-bound old first rate, the *Royal Ann*, from Aug. 1757 to Feb. 1761. While he has

Captain James Young
Captain Richard Tyrrell
Honourable Captain George Edgcumbe
Captain Samuel Graves
Captain William Parry
Captain Lucius O'Bryen
Captain Jervis Henry Porter
Right Honourable Lord Viscount Howe
Captain Washington Shirley
Honourable Captain John Byron

Pursuant to an order from Sir Edward Hawke, Knight of the Bath... The court, being duly sworn, proceeded to inquire into the conduct of Captain Alexander Hood of His Majesty's ship *Minerva*, charged by Mr Samuel Swinton, first lieutenant of the said ship, for not having done his utmost in endeavouring to destroy three of the enemy's ships and two smaller ones on the 17th September 1759; and also to inquire into the captain's reasons for his public declaration respecting the backwardness of some of his officers in not offering themselves for the service of boarding the enemy's ships.

After having maturely considered the evidences on both sides [the court] is of opinion that the said Captain Alexander Hood did on that occasion his duty in every respect as an able and diligent officer in order to take or destroy the said ships, and do therefore acquit him of any censure on that account; and as there does not appear any just grounds for the injudicious declaration of the captain's abovementioned, they do likewise acquit the other officers of any backwardness or misconduct, and they are hereby respectively acquitted accordingly.

CHAS. HARDY
etc.

[Excerpts of the evidence:]
... Lieutenant Samuel Swinton sworn.

On the morning of the 17th instant, the *Minerva* being cruising near Arbobrack, we saw three ships and a sloop and chased them into Arillon Bay. On our seeing them, Captain Hood did not hoist his boats out. We came to an anchor about two miles from them, without sounding with the boats, in five fathom water as the pilot

---

been rated 'an officer with stronger political contacts than professional merits' (Rodger, *Wooden World*, pp. 288–9) he rose rather swiftly to RA 1762 and VA 1770. For his role in 1759, see also Documents 285 and 297 below.

says.

Mr Charles Hay,[1] second lieutenant of the *Minerva*, sworn.

COURT   Relate the proceedings of His Majesty's ship *Minerva*, on the 17th September.

A.   Discovered in the morning about sunrise three sail. I called Captain Hood, who came up. We saw them to be three merchant ships. Soon after, we saw one more which proved to be a sloop. We chased them and got up with them to windward. They anchored in a place or bay. The two first run on shore before the ship which we endeavoured to get off. A small battery, before we came round the point, I believe of two guns, fired upon us. I went to my quarters forward. We fired on this battery which soon ceased firing. We then, on coming round the point, saw another battery. Captain Hood asked the pilot what water. He said five fathom. We prepared to come to an anchor but continued firing. Mr Swinton came forward and said he was going to his quarters in the cabin and I must stay at my quarters. Captain Hood said I need not fire any more. He believed we could take them without. It was a clear day and smooth water. The master went in a cutter before, and I was ordered in the barge to board a ship. I went in her, boarded the ship, and found her aground. I saw the ship the master was in [was] likely to tail the shore. I went to his assistance, then came on board to Captain Hood and told him, and returned to the ship with an anchor and hawser. I came again to Captain Hood and told him the ship had taken the ground... The captain ordered me to go and burn her—the ship the master was in—which I did and came on board again... The captain said he was extremely lucky to get out of so dangerous a bay and I said I thought so too, the wind being nearly in...

COURT   What became of the ship you was on board of?

A.   She was on her beam ends on the side of a very sharp rock and [I] believe she could not get off. Many of the *Minerva*'s shot reached her.

COURT   Was there any musketry fire from the shore?

A.   A great many ... the shot came very thick over us, but nobody was wounded. They fired stones instead of shot...

LIEUTENANT SWINTON'S QUESTION   Was there any other cannon, besides the two batteries, that fired?

A.   I believe there was... I saw some cattle, as I believe, drawing cannon...

[1] Charles Hay: L 1759, CR 1771.

280.   *Swinton to Hawke*

Minerva at sea
24 September 1759

Sir,

I beg leave to acquaint you that for several months past I have been in a bad state of health and of late have been so ill that since the 13th of this month I have been rendered incapable of executing my duty. I therefore humbly beg you would be pleased to grant me leave to quit the *Minerva* till such time as I may recover my health and strength to enable me to execute my duty. I am etc.

[Swinton's request was granted by Hawke on the 25th.]

281.   *Hawke to Reynolds*

Ramillies at sea
26 September 1759

Sir,

By the *Success* last night I received your letter of the 19th and am very well satisfied with your proceedings. I am etc.

[On the 26th, Hawke likewise acknowledged Duff's letter of the 22nd and approved his dispositions. See Documents 282a and 282b below.]

282.   *Hawke to Clevland*

Ramillies at sea
26 September 1759

Sir,

Last night I was joined by the *Success* and here enclose you copies of letters from Captains Duff and Reynolds. I am etc.

Enclosure 1:

282a.   *Duff to Hawke*

Rochester in Quiberon Bay
22 September 1759

Sir,

On the 20th instant I met with His Majesty's ships *Colchester* [Captain Roddam], *Actaeon* and *Coventry* off Port Louis. Captain

Roddam acquainted me that Captain Reynolds with the other ships were in Quiberon Bay, having on the 18th instant chased a convoy that came from Nantes consisting of about sixty sail into the harbour of Morbihan, the particulars of which Captain Reynolds sends you. Last night I arrived in Quiberon Bay and, as the blowing weather makes it uncertain when the victualler can be cleared, I thought it my duty immediately to send you by the *Success* an account of that convoy's being in the Rivers Vannes and Auray. There are only two of the pilots in the ships here that have ever been in the harbour and they have declared to me that they are not acquainted farther than the entrance of the harbour of Morbihan.

I have sent the *Pallas* to join Captain Roddam and to order the *Coventry* forthwith to join Captain Denis [off Rochefort (269)]. As the *Colchester* is very foul, I intend cruising off Port Louis with the *Rochester* and four frigates, and leaving Captain Reynolds with the other ships in Quiberon Bay to watch the enemy's ships in the Rivers Vannes and Auray till I am honoured with your farther orders.

George Mercy, master of the *Burnet* privateer of Jersey, informs me that the men in a fishing boat, which he took yesterday, say they saw on the 17th instant seven sail which they took to be French frigates at an anchor in the Pertuis Breton [just N. of Ré and Rochelle]...

Enclosure 2:

282b.   *Reynolds to Hawke*

Firm in Quiberon Bay
19 September 1759

Sir,

Admiral Boscawen's action with the French which you are pleased to notify to me by the *Prince Edward* cutter gives vast pleasure to all the squadron. I have also your letter of the 11th [266a] by the *Juno* which I shall duly observe. The *Actaeon* and *Coventry* have looked into Basque Road and I have enclosed a copy of Captain Jacobs' letter thereupon [282c].

On the 16th, I had an account from a Guernsey privateer that on the evening before, being in Quiberon Bay, he saw sixty sail under convoy of three or four men of war, one of which wore a white flag at his main topmast head, come to an anchor in Quiberon Bay from Nantes. I immediately went in pursuit of them with the whole squadron, but could not reach the Bay before all the transports got into the harbour of Morbihan... I found it necessary to anchor here, having ordered the *Colchester, Actaeon, Coventry, Adventure* and *Juno* to proceed immediately to guard Port Louis; but the two last could not get out that night and the next morning I judged it proper to have the opinions of all the captains present whether or not it was advisable to attempt the burning the enemy's ships in the harbour, and I enclose their opinions thereupon, together with my own... Upon the whole I think it is now become necessary for most of us to remain here, as I am informed that there is another convoy in this harbour that was chased by the *Rochester* some months ago, in order to keep them in or destroy them if they venture out. I shall therefore immediately send the *Juno* and *Adventure* to join the *Colchester, Actaeon*, and *Coventry* off Groix; another frigate to look into Nantes, as I am informed there are twenty more transports there that were not quite ready to sail with these; and shall remain here with the other ships where we can effectually prevent the enemy from executing their plan of invasion, until I receive your further orders.

The *Penguin* [(20)] arrived with the wine vessel this evening after dark and she shall return according to your orders of the 14th.

The ships are very short of butter and cheese, as well as water, purser's necessaries, and boatswain's and carpenter's stores. A great deal of beer has been condemned, and what they would not condemn is so bad that it disagrees with the people's health; but I hope the wine will relieve them...

Enclosure 3:

282c.   *Jacobs to Reynolds*

Actaeon at sea
16 September 1759

Sir,

Agreeable to your orders of the 11th instant, I run into Basque Road yesterday with the wind at north and brought the Island of Aix to bear S. by E. distant about two leagues, when I could plainly discover that there was none of the enemy's ships laying near that island or in St Martin's Road [N. of Ré], except one frigate (as I judged) of 30 guns with two store ships under her convoy, which I believe were intended for sea. But on our getting within three miles of them, they tacked and stood in when (having reason to expect a change of wind) I did not think it prudent to pursue them any farther [and] accordingly tacked and run out of the road...

Enclosure 4:

282d. *Minute of a Consultation*

Success in Quiberon Bay
19 September 1759

Present: Captains Reynolds [*Firm* (60)], Moore [*Adventure* (32)], Strachan [*Sapphire* (32)], Drake [*Falkland* (50)], Philips [*Juno* (36)], Ourry [*Success* (24)], Hotham [*Melampe* (36)], Clements [*Pallas* (36)], Johnston [*Pluto* fireship].

After reconnoitring the mouth of the river of Vannes, the question being put whether or not it is advisable, with the force we have here, to attempt the burning and destroying the enemy's ships in the said river:

CAPTAIN JOHNSTON: Thinks it is impracticable.

JAS. JOHNSTON

CAPTAIN CLEMENTS: Thinks it is practicable with the loss of some ships. MICHL. CLEMENTS

CAPTAIN HOTHAM: According to the best of my judgement, it appears to me impracticable to enter the harbour without great risk of losing the ships, the situation of it being by nature sufficiently strong to render it very hazardous supposing there were no batteries, nor do I think that, even if the ships were so far to succeed as to get in, they would be able to do the service intended without a sufficient land force; but a part of the squadron being kept at an anchor in Quiberon Bay will be a much more certain method of distressing the enemy and of answering the service the ships are sent upon.

W. HOTHAM

CAPTAIN OURRY: It's my opinion the batteries may be destroyed with the risk of some ships, but I cannot judge what we have to expect when [we have] entered that rapid and narrow river which may be defended from both sides by troops and cannon. We may burn some few ships which I think will not answer the loss of the few ships which we may suffer in destroying the batteries at the entrance of the port. I think it impracticable without troops to cover the boats which must go on that service. PAUL H. OURRY

CAPTAIN PHILIPS: According to my judgement, I think it may be undertaken with a great probability of success and that the advantage will overbalance the risk. H. PHILIPS

CAPTAIN DRAKE: As you have thought proper to communicate your orders to me, I can by no means give my voice for entering the harbour to destroy the transports, so contrary to the tenour of your instructions... Every service wished for and pointed to you by your instructions is in my opinion answered by keeping them in, which may be easily and certainly done by anchoring off the entrance of the Morbihan...   FRA. S. DRAKE

CAPTAIN STRACHAN: Thinks the batteries must not only be silenced but destroyed, in order to secure the retreat, should we succeed in going in which cannot be done without landing...
                                                    JNO. STRACHAN

CAPTAIN MOORE: Thinks it not practicable to destroy the ships (though we enter the harbour) from their situation; but by keeping part of the squadron off the port, we answer the service we are sent on.   M. MOORE

CAPTAIN REYNOLDS: Is of opinion from the examination of the two pilots who are acquainted here, that as the entrance is not above two or three cables length in width, with a rock in the middle and a tide running six knots (and rises and falls four fathom), the ships in the harbour [are] dispersed up the rivers and separated so that the fireship could not perform any important service upon them; and though the batteries are insignificant, a number of troops, as we are informed, being upon the spot might be so disposed as to render our attempt not only fruitless but disable the ships that might get in, so as to prevent their getting out again, by landing the guns of the ships, which appear to be large ones; and especially he does not think it advisable to attempt them as his orders make the keeping the transports in, or destroying them if they come out, the principal object of this squadron's service.   J. REYNOLDS

283. Hawke to Clevland

Ramillies at sea
28 September 1759
'Recd. 3 Oct. by express at ¼ past 1 o'clock p.m.'

Sir,

Since my last of the 26th, I have sent directions to Captain Duff by the *Gibraltar* to reconnoitre once more the entrance of the Morbihan and to try what can be done with the enemy there.

I have sent the *Magnanime* into Plymouth to clean and detached Rear-Admiral Geary in the *Sandwich* (she and the *Belliqueux* having joined yesterday) with the *Chichester* and *Anson* off Rochefort. He will have then, with the *Dorsetshire* and *Resolution*, five ships of the line and the *Coventry* frigate till I can reinforce him. I have, for the better conducting of the twenty-two sail remaining, directed Sir William Burnaby [in the *Royal Ann*] to hoist a distinguishing pendant and command the third division, which I hope will meet their Lordships' approbation. I am etc.

Minute: 4 October. Let him know I have communicated his letter to the Lords who ... think the number of ships stationed off Rochefort too many... [Clevland's actual letter is dated 5 October and comprises Document 289 below.]

284.   *Hawke to Anson*

Ramillies off Brest
29 September 1759

[This is a draft in Hawke's hand except for the words underlined. These words are supplied by Hay in substitution for the Admiral's more involved alternatives.]

My Lord,
I am under great obligations to your Lordship for the favour of your letter of the 22nd and in particular for thinking of me upon this occasion, <u>as I was</u> yesterday joined by the *Sandwich* and *Belliqueux*, which made six and twenty sail of the line. I have thought it most advisable to send Mr Geary in the first of these ships off Rochefort with the *Chichester* and *Anson* to join the *Resolution*, *Dorsetshire* and *Coventry* who are cruising there already [see 269]; and I have <u>promised to send</u> the *Torbay* and *Windsor* to him as soon as they shall arrive. I shall likewise reinforce him with some more ships of the line the instant any shall come from Portsmouth and I shall send him another frigate the moment I have it in my power. I have given him all the hints that I could possibly think of upon this subject, as well as those your Lordship is so good as to mention to me, and which I have desired him to pay a particular regard to, as being very material. I have directed him to endeavour to procure all the intelligence he can and to regulate himself accordingly. I have great hopes of his falling in with the enemy and, as he goes upon this service with the highest good will and inclination and as he is an honest man and a good plain officer, I have not the least doubt but he will do his duty greatly to his own honour and your Lordships' satisfaction.
I hope my sending Mr Geary on this service will have your Lordship's approbation. I declare I have no view in it but that of

serving my country, and of acquitting myself in the most faithful manner both to that and your Lordship.

As I have two and twenty sail of the line with me (a force but equal to that of the enemy, allowing for accidents and incidental service) I find myself under the necessity of keeping up three divisions. I have therefore ordered Sir William Burnaby to hoist a broad pendant and to command one of them till farther orders, which I hope your Lordship will approve of...

When I am obliged to return into port, I hope your Lordship will be so good as to permit me to go to Spithead in the *Ramillies* as it will be very inconvenient to go to Plymouth; and if I may take the freedom to say it, that place is certainly very improper for three deck ships either to lie or to fit at.

I have hitherto kept as close a lookout upon the enemy at Brest as was possible, and I shall use my utmost endeavour to do so while I am on this service; but I am much afraid now it begins to grow late in the year, that the weather will grow bad and not permit us to watch them so narrowly as we have done; but your Lordship may be assured that we will do all we can...

Permit me to say, my Lord, that I shall retain the highest sense of your Lordship's goodness and civility to me, and that I am with all imaginable truth etc.

285. *Hawke to Clevland*

Ramillies at sea
1 October 1759
'Recd. 5th'

Sir,

The supplies of beer and water arrive so slow, and the continual disappointments I meet with from the Plymouth beer, with which the clean ships are supplied, not lasting in a condition to be drank above a week, I am afraid may occasion the breaking up of the squadron. I am now obliged to send in the *Revenge* before the time I intended; and if I should be obliged to do so with more, it may put it out of my power to reinforce Rear-Admiral Geary, even when the ships from Portsmouth shall join me.

The enemy's ships at Brest continue the same as to number and position. They have had, ever since we came here, a schooner in the Goulet to watch our motions. On the evening of the 28th she came to an anchor off Camaret within half musket shot of their batteries. After dark, Captain Hervey went with five barges and about half past one in the morning boarded her, notwithstanding a continual fire from the batteries of great guns, mortars and small arms from the shore, and brought her away. She was commanded by two ensigns of one of the line of battle ships and had thirty-six men in all on board. None of our people were hurt, but ten of the enemy [were] wounded. Except the officers who were in the number, Captain Hervey sent the wounded, after being dressed, into Brest in a small boat he had taken the night before.

The ensigns say the four first ships which came out the 23rd July were the *Dauphin Royal* 70, *Glorieux* 74, *Dragon* 64 and *Inflexible* 64. The three which came out the 17th September were the *Bizarre* 64, *Sphinx* 64 and *Aigrette* 32, directed to join their transports at Port Louis and Nantes. I acquainted their Lordships before that they were drove in again the 20th of the same month.

Enclosed I send you an extract of a letter I received this day from Captain Duff.

I have sent the *Pallas* in to clean. I am etc.

Enclosure:

285a.   *Extract of Duff to Hawke*

Rochester off Groix
30 September 1759

Sir,

Last night I was honoured with your letter by the *Gibraltar* [mentioned in Document 283].

In my letter to you dated the 23rd instant [277] which I sent by the *Penguin* and also in my letter dated the 26th by the *Vengeance*, I acquainted you that Captains Reynolds, Philips, Hotham, Johnston and myself had been on the Island Méaban to reconnoitre the situation of the enemy's ships; that a great part of them were gone far up the different branches of the Rivers Vannes and Auray where, in our opinion, it would be very difficult to come at them; and that there were between thirty and forty ships and vessels in the lower branch of the River Auray. But as they lay much farther up the river than any of our pilots were acquainted and could, on a flood tide, move farther up if we attempted to attack them (which attempt must be made on a flowing tide) and as the enemy had had several days before my arrival in Quiberon Bay to fortify the mouth of the rivers, it was the opinion of those gentlemen, as well as mine, that in the situation we saw them, they could not be attacked with any prospect of success without a much greater force than is on this station and pilots that are well acquainted with the different branches of the two rivers.

Finding the situation of the Rivers Vannes and Auray to be such as makes it impossible for the enemy's frigates and transports to get from thence while we have a superior force in Quiberon Bay, was my reason for leaving the greatest part of the force there, and going with the *Rochester* and some of the best sailing frigates to cruise before Port Louis.

286.   Hawke to Clevland

Ramillies at sea
3 October 1759
'Recd. 7th & answd.'

Sir,

This morning I was joined by the *Windsor* from Plymouth and immediately dispatched her and the *Fame* to reinforce Rear-Admiral Geary.

At the same time I was joined by the *Penguin* which left Captain Duff the 23rd September. Enclosed I send you a copy of his letter of that date [277].

I am obliged to send the *Minerva* in for a recruit of beer before I can detach her on any service...

287.   Clevland to Hawke

3 October 1759

Sir,

I have received and communicated to my Lords Commissioners of the Admiralty your letter of the 23rd of last month [278], giving an account of the proceedings of the squadron of His Majesty's ships under your command and of the enemy's motions at Brest, by which their Lordships observe the enemy's designs to endeavour to send some of their ships to Vannes in order to escort the embarkation from thence to its place of destination...

Therefore their Lordships command me to recommend it to you, in the strongest manner, to do everything in your power to prevent any ships from getting out of Brest and to intercept such as may attempt to get to sea from Vannes, for which purpose they desire you will appoint a sufficient force to guard that part of the Bay, directing the commanding officer to be particularly vigilant whilst he continues on that service.

Their Lordships are sorry to hear any complaint has been made of the conduct of Captain Hood, who they always looked upon as a good officer, and they recommend it to you to cause the same to be inquired into at a court martial as soon as a convenient opportunity presents of assembling one. With regard to withdrawing their order to you for holding courts martial, their Lordships think the same improper and likely to be attended with inconveniences, as occurrences may happen that may require your having that power; but as the intention of it is only to empower you to do it when the necessary services of the squadron will admit, and not to oblige you to do it otherwise, their Lordships conclude you will make use of it accordingly.

In relation to the masters whose duty you represent to be rendered hard by the scarcity of proper pilots, their Lordships command me to acquaint you that they will be considered when the service you are employed upon is over, upon producing proper certificates of their deserving it.

Their Lordships have no doubt of the good conduct of Captain Reynolds and conclude, with you, that he will have done everything that may have been found practicable to destroy the enemy's ships in Pierre Percée Road [at Nantes]; but, as it is very proper and necessary at this critical conjuncture that their Lordships should know as exactly as possible what he may have done and the orders he has received from you, their Lordships desire you will please inform them thereof by the first opportunity.

As their Lordships are desirous of having, as well for their own information as for that of their successors, as accurate draughts and surveys of the French coast as may be, they desire you will please to send them such as you may have collected and that you will order the commanders of all the ships and vessels of your squadron, whom you shall hereafter detach to cruise upon the coast, to make the best remark they can of the soundings, dangers, anchoring ground, and batteries within the limits of their cruise, with their bearings, the flowing of the tides, their setting and the heights they rise, and to make draughts thereof when they have artists on board to draw them, which their Lordships would be glad to have sent to them from time to time, as opportunity offers.

Their Lordships will take care the young gentlemen, whom you mention to have appointed to act in the room of absent lieutenants, shall be provided for when there is a proper opportunity. I am etc.

288. *Hawke to Duff*

Ramillies at sea
4 October 1759

Sir,

I think it proper to acquaint you that M. Bompar, with the ships named in the accompanying list and a numerous convoy, is daily expected to some port in Old France. As the convoy may separate, you'll give directions to the captains under your orders to keep a good lookout for them. As to the remainder of La Clue's squadron, you need not be under the least apprehension, as Vice-Admiral Brodrick blocks them up in Cadiz and Rear-Admiral Geary cruises east and west from the Pertuis d'Antioche, from ten to twenty-five leagues, in the *Sandwich*, with the *Dorsetshire, Fame, Resolution, Chichester, Anson, Windsor* and *Coventry*.

The *Penguin* only joined me yesterday [286]. In case you should find it practicable to attempt the enemy in Morbihan, I have sent the *Prosperine* to you. But if there should be no occasion for them, I desire you will send the *Pluto* and her back to me. I am etc.

List of M. Bompar's squadron transmitted to Captain Duff in this letter:

Le Défenseur	74	*Le Sage*	64
Le Diadème	74	*L'Amphion*	50
Le Hector	74	*La Fleur de Lys*	30
Le Vaillant	74	*L'Améthyste*	30
Le Courageux	74	*La Valeur*	20
Le Protée	64		

289. *Clevland to Hawke*

5 October 1759

Sir,

I have received and read to my Lords Commissioners of the Admiralty your letter of the 28th past [283], giving an account of your proceedings with the squadron of His Majesty's ships under your command. Their Lordships command me to observe that they think the number of ships stationed off Rochefort is too great, since the particular objects of attention at this time are the intercepting the embarkations of the enemy at Morbihan and keeping their ships of war from coming out of Brest, wherefore they recommend it to you to station the ships under your command accordingly; and, having this day received a letter from Vice-Admiral Cotes [at Jamaica] informing them that, on the 26th July, he received certain intelligence of M. Bompar's arrival at Cap François with seven ships of the line, which the Vice-Admiral being of opinion will remain there the hurricane months of August and September before they attempt to return to Europe, the Lords have therefore the greater reason to be of opinion that such a force at present at Rochefort will be unnecessary; but as it will be proper to be early informed of what may be coming into the Bay, they recommend it to you to keep small cruisers to the westward for that purpose.

Enclosed is the intelligence received this day of the enemy's motions at Vannes, by which you will see the necessity of keeping a full sufficient force before that place.

Their Lordships are under great concern at your apprehension of being obliged to break up your squadron on account of the disappointment you meet with in the supplies of beer and water, which they will endeavour to prevent by ordering further supplies of those species, as well as wine from Portsmouth and Plymouth; and they have the satisfaction to hear from Vice-Admiral Holburne that several ships laden with wine and beer sailed from Spithead yesterday, which will enable you to continue on your station, where it is more necessary than ever for you to remain as long as possible at this very critical conjuncture; and that you may be able to do it with a superior force to the enemy, you may expect a reinforcement of three or four ships of the line in a few days. I am etc.

290. *Hawke to Clevland*

Ramillies at sea
7 October 1759
'Recd. 10th Oct. at 7 p.m.'

Sir,

As soon as possible after the receipt of Captain Duff's letter of the 23rd September by the *Penguin*, a copy of which I sent you by express [286], I detached the *Proserpine* to Captain Duff.

Rear-Admiral Geary not having met with the *Dorsetshire* and *Resolution* which rejoined me this morning, I gave orders for the *Hercules* and *Belliqueux* (the only two ships I could detach for want of beer, water and wine) to reinforce him. Before they parted company, by a cutter from Plymouth I received your letter of the 3rd instant and sent a copy of the intelligence which accompanied it to

Mr Geary and another to Captain Duff, directing a proper communication to be kept up between them, in order to settle which, as well as to intimidate the enemy, I have directed the rear-admiral to stand in with his squadron to Quiberon Bay and then return to his station.

Enclosed I send you the only two draughts I have yet received — No. 1 from Captain Ourry [of the *Success* (24)], the other from Captain Philips [of the *Juno* (36)]. Captain Hervey has been some time, by my order, employed in making proper draughts, taking the soundings, etc., about Brest, which, as soon as completed, shall be transmitted to you.

I have sent an express to Captain Hanway for a bomb-vessel, if any at Plymouth.

The officers and company of the *Foudroyant* being very sickly, I am under a necessity of sending her into port tomorrow or next day. As Captain Tyrrell is senior to Captain Hanway, I beg their Lordships will, by express, give such directions as to prevent disputes and the service suffering thereby. I am etc.

Minute: Own receipt. Approve of what he has done. And acquaint him the Lords have writ to Captain Tyrrell not to interfere in the command at Plymouth.

Enclosure:

290a. *Copy of Hawke to Duff*

7 October 1759

Sir,

Enclosed I send you a copy of intelligence which came from Vannes the 18th September. I hope from the position of your ships, should they [the French] have embarked, they have not been able to have sailed. And in case they should attempt it after your receiving this, I desire you will immediately dispatch a cutter with advice of it to Rear-Admiral Geary and another to me. Unless on this service, the cutters must not stir from your station, but must be victualled from some of the ships. If foul, can they not be laid on shore on Méaban?

I hope the *Proserpine* has joined you and that, if it could at any rate be attempted, you have destroyed the three frigates in the mouth of the river or obliged them to move farther up. The fireships you must keep with you. In case of the enemy's attempting to move, it will be most advisable to attack them in the Goulet of the river. I have not a frigate of any kind with me, but the moment any shall arrive, they shall be sent to you.

You must continue in Quiberon Bay yourself and call off all the force that can be spared from before L'Orient. Depending on your vigilance, I am etc.

291. *Hawke to Duff*

Ramillies at sea
8 October 1759

Sir,

This will be delivered to you by Captain Lockhart of the *Chatham* [(50)] whom you are to take under your command and send the *Colchester* [(50)] to my rendezvous as soon as she can be spared.

I also desire you will give directions to all the commanders of the ships and vessels under your orders to make the best remarks they can of the soundings, dangers, anchoring ground and batteries on the coast where they cruise, with their bearings, the flowing of the tides, their setting and the height they rise; and if they have artists on board, to make draughts thereof and send them to me by every opportunity. I am etc.

292. *Instructions from Hawke to Duff*

Ramillies at sea
8 October 1759

Whereas the destroying all or part of the enemy's frigates and transports in the River Morbihan is of the utmost consequence and it has been represented to me that there are on board the King's ship *Achilles* two Frenchmen in whose honesty Captain Barrington can confide, who have undertaken to carry frigates as far up in Vannes and Auray as where the enemy transports lie; you are hereby required and directed to take under your command His Majesty's ship *Achilles* and by every practicable means in your power, with the ships, frigates and fireships under your orders, attempt the destruction of the enemy's frigates and transports in the above-mentioned rivers. For which this shall be your order. Given etc.

293.   *Hervey to Hawke*

Monmouth off the Black Rocks
9 October 1759

Sir,

Since my last the winds have continued southerly till yesterday, about noon, I got in as far as the Parquet when it fell very little wind. We saw two French men of war at anchor between the Goulet and Camaret who immediately got under sail and run in before the wind and anchored with their fleet, who were all in the same position as usual ...

You will give me leave to observe, Sir, that the season comes on fast when I fear, if the enemy is so intent on getting out two or three ships, they must at last find an opportunity of a shore wind and thick weather, when our ships have been obliged to stand off, by which means the greatest vigilance and boldest perseverance to keep this dangerous coast on board may be frustrated ...

P.S.   At noon. Sir, I have just received your order by the *Montagu* ... I am thoroughly convinced of the necessity of keeping in here when it is possible; but I am as thoroughly convinced that this season greatly increases the hazard of it, as you must be sensible. However, Douarnenez [Bay] must be the resource if catched with any sudden gale westerly.

I hope you will send the *Achilles* [Captain Barrington] back with her pilots if you don't need them. The *Dunkirk* has none. This obliges me to keep her constantly by me ... I am now not two leagues from the Black Rocks.

294.   *Hawke to Duff*

Ramillies at sea
10 October 1759

Sir,

The enemy seem determined to carry their plan into execution, if possible, from Morbihan ... [Duff would be reinforced by the *Fame, Chichester* and *Windsor* and he could keep the *Colchester* if he still had her.]

You will see by the enclosed copy of intelligence that the entrance of Morbihan is not very strongly fortified, so that I would fain hope it will be no difficult matter either to destroy the seven frigates or drive them up the river, where the pilots of the *Achilles* are well acquainted. Either will be a very material service at this critical juncture. I am etc.

Enclosure:

294a. *Intelligence*

All things are disposing for the embarkation, the troops arriving and joining. But how are they to get out? We see every day within a league and a half of this, two large English ships with nine frigates of different sizes waiting for us ...

We see distinctly, and without spectacles, the English walking upon the decks of their ships. Our little forts fire from time to time on such as come near. We have raised a battery of twelve 24-pounders in the road of Locmariquer, on a point which faces the entrance of the river, and placed as a guard a detachment of fifty grenadiers. The precise day of embarkation is not determined, but every disposition for it is made.

295. *Hawke to Clevland*

Ramillies at sea
10 October 1759

Sir,

On the morning of the 8th I was joined by the *Chatham*, Captain Lockhart, whom I immediately dispatched to reinforce Captain Duff in Quiberon Bay.

In the evening of the same day, Captain Hervey sent the *Achilles* out to me with two Frenchmen, in whose honesty and honour Captain Barrington declared he could entirely confide. They cheerfully, on promise of a suitable reward, undertook to carry our ships as far up in the Rivers Vannes and Auray as where the enemy's transports lie. I only detained Captain Barrington half an hour and, as his ship's company is in perfect health, detached him directly to Quiberon. Enclosed in my last I sent you a copy of my last order to Captain Duff by the *Belliqueux* on the 7th [Document 290a].

By the *Cruiser* cutter very late last night, I received your letter of the 5th [289]. As to Morbihan, I beg leave to observe that, in my opinion, the enemy cannot stir from thence and that, should they attempt it, Captain Duff has sufficient force to destroy them in the entrance of the river, from whence such a number of ships cannot pass with safety in face of an enemy determined to attack them.

On the 8th about noon, after some foggy weather, Captain Hervey discovered two of the enemy's ships at anchor between the Goulet and Camaret. As soon as they descried him, they run in again and anchored with the rest of their fleet, who now continue in their former position, with the wind at S.W. Their Lordships may depend on the strictest watch being kept upon them that winds and weather will permit.

I was under a necessity of sending in the frigates for beer and water. For had I supplied them from the great ships, we should all have been rendered incapable of staying out, not having upon an average at this time more than three weeks for the whole. The victuallers I hear are sailed from Plymouth and, I hope, in such numbers as will supply us for three months. I am anxious to have this done before the season grows worse.

On the intelligence sent me in your letter of the 21st September relating to M. Bompar [275], I thought the intercepting him a very material object. For if the alarm [in England] is great now, it must be much greater, should he get into Rochefort; and therefore, in obedience to what I thought was their Lordships' intentions, I sent a squadron able to perform that service. But since their Lordships rely on the opinion of Vice-Admiral Cotes [see 289], I have sent orders this morning by a letter to Rear-Admiral Geary to return to me with the *Sandwich, Hercules* and *Anson*, [and] to send the *Fame, Chichester, Windsor, Belliqueux* and *Vengeance* to Captain Duff.

The ships' companies, except the *Foudroyant*, are in very good health; and as to myself, I shall give their Lordships timely notice to supply my place should my return into port be necessary—which, thank God, there is not the least appearance of at present. I write not about His Royal Highness as he writes by every opportunity himself.

Their Lordships will pardon my observing that, from the present disposition of the squadron, I think there is little room for alarm while the weather continues tolerable. As to Brest, I may safely affirm that, except the few ships that took shelter in Conquet, hardly a vessel of any kind has been able to enter or come out of that port these four months. We are as vigilant as ever, though we have not so much daylight. And if we can give credit to their own people, they have suffered greatly, having even been obliged to unload near forty victuallers at Quimperlé and carry their cargo by land to Brest. It must be the fault of the weather, not ours, if any of them escape.

The gunner of the *Falkland* [(50)] being dead, I have appointed the gunner of the *Melampe* [(36)] to her and Mr John Brewer, [gunner's] mate of the *Ramillies*, to the *Melampe*. He has passed a regular examination and is a sober, diligent, intelligent man; and [I] therefore take the liberty of recommending him to their Lordships.

Enclosed I send you the copy of a letter I received last night from Captain Duff, and am etc.

Minute: Own receipt of Sir Edward Hawke's letter of the 10th of October and let him know the Lords very much approve of his whole proceedings and particularly of the orders given to Captain Duff. Acquaint him the Lords will confirm the gunners as he desires.

Let it be done.

Enclosure:

295a. *Duff to Hawke*

Rochester in Quiberon Bay
7 October 1759

Sir,

In pursuance of your orders for the *Firm* to cruise off Port L'Orient and the *Rochester* to take her station in Quiberon Bay, I arrived here the 4th instant. The 5th, the weather was so bad that we could not reconnoitre, but yesterday being a fine day, all the captains of His Majesty's ships in Quiberon Bay went on the island of Méaban from whence we discovered the situation of the enemy to be as follows:

> Seven ships (which we believe to be the four frigates that were with the convoy I chased into Morbihan the 30th of July and three that were with the last convoy) lying near the mouth of the River Auray, where they appear to be placed for the defence of the entrance of the river. All the other ships and vessels are gone so far up the rivers that we could only see a few of their mastheads over the land.

By the men in a small boat which was intercepted yesterday going across the bay, we are informed that the enemy has brought several guns and mortars from Port L'Orient for the defence of Morbihan. I have the honour to be etc.

[With his above letter to Clevland, Hawke also enclosed a copy of his letter to Duff of 4 October (Document 288).]

296.   *Clevland to Hawke*

10 October 1759

Sir,

I have received and communicated to my Lords Commissioners of
the Admiralty your letter of the 3rd instant [286], informing their
Lordships of your being joined by the *Windsor* and of your having
detached the *Fame* to reinforce Admiral Geary, also enclosing a
letter from Captain Duff of the 23rd past, by which last they observe
that the enemy convoy of sixty-eight sail had got into Vannes and
Auray, having been seen by Captain Philips of the *Juno* who was
within gunshot of them when they came out of Nantes; but as it does
not appear what number of frigates escorted them, nor where His
Majesty's ships were stationed when the enemy got into those rivers,
their Lordships expect to be more particularly informed of the whole
transaction [and] therefore recommend to you to inquire into the
same and report how it shall appear, that they may see in what
manner this convoy could escape the cruisers, which gives their
Lordships the greater concern lest by any means they might get to
sea after the enemy's troops are embarked, and convinces them of
the necessity of your keeping a sufficient force to guard the entry of
the Morbihan to intercept any embarkations coming from thence, it
being of the highest importance at this critical conjuncture to defeat
the designs of the enemy from those ports where their preparations
are very great to attempt an invasion upon some part of His
Majesty's dominions, which, with preventing their ships of war from
sailing out of Brest, their Lordships command me to observe to you
must be the great and principal object of your attention. For, though
there may be other very necessary services, they cannot be attended
to at this time, lest those of more importance should suffer thereby.
Wherefore I have it in command from their Lordships to enjoin you
to employ the force under you for the aforesaid purposes and at the
same time to signify their directions to you that in case the enemy
should escape, you do not bring the squadron of the King's ships
further to the eastward than Plymouth or Torbay, unless in pursuit
of the enemy upon well grounded intelligence of their having passed
by those places. I most heartily wish you success, being with very
great regard and esteem etc.

297. *Hawke to Clevland*

Ramillies in Plymouth Sound
13 October 1759
'Recd. 15th'

Sir,

In the evening of the 11th, we had a hard gale at W.S.W. Next morning the *Royal Ann* made the signal of distress and parted company. Yesterday and this day, the gale rather increasing, I thought it better to bear up for Plymouth than run the risk of being scattered and driven farther to the eastward. While this wind shall continue, it is impossible for the enemy to stir. I shall keep the ships employed night and day in completing their water and provisions to three months, for at this season there can be no dependence on victuallers coming to sea. The instant it shall be moderate, I shall sail again. There are only come in yet the *Ramillies, Union, Royal George, Duke, Montagu, Foudroyant, Dorsetshire, Essex, Kingston* and *Mars*. I expect the rest in immediately and am etc.

P.S.   His Royal Highness is in so great a hurry to send his express away that I have not time to collect the weekly accounts.

298. *Hawke to Clevland*

Ramillies in Plymouth Sound
14 October 1759

Sir,

Yesterday afternoon, after sending an express to acquaint their Lordships of my arrival, came in here His Majesty's ship *Mars*, the *Success* frigate and *Swallow* sloop. The two latter kept company with the victuallers as long as they were able. About twenty of them have arrived here within these two days. No vessels can come off to us, but I am in hopes the weather will soon moderate. I understand the *Torbay* is ready to come out of Hamoaze, but the *Magnanime* and *Revenge* could not save the last spring.

Last night I received your letter of the 10th [296]. That their Lordships might be enabled to judge properly of what happened off Port Louis and Morbihan I have, from time to time, transmitted copies of the letters I received from Captains Reynolds and Duff, and duplicates of my orders and directions to each. Further lights I cannot give them.

Brest, Port Louis, Morbihan and Nantes I did consider my principal objects till I received your letter of the 21st September [275], wherein you say 'They command me to recommend it to you to keep a proper strength down the Bay to intercept them', meaning Bompar's squadron. In consequence I detached Rear-Admiral Geary with the proper strength I could spare in obedience, as I thought, to their Lordships' commands. As the list of Bompar's squadron which you sent me named five 74, two 64, one 50 gun ship and three frigates, their Lordships could not think Mr Geary's squadron of a force more than proper for the service they prescribed in your letter. I also directed a communication to be settled between Rear-Admiral Geary and Captain Duff, that they might mutually assist each other.

As soon as I received your letter of the 5th [289], I ordered Rear-Admiral Geary to join me with the *Sandwich, Hercules* and *Anson*, and the rest of his squadron to reinforce Captain Duff. I am not the least in pain about the enemy's getting out of Morbihan or out of Brest while these winds last. As the *Pallas* and *Sapphire* are clean they shall, the first moderate weather, sail for Quiberon Bay to relieve the two in greatest want of water and provisions and detach the other frigates that are ready for intelligence.

I shall not stir out of the *Ramillies* myself and hope to be at sea again in a few days in a condition to keep there without depending on victuallers. Some, if the weather will permit, I must send to Quiberon with beer and water.

I wish the ships were hastening from Portsmouth.

Since writing the above, I have received your letter of the 11th by express. Their Lordships may depend upon there being little foundation for the present alarms. While the wind is fair for the enemy's coming out, it is also favourable for our keeping in; and while we are obliged to keep off, they cannot stir. I own it was with regret I called off Rear-Admiral Geary. But as there are many ships now in England, I hope their Lordships will soon put it in my power to block up Rochefort, which will effectually distress the enemy everywhere ...

It blows so very fresh at W.N.W. that we can get neither water nor provisions off ...

P.S. Just arrived the *Temple* and *Nottingham*.

299. *Clevland to Hawke*

15 October 1759

Sir,

I have received and read to my Lords Commissioners of the Admiralty your letter of the 13th instant and am commanded by their Lordships to acquaint you they are extremely glad to hear the ships of your squadron are safe after the late bad weather. They very well approve of your victualling them in the manner you propose and do not doubt but you will take the first opportunity that the weather will admit of to return to your station.

Herewith you will receive a letter for His Royal Highness Prince Edward and their Lordships command me to signify directions to you to permit him to come on shore immediately, agreeable to the enclosed order. I am etc.

300. *The Navy Board to Hawke*

Navy Office
17 October 1759

Sir,

It having been represented to us some time ago that His Majesty's ship the *Nottingham* was in want of a surgeon in the room of Mr David Wright, we thereupon appointed one, not knowing the reason of the vacancy till last post we received a letter from Captain Lendrick acquainting us that you had directed Mr Wright to be discharged for disobedience to command, which we cannot help thinking must be a mistake, as we can recollect no precedent for a warrant officer being discharged from his employment by any commanding officer for any fault committed by him, unless he had been tried and found guilty by a court martial. Therefore we are obliged to trouble you to desire you will inform us of the particulars of this Mr David Wright's offence, that we may determine what to do with him hereafter. We dare say you will agree with us in opinion that officers may labour under very great hardships if discharged without a trial as their offences may not always be impartially stated to you, or any other commanding officers, nor the truth so thoroughly sifted as at a court martial; and indeed we cannot help observing to you that, though a commanding officer has power to suspend, we apprehend he has not to discharge, without a trial, and therefore beg for the future, when any officer appointed by us transgresses the rules of the Navy, you be pleased to order a court martial upon him to determine his fate, as any other method of dismission must, if attended with no prejudice to the parties or other inconveniences, make it impossible for us to judge what to do with such people afterwards, who will probably deny the charge and assert they could have cleared themselves had they been tried. We are etc.

G. COKBURNE [and five others]

301. *Hawke to Clevland*

Ramillies in Plymouth Sound
17 October 1759

Sir,

At 11 o'clock last night a messenger arrived at Plymouth Dock with your letter of the 15th [299], but the weather was so bad that it did not reach me in the Sound till about 8 this morning. In obedience to their Lordships' order of the same date, I have acquainted His Royal Highness Prince Edward with my having directions to permit him to go on shore. I should be glad to know whether it is their Lordships' intentions that he and his retinue should continue to be borne as part of the allowed complement of the *Ramillies*.[a] As His Royal Highness's equipage and furniture were consigned by order and inventory to me, I have given directions to send them on shore to the storekeeper of the dockyard.

The weather continues to grow worse or I should have been at sea again with the *Ramillies, Mars, Foudroyant, Torbay, Duke, Royal George, Dorsetshire, Temple, Essex, Montagu, Kingston* and *Nottingham*, which are completed for sea in every respect except their quantity of beer, which the port could not supply. The *Union*'s rudder, being bad, must be unhung and repaired[b] for which purpose she must go, as soon as the weather will permit, between the Island and the main. It will take up eight or ten hours in repairing. As the *Monmouth, Dunkirk, Bienfaisant, Hero, Resolution* and *Defiance* are not come in, I am apprehensive some of them may be got to the eastward.[c]

I hope directions will be given to the ships at Portsmouth to take on board all the beer they can possibly stow;[d] and that, whenever the weather will permit, a large quantity [will] be sent to this port ready for an exigency.[e] At present the brewhouse can supply only seventy tons a day, a quantity not far exceeding the daily expense.

Yesterday I received advice of the *Venus* and *Penguin*'s being in Torbay and this morning that the *Arethusa* [frigate] had got into Spithead, greatly shattered.

I have ordered the *Minerva*, the instant the weather shall moderate, to proceed before me to my rendezvous and the *Pallas* and *Sapphire* to Quiberon where, from the nature of that Bay, I hope the ships under Captain Duff's orders have rode in safety.

In case it shall appear practicable from the weather at this season, I shall leave directions for the *Swallow* to proceed to Captain Duff with victuallers loaded with water, beer and dry provisions.[f]

If their Lordships will consider how necessary it is not to alter my rendezvous, on which I must always keep the channel open, and that consequently, in strong westerly gales, I cannot keep the sea, they will readily lay their account with my putting often into this port.[g] At the same time, they may depend on my keeping the strictest guard over the motions of the enemy that the weather will permit.

Captain Young has applied to me for a court martial on the boatswain of the *Mars* for drunkenness and neglect of duty. Beside that it might retard my sailing should the winds and weather prove favourable, I am at a loss how to act with regard to Captain Hanway's commission. So I think it would be most advisable for their Lordships to send another boatswain to the ship.[h] I am etc.

Minute: In answer to Sir Edward Hawke's letter of the 17th October:

[a]Order him to bear [the Prince's retinue] on a supernumerary list for wages but not as part of the complement of the ship.

[b]Approve.

[c]Acquaint him that not any of the ships are got to the eastward, but the Lords hope on return to his station he will meet them without any accident.

[d]Orders to Admiral Holburne and the Commissioners of the Victualling to cause it to be done.

[e]Direct the Commissioners of the Victualling accordingly. Acquaint Sir Edward Hawke with the directions given in the two preceding articles.

[f]Approve.

[g]The Lords conclude he will not put oftener into port than is necessary and leave it to his discretion.

[h]The Lords desire he will move another boatswain and they will give warrants to such as he shall appoint on the occasion.

302. *Clevland to Hawke*

19 October 1759

Sir,

I have received and communicated to my Lords Commissioners of the Admiralty your letter of the 14th instant [298], informing their Lordships of your arrival in Plymouth Sound with part of the squadron under your command, which gives them great satisfaction to find the ships in safety after so violent a storm.

Their Lordships direct me to observe that they are very well satisfied your sending the ships to Rochefort was in consequence of their letter of the 21st September, at which time there was reason to expect M. Bompar home [from the West Indies], but since that, it being more probable to think the designs of the enemy were more ready to be put in execution from Morbihan and Brest, it became necessary to collect the whole force at those places, which occasioned their Lordships' subsequent letters, and they are still of opinion that those places must be the first and principal object of your attention; but if, after providing sufficient force for those purposes and your being reinforced by the ships that came home with Admiral Boscawen, you shall find a number of ships can be spared to cruise off Rochefort, their Lordships recommend it to you then to detach them, especially as it is not improbable the five ships of Monsieur de La Clue's squadron which put into Cadiz [one 64, two 60s, and two 50-gun ships] may endeavour to get into that place.

Their Lordships very much approve of a communication being settled between the commanders of the several squadrons on the enemy's coast.

The Lords have appointed Lieutenant Sharpe to be 6th of the *Ramillies* and have removed the others up. I am etc.

303. *Hervey to Hawke*

Monmouth off Brest
20 October 1759

Sir,

As soon as the wind came easterly, I lost no time in getting off the Black Rocks where I was seven hours afterwards on the Thursday morning [the 18th], but being thick weather with rain had no opportunity to look well in till this morning ...

I can only add that I think them exactly as they were, and as I am certain nothing whatever has got out since I have been on this station, so I believe this hard westerly wind has not brought anything in ...

I was taken very ill of the gout in both my feet the 11th instant, which has confined me since; and though I am much better, I am far from being well, being only able to be carried from gallery to gallery as I want to look out, from whence I took the view of the enemy's ships this morning ...

304.   *Hawke to Hervey*

Ramillies at sea
21 October 1759

Sir,

This morning I received your letter of the 20th and greatly approve of your proceedings.

At the same time, give me leave to assure you I am very sorry for your indisposition and heartily wish you a speedy recovery of your health. As I am in daily expectation of a reinforcement from Portsmouth I intend, as soon as it shall arrive, to send the *Monmouth* in to refresh or clean, and the *Bienfaisant* to recruit ...

305.   *Hawke to Commissioner Pett at Plymouth*

Ramillies at sea
21 October 1759

Sir,

On considering the state of the King's ships now with me, I find I shall want 800 tons of beer and 300 tons of water, which I desire you will send me out with the utmost dispatch. If the victuallers from Portsmouth are arrived, send them away directly without waiting till the whole shall be ready. I am etc.

306.   *Hawke to Clevland*

Ramillies off Ushant
21 October 1759
'Recd. 24th at 10 at night'

Sir,

At 4 in the afternoon of Thursday last the 18th instant, with very little wind, I weighed and, by the help of our boats, got out of the Sound. Night coming on, I could not tell what ships had followed me except the *Royal George, Torbay* and *Essex*, which was the reason I did not then acquaint their Lordships with my sailing, but left it to Sir Charles Hardy. In the morning of the 19th off the Lizard, I found in company the *Mars, Duke, Foudroyant, Dorsetshire, Kingston, Nottingham, Montagu* and *Success*. On the 20th I was joined by the *Union* and *Temple*. The first remained after me to repair her rudder and the latter to get her coppers up. Also by the *Venus* and *Penguin*. In obedience to their Lordships' orders I have sent the latter to Spithead.

At 12 p.m. of the 19th I brought to, Ushant S.W. by W. ten leagues. Not knowing whether Captain Hervey had been able to recover his station, at 9 the next morning I sent the *Torbay* to look into Brest and followed in with the squadron till I discovered the *Monmouth, Dunkirk*, and *Bienfaisant* at anchor off the Black Rocks. The wind casting to the eastward and the tide of ebb coming down, the *Torbay* could not get nearer than to discover the enemy's four flags and sixteen sail of large ships. But Captain Keppel brought me this morning the accompanying apparent state of the enemy from Captain Hervey, who had been off the Black Rocks from Thursday morning but was prevented by thick weather from looking into Brest Road till the morning of the 20th .

This is the third day we have had fresh gales from the eastward and not the least appearance of the ships from Portsmouth.

This morning I have been joined by the *Hero* and *Resolution*.

On Thursday morning Captain Tyrrell acquainted me by letter that his bad state of health would not admit of his going to sea, of which he said he had informed their Lordships. So I gave him leave to go on shore and appointed Captain Hill of the *St Florentine*[1] to act in the *Foudroyant* till their Lordships shall appoint another to command her.

Enclosed is the state and condition of His Majesty's ships now with me. I am etc.

307.   *Instructions from Hawke to Captain James Young of the*
           MARS

Ramillies at sea
22 October 1759

You are hereby required and directed to hoist a distinguishing pendant at your main topmast head and take the *Royal Ann*'s place [see 297] in the line of battle, with the command of the King's ships

---

[1] Hill: L 1740, C 1747, RA 1778; and, having been given his flag after some thirty-one years as a post captain, he died in the same year.

named on the margin [*Duke, Torbay, Essex, Temple, Defiance*], the captains of which are hereby required to follow your directions till farther order ...

308. *Hawke to Hervey*

Ramillies at sea
23 October 1759

Sir,

... I desire you will transmit to me, as soon as possible, the best remarks you have made of the soundings, dangers, anchoring ground and batteries within the limits of your station, with their bearings ... and direct all the captains under your orders to do the same. I am etc.

309. *Hawke to Hervey*

Ramillies at sea
23 October 1759, 11 a.m.

Sir,

Since writing to you in the morning I have received your letter of the 22nd. [In this Hervey reported that he had sent in the *Bienfaisant* because she was short of stores and had many sick men.] As I have but seventeen sail of the line, I desire you will not send any ships in without giving their captains positive orders to join me first, as I must be left to judge of the necessity of their going in and often have resources you can have no knowledge of.

I have sent you water, wine, bread and seventeen butts of beer.

I congratulate you on the recovery of your health and shall be glad you may be able to stay out as long as I do. I am etc.

310. *Hawke to Clevland*

Ramillies at sea
24 October 1759

Sir,

Yesterday I was joined by the *Fortune* sloop with five vessels with beer and one with wine from Portsmouth and, about noon, by the *Namur* [(90)] which brought me the agreeable news of the surrender of Quebec, on which I beg leave heartily to congratulate their Lordships. In the evening the *Prince Edward* cutter brought me an account from Captain Duff of his proceedings, copies of which you have enclosed.

This morning I have been joined by the *Warspite* [(74)] and *Hercules*. Enclosed is a copy of Captain Porter's account of his falling in with a French 74-gun ship [the *Souverain*] on the 10th instant in latitude 46.40 and about twenty-five leagues WbN½N from Oléron. As [the *Hercules*, also of 74 guns] wants a great deal of refitting, I have taken out her provisions and sent a cutter by express to Plymouth, that everything may be possible may be ready for her. I am afraid Captain Porter will not be able to come out in her again.

The *Bienfaisant*, being in want of everything, was sent in by Captain Hervey. I hope she will join him again in a few days.

This afternoon I have been joined by the *Sandwich* and *Anson*. Agreeable to my order [see 298] Rear-Admiral Geary detached the *Fame, Chichester, Belliqueux, Windsor* and *Vengeance* [(28)] to Quiberon Bay. I am etc.

Enclosure 1:

310a. *Duff to Hawke*

Rochester in Quiberon Bay
18 October 1759

Sir,

On the 11th instant I was honoured with your orders dated the 8th instant [292].

It is with very great concern I acquaint you how much reason Captain Barrington has to be sorry for having placed so much confidence in the two Frenchmen he recommended to you as qualified to pilot His Majesty's ships up the Rivers Vannes and Auray to where the enemy's frigate and transports lie.

About 10 o'clock in the forenoon on the 11th instant the *Achilles*, in coming through the Passage of the Teignouze in charge of those pilots, run upon the Gouivas [Goué Vas] Rock and received so much damage that, as she lies at anchor, she makes twelve foot water in an hour. The *Chatham*, who had no pilot on board and was following the *Achilles*, nearly escaped being on the same rock by instantly hauling her wind and standing to the N.W.

The *Proserpine* did not arrive here till the 11th in the afternoon, when I had the honour to receive your letter dated the 4th instant [288].

It blowing hard in the S.W. quarter Captain Reynolds, with the ships that were cruising with him off Port L'Orient, anchored in Quiberon Bay the 11th in the evening to prevent being drove farther off their station. Captain Reynolds brought me your letter dated the 7th instant [290a] which he received at sea ...

The 12th, Captain Lockhart [of the *Chatham*] got in here, from whom I received your letter dated the 8th [291] directing me to send the *Colchester* to your rendezvous as soon as she can be spared. The 12th, 13th and 14th it blew so hard that boats could not pass. On the 15th I called a council of war, a copy of which comes enclosed.

[A copy of this record comprises the second enclosure with Hawke's above letter to Clevland. The assembled captains duly examined Barrington's French pilots and unsurprisingly concluded that their knowledge of that part of the coast was not to be trusted.]

It had blown very hard westerly for several days, which I fear has dispersed and distressed Mr Geary's squadron.

The enemy's ships in Morbihan remain in the same situation ... The frigates near the entrance of the River Auray cannot be attacked unless we had pilots to carry the ships into the harbour of Morbihan, and then it must be done with a leading wind and a flood tide, which would give them an opportunity to go further up the river than we could follow them; and, as the ships which performed that service must continue in Morbihan till they got a fair wind to bring them out, the narrowness of the harbour, the strength and irregular settings of the tide making it impossible to work out, the other captains, as well as myself, are of opinion the risk would overbalance the hurt we could do to the enemy ...

By the weekly accounts which come enclosed you will see His Majesty's ships here are short of water, butter and cheese.

The damage the *Achilles* has received making it necessary to send her immediately to England, and judging it very hazardous to let the *Achilles* go to sea without other ships in company, I have ordered the *Actaeon* [(28)] and *Gibraltar* [(24)] to proceed with her, which I hope you will approve of.

As soon as the weather permitted of it, I ordered the *Firm* [(60)], *Maidstone* [(28)] and *Juno* [(36)] off Port L'Orient and shall send a 50-gun ship to them as soon as the ships mentioned in your orders of the 10th [294] join me. I have the honour etc.

[Enclosures 3 to 5 are not reproduced here.]

Enclosure 6:

310b.   *Captain Jervis Porter to Hawke*

Hercules

[This is his undated account of his action on 10 October with the *Souverain* (74) which was escaping to Rochefort after the Battle of Lagos.]

On the 10th instant at 8 in the morning, being in the latitude of about 46.40, steering S.E. with the wind at S.W., we saw a sail to windward which we chased ... About noon, the chase hoisted a blue flag at her main topmast head which we answered by hoisting an English ensign at the mizen topmast head (a signal which is sometimes made between two French ships of war upon meeting after parting company). She neared us very fast and we plainly discovered her to be a large French ship of war ... At ½ past 5, being about one mile to windward of us and abaft our beam, with an intention of coming to action as her guns were run out below, she hauled her jack down and hoisted her ensign and pendant. We shortened sail by bunting our mainsail, hauling up the foresail and hauling down the staysails, but kept the jib up. We then hauled down our French jack, hoisted our colours, hauled our ports up which were until this time down, and run our weather guns out, upon which she immediately hauled her wind and set her mainsail and staysails. We then discovered her to be a 74-gun ship ... About ¾ after 9, being pretty near up with her though not near enough to engage, she put her helm hard a-starboard and gave us her larboard broadside, and then kept on as before and gave us her starboard broadside. We then immediately starboarded our helm and ran right down upon her whilst she was loading her guns and, getting close to her, ported our helm and began to engage as the guns bore upon her. At ½ past 10, we was so unlucky as to have our main topmast head shot away, which she took the advantage of and made all the sail she could from us. We did the same after her and continued to chase until 8 the next morning when we saw the north end of Oléron about five leagues distance. The chase was about four or five miles from us.

Finding it impossible to come up with her in so short a run and engaging ourselves with a lee shore, with our foreyard shot through in two places [and] our fore topsail yard so badly wounded that, when we came afterwards to reef the sail, it broke; and having all our sails and rigging very much shattered (at which the enemy only aimed) we left off the chase and wore ship—having one man killed and two wounded, including the captain, who was shot in the head and has lost the use of his right leg by the wind of a shot.

N.B.   When we began to engage, Oléron bore EbS¼S., twenty-five leagues. The officers and men behaved with the greatest spirits and alertness, without the least confusion.

311.   *Hawke to Clevland*

Ramillies at sea
25 October 1759

Sir,

By the *Dorset* cutter, which joined me this day from Plymouth, I have received your three letters of the 18th and 19th ...

Their Lordships will perceive by my letter of yesterday [310] that a considerable reinforcement is gone to Quiberon Bay. But still being of opinion that the best security will be a squadron off Rochefort, as soon as I shall have ships to spare I intend sending one to cruise in the tract of it.

This morning I was joined by the *Chichester* whom, her bowsprit being sprung, I am under a necessity of sending in to refit. I am etc.

[Clevland's minute of 29 October is formalized in Document 314 below.]

312.   *Captain Lendrick to Hawke*

Nottingham at sea
26 October 1759

Sir,

In answer to yours of the 25th instant, desiring me to transmit to you the reasons of my confining Mr David Wright, late surgeon of the *Nottingham*, I am to inform you:

That Mr George Bowyer,[1] second lieutenant of the *Nottingham*, having the watch upon deck between 8 and 12 p.m. the 23rd August 1759 and the ship at sea, and having occasion to tack the ship between 10 and 11, ordered John Harris, boatswain's mate, to go down and turn up all the idlers in and about the cockpit to assist in tacking; that whilst said Harris was in the execution of his duty and, among others, ordering up the loblolly man [literally the 'gruel man'

---

[1] Bowyer: L 1758, CR 1761, C 1762. Served with distinction in four battles in the W. Indies 1779–80. RA 1793. Lost a leg at Battle of the First of June 1794. Created baronet; VA 1794. Adm. 1799.

and otherwise the surgeon's assistant], the surgeon, Mr David Wright, called out to him from his cabin, 'Get you gone, you rascal. He shan't go for you, and if you don't be gone instantly from this, I'll kick you up the ladder. I'll make you know you have not Captain Marshall to deal with.'[1]

Upon this, said Harris came to his officer Mr Bowyer and complained that the surgeon would not suffer him to do his duty, upon which said lieutenant sent William Wallace, quartermaster, to acquaint the surgeon that he wanted to see him immediately upon the quarter-deck, when the surgeon returned for answer he would not come for him. Said lieutenant, on this answer being brought, and said lieutenant, thinking his authority called in question, ordered Mr Fairman, midshipman, to go down to said surgeon and deliver the above orders, viz. that he wanted and ordered the surgeon to attend him on the quarter-deck, when said surgeon replied for answer he would not on any account, without said lieutenant's orders conveyed to him in writing, nor did he know what right he had to obey Mr Bowyer, said lieutenant. On this second answer, he sent down said midshipman down [sic] again to the said surgeon with his orders as before, and said surgeon returned same answer as before, which was delivered said lieutenant by said midshipman.

Upon this, Mr Bowyer, lieutenant of the watch, came in to me and complained of the surgeon's disobedience to his command, and I ordered said lieutenant to send the mate of his watch with his orders as above to the surgeon to attend him, which said lieutenant did by sending Mr McLeod, master's mate, who brought him the surgeon's answer that he, the surgeon, would not come without a written order from the lieutenant, nor even then without his signifying to him that he himself or some other person had met with an accident which prevented their being brought down to the cockpit to him.

The lieutenant acquainting me with this answer from the surgeon, I ordered the above master's mate to go down in my name and acquaint the surgeon I wanted him, which order he complied with and came to me. When inquiring into his reasons for disobeying the lieutenant, his superior officer's, command who then commanded the watch and represented me, his answer was he did not know any person had a right to give him orders except myself and that he would not obey any lieutenant.

On this, Sir, I ordered him to be confined to his cabin for disobedience and mutiny, and wrote to you for a court martial on said

[1] Marshall had been relieved by Lendrick two months earlier. See p. 217, n. 2.

surgeon, when, the service I was ordered upon [off Brest with Hervey] not admitting of a court martial, you granted me an order to discharge him into the *Sandwich*, which I did, giving him a certificate accordingly that he was discharged for disobedience to command.

I have stated the whole affair so as to make up one single charge ...

There are other parts in the surgeon's character, such as exacting sums of money for the cure of venereal disorders for the common men over and above the government's allowance in that case provided, which in my opinion would be sufficient to have him discharged from the service. But this I have not touched upon. I am etc.

313. *Hawke to the Navy Board*

Ramillies at sea
29 October 1759

Gentlemen,

I have received your letter of the 17th [Doc. 300], in answer to which I am to acquaint you that there was no mistake in Mr Wright's being ordered by me to be discharged and the reason marked on the pay list. The *Nottingham* was wanted at a moment's warning to cruise in the Goulet at Brest, a station which required every man in her to be ready at a call. No probability [offered] of being able to try Wright at a court martial for his disobedience of orders, and other dirty crimes. Nor could I, in the circumstances the ship was then in, admit of sentries being kept on so worthless a fellow ... Enclosed I send you a letter from Captain Lendrick [see 312] relating to Wright ...

By the *Melampe* this day I have sent in Mr James Cock whom you appointed surgeon of the *Duke*. His infirmities rendering him incapable of his duty, he applied to be sent home. The surgeon he was to supersede, though very old, still continues in the ship. I am etc.

314. *Clevland to Hawke*

29 October 1759

Sir,

I have received and read to my Lords Commissioners of the Admiralty your letter of the 25th instant [311], giving an account of your proceedings with His Majesty's ships under your command.

Their Lordships are of opinion that the force you have sent to Quiberon Bay is very sufficient and they concur with you in opinion of the utility of a squadron off of Rochefort, but the advices by the last mail all concurring that positive orders are sent to M. Conflans to put to sea directly and at all events to engage His Majesty's ships under your command, their Lordships have directed all the ships that can possibly be got ready to join you with the utmost expedition. Wherefore, till you have a sufficient number to deal with M. Conflans, their Lordships recommend it to you not to make the detachment you mention to cruise off Rochefort. When you have, they approve of your doing it. I am etc.

315.   *Hawke to Clevland*

Ramillies at sea
29 October 1759

Sir,

This day I was joined by the *Portland* [(50)], with the *Firedrake, Furnace* and *Thunder* bombs, with their tenders, all which I have detached to Quiberon Bay ...

I have sent the *Melampe* in to clean and, in room of her, the *Actaeon* and *Gibraltar* [see 310a], sent the *Venus, Southampton* and *Minerva* to Captain Duff.

By the *Melampe*, Captain Duff acquaints me that the master of a Spanish vessel, which came out of Auray the 20th instant, informed him that there were five regiments at Auray and eight at Vannes and about sixty vessels lying near Auray with their sails unbent. Two of the enemy's transports went from the River Vannes to Auray the 21st instant, which is all the alteration since his last account.

Enclosed is Captain Lendrick's report of the soundings, etc., of the Bay of Brest. I am etc.

Minute: 5 November. Own receipt.

316.   *Clevland to Hawke*

30 October 1759

Sir,

My Lords Commissioners of the Admiralty considering it is very probable you may at this season be drove from your station off Ushant up the Channel and that the enemy may take such opportunity of coming out of Brest, their Lordships therefore command me to recommend it to you, whenever that happens, to endeavour to leave some of your frigates to the westward of Ushant to observe the motions of the French ships in Brest and, in case of their coming out, to see which way they stand and then repair to such rendezvous as you may appoint with the intelligence; and that you may receive it as early as possible, and to enable you to follow them with the greater dispatch, you should give them a signal to make if the ships are sailed.

And as it is possible, if the enemy come out, they may attempt to destroy His Majesty's ships in Quiberon Bay, their Lordships likewise recommend it to you to keep a cruiser off Belle Isle, that she may give the most early intelligence of the enemy's motion to the ships of His Majesty in Quiberon Bay and thereby prevent their being surprised. I am etc.

317. *Hawke to Clevland*

Ramillies at sea
5 November 1759
'Recd. 9th by express'

Sir,

By the *Gibraltar*, which joined me from Plymouth on the 1st instant, I received your letters of the 21st and 22nd ultimo.

Beside the risk the furniture runs of being spoiled at sea in a winter's cruise, I must beg leave to acquaint their Lordships that it was His Royal Highness's desire that I should send it ashore to the storekeeper.

I hope their Lordships did not conclude from that remark on my rendezvous in my letter of the 17th [301] that I should come into port while there should be a possibility of keeping the sea. Single ships may struggle with a hard gale of wind when a squadron cannot. It must always from wearing lose ground in working against a strong westerly wind in the Channel where it cannot make very long stretches, but more especially if it should blow so as to put it past carrying sail. If for the future this should happen, I shall put into Torbay, as I cannot be induced to think there is sufficient room for so large a squadron, or water for the three-decked ships, in Plymouth Sound at this season of the year ...

Falling in with some of the victuallers destined for Quiberon, which had lost company with the *Swallow*, I sent the *Gibraltar* to see them safe there and then return to me.

By the *Thames* from Plymouth on the 2nd instant, I received your letter of the 25th. She brought with her five victuallers from Plymouth and four large ones from Portsmouth with beer and water. The four last brought us a seasonable and large supply ...

Keeping the sea in the last gale of wind has greatly shattered the *Monmouth*, as their Lordships will perceive by the accompanying copies of letters and reports. Captain Hervey has also suffered much in his constitution by the fatigues and watchings of the critical station he has been on since the 1st of July. Through the whole he has given such proofs of diligence, activity, intrepidity and judgement that it would be doing injustice to his merit as an officer not to acknowledge that I part with him with the greatest regret. He has also been, during that time, well seconded by Captains Barrington [*Achilles*], Digby [*Dunkirk*], Lendrick [*Nottingham*] and Balfour [*Bienfaisant*]. Captain Digby [just now] with the *Intrepid* is still on that station and I expect the *Bienfaisant* every day to return to it. During the last southerly winds, there was no looking into Brest Road but, from the position of the ships under Mr Hervey and that of the squadron, I may venture to give it as my opinion that nothing has got out from thence.

I was obliged to send the *Nottingham* and *Monmouth* in; also the *Foudroyant* and *Anson* on account of the sickly state of their companies. I am etc.

Minute: Let him know I have communicated his letter to the Lords who have great satisfaction in the account he gives of the conduct of Captain Hervey and the other officers mentioned.

Enclosure 1:

317a. *Copy of Hervey to Hawke*

Monmouth off the Black Rocks
2 November 1759, at 8 at night

Sir,

The wind and weather have been so perverse that I have not been able to look in since the taking provisions on board ... There has been nothing stirring out, however.

The purport of my sending this to you so suddenly is to enclose you my carpenter's report of the ship. You may imagine 'tis with the greatest reluctancy I do it, as it is near a month that the officers had reported to me her making eighteen inches an hour, even at anchor;

but I was in hopes of stopping some of [the leaks] when I got to an anchor. I now find it increases fast and that, when she takes in a great deal, there will be no getting at it for the timbers. As she makes this twenty-one inches in the present fine weather and at anchor, 'tis to be feared it will greatly increase in any bad weather.

I am myself much as I was when I wrote last—not able to put either foot to the deck ...

Enclosure 2:

317b. *Copy of Lendrick to Hawke*

Nottingham at sea
4 November 1759

Sir,

His Majesty's ship *Nottingham* under my command having sprung a leak the 1st November ... and having applied to Captain Hervey, I am ordered by him to wait for you to know your further pleasure.

The carpenter's opinion I enclose you. I am excessively sorry this accident should have happened at a time the service seems to require our greatest attention; but as the ship is old and infirm, I can't think that a narrow and strict inspection can be dispensed with, and more so at this season of the year ...

318. *Instructions from Hawke to Mr Methell, Butcher*

Ramillies in Torbay
10 November 1759

I desire you will supply as many of His Majesty's ships [as are] now in this road with fresh beef at the current price of the country, taking proper receipts from the purser or purser's steward of each ship for the quantity you shall supply her, which receipts you are to transmit to the Commissioners for Victualling His Majesty's Navy, with certificates from two respectable persons of the meats being charged at a market price, in order that you may be paid for the same. For which this shall be your warrant. Given etc.

319. *Hawke to Clevland*

Ramillies in Torbay
10 November 1759
'Read & ansd. 13th' [Document 321]

Sir,

By a cutter from Plymouth late in the night of the 5th, I received your three letters of the 29th and one of the 30th October [316]. At that time the captain of the *Anson* had my orders to proceed next morning with the empty victuallers to Plymouth; but from the advices mentioned in one of yours [314] of the orders given to Monsieur Conflans, I stopped her. On the 6th in the morning with a fresh wind at W., we tried to weather Ushant which then bore S½E four leagues. But the gale increasing and veering to N.N.W., I made her signal to go into port; and, after several efforts not being able to get to the westward of the island with the squadron, I was obliged on the 7th to carry all the sail I could to the northward. The gale continued very hard between the N. by W. and N.W. by N., and at noon of the 8th the Start bore N. by W. distant nine leagues. Moderating a little in the evening, I worked under the Start by 8 in the morning of the 9th and, till afternoon, entertained some hopes of being able to keep the sea and get to westward. But the wind increasing at W. by N., I was obliged and lucky enough to get in here late last night in the *Ramillies*, with the *Union, Mars, Warspite, Hero, Kingston, Torbay, Dorsetshire, Namur, Swiftsure, Temple, Royal George, Revenge, Resolution* and *Success*. This morning came in the *Montagu*, the *Essex* is at anchor about two leagues without and, in sight, the *Sandwich* and *Duke* working up under their courses. If the wind does not abate, I am in doubt whether the two latter will be able to fetch this place. I have found the *Anson* here, not having been able to get into Plymouth.

As to their Lordships' particular directions signified in your letter of the 30th, be so good as [to] lay before them the copy of the orders I left with Captain Duff ... On the 27th October, I sent directions to Captain Duff to keep a cruiser off Belle Isle and another off Basque Road in order to give him timely notice of the motions of the enemy.

Considering as their Lordships will perceive by my former letters how material and critical a service it would be at this time to intercept Bompar, while Auray and Vannes were more than sufficiently secured and the enemy's squadron blocked up at Brest, I had come to a resolution, as soon as the *Magnanime, Revenge, Burford, Chichester, Hercules* and *Defiance* should join me from Plymouth, to have sent Rear-Admiral Geary with seven sail of the line to cruise from ten to twenty leagues N. from Cape Ortegal, as the season of the year rendered it impracticable to cruise in the bottom of the Bay; to station one frigate off Cape Finisterre, one fifty leagues to the westward of Belle Isle, and one off Cape Clear for intelligence. When I sent the *Portland* to Quiberon, I intended she should have been followed by the *Intrepid* [(60)]; and therefore I sent the *Thames* [(32)] off Cape Finisterre and directed Captain Byron in the *Fame* [(60)], with the *Windsor* [(60)], as soon as they should be completed from the victuallers, to proceed off Cape Ortegal till he should be joined by the Rear-Admiral. The weather driving me from my station and keeping the ships still at Plymouth has prevented the farther execution of my plan for the present. The *Monmouth* and *Nottingham* being obliged to go into port obliged me to detain the *Intrepid*.

As to Quiberon, I submit it to their Lordships whether or not, considering the season of the year, the *Belliqueux* [(64)] and *Firm* [(60)] should not be called off. If, which is very improbable, the enemy should escape me and make their push there with their whole squadron, these two ships would be of little avail and, without them, the five 50-gun ships and nine frigates would be a much more manageable squadron and therefore better able to preserve itself until my arrival. It is my opinion also that the two fireships and three bomb vessels should now be called off. On the 30th October I sent directions to Captain Duff to try if the latter could do any execution on the enemy's frigates in the mouth of Morbihan.

It blows a mere fret [i.e. hard gale] of wind from the N.W. Bompar, if near, may get in, but no ship can stir from any port of the enemy in the Bay. The instant the weather will admit of it, I shall get to sea again.

As the boats cannot easily pass, I cannot collect the state of the ships. I am etc.

320. *Hawke to Clevland*

Ramillies off the Start
12 November 1759

Sir,

The weather moderating all night and a light breeze springing up easterly, I weighed this morning at 7 o'clock and am making all the haste possible to my station.

I was joined here by the *Magnanime*, *Hercules*, and *Actaeon*. The *Duke* being in want of courses and other sails, I have ordered her

into the Sound to be supplied from the *Barfleur* with directions not
to remain there a night. I am etc.

321.   *Clevland to Hawke*

13 November 1759

Sir,

I have received and read to my Lords Commissioners of the
Admiralty your letter of the 10th instant [319], giving an account of
your being forced into Torbay, with several of the ships under your
command, by hard gales of wind; and am to acquaint you their
Lordships are very glad to find the ships escaped so well from the
weather.

Their Lordships well approve of the disposition you propose to
make of the ships under your command in order to intercept Monsieur Bompar and they recommend it to you to pursue your plan
when you shall judge, by the reinforcements you may receive from
Plymouth, that you have force enough with you to enable you to do
so; and their Lordships are persuaded that Commodore Hanway
will hasten those reinforcements out to you with all the dispatch that
is possible.

Their Lordships agree with you in opinion that it may be very
proper to call off the *Belliqueux, Firm*, fireships and bomb vessels
from Quiberon, and they recommend it to you to do so accordingly
and to send the bomb vessels into port.

Enclosed I send you an extract of a letter from Vice-Admiral
Cotes and another from Captain Wyatt of the *Wager* containing
intelligence of the squadron under the command of Monsieur Bompar; and, wishing you all success in your undertakings, I remain etc.

[The enclosed letter from Cotes was dated at Port Royal, Jamaica,
on 9 September. He thought the French would sail from Cap
François by mid-October, 'their men being very sickly'.]

322.   *Hawke to Geary*

Royal George at sea
17 November 1759

[Because of sickness on board the *Sandwich*, Hawke on 14
November ordered Geary to go into Plymouth and collect replace-
ments for his sick men from the ships in that port. On 17 November
Geary was back at sea. At 3 p.m. he was informed by a returning

victualler that Conflans's squadron was out and that Hawke was in hot pursuit in the direction of Belle Isle. Geary, in company with the *Foudroyant* and *Bienfaisant*, tried to follow but the winds were so contrary that on the 20th—the day of battle in Quiberon Bay—the three ships were to be found abreast of Start Point! Meanwhile, on the 17th Hawke had written a short letter to Geary; and, when reporting to Clevland from off Ushant on the 26th, the rear-admiral enclosed the following extract (excluding Hawke's opening sentence: 'I am heartily vexed you was left behind.')]

The same wind which carried us from Torbay carried Conflans from Brest with eighteen sail of the line and two frigates. In the evening of the 15th they were seen by the *Swallow* sloop, Belle Isle E. by S. 22 leagues, wind also E. by S. The *Swallow* and the *Juno* returned to acquaint Captain Duff in Quiberon. I am making all the sail I can thither.

As it is uncertain where we may follow them, I desire you will collect as many ships as you can of my squadron and cruise on my rendezvous off Ushant till farther order. I am etc.

323. *Hawke to Clevland*

Royal George off Ushant
17 November 1759
Wind south, Ushant E ½ N 21 Leagues
'Recd. the 21st express at 5 p.m.'

Sir,

On the 12th I had great hope of getting on my station, but in the night between that and the 13th off the Bolt met with a hard gale at S.W. which obliged me to bear up for Torbay again, where I anchored in the afternoon with the ships mentioned in my former, and the *Dunkirk, Intrepid, Burford*, and *Defiance*. The wind proving fair on the 14th, I made the best of my way to my station. The *Sandwich* being very sickly, I directed Rear-Admiral Geary to stop in Plymouth Sound, send his sick to the hospital,[1] receive others in their room and then join me on the rendezvous.

The *Ramillies* having for some time past complained greatly and been waterlogged whenever it blowed hard, on a complaint from her carpenter to Captain Taylor I ordered her defects to be inspected by the carpenters of the *Union, Namur* and *Royal George*, who declared

[1] At Plymouth, hospital facilities were still on the old contract basis. Stonehouse Hospital came into use in 1760.

her not fit to keep the sea at this season of the year. On this, I shifted
my flag to the *Royal George* and sent the *Ramillies* to clean and refit
at Plymouth ...

On the 14th, a little before I got under way, Captain Parry of the
Kingston acquainted me by letter, and by his surgeon, of his being in
so bad a state of health as not to be able to proceed to sea. I ...
therefore ... appointed Captain Shirley[1] of the *Fortune* sloop to
command the *Kingston* and Lieutenant Nathaniel Stuart,[2] second
of the *Ramillies*, to command the *Fortune* till farther order.

On the 16th in the morning, I dispatched the *Fortune* to Captain
Duff with orders to leave only four frigates, two fireships and the
bombs in Quiberon, three frigates off Port Louis, and cruise himself
with the rest in such station off Belle Isle as best to cover Quiberon
and guard against being surprised. But now I find my orders would
come too late, for in the evening of the 16th one of the victuallers
from Quiberon joined me. The master acquainted me that about
dusk [on the 15th] the *Swallow* was spoke with by the *Juno* [Captain
Philips] and ordered to return to Quiberon, as did the *Juno*, to
inform Captain Duff that the French fleet was then in sight, consisting of eighteen sail of the line and three frigates. Belle Isle bore E. by
S. twenty-two leagues from the victuallers, the French squadron W.
by N. from them about three leagues, with the wind E. by S. They
were working to the eastward. I have carried a pressure of sail all
night, with a hard gale at S.S.E., in pursuit of the enemy and make
no doubt of coming up with them either at sea or in Quiberon Bay.

I have sent directions [322] to Rear-Admiral Geary to keep on my
rendezvous off Ushant.

The squadron now with me consists of twenty-three sail of the line
and [the] *Success* frigate.

This morning I received your letter of the 13th [321] with the
enclosed intelligence from Vice-Admiral Cotes and Captain Wyatt,
and am etc.

Minute: 23 November. Own receipt. Approve [his shifting his flag
to the *Royal George*] and acquaint him the Lords have ordered
one of the Surveyors of the Navy to see that what is necessary
be done to the *Ramillies* ... The Lords sincerely wish he may be

---

[1] Thomas Shirley: L 1755, CR 22.2.59, C 19.11.59. Superannuated RA.

[2] Stuart (L 1745) was killed a few days later. This case, like that of Robert Hay in
1747 (Document 27), illustrates the lack of protection for a commanding officer on his
quarterdeck, especially in a close engagement entered by a small ship. Documents
327, near the end, and 328, with n. 1 on p. 350, also refer to Stuart.

able to come up with the enemy, not doubting but in that case everything which can be expected from an experienced and gallant officer will be done by him.

324. *Captain Matthew Buckle to Hawke*

Namur in Quiberon Bay
22 November 1759

Sir,

Agreeable to your directions which I received by the lieutenant of the *Hercules*, I proceeded up this bay in order, if it was in my power, to destroy the two French ships he mentioned to you, but upon my opening the bay which he thought he saw them in, I plainly perceived that they were in the entrance of the river that goes up to Vannes or Auray with eight others. Two or three of them are large frigates or may be of the line. The rest appears to be transports by what I can judge by the distance of their masts, as I can only see them over the land; and, night coming on, I have anchored here till I hear your farther directions what you shall be pleased I shall do farther. For, they being in the river, and as I have no pilot, I don't know whether it is practicable to attack them there. I am etc.

325. *Instructions from Hawke to Captain Arbuthnot[1] of the PORTLAND*

Royal George off Penvins Point
23 November 1759

You are hereby required and directed to take under your command His Majesty's Ship *Chatham* and proceed with her as near as you can with safety to the *Essex* and, after taking out the stores and what things can be saved from her and the *Resolution*, you are to set them both on fire. For which this shall be your order. Given etc.

326. *Commodore Young to Hawke*

Mars
23 November 1759

Sir,

Enclosed is the report of Captain Willett and Captain Hood. The other ship is just got in, and a frigate layed at the mouth of the river

---

[1] Arbuthnot: L 1739, CR 1746, C 1747. Served at Havana 1762. RA 1778, VA 1779, A 1783. For most of 1779–81 he was c.-in-c., N. America.

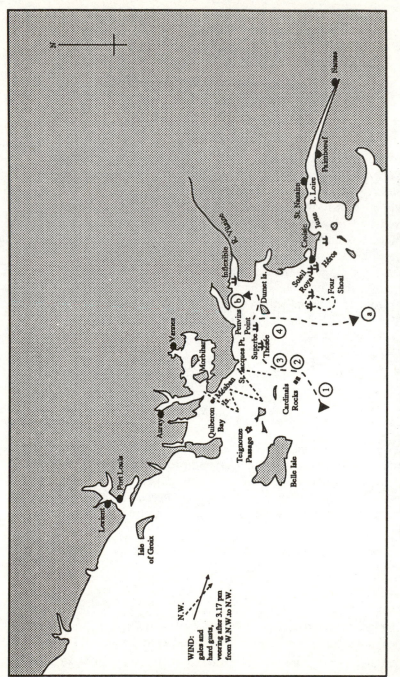

The Battle of Quiberon Bay, 20 November 1759 and the nearby coast

(Reproduced by kind permission of Dr. J. Sweetman, editor of *The Great Admirals*, U.S. Naval Institute Press [1991], which includes 'Edward Hawke' by R. F. Mackay.)

Approximate tracks of the French

Conflans's intended course

Track of chasing British van

⊥ A wrecked or sunken ship. On the Four Shoal
are the *Resolution* and *Essex*.

0   12.5   25

miles

① At about 2.45 p.m., French rear is engaged
(Two hours later, *Formidable* taken.)

② At 3.17 p.m., French line thrown into
disorder by a hard northerly gust. Thereafter,
wind at N.W.

③ From 4 to 5, a pell-mell action between here
and Dumet Is.

④ At 5.30, Hawke anchors here. French group
ⓐ steers for Rochefort and ⓑ stands towards
the R. Vilaine.

with an armed brig. The *Sapphire* [Captain Strachan] will be ready to proceed by the time appointed, if you choose we should persevere, as circumstances are something altered since I received your last directions. I am etc.

Enclosure:

326a. *Report by Willett and Hood*

Sir,

Agreeable to your directions, we have surveyed the entrance of the River Vilaine and seen the number of the enemy's ships there and find as follows. There are seven sail of the line and two frigates in the river and another on the starboard entrance on her beam ends, which we judge to be a frigate. One of the frigates weighed and came out to the mouth of the river, which appeared to be small. There is also a brig with a number of men in her — we think she mounts 6 or 8 guns—which got under way and fired several guns at our boats. The depth of water, going in from the inner buoys, was from three fathom to eleven feet at low water, and then we judged ourselves to be two miles from the shore. There are two guns mounted on the starboard entrance, going into the river, and one gun on the larboard shore, which also fired at our boats. We think the ships are about half a mile up the river and appear to be afloat. We are ...

WM. SALTREN WILLETT
ALEXR. HOOD

327. *Hawke to Clevland*

Royal George off Penvins Point
24 November 1759

Sir,

In my letter of the 17th by express, I desired you would acquaint their Lordships with my having received intelligence of eighteen sail of the line and three frigates of the Brest squadron being discovered about twenty-four leagues to the N.W. of Belle Isle, steering to the eastward. All the prisoners, however, agree that on the day we chased them their squadron consisted, according to the accompanying list, of four ships of 80, six of 74, three of 70, eight of 64, one frigate of 36, one of 34 and one of 16 guns, with a small vessel to look out. They sailed from Brest the 14th instant, the same day I sailed from Torbay. Concluding that their first rendezvous would be

Quiberon, the instant I received the intelligence I directed my course thither with a pressed sail. At first the wind, blowing hard at S. by E. and S., drove us considerably to the westward; but on the 18th and 19th, though variable, it proved more favourable. In the meantime having been joined by the *Maidstone* [(28), Captain Dudley Digges] and *Coventry* [(28), Captain Francis Burslem] frigates, I directed their commanders to keep ahead of the squadron, one on the starboard and the other on the larboard bow. At ½ past 8 o'clock in the morning of the 20th, Belle Isle by our reckoning bearing EbN¼N, the *Maidstone* made the signal for seeing a fleet.

I immediately spread abroad the signal for a line abreast in order to draw all the ships of the squadron up with me. I had before sent the *Magnanime* [Captain Lord Howe] ahead to make the land. At ¾ past 9 she made the signal for an enemy. Observing, on my discovering them, that they made off, I threw out the signal for the seven ships nearest to them to chase and draw into a line of battle ahead of me and endeavour to stop them till the rest of the squadron should come up, who were also to form as they chased, that no time might be lost in the pursuit.

That morning they [the French] were in chase of the *Rochester, Chatham, Portland, Falkland, Minerva, Vengeance* and *Venus*, all of which joined me about 11 o'clock (and [in] the evening the *Sapphire*) from Quiberon Bay. All the day we had very fresh gales at N.W. and W.N.W., with heavy squalls. Monsieur Conflans kept going off under such sail as all his squadron could carry and at the same time keep together, while we crowded after him with every sail our ships could bear. At ½ past 2 p.m., the fire beginning ahead, I made the signal for engaging.

We were then to the southward of Belle Isle and the French admiral, headmost, soon after led round the Cardinals while his rear was in action. About 4 o'clock the *Formidable* [(80), flagship of Saint-André du Verger] struck; and a little after the *Thésée* [(74)] and *Superbe* [(70)] were sunk. About 5, the *Héros* [(74)] struck and came to an anchor; but, it blowing hard, no boat could be sent on board her. Night was now come and, being on a part of the coast among islands and shoals of which we were totally ignorant, without a pilot, as was the greatest part of the squadron, and blowing hard upon a lee shore, I made the signal to anchor and came to in fifteen fathom water, the Island of Dumet bearing E. by N. between two and three miles, the Cardinals W½S, and the steeples of Croisic S.E., as we found next morning.

In the night we heard many guns of distress fired; but blowing hard, want of knowledge of the coast, and whether they were fired by a friend or an enemy, prevented all means of relief.

By daybreak of the 21st we discovered one of our ships [the *Resolution* (74)] dismasted ashore on the Four [shoal], the French *Héros* also, and the *Soleil Royal* [(80)], flagship of Marshal Conflans], which under cover of the night had anchored among us, [now] cut and run ashore to the westward of Croisic. On the latter's moving, I made the *Essex*'s signal to slip and pursue her; but she unfortunately got upon the Four and both she and the *Resolution* are irrecoverably lost, notwithstanding we sent them all the assistance that the weather would permit. About fourscore of the *Resolution*'s company, in spite of the strongest remonstrances of their captain [Henry Speke], made rafts and, with some French prisoners belonging to the *Formidable*, put off and I am afraid drove out to sea. All the *Essex*'s are saved with as many of the stores as possible, except one lieutenant and a boat's crew, who were drove on the French shore and have not since been heard of. The remains of both ships are set on fire.

We found the *Dorsetshire, Revenge*, and *Defiance*, in the night of the 20th, [had] put out to sea—as I hope the *Swiftsure* did, for she is still missing. The *Dorsetshire* and *Defiance* returned the next day and the latter saw the *Revenge* without. Thus what loss we have sustained has been owing to the weather, not the enemy, seven or eight of whose line of battle ships got to sea, I believe, the night of the action.

As soon as it was broad daylight in the morning of the 21st I discovered seven or eight of the enemy's line of battle ships at anchor between Point Penvins and the River Vilaine, on which I made the signal to weigh in order to work up and attack them. But it blowed so hard from the N.W. that, instead of daring to cast the squadron loose, I was obliged to strike topgallant masts. Most of those ships appeared to be aground at low water. But on the flood, by lightening them and the advantage of the wind under the land, all except two got that night into the River Vilaine.

The weather being moderate on the 22nd, I sent the *Portland, Chatham* and *Vengeance* to destroy the *Soleil Royal* and *Héros*. The French on the approach of our ships set the first on fire and soon after the latter met the same fate from our people. In the meantime, I got under way and worked up within Penvins Point, as well for the sake of its being a safer road as to destroy, if possible, the two ships of the enemy which still lay without the Vilaine. But before the ships I sent ahead for that purpose could get near them, being quite light and with the tide of flood they got in.

All the 23rd, we were employed in reconnoitring the entrance of that river which is very narrow and [has] only twelve foot of water on the bar at low water. We discovered at least seven, if not eight, line of battle ships about half a mile within [and] quite light, and two large frigates moored across to defend the mouth of the river. Only the frigates appear to have guns in. By the evening I had twelve longboats fitted as fireships, ready to attempt burning them under cover of the *Sapphire* and *Coventry*. But the weather being bad and the wind contrary obliged me to defer it till at least the latter should be favourable. If they can by any means be destroyed, it shall be done.

In attacking a flying enemy it was impossible, in the space of a short winter's day, that all our ships should be able to get into action or all those of the enemy brought into it. The commanders and companies of such as did come up with the rear of the French on the 20th behaved with the greatest intrepidity and gave the strongest proofs of a true British spirit. In the same manner I am satisfied would those have acquitted themselves whose bad going ships, or the distance they were at in the morning, prevented from getting up.

Our loss by the enemy is not considerable for, in the ships which are now with me, I find only one lieutenant and thirty-nine seamen and marines killed and about two hundred and two wounded. When I consider the season of the year, the hard gales on the day of action, a flying enemy, the shortness of the day, and the coast we are on, I can boldly affirm that all that could possibly be done has been done. As to the loss we have sustained, let it be placed to the account of the necessity I was under of running all risks to break this strong force of the enemy. Had we had but two hours more daylight, the whole had been totally destroyed or taken, for we were almost up with their van when night overtook us.

Yesterday came in here the *Pallas, Fortune* sloop, and the *Proserpine* fireship. On the 16th I had dispatched the *Fortune* to Quiberon with directions to Captain Duff to keep strictly on his guard. In her way thither she fell in with the *Hébé*, a French frigate of 40 guns under jury masts, and fought her several hours. During the engagement Lieutenant Stuart, second of the *Ramillies*, whom I had appointed to command her, was unfortunately killed. The surviving officers on consulting together resolved to leave her, as she proved too strong for them.

I have detached Captain Young to Quiberon Bay with five ships and am making up a flying squadron to scour the coast to the Isle of

Aix and, if practicable, to attempt any of the enemy's ships that may be there. I am etc.

Enclosure 1:

327a.   *'List of the French Squadron which came out of Brest, November 14th, 1759'*

	Guns		Men
Le Soleil Royal	80	Monsr. Conflans, admiral	1200
Le Tonnant	80	Monsr. Bauffremont, vice-admiral [chef d'escadre]	1000
Le Formidable	80	Monsr. Saint-André du Verger, rear-admiral [chef d'escadre]	1000
L'Orient	80	Monsr. Guébriant [chef d'escadre]	1000
L'Intrépide	74		815
Le Glorieux	74		815
Le Thésée	74		815
Le Héros	74		815
Le Robuste	74		815
Le Magnifique	74		815
Le Juste	70		800
Le Superbe	70	Monsr. Montalais	800
Le Dauphin	70		800
Le Dragon	64		750
Le Northumberland	64		750
Le Sphinx	64		750
Le Solitaire	64		750
Le Brillant	64		750
L'Eveillé	64		750
Le Bizarre	64	Le Prince de Montbazon	750
L'Inflexible	64		750
L'Hébé	40	Gave chase the 2nd day after coming out and lost company, and was engaged by the *Fortune* sloop where Lt. Stuart, 2nd of the *Ramillies*, was killed.	
La Vestale	34		
L'Aigrette	36		
Le Calypso	16		
Le Prince Noir [actually, *La Noire*]		A small vessel to look out.	

The above ships were all in company when the action began, except the *Hébé* frigate.

Enclosure 2:

327b. *Line of Battle*

[20 November 1759]

The *Warspite* to lead with the starboard and the *Hero* with the larboard tacks on board.

Frigates	Rate	Ships	Commanders	Guns	Men	Division
Rochester [Duff]	3	*Warspite*	Sir John Bentley	74	600	
Portland [Arbuthnot]	4	*Kingston*	[Thos.] Shirley	60	400	
Falkland [Drake]	3	*Swiftsure*	Sir Thomas Stanhope	70	520	
Chatham [Lockhart]	2	*Duke*	Capt. Graves	90	750	
Minerva [Hood]	2	*Union*	Sir Chas. Hardy, Capt. Evans	90	770	Sir C. Hardy Vice-Ad. of the Blue, etc.
Venus [T. Harrison]	3	*Hercules*	Fortescue[1]	74	600	
Vengeance [Nightingale]	4	*Intrepid*	Maplesden[2]	60	420	
Coventry [Burslem]	4	*Montagu*	Rowley	60	420	
Maidstone [Digges]	3	*Revenge*	Storr	64	480	
Sapphire [Strachan]	3	*Dorsetshire*	Denis	70	520	
[The above frigates] joined us between Ushant and Belle Isle.	3	*Torbay*	Hon. Capt. Keppel	74	700	
	1	*Royal George*	Sir Edward Hawke, Capt. Campbell	100	880	Sir Edward Hawke, Kt of the Bath, Ad. of the Blue.
	3	*Magnanime*	Rt. Hon. Lord Howe	74	700	
	3	*Burford*	Gambier[3]	70	520	
	3	*Chichester*	Willett	70	520	
	4	*Dunkirk*	Digby	60	420	
	3	*Temple*	W. Shirley	70	520	

[1] Fortescue: CR 1746, C 1757. He died in 1775.
[2] Maplesden: L 1739, CR 1746, C 1756.
[3] James Gambier was the grandson of a Huguenot refugee and the uncle of the future Adm. of the Fleet Lord Gambier; L 1743, C 1747. Commodore and c.-in-c., N. America 1770–3. RA 1778, VA 1780; c.-in-c., Jamaica 1783–4.

2	*Namur*	Buckle	90	780	
3	*Mars*	James Young Esq.	74	600	Jas. Young Esq. Com-
3	*Resolution*	Speke	74	600	modore
3	*Essex*	O'Bryen	64	480	
4	*Defiance*	Baird	60	420	
3	*Hero*	Hon. Capt. Edg-cumbe	74	600	

328.   *Hawke to Anson* (a draft)

Royal George in Quiberon Bay
[late November 1759]

My Lord,

I thought it would be a satisfaction to you that some person should be sent home with my express on whom your Lordship might rely for a faithful and impartial account of our action with the French fleet on the 20th instant. I therefore made choice of Captain Campbell who proved himself to me an honest, brave, good officer in all respects and fully answered the good opinion I had ever conceived of him. As I could then say little to your Lordship, having sent a full account of the proceedings of the squadron to the Board of Admiralty, I believed it would be of little import to trouble you with a letter by him.

I took the freedom to desire Captain Campbell to request two favours of your Lordship for me. The one was that Lieutenant Stuart, whom I had appointed to act as captain of the *Fortune* sloop and who unfortunately lost his life in her, might be confirmed in humanity to his widow, who he has left starving with three or four children. The other was to make Lieutenant Ogle of the *Ramillies* a captain for me.[1] He has been a long while an officer and is truly deserving of promotion, being a sober, sensible, diligent, good young man. He is a first cousin to Lady Kingston and is well known to Lord Scarborough and Sir George Saville, both of whom have a great regard for him.

I have now the pleasure to acquaint your Lordship that the *Swiftsure* and *Revenge* are come in safe, excepting the few damages they received from the enemy, which may soon be repaired in port,

[1] Some three months later, the Ady. confirmed Stuart as commander of the *Fortune* sloop from 14.11.59 (Adm. 6/19, p.140). Meanwhile on 27.12.59 Ogle had been appointed to command the *Strombolo* fireship.

but they must both come home for that purpose; and that we have heard of the loss of another of the enemy's ships. She was called the *Juste*, of 70 guns. Indeed, my Lord, had you been in the action, I am of opinion that you would have thought it a miracle that half our ships were not on shore, they were all so keen in the pursuit of the enemy, in a winter's day and hard squalls, upon their own coast, which we were all unacquainted with. The loss of our two ships was owing to their not having the *Neptune François* on board, and they had neither of them anything to direct them what to do. This leads me to offer to your Lordship's judgement whether it would not be greatly for the benefit of the service to have that book correctly printed on a large scale, and translated, at the King's expense, and given to all the ships that are employed, as well as the best draughts that can be had of the different coasts in any part of the world where our ships may be sent.

I have consulted all the young, active men of spirit in the frigates, besides others, about the enemy's ships lying in the Vilaine harbour and have made them reconnoitre them as they lie, over and over again; but am sorry to tell your Lordship that they positively assure me we can do nothing with them, either with fireships or bombs. However they will be rendered entirely useless to the enemy, as I shall keep a watch upon them to prevent anything going to or coming from them—and have reason to believe most, if not all of them, have broke their backs. [On this, see Document 330a together with Note 1.]

As soon as the weather would permit, I detached Mr Keppel away with a squadron to run along the coast to the southward as far as Rochefort with directions to return to me again in Quiberon.

Now that the principal service is at an end, I should be glad of your Lordship's permission to return into port with the three deck ships and such others of two decks as require to be cleaned and are not in a fit condition to stay out. Sir Charles Hardy, who has been out as long as myself, would be glad if your Lordship shall approve of his coming in at the same time.

I beg leave to offer for your Lordship's consideration whether it would not be proper to keep about twelve sail of the line constantly lying in this place with three 50-gun ships and four or five frigates, under the command of an admiral, which will be, I should think, a sufficient guard for their whole coast from Port Louis to Rochefort. A couple of these ships with a frigate may keep constantly cutting across each other from one port to the other, by which means their whole coast [at] Port Louis, the River Vannes and Auray, Vilaine,

Nantes and Rochefort will be in a great measure blocked up. And four or five sail, of great and small, will, I should think, be enough to cruise off Brest.

In regard to the whole I can truly say that I have in all respects, strictly and faithfully complied with my duty, and that I have nothing more sincerely at heart, at all times, than to use my utmost endeavours to merit your Lordship's approbation, being with the highest and sincerest truth and respect etc.

329.   *Court Martial on the loss of the RESOLUTION*

Union in Quiberon Bay
29 November 1759

Present:

> Sir Charles Hardy, Knight, Vice-Admiral of the Blue
> Sir John Bentley
> Honourable Captain George Edgcumbe
> Captain Samuel Graves
> Captain Peter Denis
> Captain Robert Duff
> Captain John Reynolds
> Captain John Storr
> Captain Dudley Digges[1]
> Captain John Lockhart
> Captain John Evans

Pursuant to an order from Sir Edward Hawke, Knight of the Bath, Admiral of the Blue, etc., dated the 27th November 1759 directed to Sir Charles Hardy, Knight, Vice-Admiral of the Blue. The court, being duly sworn, proceeded to the trial of Captain Henry Speke for the loss of His Majesty's ship *Resolution*, she being unfortunately stranded on a shoal called the Four during the night of the 20th instant and irrecoverably lost.

LIEUTENANT CHARLES FIELDING[2] sworn.

> COURT   Relate to the court what you know of the loss of the ship and what orders you received from the captain.
> A.   I had the first watch and received orders to knot and splice the rigging with all possible dispatch and, when in a condition to make sail, to tack and join the Admiral … At half past 9 we put

---

[1] Digges: L 1745, C 1753. Died in 1779.
[2] Fielding: L 1757, CR 14.4.60, C 27.8.60. Died in 1782.

the ship to stays; but, missing stays, we wore and, in standing to the fleet, the ship struck in about half an hour upon a sand we knew nothing of. After she was aground, everything was done that was possible to preserve the ship.

MR JOHN PIERCY, master, sworn.
COURT   What orders did you receive?
A.   To put about to join the Admiral as soon as we could.
COURT   What time was that?
A.   About 9.
COURT   Did you apprehend being near any sand?
A.   No.
COURT   Did you know anything of the sand you was grounded upon?
A.   No. I am wholly unacquainted with the coast.
COURT   Had you a *Neptune François* on board?
A.   No ...

MR DAVID MARTIN, carpenter, sworn.
COURT   Give the court an account of what you know of the loss of the ship.
A.   I believe we did not know we were so nigh any sand. When she first touched, I was down below and run up immediately. We soon got over that sand, but after we came to an anchor, she tailed on shore and struck very hard. At high water, she floated and we did all we could to save her, but could not. At low water, she struck again very hard and was bulged.

After examining the officer of the watch, master, and others, it appears to the court that the *Resolution's* grounding was an unavoidable accident, they being wholly unacquainted with the coast and not knowing there was any such sand, or shoal, in their way when they tacked to join the Admiral; and that Captain Speke did personally and, by his orders, use every means possible for her preservation, which became impracticable from her soon bulging. And the court do therefore acquit Captain Speke and all the officers for the loss of the said ship; and they are hereby acquitted accordingly ...

[The necessary court martial on the loss of the *Essex* was held at Portsmouth on 22 January 1760—after Hawke's return to England.]

330. *Hawke to Clevland*

Royal George in Quiberon Bay
1 December 1759
'Recd. 29th by express'

Sir,

The manoeuvres of the enemy crowding away on the 20th prevented our being able to reckon their number exactly. Now I can with certainty assure their Lordships that their squadron consisted of twenty-one sail of the line and four frigates, with more seamen and soldiers than I gave in the list [327a] which accompanied my last. To the number destroyed I can also add the *Juste* of 70 guns; and I am in hopes, too, to find the *Magnifique* run ashore or lost, for she was terribly shattered.

The *Dorsetshire, Swiftsure, Revenge* and *Magnanime* wanting great repairs, I have ordered the *Revenge* to Plymouth and the rest to Portsmouth with the *Proserpine* and *Formidable*. I have detached the *Maidstone* with orders to Rear-Admiral Geary to join me here with the *Foudroyant, Valiant* and *Bienfaisant*, leaving the smaller ships to cruise off Brest, as I am clearly of opinion that this is the most proper rendezvous for the squadron.

Enclosed is a list of the ships off Rochefort under Mr Keppel's orders. I have sent the *Rochester* to join the *Fame* off Cape Finisterre, the *Coventry* off Nantes, the *Southampton* off Belle Isle, and the *Falkland* off Groix.

Since my last I have been joined by the *Firm, Success, Firedrake* [bomb vessel], and last night by the *Actaeon*. Captain Ourry [of the *Success*], not knowing where the French squadron was gone, sent the *Gibraltar* to put the ships off Cape Finisterre and Calais on their guard.

Enclosed is a list of officers I have appointed to act in vacancies. I must only add that I should be greatly obliged to their Lordships to remember Lieutenant Thomas Neilson,[1] first of the *Ramillies*, now commanding the *Success*. He has been nineteen years a Lieutenant, upwards of three of which he has been an officer with me. And Mr William Pearce, my first clerk, to be made a purser.[2] I am etc.

Enclosure:

---

[1] Neilson (L 1741) was appointed commander on 1.3.60.
[2] No warrant seems to have been issued for Pearce in the course of the following six months.

330a. *Copy of Young to Hawke*

Mars off Quiberon Bay
30 November 1759

Sir,

I beg leave to acquaint you that there is no alteration in the situation of the French ships here [in Morbihan harbour] since my arrival. Their sails are all bent, which Captain Arbuthnot thought they were not when they lay here before. Yesterday our boat, in sounding the passage, spoke with a dean from Port L'Orient where there is three frigates and about thirty merchantmen. They say there is seven of their ships destroyed and three of ours;[1] but that is all they could get out of them, as they are very silent. But all their shops were shut up and they appeared in great consternation. We have taken up the *Venus*'s cable and anchor, [cut away when Duff was alerted on 19 November], and *Thunder* bomb's. The *Portland* has also taken up hers. The buoy ropes of some of them break, but we leave slip ones on the cables, when you think proper to send the ships they belong to to take them up. I am etc.

331. *Hawke to Clevland*

Royal George in Quiberon Bay
2 December 1759
'Recd. 26 December'

Sir,

The day after I came to an anchor off Penvins Point, [being] anxious for the safety of the lieutenant of the *Essex* and the *Resolution*'s people who went away on the raft, I wrote to the Duke d'Aiguillon [the general commanding the French expeditionary army] begging he would cause inquiry to be made for them on the coast, that I might exchange them. As the number of men much wounded on board the *Formidable* was very great and very nauseous, I desired at the same time he would send vessels to take them on shore. I received a very polite answer and the wounded were sent for. He also sent an officer to desire that I would send on shore five companies of the regiment of Saintonge and one hundred and forty militia on the

---

[1] The number of French ships of the line lost was indeed seven. The *Formidable* had been taken and the *Soleil Royale*, *Thésée*, *Superbe*, *Héros*, *Juste* and *Inflexible* were sunk in battle, wrecked, or otherwise destroyed. Of the ships seeking refuge in the Vilaine, only the *Inflexible* was lost. The British, for their part, lost two of the line, as reported by Hawke (Documents 327 and 328 above).

terms of the cartel settled by General Conway in February last. On this, I sent Lord Howe on shore to him and enclose you a copy of the agreement between them, which I have approved and consented, as only about one hundred and twenty of the French soldiers survive; that they shall go on shore on parole given that they shall not serve against His Majesty for one year to come; also that the officers and gardes-marine, in number five, shall be sent on shore on their parole ...

The *Coventry* is just returned from the wreck of the *Juste* on the Charpentier [near St Nazaire]. She is irrecoverably lost, and all her crew, excepting about 250 men.

Captain Keppel is also returned and enclosed I send you a copy of his report.

This morning came in here the *Aeolus* [(32), Captain John Elliot[1]]. I am etc.

Enclosure:

331a. *Keppel to Hawke*

Torbay in Quiberon Bay
2 December 1759

Sir,

In pursuance of your directions to me, I proceeded with the squadron under my command to the southward in quest of the enemy's ships and on the 29th anchored off Aix Road. The *Minerva* joined in the evening and her captain informed me that he had stood very near the Isle of Aix and that from his mast head, over the island, he perceived seven large ships of the line, one with a flag at her fore topmast head, besides another ship that was dismasted and in tow of a small vessel. The situation of the enemy's ships, as described by Captain Hood, gave me some reason to imagine they had got up very near the mouth of the Charente.

At daybreak the following morning, I weighed with the squadron and proceeded to the Isle of Aix and, as I passed the Point, I discovered the enemy's ships as follows: three frigates and four line of battle ships close in between Fort la Pointe and Isle Madame, and three line of battle ships within Fort la Pointe. This appearance

[1] John Elliot was a younger brother of Gilbert Elliot (p. 151, n. 2). Having been first in the merchant service, he became L 1756, C 1757. He had a brilliant record as a frigate captain in the Seven Years War and commanded at the defeat of Thurot in Feb. 1760. In the American War, as a senior captain, he was again to the fore — notably at Rodney's relief of Gibralter 1779–80. RA 1787, VA 1790, A 1795.

agreed exactly with Captain Hood's description excepting the dis-masted ship, which I did not see. There appeared four more very large and rigged [ships] as high up the Charente as the Vergeron. The situation and distance of the nearest of the enemy's ships was such as rendered it impracticable to offer an attempt upon them, they being farther up by miles than any ship can go without warping through the mud and being dismantled ...

The seven line of battle ships that I suppose to be part of the enemy's fleet dispersed by you, Sir, the 20th November seemed, as to their rigging, somewhat shattered ...

I was within musket shot of the point of the Isle of Aix, and the fortifications are now in the same ruined condition that you left them in, Sir, in April 1758.

I am, with the greatest respect, Sir, etc.

332. *Anson to Hawke* [holograph]

Admiralty
1 December 1759

Dear Sir Edward,

I have the utmost satisfaction in assuring you that the arrival of Captain Campbell with the good news of the success and glory which has just crowned your long and worthy labours for the public service has given the most general joy and satisfaction here. His Majesty extremely approves every part of your conduct and the behaviour of your whole fleet, and is fully satisfied that nothing was omitted which could be done to gain and improve the victory.

It is his gracious intention to recompense a service of so much honour and importance. I am authorized by the Duke of Newcastle to acquaint you that a grant is proposed and agreed to of fifteen hundred to you and your family for thirty-one years, the longest term the King can grant.[1] I must by no means omit informing you of the Duke of Newcastle's ready proposal and Mr Pitt's support of what it is hoped will be agreeable to you, and I am sure you know how zealously I have always endeavoured to contribute towards what might give you satisfaction. Indeed all the King's servants are as desirous as possible of taking this opportunity of showing their regard for you.

I must add that nothing makes me so happy as every instance of

---

[1] In March 1760, Hawke was officially informed that his pension would amount to £2,000 a year for his own life and for the lives of his two older sons in succession after him.

the truly gallant and skilful behaviour of the English Navy; but it is impossible not to feel a peculiar joy upon an occasion which has enabled so many of my particular friends to give the world fresh proofs of the merit I have so long esteemed. I must beg of you to express my sentiments to all of them and how much I rejoice in their safety. My congratulations on everything honourable and advantageous to you proceed from the sincerest friendship with which I am always,

Dear Sir,
Your most faithful humble servant

ANSON

333. *Clevland to Hawke*

3 December 1759

Sir,

I have communicated to my Lords Commissioners of the Admiralty your letter of the 24th past [327], with an account of the proceedings of His Majesty's ships under your command in coming up with and defeating the French squadron commanded by Monsieur le Maréchal de Conflans on the 20th instant near Belle Isle, which letter has been placed before His Majesty, who was graciously pleased to approve of your conduct on that glorious occasion, where you have rendered the highest service to your country and acquired so much honour to yourself which, their Lordships command me to acquaint you, they, as well as the whole nation, are sensible of, and that they return you thanks for the same. I have it also in command to express their Lordships' satisfaction in the behaviour of the several captains and companies of His Majesty's ships which they recommend to you to make known to them.

Their Lordships extremely approve of the judicious disposition you have made of your squadron and, as you will soon come into port, they command me to acquaint you that you have their leave to come to Town to recover the fatigue of your long and attentive cruise, which has ended with so much success and honour.

I beg you will permit me to add my sincere congratulations hereon and to assure you that I am with very great esteem and regard etc.

[During the next few weeks the weather was so bad that this letter did not reach Hawke till 6 January. Anson's letter dated 1 December (Document 332) probably came out with Clevland's but, being personal, was not acknowledged in Hawke's official dispatch of 7

January (Document 338).]

334. *Hawke to Clevland*

Royal George in Quiberon Bay
9 December 1759

Sir,

Since my last of the 2nd [331] the wind has blown so hard easterly that it has prevented all operations against the enemy, except sending the *Sapphire*, *Aeolus* and *Coventry* to reduce the Island of Yeu, which you will see they have effected by the enclosed copy of a letter from Captain Strachan. Besides distressing the enemy, I had in view the watering the squadron from thence in case of want.

I have sent the *Defiance* and *Dunkirk* to look into Basque Road and off the Isle of Aix. For, ever since Mr Keppel's report [331a] of the situation of the enemy there, I have been of opinion that the most effective way to block up all the French ports will be to divide the squadron and send at least twelve ships of the line, with two or three frigates, to lie in the Basque Road, or at Aix, and eight or nine here to guard Morbihan and Vilaine, with cruisers off Brest where nothing can be ready soon. Cutters, at least eight or ten, will be wanted for these two squadrons, while the frigates and 50-gun ships cruise off Belle Isle, Groix and Bordeaux. The better to enable me to prosecute this plan, I have directed Rear-Admiral Geary to send back to England all the ships that might have been sent out with orders to return as soon as they should receive certain intelligence of the fate of the Brest squadron; to leave a 60-gun ship and one or two frigates off Brest; and to repair to this bay with all the other ships under his orders. Lying at anchor here and in Basque Road, with frigates cruising, will distress the enemy more effectually than keeping the sea and at the same time be a great saving to the government in wear and tear of ships and their furniture.

As soon as Mr Geary shall join me, I shall detach Captain Edgcumbe with a squadron to Basque ... The *Portland*, *Pallas* and *Fortune* lie off Vilaine where four of the French men o' war have been aground; and none of them, though we cannot come at them, seem to lie there in great safety. The *Actaeon*, *Chatham*, *Success* and *Firedrake* are off Croisic to cover the vessels attempting, if possible, to weigh the guns of the *Soleil Royal*. I have with me the *Royal George*, *Union*, *Namur*, *Duke*, *Torbay*, *Hero*, *Warspite*, *Hercules*, *Mars*, *Belliqueux*, *Burford*, *Chichester*, *Firm*, *Montagu* and *Kingston*. We have taken all the wine out of the two cats from Guernsey. There is great want of bread, beer, butter and cheese, and a month of other species in the squadron. I am etc.

335. *Hawke to Clevland*

Royal George in Quiberon Bay
16 December 1759
'Recd. 24th'

Sir,

The hard easterly gales, which have blown here above these fourteen days, I am apprehensive have prevented either the dispatches I sent to Rear-Admiral Geary from reaching him, or drove him so far to the westward that I have little reason to expect him here soon. In the present state of the ships with me, which on an average have not above one months' provisions on board, a fortnight or three weeks breaks greatly into my plan and I shall not be able, till a fresh squadron shall arrive, to send any ships to Basque Road. Even in that case, few of the squadron now in this bay will be able to remain for want of wood, coals and candles, where a strong one is absolutely necessary.

I am also afraid the strong easterly winds have drove the *Dorsetshire, Revenge, Swiftsure, Magnanime, Temple* and *Colchester* to the westward or to Ireland. I therefore enclose you duplicates of the letters I sent by them.

I have now been thirty-one weeks on board without setting my foot on shore and cannot expect my health will hold out much longer. I therefore hope to be relieved. Sir Charles Hardy and Rear-Admiral Geary are in the same condition.

Large cats are the only vessels proper to bring provisions at this season of the year. I am etc.

336. *Hawke to Clevland*

Royal George in Quiberon Bay
26 December 1759
'Recd. 1st January'

Sir,

The *Falkland* cruising off Groix being very short of provisions and necessaries, I sent the *Intrepid* to relieve her, with orders to Captain Drake to repair to Plymouth to clean and refit; but, missing each other, the *Falkland* put in here and sails today for England.

The *Defiance, Dunkirk* and *Aeolus* are also returned without having been able to look into Basque Road.

Enclosed is the state and condition of His Majesty's ships under my command, by which their Lordships will perceive that few, if any, of them can now remain here above a fortnight longer for want of water, provisions and necessaries, unless these articles be already on the way hither. Very little water, and that very brackish, can be procured from the Isle of Yeu, as they have it only in draw wells in their houses.

This comes by the *Venus* and I propose, in order not to distress the rest, to send hence tomorrow the *Duke, Kingston, Montagu, Swallow* and *Fortune* to clean and refit at Plymouth.

The *Intrepid* [Captain Jervis Maplesden] having been drove in here on the evening of the 24th, I have ordered Captain Maplesden, with the *Aeolus*, to return to his station off Groix.

The *Swallow*, one of the cruisers which I sent with orders to Rear-Admiral Geary, returned yesterday without having met with or heard of him.[1]

Whatever ships shall be sent on this station must be furnished with four months provisions of all species and more especially with necessaries for that time. I am etc.

337.   *Hawke to Clevland*

Torbay in Quiberon Bay
2 January 1760

Sir,

By want of provisions and water I am reduced to the necessity of sending the *Royal George, Union, Namur, Mars* and *Belliqueux* into port. I have hoisted my flag on board the *Torbay* [Captain Keppel] and shall remain in this bay with the *Hero, Warspite, Hercules, Chichester, Burford, Defiance, Dunkirk, Intrepid, Portland* and *Chatham* till their Lordships shall relieve me, which I beg may be as soon as possible, or till our water and provisions shall be gone, which will be in twenty days more. If their Lordships will consider how long all these ships have been out, they will perceive they can only be relieved by clean ships.

The *Aeolus* is off Groix, the *Coventry* off Bordeaux and the *Southampton* going off Basque. I am etc.

[1] Having lost sight of the rest of his labouring squadron, Geary took account of the battered, sickly and depleted state of the *Sandwich* and went into Spithead on 26 December.

338. *Hawke to Clevland*

Torbay in Quiberon Bay
7 January 1760
'Recd. 23 January'

Sir,

On the 5th arrived the two cutters from Plymouth but without bringing any dispatches. Last night I was joined by the *Anson* and *Monmouth*, by whom I had the satisfaction of receiving your letters of 23rd November and 3rd December 1759 [333]. The last has communicated to me the most substantial pleasure that I could enjoy in this world, my Royal Master's most gracious approbation of my conduct. I shall long for an opportunity to throw myself at his feet with the most loyal assurance of the dutiful sense I do, and ever shall, entertain of his goodness.

Their Lordships, too, may depend on my constant gratitude for their kind sentiments of my behaviour on that occasion.

Every plan of operation I formed after the 1st December has proved abortive through bad weather and want of provisions and necessaries. I have, from the small number of ships that could stay out, been confined to one object, the troops at Vannes. I am now informed that one regiment of dragoons has marched on foot from thence to Broglie's army and that all the transports in the Rivers Vannes and Auray were discharged from the French King's service the last day of December.

I hear by the *Anson* that the victuallers were to sail on Wednesday last. I am much afraid they will hardly get to this place. Yet I shall wait with patience some days longer in expectation of them or of Admiral Boscawen, who will bring the surest relief. I am etc.

[Leaving Sir John Bentley in command, Hawke sailed in the *Torbay* on 11 January. He was soon in the Channel but, having then been held up for some days by contrary winds, he finally put into Plymouth on the 16th.]

339. *Admiralty Minute*

7 February 1760

Present: Anson, Hay, Elliot, Forbes.

Sir John Bentley, left by Sir Edward Hawke commander-in-chief of His Majesty's ships in Quiberon Bay, having represented that the men are very much afflicted with the scurvy, and Admiral Boscawen, who is gone thither, having desired that they have a constant supply of beef, mutton, onions, etc., the Commissioners for Victualling are to be directed to cause the same to be done accordingly ...

340. *Hawke to Anson* [holograph]

[? late February 1760]

[On 15 February 1760 the *Ramillies*, still commanded by Captain Witteronge Taylor (Hawke's flag captain from 1756 till November 1759), was wrecked on Bolt Head in a great gale. All her company perished except for a midshipman and twenty-five others.]

Sir Edward Hawke presents his compliments to Lord Anson and hopes he will be so good as to pardon his taking the freedom of reminding his Lordship of the four poor unhappy women, the warrant officers' widows of the late *Ramillies*. They are left destitute of everything, and both them and their children must infallibly starve unless the Board will commiserate [with] their unfortunate situation.

Sir Edward has lately received a letter from the widow of Captain Taylor wherein she begs him to intercede with his Lordship in her behalf. She is truly a very deserving, good woman and well worthy of his Lordship's compassion. Sir Edward would have delivered a petition for her to the King and Council when he gave the others to Mr Sharp, but he told him there was no occasion for it because the Board had it in their power to settle what pension they should think proper upon her. Poor woman, she has no friend in Town to solicit for her but himself; and as she is the unfortunate widow of his captain, he trusts in Lord Anson's goodness to excuse his being so troublesome.

Sir Edward has been confined this week past with a very troublesome cough or otherwise he would have waited on his Lordship to have implored his goodness for these poor unhappy women.
George Street, Monday night.

PART IV(f)

AUGUST 1760—AUGUST 1762
HAWKE'S LAST CAMPAIGNS

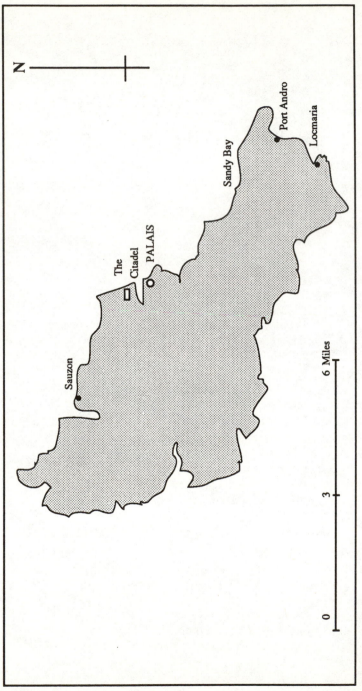

Belle Isle

INTRODUCTION

After returning to England in January 1760, Hawke duly received his pension and the thanks of the House of Commons. Having recovered his health, he was instructed in August to relieve Boscawen who had been enforcing a system of blockade now based on Quiberon Bay. Hawke was to attend especially to Rochefort and the estuary of the Vilaine from which six surviving French ships of the line and several frigates might try to escape [Document 341]. Indeed, in January 1761, a thick fog presented them with a good opportunity, as we shall see.

Meanwhile Hawke became a good deal preoccupied with Pitt's plan to seize Belle Isle. The island was big enough to harbour a fairsized military force and Pitt believed that, once based there, it would compel the French to deploy troops along much of the Biscay coast. Early in the autumn of 1760 the cabinet heard evidence from Captain Keppel that, while the north-easterly beaches of the island seemed those best suited for a landing, they were close to the guns of the citadel. Also the water offshore might not be deep enough to permit close naval support. On 9 October Anson wrote to Hawke asking him to report on these and other items [342]. In an accompanying note of the same date Clevland wrote that Anson 'would be glad to be favoured' with Hawke's 'private thoughts' on the project 'in a separate letter'. Hawke, however, replied in a single letter [343]. This forced Anson to put before the King and cabinet Hawke's own preference for a landing on the mainland in Quiberon Bay. This resulted in a major conflict of opinion at the top political level. Pitt was extremely annoyed at what he regarded as Hawke's improper interference with his plans. Then, on 25 October, King George II died and the Belle Isle question fell into abeyance for a few weeks.

Pitt, however, re-established his leadership and, in consequence, Hawke is to be found on 15 December preparing for the unseasonable arrival of the invasion force [344]. But by 27 December he was informed that more sensible views had prevailed and a landing would not be attempted during that winter.

In France the navy minister had meanwhile offered a full captaincy to any subordinate officer who could bring a ship of the line from the Vilaine to Brest. It was the Chevalier de Ternay who proceeded to accomplish this feat in January 1761 under the cover of a dense fog. The account given by an officer of the detached force watching the Vilaine is embodied in Hawke's dispatch of 13 January, written from his anchorage some twenty miles away in Quiberon Bay [347]. Ternay brought out not one ship of the line, but two, together with two frigates. However, one of the frigates was soon captured by the British after a fierce exchange. But it should be noted that, in January and April 1762—when Hawke was not on the Quiberon station—Ternay succeeded in extricating the remaining four serviceable ships of the line from the Vilaine, two at a time, and carrying them to Brest. With two of the rescued ships of the line and two frigates he carried out his notable raid on Newfoundland. Ternay's exploits illustrate the fact that, even with the advantage of a degree of shelter, a close blockade might well prove less than perfectly effective at all seasons of the year. On the other hand, in Ternay's case at least, the enemy could emerge only in small numbers and on occasions which were hardly predictable—by either side—more than a few hours in advance.

Having completed five months of service, including the winter, Hawke returned to Spithead in the *Royal George* on 10 March 1761 and was granted extended leave for the re-establishment of his health [348–9]. In January 1762, while the Admiral was still recuperating, the strategic picture was considerably changed when the long-threatened entry of Spain into the war on the side of France was officially declared. This led in the summer to a British military force being sent to Portugal. Hawke, having meanwhile been called back to Portsmouth in April, was charged with the safeguarding of the transportation [359]. He had been furnished with a commander-in-chief's commission which gave him wide powers [352]. This, however, caused a certain lack of smooth co-ordination. The Admiralty soon found it inconvenient to issue all orders for ship movements in the Channel through Hawke but failed to avoid causing him a degree of annoyance [358].

Soon afterwards, on 6 June, Anson died quite suddenly at his home in Hertfordshire. Combining professional knowledge with political and administrative skills, he had, as First Lord, made a great contribution to the remarkable successes achieved by the Navy during the war and his loss was hardly reparable. There were rumours that Hawke would replace him. However, the orders issued to that admiral on 5 May to make ready for the sea [353] remained in force and, towards the end of June, he sailed with ten of the line for his final cruise in the Bay of Biscay. In view of his successful interceptions of 1747 and 1759, the detailed reasoning behind Hawke's movements (given in his dispatch of 9 July) is of interest [366].

Meanwhile, the maritime dominance exercised by Britain over France and Spain combined had already been quietly underlined on 11 May 1762 when Hawke, as commander-in-chief, ordered a mere sloop of 8 guns to escort a convoy of six troop transports from Portsmouth to Belle Isle, after also safeguarding some of the trade in the Channel during the early part of her voyage [354].

341. *Secret Instructions from the Lords of the Admiralty to Hawke*

8 August 1760

Whereas we intend that you shall proceed forthwith to Quiberon Bay in order to relieve Admiral Boscawen in the command of the squadron of His Majesty's ships employed there and in the adjacent parts, you are hereby required and directed to repair immediately to Spithead and hoist your flag on board His Majesty's ship the *Royal George* and then proceed down the Channel off Plymouth where you are to take under your command His Majesty's ships and vessels named in the margin [*Hero* (74), *Burford* (70), *Monmouth* (64), *Edgar* (64), *Sapphire* (32)] whose captains are directed to join you on your appearance and follow your orders and then make the best of your way to Quiberon Bay.

You will receive herewith a list of the ships and vessels now under the command of Admiral Boscawen; and whereas we intend you shall have seventeen ships of the line and twelve frigates and sloops ... and whereas it is designed you should with this squadron keep a very diligent watch over the enemy's ships of war and use your utmost endeavour to prevent their joining each other, or getting to sea separately, with any number of transports, and also to take or destroy their convoying stores, provisions, arms and ammunition to any of their ports at home or colonies abroad, you are to apply the utmost attention to the well performing those services, and in particular to be very attentive to the enemy's ships at Rochefort and in the River Vilaine ...

Given etc.

ANSON
GEO.HAY
THOS. ORBY HUNTER

342. *Anson to Hawke* (a copy)

9 October 1760

The situation of the King's affairs in Germany requiring a diversion to be made on the enemy's coasts, His Majesty's servants have considered which may be the properest place for that purpose and, having examined Mr Keppel who, having been lately in the bay, had an opportunity of making the observations that I send herewith on part of the coast of the isle of Belle Isle which it is thought may be attacked with the best prospect of success; and the King, as well as his servants, reposing great confidence in you, I have it in command to let you know that a very considerable body of troops, with a train of artillery, are collecting together and transports getting ready to embark them, whenever it shall be thought proper.

Wherefore you are desired to use every means in your power to inform yourself how near ships can lie to batter the several works in the sandy bays of Belle Isle mentioned by Mr Keppel, and what depth of water there is close in to the shore, and to ascertain the distance of the citadel from the said sandy bays.

You will also inform yourself whether troops can be landed at Locmaria or any other parts of the island besides these described in Mr Keppel's paper and how far they may be from the citadel. You will likewise please to learn whether the enemy's ships in the River Vilaine are disarmed and, if so, whether their artillery, ammunition and stores have been sent to Paimboeuf [in the Loire estuary] or how disposed of.

It will also be necessary to know what numbers of regular troops and militia there may be in the island and if the town of Palais is fortified, to come at which knowledge I would recommend to you to cause some coasting or fishing vessels belonging to the enemy to be taken, and by every proper means to get the best intelligence you can from them.

When you have satisfied yourself with all that is necessary to be known, I must desire you will send me your answer by a good sailing frigate to the first port she can make in England and to forward the same by express.

I hope it is needless for me to repeat the confidence that is reposed in you on this occasion and the necessity there is for the strictest secrecy.

343. *Hawke to Anson* (a copy)

Quiberon Bay
17 October 1760

Late in the evening of the 14th I had the honour of your Lordship's letter of the 9th by the *Melampe*. Before I give my opinion on the subject of it, you will give me leave to assure your Lordship that, whatever plan of diversion shall be fixed on, I shall cheerfully contribute my utmost to carry it into execution, whatever my own sentiments of it may be.

As I only had cursory views of Belle Isle as I passed by it, I dispatched Captain Hotham [of the *Melampe* (36)] immediately to reconnoitre it and in the meantime examined a sensible French pilot, whom I took out of a Spanish ship, and the master of a *chasse-marée*. Their accounts agree with Captain Hotham's observations that no vessel can lie nearer to citadel, which stands very high, than two miles at least; that they may approach Point Andro but not be able to injure the high batteries that defend it. So they may [approach] the Sandy Bay defended by the batteries I, K, L, M in Captain Hotham's sketch, but that and every other place accessible by boats is defended by palisades and walls. By all accounts, from the first of our coming here the enemy has been particularly attentive to the fortifying the little of this island which is not impregnable by nature. They, by the accounts I have, keep the citadel well stored and, besides two battalions of militia, have three regiments of regulars on it. But suppose it taken, will the possession of a place detached by water from the continent draw troops from any part of that continent to retake it while we are masters at sea? On the contrary, I think it may prove a great accession of strength to them, as by the cartel settled last year with General Conway, within a few weeks we must deliver up three regiments and two battalions of militia, now useless in a detached isle, to be employed against Hanover.

Your Lordship will readily conclude that I cannot subscribe to Belle Isle's being the properest place for making a diversion.

For your Lordship's satisfaction, I send this express by Captain Hotham.

The short stay I made here last winter, together with the tempestuous weather, prevented my making the necessary observations on the enemy's coast. But ever since my last arrival I have not been idle and employed my officers in sounding and reconnoitring Morbihan, the Rivers Auray, Vannes and Vilaine, with an intention to attempt destroying the men of war in the last and the transports in the two first. For this purpose I have also got what intelligence I could from the crews of several *chasse-marées* who, by promises of rewards, have been pretty open. From the whole I formed sanguine hopes of success as, by all accounts, there are not above 1400 regulars to defend the coast from Morbihan to Nantes. Croisic, with the Salt Pans, I had also included in my plan. But your Lordship's letter has opened a wider view to me and induced me to lay aside for the present the execution of my own. The batteries at the mouth of the Vilaine and Morbihan may be attacked at the same time, while the boats may push on to fire the ships in the one and the transports in the other. In the meantime about a thousand marines or other troops may land and secure the neck of land on which stands St Jacques where, in the case of a disaster, our troops from the Morbihan and Vilaine may retreat, meet, and defend themselves against all the force of France, in case of succeeding in the first attack. I think there will be little hazard against making a lodgement at Vannes, Auray and Croisic, or, according to the number of troops, advancing to L'Orient.

From Vilaine to Vannes is twelve miles, from Vannes to Auray nine miles, and from Auray to L'Orient twelve miles. Croisic is about fifteen miles from Vannes, but may be easily defended by itself.

Enclosed are sketches of some part of the coast.

I have some Frenchmen who will serve for pilots for the Rivers Vannes and Auray.

Whichever plan shall be approved of, I shall have everything in my power ready for the troops to enter on action the instant they arrive. The better to enable me to do this, I hope your Lordship will send by a clean frigate beforehand the number of troops, transports, frigates, bomb vessels, fireships, cutters and flat-bottomed boats.

The transports must have good ground tackling or they will be liable to be drove on shore if we should have a run of bad weather.

Enclosed is part of Captain Gambier's letter in consequence of the directions I gave him before the arrival of the *Melampe*, dated this day.

344. *Hawke to Pitt*

Royal George in Quiberon Bay
15 December 1760

Sir,

By Sir John Bentley of the King's ship *Warspite*, who joined me in Quiberon Bay the 26th November, I had the honour of your letter with the secret instructions which His Majesty had been pleased to sign for my guidance and direction in the attempt to be made on the island of Belle Isle. I beg leave, Sir, by you to throw myself at His Majesty's feet with the deepest and most grateful sense of the confidence he is graciously pleased to repose in me by entrusting me with the execution of the maritime part of that important attempt.

As I received no plan of operation nor so much as a hint of the general or Captain Keppel being acquainted with the soundings or proper landing places, I presumed from thence that my first duty was attentively to reconnoitre and sound the accessible side of Belle Isle on the north, [that is] from Point Locmaria on the S.E. to Point Daubourg on the N.W. end of the island. For this purpose I dispatched Captains Peyton,[1] Lendrick, Evans, Bennett [now Hawke's flag captain], and Lee in a sloop and cutter to examine that coast with the utmost care and attention. They had the advantage of very fine weather and of meeting with no obstruction from the enemy, who either did not perceive them or did not penetrate their employment. Enclosed is a copy of the report they made to me on their return. After maturely considering it, I formed the enclosed plan of attack, under cover of which the troops are to land immediately on arrival, if the weather will permit. That it may be the easier understood, I have taken the liberty to enclose you a sketch of the north side of the island with the ships placed in their stations of attack, purposing while they are engaged to make a diversion with bombs and frigates at Palais and with frigates at Sauzon. I have dispatched the *Tamar* [sloop] to cruise nine or ten leagues N.W. of Belle Isle with like copies and sketches, and the necessary orders to Captain Keppel.

In case he should come in more to the southward I have sent duplicates in the *Warspite* whose station lies that way. I have only made some little deviation from the plan sent to Mr Keppel with regard to the diversion off Sauzon, but such as by no means affects the principal attack. I shall also take out from this bay the *Princess Amelia* [(80)] and have five or six hundred seamen and all the

[1] Joseph Peyton: L 1743, CR 1756, C 1757, RA 1787, VA 1790, A 1798.

marines belonging to her and the *Royal George* and *Union* ready to perform any necessary service.

As to their Lordships' second injunction, not having proper vessels (I mean cutters) for that service, I made the best shift I could, which was fitting four victuallers to prevent the enemy's sending supplies from the continent.

The enemy on the island, or indeed on any part of this coast, did not show the least sign of alarm till, on the 3rd instant, one of the cruisers perceived a Dutch dogger send a boat ashore on the S.E. end of Belle Isle and immediately stand out to sea again. The islanders were presently in motion and began to blow up rocks for a ramp and draw somewhat like lines round the citadel. But both along the coast and on Belle Isle there seems to be again a perfect state of tranquillity.

On the 7th instant the first battalion of the Royal Scott's and Handyside's regiment arrived safe in this bay from Cork. They escaped a violent gale of wind, in which the *Southampton* lost her fore and mizen masts, only by a few hours.

The weather appearing settled and the winds fair for bringing the troops from Spithead, I purpose moving to the Great Road of Belle Isle to be ready on their arrival. I shall not move the transports, however, till a greater likelihood of the rest being near.

I hope you will do me the justice to assure His Majesty that no means in my power shall be wanting to conduce to the success of the expedition. I am etc.

P.S.   Since writing the above, I have received intelligence by the master of a Spanish brig from Croisic that the enemy are collecting three thousand men to be transported from thence to Belle Isle. You may depend on my doing my utmost to intercept them with such vessels as I have.

345.   *Hawke to Clevland*

Royal George in Quiberon Bay
15 December 1760

Sir,

On the 21st last month Captain Hunt[1] in the King's frigate *Unicorn* brought me your letter of the 14th November, acquainting me with the number of troops and ships to be employed in an

---

[1] Hunt: L 1757, CR 1767, C 1771. Captain of Greenwich Hospital from 1781; died in 1796.

attempt upon Belle Isle. Also copies of their Lordships' orders of the same date to Captain Keeler of the *Terpsichore*,[1] who had been dispatched to embark that part of the troops which were at Cork.

In obedience to their Lordships' directions signified in the last part of that letter to make all necessary preparation for entering into immediate action on the arrival of the troops, I sent Captains Peyton, Lendrick, Evans, Bennett and Lee carefully and attentively to reconnoitre and sound the north side of Belle Isle, from Point Locmaria on the S.E. and to Point Daubourg on the N.W. end, in order for finding out the properest landing for the troops. No.1 is a copy of their report. In consequence of that I made the disposition of the attack under cover of which troops are to land [on a beach half a mile N.E. of Locmaria] contained in No.2. Copies of these, with orders to Captain Keppel, I have dispatched by Captain Lee in the *Tamar*, who cruises for him nine or ten leagues N.W. from Belle Isle. The *Warspite* being stationed somewhat more to the westward in case of the *Tamar* not falling in with Captain Keppel, I sent copies also to be delivered him by Sir John Bentley.

For want of cutters, the only proper vessels and which I wrote for on the 11th October last, I had no other way of obeying their Lordships' directions for preventing the enemy from sending any supplies to the continent but by putting officers and men on board four of the best empty victuallers[2] to cruise in the tracks of their *chasse-marées*. Two of these vessels, the *Friendship* and *Minerva*, had part of their cables rubbed at anchor in a gale of wind, of which I have given the masters certificates, that allowance may be made to the owners for the damage, if consistent with their contract. Since that, I have had the addition of the *Unicorn* [(28)], *Postillion* [(18)], *Terpsichore* [(24)], and *Mortar* bomb, a number still too small for the effectual performance of that service.

We did not perceive any alarm at Belle Isle or any part of this coast till the 2nd instant, when a Dutch dogger sent a boat ashore on the S.E. end of Belle Isle, on which they began to blow up rocks near the shore to form a camp on the top of the island and draw their lines around the citadel ...

On the 26th ultimo Sir John Bentley, in His Majesty's ship *Warspite*, brought me their Lordships' order of the 17th to obey all such

---

[1] Keeler: L 1756, CR 1759. The *Terpsichore* (24) was one of Thurot's squadron captured in Belfast Lough by Elliot's force in Feb. 1760. Keeler was posted in 1761. Superannuated RA 1790.

[2] On 27 Nov., for instance, Hawke had ordered two of these vessels each to be manned with 1 lieutenant, 3 petty officers, and 50 men.

orders and instructions as I should receive from His Majesty by one of his Secretaries of State, with which I shall strictly comply. By the same ship I received His Majesty's secret instructions for the attempt on Belle Isle and a letter from Mr Secretary Pitt ...

346. *Extract from Hawke to Pitt*

Royal George in Quiberon Bay
21 December 1760

... Four and twenty frigates, privateers and armed vessels went into the Morbihan last year to have attended the French embarkation. Only one that I have heard of has hitherto escaped. As I have the greatest reason to believe that their being sold to Spaniards and wearing Spanish colours is all collusion, and incidents of this kind, being unforeseen, could not be provided against in my orders, I hope you will think with me that I do my duty to my King and country in stopping so great a number of armed ships sallying out at once against the British trade till I receive positive directions for my conduct in this affair ...

347. *Hawke to Clevland*

Royal George in Quiberon Bay
13 January 1761

'Recd. 31st'

Sir,

As it is now about a month since the *Minerva* sailed from St Helens with the account of the expedition being deferred, I confess I flattered myself, considering the state of the ships under my command, that she would have been soon followed at least by some frigates. My instructions afford me reason to expect that, in order effectually to do the duty of my station, I should instantly be furnished with seventeen sail of the line and twelve frigates [see 341]. Their Lordships know whether I have had them or not, and whether those I have had have been relieved every four months to preserve their companies, be enabled to perform the duties of the station, and save the exorbitant expense of victuallers which, after all, but little answer their intended purpose. After thirty weeks, I am under a necessity of sending home the *Prince* for want of water. If the easterly wind holds, we must soon follow in a body.

At noon of the 8th, Lieutenant Lawes of the *Prince Edward* cutter arrived from Dumet and acquainted me that about 8 o'clock the night before, as he lay in his station on the north shore, he heard one gun and about ten minutes after another, and saw a light at the *Burford*'s ensign staff. Not knowing the meaning of the signal, he lay quiet all night without perceiving that the *Burford* [(70)], *Prince Frederick* [(64)] and *Modeste* [(64)] had slipped and gone to sea, which he found the next morning. As, for several days before and particularly that day, there happened a very thick fog on a spring tide, I can only conjecture that the two French ships or frigates, that have lain in readiness all along near the mouth of the Vilaine, had at noon got under cover of the thick fog over the bar, in the afternoon taking in what they could, and, after dark, sailed; but, it seems, not without being perceived by our guard ships. I am confirmed in this my opinion by the people of the *Friendship* cutter who, at 11 that night, six or seven leagues S.W. of the Four, fell in with a frigate steering to the westward with topgallant sails set. She was close alongside of the frigate and hailed her, but received no answer. On the 9th I sent my first lieutenant in the *Friendship* close in with the Vilaine—so as to be fired over in the *Friendship* cutter. He found no two ships as usual near the mouth of the river and only a great number of *chasse-marées*.

As the wind continues easterly, I cannot expect any of these three ships here again, more especially as they will want water.

I have sent the *Princess Amelia* [(80)] with two cutters to lie guard off Dumet, a very improper station for a three-decked ship at this season; but I have no other resource till the arrival of the *Mars* [(74)] and *Orford* [(66)], whom I have sent a *chasse-marée* to call off from the station before Basque Road.

The *Union* lies off St Gildas to guard the Morbihan.

Enclosed is the state and condition of His Majesty's ships under my command in this bay. I am etc.

348. *Extract from Hawke to Clevland*

Royal George in Quiberon Bay
28 February 1761

... On the 8th anchored here His Majesty's frigate *Stag* from Plymouth. She brought me your letter of the 8th January with copies of intelligences received by the Lords Commissioners of the Admiralty; likewise their Lordships' order of the 31st January directing me to return home with the three-decked ships and such other of inferior classes as should be unfit to continue longer at sea, and to detach such as should be in a condition to cruise very diligently, either jointly or separately, in certain latitudes in order to take or destroy the enemy's ships, either homeward or outward bound. In obedience to these orders I prepared immediately for my departure from thence, having first fitted the *Mars, Orford* and *Melampe*, who sailed hence the 10th instant to cruise as long as their water and provisions would last between Cape Finisterre and Belle Isle, looking frequently into Basque Road, the Vilaine, Morbihan and Port Louis to observe the enemy's motions in those places and then repair to Plymouth Sound for farther orders. On the 18th, I detached the *Swallow* to join them.

Having also supplied the *Warspite*, I directed Sir John Bentley to proceed and cruise, while his water and provisions lasted, between Cape Finisterre and Cape Clear and then return to Plymouth.

On the 13th arrived the *Ripon* [(60)] from accompanying the West Indian convoy to the westward. I supplied her with water, wine, bread and butter, and detached her to the rendezvous off Brest.

Captain Angel[1] in the *Stag* [(32)] I have ordered to cruise off the body of Belle Isle for the *Bedford* [(64)] with orders to Captain Dean[2] also to repair to that rendezvous.

The wind coming easterly on the 18th, I put to sea with the *Union, Princess Amelia, Coventry* and the convoy. But next day meeting a hard gale from the W.S.W. to the N.W. obliged me to bear up again for this bay, where we have been detained by the winds continuing to blow westerly ...

As my health is much impaired by my long continuance on this station, I hope to find orders on my arrival at Portsmouth to come on shore for the re-establishment of it in the country ...

Minute: 9 March ... The Lords are concerned for his ill state of health and wish him a speedy and perfect recovery, for which end he has their leave to go into the country from which they hope he will find benefit.

---

[1] Angel: L 1739, CR 1755, C 1756. Died in 1777.
[2] Dean: L 1755, CR 1758, C 1758. Died in 1779.

349. *Hawke to Clevland*

Royal George at Spithead
10 March 1761

Sir,

On the 5th instant I sailed from Quiberon Bay with the wind at
N.N.W. and arrived here this day at noon.

Enclosed is a duplicate of my letter of the 28th February. I am etc.

350. *Hawke to Clevland*

Royal George at Spithead
11 March 1761

Sir,

I have received your letter of the 9th and thank their Lordships for
giving me leave to strike my flag and go into the country for the
recovery of my health ...

I shall be obliged to their Lordships if they will grant Monsieur
Tortain, who commanded the *Anémone*, leave to return on his
parole to France, on condition he does not serve against Britain
during the war, as he has been prisoner in England several years this
war, and his wife and a large family of children. I am etc.

Minute: 16 March. Own receipt. Order it to be done. Let Sir
Edward know it.

349.   *Hawke to Clevland* (holograph)

George Street
9 April 1762

Sir,

This morning I received their Lordships' order of yesterday's date,
requiring me forthwith to repair to Portsmouth and hoist my flag on
board His Majesty's ship *Blenheim* or any other ship there or at
Spithead that I should think more proper, they having appointed me
commander-in-chief of the King's ships and vessels employed and to
be employed in the Channel, Soundings, Coast of Ireland, and Bay
of Biscay.

As I have some private affairs to settle which will require a few
days, if the service I am to be sent on will admit of it, I shall be much
obliged to their Lordships if they will be kind enough to indulge me
with leave to remain in Town for ten days. I am etc.

Minute: The Lords have not any objection to his staying for the time he desires, and should there be occasion for his going down, he will be informed of it.

352. *Hawke to Clevland*

Ocean at Spithead
5 May 1762

Sir,

... From the tenour of my commission I did conclude that the destination of the King's ships within the limits of my command rested with me and, among others, for this good reason that otherwise, in pressing exigencies of service, too much time would be lost in apprising their Lordships of the destination of ships and receiving their answer. Beside, this would in fact be destroying their Lordships' intentions in giving me this commission and put it out of my power to answer for any event on any station within my command. They may depend on my paying the greatest regard to convoys and not sending out ships improperly ...

[No minute is written on this dispatch.]

353. *Instructions from the Lords of the Admiralty to Hawke*

5 May 1762

Whereas the intelligence concerning the enemy's preparation at Brest [reportedly aimed at Ireland] transmitted to you in our Secretary's letter of yesterday's date is corroborated by advices received from abroad and whereas we think fit that some of the King's ships should be forthwith stationed to intercept those of the enemy if they should happen to come out of Brest, you are hereby required and directed to order the captains of His Majesty's ships named in the margin [*Ocean* (90), *Swiftsure* (70), *Lancaster* (66), *Brilliant* (36), *Aeolus* (32), *Arethusa* (32)] to cruise with them for three weeks or a month betwen Ushant and Cape Clear as you shall judge most advisable to answer this purpose. Given etc.

354. *Instructions from Hawke to the Hon. John Luttrell,[1] captain of the DRUID sloop (8)*

Blenheim, Portsmouth Harbour
11 May 1762

By Sir Edward Hawke, Knight of the Bath, Admiral of the Blue and commander-in-chief, etc.

Notwithstanding my former orders, you are hereby required and directed to take under your convoy all the [six] transports bound to Belle Isle[2] and proceed with them, as soon as they are ready, to that island. You are also to take under your convoy the vessels named on the other side bound to the westward and see them in safety off Plymouth in your way down Channel. For which this shall be your order. Given etc.

E.H.

By command of the Admiral,
J.H.

355. *Hawke to Clevland*

Blenheim in Portsmouth Harbour
12 May 1762

Sir,

... I was cautious of making any addition to their Lordships' order of the 5th but, in my humble opinion, to cruise between Ushant and Cape Clear is too extensive a station and should Captain Sayer [of the *Lancaster* (66)] think that keeping on the rendezvous eight leagues W.S.W. from Ushant would keep them in,

[1] Luttrell (later the Hon. John Luttrell Olmius): L 1758, CR 4.3.61, C 25.8.62.
[2] The island had been occupied by the British since June 1761.

he might be deceived by their escaping through the Raz. The only way to prevent this is to station the frigates off St Matthews Point while the ships of the line keep the rendezvous. Beside, he will want a cutter or two ...

[But an effective watch on Brest was not, in the event, maintained and Ternay brought a squadron out. See Document 360 below.]

356. *Hawke to Commodore John Moore, commanding in the Downs*

Royal George at Spithead
18 May 1762

Sir,
The *Cormorant* [(16), fireship] put to sea with an easterly wind which might have been the reason for my letter's not reaching you earlier. It gives me sensible pleasure to find you are so well recovered as to be able to return to your command ...

As the summer season advances, I would recommend it to you to station at anchor a sufficient number in each passage with cutters, and some without the intermediate flats [i.e. level ground], unless you shall have numbers enough to relieve them every six weeks. I desire you will apply for vessels to carry beer and other species of provisions to them as they shall want, that the entrance to Dunkirk may never be left without a proper guard. I am etc.

357. *Hawke to Clevland*

Royal George at Spithead
26 May 1762

Sir,
In the conversation I had with Lord Anson with regard to Dunkirk before I left Town, I gave it as my opinion, which was acquiesced in, that the surest way to prevent any vessels of the enemy from coming out of that port was to block it up, which was very practicable during the summer. One or two frigates and cutters off there, with cruisers scattered off Dieppe, Beachy Head, St Valéry [en Caux] and [St Valéry] sur Somme, etc., did not appear to me likely to answer the end proposed. For should they venture out, our small force must run with the intelligence to the Downs and much time after arriving there be lost in collecting the scattered cruisers. As, therefore, this place was recommended to my particular attention, I

have sent Commodore Moore orders, now [that] he has got so many frigates, sloops, bombs, fireships and cutters, to station first a sufficient number to the westward between the Splinter and the west end of the Brake Sand; secondly, a sufficient number to the eastward between the Broad Bank and the Cames, keeping some cutters continually moving off Round Hill and the entrance to the harbour in order to make signals by day with guns and by night with rockets, which Lord Anson assured me should be prepared for that purpose; in the third place, a sufficient number at proper distance from each other, along the front of the Brake to the northward to prevent the enemy from running over that flat.

The vessels thus stationed might from time to time be supplied in small craft with beer, water, and provisions; and thus, in case of any motions of the enemy, there would always be a force ready to fall on them immediately, whereas they might not be so soon overtaken should they once get out.

I hope this will meet their Lordships' approbation. If not, I can only say that I have done what appeared to me to be my duty and at the same time to be the best means of securing what was recommended to me as an object of the greatest importance.

Yesterday sailed for the Downs the *Rainbow* [(40)] and *Carcass* [bomb], also the *Proserpine* [fireship] and *Pelican* [bomb] who had put back with contrary winds. I am etc.

Minute: 27 May. The Lords are of opinion that the plan may be a very good one, but that the motions of the enemy do not at this time make it necessary to be carried into execution, but whenever it does the Lords will inform him of it; and there not being a sufficient number of ships at present in the Downs to answer the various services, the Lords recommend it [to him] to continue the ships on their present station.

358.   *Hawke to Clevland*

Royal George at Spithead
31 May 1762

Sir,

Yesterday after post sailed the King's ships *Portland* [(50)] and *Niger* [(32)] to the Downs in pursuance of their Lordships' orders to their respective commanders which came under cover to me and were delivered on the evening of the 29th. These ships were under my command till the receipt of the above orders. I therefore submit it to their Lordships' reflection whether it would not be more proper that they should signify their directions to me with regard to the King's ships under my command and leave me to give the orders in consequence ...

Minute: 1 June. In answer to this part, acquaint him the Lords will signify all their directions through him whenever it can be done consistent with the service. And acquaint him I have communicated the whole to the Lords.

359.   *Instructions from the Lords of the Admiralty to Hawke*

12 June 1762

[By 1762 the French minister Choiseul was planning a Franco-Spanish invasion of Portugal. His underlying purpose was to divert British troops to Portugal in sufficient number to allow 50,000 Frenchmen to be landed in England and thus secure favourable terms at the peace settlement. In April, Portugal duly rejected a Franco-Spanish ultimatum. The British government decided to adopt Frederick of Prussia's suggestion that the garrison of Belle Isle might be transported to Lisbon. Lord Tyrawley was chosen as the British commander-in-chief but, in the event, the active command devolved upon Lord Loudon.]

You are hereby required and directed to cause the battalions named in the margin [Oswald's, Deaken's, Nairne's and Hamilton's] to be embarked on board the seven transports following them and proceed directly to Belle Isle, under convoy of His Majesty's ships the *Essex* [(64)] and *Dreadnought* [(60)] ...

You are to direct the captain of the *Essex* to receive on board the Earl of Loudon[1] with his suite, servants, baggage, etc., and the captain of the *Dreadnought* to receive on board Colonel Forrester, Governor of Belle Isle, with his suite ...

You are to send orders to Captain Man,[2] or the senior officer of the King's ships at Belle Isle, to prepare, so soon as the six battalions above-mentioned [the fifth and sixth being Wedderburn's and Ogle's] shall be debarked, a sufficient number of the transport vessels at that island and, if necessary, any of those that carry over the said

---

[1] General John Campbell, 4th Earl of Loudon, had joined the Army in 1727. As C.-in-c. in N. America 1756–7, he had seemed indecisive and slow to move, but he was to do better in Portugal.
[2] Robert Man: L 1740, C 1745; commanded a squadron off Brest in 1762. RA 1770 (see Document 469), VA 1775, A 1780.

battalions, to receive on board the troops destined to proceed from thence to Portugal, together with the artillery, horses, stores, and all other necessaries assigned to accompany them thither, and to have everything in readiness for their embarkation the moment he shall receive directions from you for that purpose and for the farther proceeding of the transports.

And whereas we have received intelligence that the Spanish squadron at Ferrol, consisting of seven ships of the line, has been seen cruising off that port with a view possibly to endeavour to intercept the succours going to Portugal, and whereas it is therefore necessary that a squadron of His Majesty's ships should proceed to sea to guard against any surprise of that kind, you are, whenever you can make up nine ships of the line and two or three frigates either at Portsmouth or Plymouth, exclusive of those mentioned, to proceed yourself down Channel with such squadron, and when you come off Ushant to detach a frigate with orders to the senior officer at Belle Isle to embark the troops, artillery, horses, stores, etc., designed for Lisbon, and when they are embarked to send the transports, having them on board, under convoy of the *Essex* and *Dreadnought*, to such rendezvous as you shall think fit to appoint, to which you are to repair with the squadron and wait for them; and in case the enemy's ships shall be in Ferrol, you are to see the transports in safety clear of Cape Finisterre and then send them on to the Tagus with the *Essex* and such additional convoy as you shall think necessary. But if the enemy's ships shall be at sea and not in Ferrol, you are to proceed with your whole force and accompany the said transports off the bar of Lisbon, where you are to remain till they have got safely over it ... Given etc.

J. FORBES[1]
VILLIERS[2]
T. PELHAM[3]

By express at ½ past 10 at night.

---

[1] After Anson's unexpected death on 6 June 1762, the surviving Lords remained in office till the end of the year. Halifax (p. 389, n. 1) became 1st Lord on 17 June.

[2] George Bussy Villiers was known as Viscount Grandison till he succeeded as 4th Earl of Jersey in 1769. MP 1756–69; a Ld of Ady 1761–2. Afterwards held various offices at court; noted for his fastidious dress and courtly manners.

[3] Thomas Pelham (eventually created Earl of Chichester) was a cousin and a follower of the Duke of Newcastle. MP 1749–68 when he became the 2nd Baron Pelham of Stanmer. A Ld of the Ady 1761–2, he held various lucrative sinecures. Regularly dubbed 'Tommy Pelham' by a contemptuous Horace Walpole.

360. *Clevland to Hawke*

13 June 1762

Sir,

I have received and communicated to my Lords Commissioners of the Admiralty your letter of yesterday's date, informing them of the naval proceedings under your direction and of your intention, as the station off Brest is left open by the return of the *Aeolus* [(32)] into port and the *Brilliant* [(36)] being gone off Ferrol, to detach the *Shannon* [(36)] thither and replace her off Havre by the *Tartar* [(28)], and when the *Aeolus*'s bowsprit is repaired to send her off Brest likewise; and in return I am to acquaint you that their Lordships very well approve of what you propose to do. I am etc.

[However, Ternay had already slipped out of Brest with two of the line, two frigates, and some transports on his way (as it transpired) to Newfoundland.]

361. *Commodore Moore to Hawke*

Deal
20 June 1762

Sir,

Enclosed you have the present disposition of the squadron under my command. I beg leave to acquaint you that the constant drafts the Admiralty make of ships from hence disables me from the guarding the passages into Dunkirk Road with the propriety I wish to execute your orders and, it being signified to me from the Admiralty that it is the King's pleasure I should exert my utmost vigilance to prevent any junction there of craft from the western parts obliges me, as you will see, to keep a range of ships as far to the westward as Boulogne.

The enemy have made no alteration in their craft at Dunkirk except bending the sails of one of the prams, and fourteen flat-bottomed boats are ordered to be got ready. Their camp is formed in the neighbourhood of Dunkirk of fifteen battalions, but they begin to be sickly and desertion takes place amongst them, the troops being employed in draining the great Morare of Fernes. The boats at Calais, which have laid long with their sails bent, have lately had them unbent again. I have the honour to be etc.

362. *Hawke to Moore*

Royal George at Spithead
20 June 1762

Sir,

I have been so hurried in preparing for sea that I have not had time to pay a proper attention to your several letters. I sail on Wednesday next [the 23rd]. Therefore till my return you will apply immediately to the Board for their directions. I am etc.

363. *Line of Battle*

Royal George at Sea
26 June 1762

The *Magnanime* to lead with the starboard and the *Hero* with the larboard tacks on board.

Frigates	Rates	Ships	Commanders	Guns	Men	Division
Martin [10]	3	*Magnanime*	Capt. Montagu	74	650	
	4	*Prince George*	Wallis[1]	60	420	
Mecklenburg cutter	3	*Revenge*	Vernon[2]	64	480	
Tartar [28] to repeat signals	1	*Royal George*	Sir Edwd. Hawke Capt. Bennett[3]	100	880	Sir Edwd. Hawke, Kt of the Bath, Ad. of the
	2	*Prince*	Marlow[4]	90	750	Blue
	2	*Ocean*	Langdon[5]	90	750	
Aeolus [32] to repeat signals	3	*Princess Amelia*	HRH Duke of York Lord Howe[6]	80	665	HRH Duke of York, Rear-Ad. of the Blue

[1] Wallis: Lacked patronage at entry; L 1748, CR 1756, C 1757. Commanded the *Dolphin* on a voyage of discovery 1766–8 (see Document 404 and p. 425, n. 1).

[2] Edward Vernon was not closely connected with Admiral Edward Vernon of Porto Bello, etc. Commissioned in 1743, he served in the *Berwick* with Hawke at the Battle of Toulon; CR 1747, C 1753. Commanded the *Revenge* in the Western Squadron 1760–2. Knighted 1773; RA 1775, VA 1778, A 1787. C.-in-c., India 1776–81. An early balloonist, he ascended twice from the Tottenham Court Road in 1785; came down firstly at Horsham, then at Colchester.

[3] Bennett (on whom see p. 102, n. 1 and the related documents) had been posted captain of the *Royal George*, doubtless at Hawke's behest, in Jan. 1760.

[4] Marlow: L 1743, C 1756 and fought frigate actions 1757–8. RA 1780, VA 1787, A 1794.

[5] Langdon: L 1743, CR 1753, C 1756, RA 1780. See also p. 388, n. 1.

[6] It was at Howe's own request that he was appointed flag captain to the youthful Prince Edward.

	3	Nassau	Capt. Suckling[1]	64	480
	4	Achilles	Fortescue	60	420
Shannon [36]	3	Hero	Hon. Capt. Barrington	74	650

[Given etc.]

364. Clevland to Hawke

30 June 1762

Sir,

Having communicated to my Lords Commissioners of the Admiralty your letter of the 26th instant, enclosing a copy of your rendezvous and informing them that you shall make the best of your way to the station therein prescribed, I am commanded by their Lordships to observe to you that, as the rendezvous is ten leagues N.W. from Cape Finisterre and you do not mention your intention of appearing before Ferrol, they apprehend the transports with the troops from Belle Isle may be liable to be intercepted by the Spanish ships from Ferrol; wherefore their Lordships recommend it to you in the strongest manner to keep upon such station as will most effectually prevent such misfortune and to inform them what you do therein by the return of the sloop which you are to dispatch for that purpose. I am etc.

[To] Sir Edwd. Hawke, by a messenger.

365. Secret Instructions from the Lords of the Admiralty to Hawke

1 July 1762

Whereas it is expected that the French squadron under the command of Monsieur Blénac may very probably return very soon from San Domingo and it is of the utmost consequence to intercept them; you are hereby required and directed, when you shall have seen the transports with troops on board from Belle Isle, designed for Lisbon, so far on their way as you shall judge necessary for their security, to cross the latitudes between Cape Finisterre and Cape Clear for one month in such manner as you shall judge most proper

---

[1] Suckling (Horatio Nelson's uncle and patron): L 1745, C 1755. In Oct. 1757 commodore Arthur Forrest, with Captains Suckling and Langdon, fought a very spirited action with a superior French squadron in the W. Indies. Suckling was Controller from 1775 to 1778 when he died at the age of 53.

to answer for that purpose ... and you are to return at the expiration of that time to Torbay and remain there until you receive further order, sending us an account of your arrival and proceedings. Given etc.

DUNK HALIFAX[1]
GEO. HAY
J. FORBES
H. STANLEY
VILLIERS
T. PELHAM

366. *Hawke to Clevland*

Royal George at sea
9 July 1762
Cape Finisterre SbE distant 9 leagues
'Read'

Sir,

In my last letter off Plymouth, 26 June, I acquainted you for their Lordships' information that I should make the best of my way to the station prescribed in the rendezvous, a copy of which I sent enclosed. On the 28th, having got to the westward of Ushant, I dispatched Lieutenant Fairlie in the *Mecklenburg* cutter with final orders to the captains of the King's ships at Belle Isle to hasten the sailing of the troops from thence for Lisbon, as soon as the *Lancaster* and *Essex* should arrive. That evening the wind springing up northward of the east and continuing so, enabled me to reach my station on the 1st instant, about 8 in the morning. I instantly stationed the *Tartar* between me and Cape Finisterre, that nothing might pass unobserved between it and the squadron in the night... At the same time I dispatched Captain Hotham in the *Aeolus* to look into Ferrol...

[On 6 July] the *Aeolus* rejoined the squadron. Captain Hotham had the afternoon before looked into the harbour at Ferrol where he could only observe one large ship with a flag at the mizen topmast head. As he was hauling out of the bay again, he took two Spaniards in a small fishing boat. A list of the Spanish squadron still in Ferrol

---

[1] George Montagu Dunk was the 2nd Earl of Halifax. As President of the Board of Trade (1748–61) he had promoted the North American commerce and was styled 'Father of the Colonies'. Pleaded for Byng 1757. He was 1st Ld of the Ady 17.6.62–18.10.62 (when he was succeeded by George Grenville). A Sec. of State 1762–5 (signing, with others, the warrant for Wilkes's arrest 1763) and again in 1771, when he died in office.

harbour, as delivered by the prisoners, accompanies this. [There were ten of the line, not all ready for sea.] They farther declare that seven of their line of battle ships and a frigate had been out for six days in the beginning of April...

In the evening [of the 7th] arrived on the rendezvous His Majesty's sloop *Senegal* which brought me your two letters of the 30th [including 364]. Before I fixed on a rendezvous in pursuance of their Lordships' order of the 12th June [359] I had maturely considered every circumstance, both with regard to the enemy and the transports to come from Belle Isle. As to the first, not the least fear of their being at sea filled me either with distraction or irresolution. The enemy themselves could never suppose we should be so absurd as either to appoint a rendezvous for the convoy from Belle Isle, or the commander of it shape a course for any part, within the Cape, as thereby would be run the risk of being embayed with a westerly wind. The course from that island, with a fair wind, is W.S.W. by compass, which will fall in with Cape Torriano [i.e. Cape Toriñana, just N. of Cape Finisterre] and consequently with my rendezvous. Beside, the conductor of the convoy would not, for the reason already given, in prudence keep to the southward, but rather to the westward of that course, till he should get into or near the latitude of the Cape. Under these circumstances, as well as to avoid the above risk, I could not think of being nearer Ferrol than I am. And suppose I had shown myself off that port I could not, on the same considerations, have cruised there, but immediately repaired to a more proper station. The risk and inconvenience of being so far in the Bay rendered Cape Ortegal very improper. The enemy can not come out with a westerly wind; and should they come out with an easterly, they cannot either get in again or escape the observation of the cruisers. Add to all this that, though I never leave my rendezvous naked, yet I stretch backward and forward so as always to be at hand between the two [limits]. Neither are the enemy ignorant that I am watchfully looking out for them. The fires on their beacons are lighted every night...

[There is no minute other than the word 'Read' as indicated above.]

367. *Hawke to Clevland*

Royal George in Torbay
24 August 1762

Sir,

... In my letter of the 9th July by the *Senegal* I took the liberty of putting their Lordships in mind that, should the squadron be soon wanted after its arrival at Torbay, many things would be wanting which I hope would be sent there with the utmost dispatch. On my arrival here, I did not find anything provided. Ships from a cruise want to be near a hospital, a victualling office, and a dockyard. Water can not be got easily at this place nor casks fitted to receive it. Yards, sails, topmasts, etc., are wanting. However, I have done all in my power, for I have directed the captains to cause the ships under their command to be heeled, scrubbed, and boot-hose-topped, completing their water as fast as possible, except the *Royal George* which must go into port. Notwithstanding all that can be done, I am of opinion that it will take up the space of near six weeks to refit them for service under the circumstances of this untoward bay. At Spithead they might have been fit for service in ten days and all that is gained by being here is about a day's sail.

I have now been nine weeks at sea and before the squadron can be fitted it will make up fifteen. I must therefore entreat their Lordships' order to strike my flag and come on shore. Should His Majesty's permission be necessary, I hope they will be so kind as to apply for it. I am etc.

[The Lords agreed that the squadron should go to Portsmouth. After being delayed by contrary winds, Hawke anchored at Spithead on 3 September and, in accordance with the orders awaiting him, he struck his flag that afternoon.]

PART V

NOVEMBER 1766–JANUARY 1771
FIRST LORD

INTRODUCTION

For as many as eighteen of the years between 1739 and 1783 Britain was involved in major naval conflict. Hawke's time as First Lord (from late 1766 to the beginning of 1771) forms part of a relatively long intermission of peace. At that early stage of the country's rise to industrial and commercial pre-eminence her capacity to generate revenue was, of course, undeniably limited and there was an inevitable reluctance to spend a great deal of money on the Navy in peacetime. This reluctance had marked the truce of 1748 to 1755, precarious though it was, and despite the fact that Anson presided at the Admiralty from 1751 onwards; and it was speedily re-established with the ending of the Seven Years War some three years before Hawke went to the Admiralty. Yet something had been learned from the difficulties experienced in mobilizing the Navy in 1755. Whereas in 1751 the number of enlisted men had been allowed to fall as low as 8,000, Hawke's peacetime Navy of 1766 to 1771 was provided with 16,000—and this remained the peacetime establishment for the rest of the century, emergencies apart. Shipbuilding programmes and the stockpiling of materials likewise went ahead at a slow but steady pace. But the likelihood of unreadiness in a sudden crisis was already being registered by Lord Egmont as First Lord in 1764[1]. However, it was not until the advent of the Falkland Islands crisis of 1770 that it could be clearly seen that naval provision since 1763 had been inadequate on at least three counts: firstly, because the French were now concentrating on *naval* preparations for a war of revenge against Britain and her empire; secondly, because the British Navy was suffering from the hasty construction of ships

[1] J. Steven Watson, *The Reign of George III 1760–1815*, (Oxford: Clarendon Press, 1960) pp. 103–4.

during the Seven Years War which, being built often of unseasoned timber, were now rotting quickly, especially if they were lying in reserve—and most of them were; and thirdly because the total amount of shipbuilding in recent years, both of naval and merchant vessels, had led to the exhaustion of homegrown supplies of certain vital categories of oak and to a scarcity of masts (normally obtained from North America and the Baltic).

When British sea power reached a peak towards the end of 1762, the Navy possessed 305 ships of all rates and 84,770 seamen and marines.[1] During the subsequent peace, most of these ships were laid up 'in ordinary' where, owing in part to the absence of ventilation in their holds, and especially to the aforesaid use of unseasoned timber in their construction during the war, they were subject to accelerated decay. Professor Daniel Baugh has noted, by way of contrast with the situation after 1763, that ships built before 1739 of properly seasoned timbers survived their time 'in ordinary' quite well, despite the often irrelevant routines followed by their skeleton crews.[2]

Judging by the evidence printed here, Hawke's Board was unaware of the extent of the fleet's deterioration [Documents 379, 385, 410; but see also 490]. The general picture is that, especially in his first year at the Admiralty, an effort was made to sharpen the vigilance of the Navy Board. However, that Board's attention was directed towards the administration of the dockyards rather than the condition of the ships in reserve [377, 379, 392, 398 and 450]. The Navy Board, led till July 1770 by an ageing George Cokburne, seems to have done nothing to alert the Admiralty about the condition of the ships 'in ordinary'. (See especially 379, para. 5.) However, soon after Cokburne's death in office, the Falkland Islands crisis broke (on which subject see also the General Introduction above). There arose the immediate possibility of a new war with Spain and perhaps with France as well. The Admiralty's response to this emergency contributes a series of documents towards the end of this final Part [451–489]. Among the subjects treated in that series are trade protection, bounties, exemptions from impressment, and the Admiralty's strict control of the press gangs—to say nothing of the true state of the ships which was so suddenly and starkly revealed.

Until the onset of the Falklands crisis, the Admiralty complied assiduously with the government's economical policy [373–4, 392,

---

[1] Stephen F. Gradish, *The Manning of the British Navy during the Seven Years War* (London: Royal Historical Society, 1980) pp. 46 and 53, with n.3.

[2] Baugh, *British Naval Administration in the Age of Walpole*, pp. 243–9.

397, 433]. However, despite this policy, more public money was being spent annually on the Navy from 1767 to 1770 than was the case in any of the years 1749 to 1754. For instance the figure of £1,668,356 spent in 1769 may be compared with £871,693 in 1750. Prices were not much higher in the later year.[1] But the Falklands crisis had the effect of lifting the annual expenditure above £2,000,000 for every subsequent peacetime year before 1793. Within the financial limits imposed on it, Hawke's Board tried to obtain a more adequate supply of the scarcer categories of oak and of the exotic fir trunks suitable for masts [410–413, 423, 432, 476].

As explained in the General Introduction, the length of this Part needed to be kept within bounds, in so far as Hawke was primarily a great fighting commander and not specially qualified to fill a ministerial post. However, a considerable variety of business was transacted under his leadership, ranging from an attempt to reform the Portsmouth Academy [375–6] to the issuing of instructions to Lieutenant James Cook before his first voyage of exploration in the Pacific [404, 404a and 404b]. By way of providing general coverage, the Board's minutes offered special advantages. Though succinct, they were found to be fuller and more enlightening than those appertaining to some previous and subsequent periods. A good number of them show that the Board was far from resistant to the possibility of technical improvement [372–3, 378, 383, 402–3, 410, 415–16, 418–21, 424–8, 436, 442].

368. *Lord Chatham to Hawke*

Bond Street
28 November 1766

Sir,

I am commanded by the King to acquaint you that Sir Charles Saunders and Mr Keppel having come to a resolution to resign their seats at the Admiralty, His Majesty has been graciously pleased to turn his thoughts to you, Sir, for the head of that Board. I have the honour in consequence to propose to you in His Majesty's name that very important office.

Give me leave to assure you, Sir, that I have particular satisfaction in executing the King's commands to me upon this interesting occasion, and allow me to add my sincere hopes that this letter may find you in as full possession of health as your country wishes you to

---

[1] Mackay, *Hawke*, pp. 305–6.

be.

I have the honour to be, with most respectful esteem and consideration, Sir,

Your most obedient and most humble servant

CHATHAM

369. *Admiralty Minute*

12 December 1766

Present: Hawke, Townshend, Buller, Yonge, Brett, Jenkinson.

The new commission dated yesterday and constituting and appointing the Right Honourable Sir Edward Hawke, Charles Townshend[1] and John Buller[2] Esquires, Henry Viscount Palmerston,[3] Sir George Yonge,[4] [Rear-Admiral] Sir Peircy Brett and Charles Jenkinson Esquire[5] Commissioners for executing the office of Lord High Admiral of Great Britain and Ireland, etc., being read, the Lords took their places at the Board accordingly...

370. *Admiralty Minute*

Saturday, 7 February 1767

Present: Hawke, Buller, Brett, Jenkinson.

... Commodore Willett [at Chatham] representing to the Board that Benjamin Say, a marine drummer, who was sentenced to receive two hundred lashes for desertion, has been so ill ever since as to be unable to undergo the same and that the surgeons of Rochester Hospital and of His Majesty's ship the *Yarmouth* [guardship] are of opinion that it is not in the power of medicine to relieve him while

---

[1] Charles Townshend (later the 1st Baron Bayning) was known as 'Spanish Charles' for his early diplomatic service and to distinguish him from his cousin, Chatham's Chancellor of the Exchequer. MP 1756–84, 1790–6; a Ld of the Ady 31.7.65–28.2.70 when he transferred to the Treasury.

[2] John Buller was MP for Exeter; a Ld of Ady 31.7.65–22.9.80.

[3] Henry Temple was the 2nd Viscount Palmerston in the Irish peerage and the father of the future Prime Minister. MP from 1762 till his death in 1802. A Ld of the Ady 15.9.66–15.12.77; then of the Treasury 1777–82.

[4] Sir George Yonge (1731–1812) was the 5th baronet. MP 1754–61 and 1763–96. A Ld of Ady 15.9.66–28.9.70 (Saunders having been 1st Ld 15.9.66–11.12.66). Sec. at War 1782–3 and again 1783–94. Governor of the Cape of Good Hope 1799–1801.

[5] Charles Jenkinson, who was eventually created 1st Earl of Liverpool and was the father of the long-serving Prime Minister, was a politician closely linked with 'the King's friends'. MP 1761–86; a Ld of Ady 11.12.66–8.3.68; and then held various offices (including Sec. at War 1778–82).

his spirits are so depressed as they are by the apprehension of the punishment; resolved that in consideration of what is set forth the man be pardoned...

371. *Admiralty Minutes*

10 March 1767

[Where a Saturday is not mentioned, it may be assumed that the Board was meeting on another day of the week. At any one meeting several minutes were normally recorded besides those given in this selection.]

Present: Hawke, Townshend, Buller, Brett.

... The King having been pleased to direct by his Sign Manual of the 4th instant that George Cokburne Esq., in consideration of his good and faithful services, be allowed half pay from the 1st of January last, notwithstanding his being Controller of the Navy; resolved that orders be given to the Navy Board accordingly.

A letter was read from the Navy Board of the 9th instant enclosing an account of defects discovered in the *Royal Ann* [(100)] at Portsmouth and proposing to take her to pieces and apply her serviceable remains to house carpentry uses, etc.; resolved that orders be given to them to do as they have proposed...

372. *Admiralty Minute*

23 March 1767

Present: Hawke, Townshend, Buller, Brett.

... The Lords took into consideration a report from the Commissioners of the Victualling upon a reference to them of a letter from Vice-Admiral Pye,[1] commander-in-chief of His Majesty's ships at the Leeward Islands, complaining of the newness and bad quality of the rum supplied by the contractors to His Majesty's ships on that station, and proposing, in order the better to preserve the health of the seamen, that they may be occasionally supplied with fresh provisions in the same manner they are supplied at Jamaica;

[1] Pye: L 1735, C 1741; commended for service in the Adriatic 1744. Commodore and c.-in-c., Leeward Is 1752–5, being superceded by Rear-Adm. Frankland who suspended him for fraud, peculation, etc. Court-martialled after delays, largely exonerated, and made RA 1758, VA 1762, A 1773. Again c.-in-c., Leeward Is 1766–9; c.-in-c., Portsmouth 1770–3 and 1777–83, and presided at Keppel's court martial (1779). Known as 'Nosey Pye', he deemed himself sexually irresistible.

resolved that a copy of the said report be sent to the Vice-Admiral for his information and that he be acquainted the Lords, for the reasons therein contained, do not think fit to permit him to purchase fresh meat for the seamen of his squadron, but that the Commissioners for Sick and Hurt having represented to the Lords the great advantages that have arisen from issuing portable soup to the well seamen on board His Majesty's ships on long voyages where fresh meat could not be procured, and proposed making trial of the same on board the ships at the Leeward Islands, their Lordships have ordered a quantity of the said soup to be sent out to him by the *Scarborough* [frigate] which he will cause to be served to the men agreeable to the regulations that will be transmitted to him, at the same time, by the said Commissioners...

373.   *Admiralty Minutes*

26 March 1767

Present: Hawke, Townshend, Buller, Brett.

... The Navy Board having transmitted hither an account of the defects of the *Eagle* [(60)] and *Thetis* [(32)] at Portsmouth and proposed to sell them if purchasers can be found, otherwise to take them to pieces; resolved that orders be given for doing as they have proposed...

Resolved that Vice-Admiral Pye and the captain of the *Scarborough* going out to join him be acquainted with the orders given some time since to the Navy Board for causing the larboard side of that ship's bottom to be paid with a composition invented by Mr Jackson, a chemist, to prevent the damages occasioned by the worm; and that they take every opportunity to inspect the effects of the same and to report, from time and time, to their Lordships and to the Navy Board.

A letter was read from the Navy Board of the 24th instant with a plan enclosed of the probable expense of the Navy for the present year, prepared in pursuance of their Lordships' order of the 19th past and, their Lordships observing that the same greatly exceeds the parliamentary grants, within the bounds of which the Navy Board were directed strictly to keep; resolved that the plan be returned to them with directions to send another in lieu of it, strictly conformable to the aforesaid order, taking care the retrenchments they make be such as shall be least detrimental to the service; and if they will point out any methods necessary to be taken in order to diminish the expense and reduce it within the grants of Parliament, their Lordships will give the proper orders for the same.

374. *Admiralty Minute*

3 April 1767

Present: All seven Lords.

The Navy Board, attending according to order upon the subject of their letter of the 24th ultimo and the plan of expense therein enclosed, were called in.

The Lords recommended to them to suggest the properest methods of reducing the expense of the Navy so as not to exceed the whole of the money granted for naval services for the present year and to obtain, if possible, the same quantity of work now performed at a less charge, so that the service may not suffer at all, or as little as possible, by such reduction of expense; and, being heard thereupon, they suggested several proper methods which then occurred to them for those purposes.

The Navy Board being then desired to withdraw, the Lords determined to abide by their order of the 19th of February last; and, having again called in the Navy Board, acquainted them with such determination and recommended to them that, in the answer they give to the order above-mentioned, they do suggest the heads of reduction which they have this day stated and such others as upon more mature consideration may occur to them. The Lords also acquainted them that they will be ready to enforce by their authority all such orders as may be proper and necessary to be given for the purposes aforesaid.

[This is the complete and the only minute of the meeting in question.]

375. *Admiralty Minute*

2 May 1767

Present: Hawke, Buller, Brett.

[The naval academy at Portsmouth, which came under the ultimate jurisdiction of the Admiralty, opened in 1733. Underlying this development was their Lordships' dissatisfaction with the instruction given afloat to youthful aspirants to commissioned rank. The academy duly provided instruction in mathematics and navigation, as well as in gentlemanly accomplishments. However, the feeling persisted that a naval career could be better served by direct entry into a ship under the patronage of an officer, preferably the captain. Entrants of this type, who were usually but not necessarily rated captain's servants, included Rooke, Shovell, Vernon, Anson, Boscawen, Howe, Samuel Hood, Jervis, Duncan, Cornwallis, Collingwood and Nelson, to say nothing of Hawke himself.[1] In 1767, as the following documents show, the Board tried to raise the standard of discipline at the academy and improve its curriculum.]

... A letter was read from Mr Hughes,[2] Governor of the Royal Academy at Portsmouth, dated the 23rd of last month, acquainting the Board that the Academy was then ready for the reception of scholars and would be so for the masters in a fortnight; resolved that he be directed to inform the friends or parents of the scholars belonging thereunto that proper masters and teachers are now provided for them and that it is expected they return to the Academy upon a certain day ... and that, as their Lordships shall expect the strictest discipline to be observed there for the future, they are desired to give the strongest injunctions to their children, or young gentlemen under their care, to be very obedient to their masters and cautious of their behaviour; and in particular to inform the friends or parents of the four scholars named in the margin [Philip Brotherton, Charles Everitt,[3] Thomas Worseley, Hon. William Tollemache[4]] that, before their readmittance, it is expected they make a formal recantation of their past misbehaviour in presence of himself, the masters, teachers, and other scholars, and declare their penitence for the same and firm resolution of amendment.

Their Lordships then resumed consideration of the report of Vice-Admiral Holburne[5] and Mr Hughes, of the 5th day of November last, upon the differences that has [sic] arisen between the masters and the scholars and the disturbances that had happened in conse-

---

[1] See Baugh (ed.), *Naval Administration* (N.R.S.) pp. 38, 57–62; also Michael Lewis, *The Navy of Britain* (London: Allen & Unwin, 1948) pp. 253–4.

[2] Richard Hughes (created 1st baronet 1773) was the son of the Richard Hughes who preceded him as Commissioner at Portsmouth (p. 101, n. 2). L 1726, CR 1739, C 1740. Commissioner at Portsmouth (and Governor of the Naval Academy) 1754–73.

[3] Everitt: L 1772, CR 1776, C 1777.

[4] Tollemache was commissioned in 1772 but seems to have advanced no further. Brotherton and Worseley do not appear in the invaluable 'Commissioned Sea Officers of the Royal Navy', issued to many libraries by the National Maritime Museum in 1955.

[5] Holburne was c.-in-c. at Portsmouth 1758–66.

quence thereof; and having judged it necessary to make some alterations in and additions to the articles, rules and orders established in 1733 for the good government and order of the Academy and the scholars educated therein; resolved that the same be sent to Mr Hughes and that copies thereof be likewise printed...

376. *Admiralty Rules and Orders for the Academy at Portsmouth*

2 May 1767

Whereas we have judged it necessary to make some alterations in the articles, orders, and rules established in the year 1733 for the good government of the Royal Academy at Portsmouth and the scholars to be educated therein, and have thought fit to establish the following rules and orders in lieu thereof, we do hereby request and direct the Commissioner of the Navy residing in His Majesty's dockyard at Portsmouth [Richard Hughes] and the several officers of the yard herein concerned, as also the Master of the Academy and the other teachers and ushers, as well as the scholars, strictly to conform themselves thereto, so far as the same do respectively relate to them:

Article 1.

None shall be admitted into the Academy but the sons of noblemen or gentlemen who shall not be under twelve years of age, nor above fifteen at the time of their admission, the same to be certified by the minister or church wardens from the register of the parish where they were baptized.

2.

No scholar shall be admitted into the Academy until he has been examined by the Headmaster in the presence of the Governor ... and until he produces a certificate of his morals and good behaviour from the master or person under whom he was last taught.

3.

The Lord High Admiral or Lords Commissioners of the Admiralty for the time being shall appoint the masters, ushers, and scholars, and may at any time dismiss such as they shall judge deserve it.

4.

The Commissioner of His Majesty's Navy for the time being at the dockyard at Portsmouth shall be Governor of the Academy and the masters, ushers, and scholars shall be obedient to and observe his directions.

5.

The Master of the Academy is to reside in the apartment allotted for him in the building and to have government over the teachers, ushers, and scholars...

7.

The scholars are to lodge in separate chambers and all to board with the Master to whom they are to pay the sum of twenty-five pounds a year each and no more, for which he is to keep them a decent and proper table and to find them in washing, fire, candles, towels, table and bed linen, and the necessary utensils of the house...

9.

The Master is to treat all the scholars with equal care and attention and to see that the other teachers and ushers do the like, there being no preference or distinction to be suffered among the scholars either in boarding, lodging, schooling, or in other ways, but all to be upon an equal foot, except the encouragement due to such as shall distinguish themselves from their fellows in application to their studies.

10.

No scholar shall be allowed to keep a servant...

11.

Every scholar is to be provided yearly at his own expense with a new suit of blue cloth against His Majesty's birthday, conformable with a pattern suit lodged with the Master.

12.

The Master is to take care that all the scholars go neat and decent in their apparel and that they show due respect to the commission officers of the Navy and to the officers of the yard whenever they meet with them.

13.

It being intended that the scholars be instructed in writing, arithmetic, drawing, navigation, gunnery, fortification, and other useful parts of the mathematics, and also in the French language, dancing, fencing, and the exercise of the firelock ... the said master is to settle a plan for a regular and orderly course in their several studies, and from time to time to vary it as he shall find necessary, which he is to lay before the Lords Commissioners of the Admiralty for their consent and approbation.

14.

The hours of teaching shall be the same as are appointed for the shipwrights' working, excepting that the scholars shall be allowed half an hour for breakfast and an hour and a half for dinner; and no times of intermission or holidays are to be allowed, except such as are observed in the dockyard, and except Saturday in the afternoon.

15.

On Sundays and other days of public worship, the scholars are to go constantly to church, accompanied by the Master and teachers...

18.

The fencing master is to see that arms and accoutrements be always kept clean and in good order by the person appointed for that purpose.

19.

If any of the scholars shall lose or spoil their arms or accoutrements, the Master is to provide others for them at the expense of their parents or relations, and to give them due correction...

21.

The Commissioner is frequently to go into the schools and inspect into the studies and behaviour of the scholars and the methods used by masters and teachers in instructing them, and shall represent his observations, as well of the forwardness and improvement of the former as of the diligence and attendance of the latter, to the Secretary of the Admiralty...

23.

The scholars are to be punished for their faults during the first year of their being in the Academy by the rod, by the imposition of task, or by confinement, at the discretion of the Headmaster, and for more heinous offences by expulsion by order of the Lord High Admiral or Lords Commissioners of the Admiralty for the time being.

24.

The scholars, after having been a year at the Academy and having received their accoutrements, swords, and firelocks, are to be punished for their faults by imposition of tasks or by confinement at the discretion of the Headmaster, or by confinement with a sentinel at the door at the discretion of the Governor, and for more heinous offences by being mulcted of a part of the time which is allowed to be included in the time of service necessary to qualify them to be lieutenants in the Royal Navy, or by expulsion...

25.

If any scholar shall be expelled from the Academy, he shall never afterwards be admitted to serve in the Royal Navy.

26.

Upon application from the parents or guardians of any of the scholars to the Commissioner, he may give them leave either at Christmas or Whitsuntide to be absent for three weeks...

27.

The Master is to certify the names of such of the scholars as have been a year in the Academy to the Commissioner, after which time they are to be excused from going to school two afternoons in the week, and the Commissioner shall direct one of the masters attendant to carry them one of the said afternoons into the rigging house and show them the manner of preparing and fitting the rigging of ships, as also into the storehouses and sail lofts, and likewise to take them afloat when any works are doing that are fit for their knowledge and even to employ them in such works as are proper for them.

28.

The Commissioner is likewise to direct the master shipwright, another of the said afternoons, to instruct them in the knowledge of the proportions and use of all the parts that compose a ship...

29.

The Commissioner may likewise appoint any ship or vessel in ordinary of the smallest rate to be placed as near the dockyard as may be and order the scholars to rig and unrig her frequently... He may also cause two guns to be placed in her with their furniture and some powder and shot, and order one of the most experienced gunners of the ships in ordinary to exercise and instruct them in the use of cannon.

30.

No scholar is to remain in the Academy above three years nor less than two years...

31.

When any scholars are drawn out of the Academy to be sent to sea, the Master is to give each of them a certificate of the time he has spent in the Academy...

34.

The scholars in His Majesty's ships shall be kept to the duty of seamen but have the privilege of walking on the quarter-deck and shall be allotted a proper place to lie in, without setting up any cabins for them; and they shall be rated on the ship's books with the title of Volunteers by Order and receive able seaman's pay.

35.

The captain shall oblige the volunteers to keep journals and to draw the appearances of headlands, coasts, bays, and suchlike; and the master, boatswain, and schoolmaster shall instruct them in all parts of learning that may qualify them for the duty of able seamen and midshipmen.

36.

After two years at sea, the captain of the ship shall rate them midshipmen ordinary or midshipmen, if they are qualified for it.

37.

Volunteers who have been educated in the Academy shall have liberty while their ships are in Portsmouth to frequent the school and are to be instructed both there, and in the yard, *gratis*, in the same manner as when they were scholars but without any other charge to His Majesty...

41.

Volunteers educated in the Academy and sent from thence by order of the Lord High Admiral or Lords Commissioners of the Admiralty to serve in His Majesty's ships shall be qualified in point of time for Lieutenants after so many years of service at sea as, together with the time specified in the certificate given them upon leaving the Academy, shall complete the term of six years, provided they have served two years thereof as mates, midshipmen, or midshipmen ordinary in His Majesty's ships and are not under twenty years of age; but they shall pass the usual examination of their abilities before they can be preferred.

Given etc.

15E. HAWKE
C.TOWNSHEND
J. BULLER
GEO.YONGE

377. *Philip Stephens[1] to the Navy Board*

Admiralty Office
10 June 1767

Gentlemen,

Having read to my Lords Commissioners of the Admiralty your letter of the 5th instant, containing a report of your visitation of His Majesty's several yards, their Lordships took the same into consideration and observed that, in that part of it which relates to the condition of the yards, and to the obedience paid to the instructions and orders established for the government thereof, you have expressed yourselves in too general terms, so as not to give their Lordships the information necessary for their forming a judgement of the present condition of the yards. Their Lordships therefore command me to signify their direction to you to report with respect to each yard severally whether you found the officers of the said yards diligent or remiss in their duty, whether they properly discharge their duty themselves or trust therein too much to the clerks or other persons under them; whether proper care has been taken in the receipt, preservation and issue of stores; whether the standing orders and instructions have been properly read to the officers and workmen according to the orders given on that head; and whether they have hitherto been attentive in checking, as far as was in their power, the abuse of the privilege of carrying out chips; whether you found the workmen of each yard respectively able and industrious in their several branches; and whether the under-officers were careful to see that the workmen were employed at their work during the whole of their working hours.

Their Lordships farther observing that you mention an order you have given for more effectually guarding against frauds in the receipt of timber without having specified what the same is, it is their Lordships' direction that you transmit to them a copy of the said order; and their Lordships have thought proper to defer the farther consideration of your said letter or the giving of any orders thereupon, until they receive from you the farther information of the state and condition of the yards, agreeable to the directions above-mentioned. I am etc.

[1] Stephens: A clerk at the Ady 1751–9; 2nd Secretary 1759–63 (and was also Anson's secretary when he was 1st Ld); Secretary of the Ady 1763–95. MP 1768–1806. Created baronet 1795, and granted a special pension 1806. Died 1809. He wrote his minutes in a barely decipherable hand.

378. *Admiralty Minute*

18 June 1767

Present: Hawke, Townshend, Buller, Brett, Jenkinson.

... Vice-Admiral Pye, commander-in-chief at the Leeward Islands, having represented to the Lords in his letter of 19th April last the great utility of copper sheathing in preserving from the worm the bottoms of several merchant ships trading in those parts from Bristol and Liverpool; resolved that an extract thereof be sent to the Navy Board for their information...

379. *Letter from the Lords to the Navy Board*

23 June 1767

Gentlemen,

Having taken into our consideration your letter of the 17th instant and resumed consideration of your letter of the 5th instant, containing together your report of the present state of His Majesty's yards as appeared to you upon your last visitation and of the measures taken by you for the information thereof, in consequence of our orders of 21 April last, we observe from your report that the directions so particularly enforced by your warrant of the 13th of March 1749 for reading at least once in three months all the standing orders of the Navy relating to the government of the yards and ordinaries have not of late been complied with in any of the yards except Portsmouth; and that the directions given for fixing up at the gates, and in other parts of the yards, the orders necessary for the information of the inferior officers and workmen, have not been duly obeyed in any of the yards except Plymouth; from whence it appears that the officers have been supine and negligent in this essential part of their duty.

We hope that the reproof and injunctions which you mention to have given them will be sufficient to prevent any farther negligence of this kind. But we recommend it to you to be particularly attentive to the conduct of the officers in this respect for the future and to direct them from henceforth to note upon the weekly progresses sent to this, and to your office, the days on which standing orders are publicly read. And though we are of opinion with you that the orders and instructions given for the general government of the yards and ordinaries may be sufficient for the wise purposes intended by them, yet, as they are dispersed without order or method in a variety of warrants, issued at different times, through a long course of years, we cannot think that they are well digested, so as to afford in a proper and clear manner the information necessary for the conduct of the officers and workmen of the yards. We do therefore hereby desire and direct you to proceed immediately to arrange and digest the said orders and instructions under proper heads, so as to compose one uniform body and system out of the whole, taking care where there are repetitions of the same order to adopt that where the sense is most clearly explained and best enforced; and to transmit the same, when finished, to us for our approbation, it being our intention that the orders and instructions so arranged and digested shall then be printed and thereby made more generally known.

We also observe by your said report that the officers of the yards have not been so attentive and diligent as they ought to have been in remedying the abuses arising from the privilege of chips. We hope that the reproof and injunctions given to them on this head will have their due effect. We think proper, however, to recommend this object to your future attention; and as this abuse has been suffered to increase in Chatham yard more than any other, particularly by the accumulation of a very great quantity of chips, many of them unlawful ones, near the dockyard gates for sale, we do farther desire and direct you to signify our highest displeasure to such of the officers of that yard as have been blamable by conniving at these practices and to acquaint them and the workmen that, as the privilege of carrying out of chips could never be intended to extend to the carrying out of slab or useful timber, or to authorize the sale of real chips, any workman who shall be concerned in any of these practices for the future is to be dismissed, and that any officer who shall connive thereat will be severely punished upon proper representation made thereof. And as you have represented in your said report that you remarked in the workmen of the said yard a particular degree of sloth and inactivity, you are to signify our high displeasure also on this account to the master shipwright and other officers of that yard, to whose negligence this evil must in great measure be imputed.

We farther observe from your said report that, as the numbers of old men are greater in Portmouth yard than in any other, you are desirous that the pension established by His Majesty's Order in Council upon shipwrights and caulkers superannuated in the service be extended to a greater number, and that such of the workmen unfit for farther service as have been at sea be admitted into Greenwich

Hospital, we do hereby acquaint you that we will be ready, as vacancies shall happen on the present establishment of superannuation, to admit such shipwrights and caulkers as shall be recommended to us. But we do not think fit to propose to His Majesty the alteration of our establishment so lately made with a view to meet a case which exists in only one of the yards, and that probably from accidental circumstances. And with respect to the decayed workmen who are qualified for Greenwich Hospital, you are to cause a list of their names to be forthwith prepared and transmitted to us, and we will then give orders for their being admitted into the said Hospital as soon as possible.

We observe with pleasure by your aforesaid report that the ships lying up in the several ordinaries were found in excellent order and that the regulations on that head have been well and punctually observed. We do therefore desire and direct you publicly to signify to the masters attendant of the several yards and to all others concerned in the care and preservation of the said ships our high approbation of their conduct, assuring them that they will, on that account, be the objects of our particular favour and protection.

Lastly, we observe from the whole of the said report that the present disorders and irregularities in the yards have gradually increased to their present height from a neglect and relaxation of that discipline which it is the duty of the officers of the said yards, according to their instructions and rules of the Navy to maintain; and as we cannot therefore expect that the reformation now attempted will long continue but by a regular and constant exertion of the same zeal and attention which has been shown on the present occasion, we do most earnestly recommend you by frequent inquiries into the conduct of the officers and workmen, and to the Commissioners resident in the several yards by a careful and sedulous observance of the behaviour of all who are under them, to endeavour to keep them to a diligent discharge of their duty.

We also recommend it to you to visit the yards once more in the course of the present year and not to omit doing the like once at least in every year, that you may be able from your own observation to inform this Board whether the orders now given have been duly obeyed and produced the good effects expected from them. And though upon the present occasion we have rested satisfied with the general account that has been given of the behaviour of the officers belonging to the yards, yet we shall expect upon a future visitation, after time has been allowed for reformation of what is now complained of, if any abuses or disorders shall be found to continue, that you do not fail through mistaken good nature or indulgence to represent by name such officers to whose negligence these irregularities or any relaxation of discipline is to be imputed, that we may then proceed to punish those who will not reform their conduct upon the admonitions now given.

We are etc.

ED. HAWKE
C. TOWNSHEND
PALMERSTON
P. BRETT
C. JENKINSON

380. *Moore to Stephens*

Portsmouth
20 July 1767

[From 1767 to 1769 Sir John Moore, Rear-Admiral of the Red, who had been Hawke's flag captain in 1747, was commander-in-chief at Portsmouth, usually wearing his flag in the *Dorsetshire* (70) which had been in Hawke's squadron at Quiberon Bay and was now a guardship. In July 1767 there were seven guardships at Portsmouth. Of these ships of the line, the five largest each had a peacetime complement of only 180; and out of the seven captains, three had been allowed leave of absence by the Admiralty. There were also four smaller ships at Spithead. According to Moore's returns, the *Gibraltar* was 'leaky', the *Aeolus* 'fit for sea', the *Hound* 'very foul', and the *Escort* 'fit for sea' (although her surgeon and carpenter were both 'dead'). The frigate *Solebay*, of which more below, was 'ready for dock'.]

Sir,
    In consequence of their Lordship's directions signified by your letter to me of the 18th instant to inquire into a complaint made against Captain Bremer[1] of the *Solebay* [(24)], I sent immediate notice to him that I would come on board the ship tomorrow on that business, but I find he went to Town on Saturday last [the 18th] in consequence of leave from their Lordships, so I am obliged to postpone the inquiry. I am etc.

---

[1] Bremer: L 1755, CR 1762, C 1765. Dismissed Aug. 1767 (Document 384).

381. *Moore to Stephens*

Portsmouth
27 July 1767
'Read 13th [August] & orders thereon' [see 384]

Sir,

Captain Bremer being returned to his duty, I have inquired into the complaint made against him by Mr Whitlock Nicholl;[1] and, in regard to what he says of himself, I find the circumstances to be as follows:

That he was never rated mate, though he did the duty of such, but was rated midshipman when Captain Bremer came to the command of the ship and continued so till the 31st of March, when he was rated able [seaman].

I find by the general muster book that the date of pay lists is the 23rd of June last when the ship was in Plymouth Sound, but they were not given to him till the 29th, at which time she was in Portsmouth Harbour. It is true that Captain Bremer did not write to me for his discharge till the 3rd of July and sets forth in his letter that Mr Nicholl was recommended by his friends to Captain [Thomas] Collingwood[2] [of the *Tweed* (28)] who was ready to receive and rate him in the same capacity, upon which I gave an order for his discharge into the *Tweed*. But I now find that Captain Collingwood could not receive him, his complement being complete, and that therefore, of course, the Commissioner would not pay him his wages.

It does not appear that Mr Nicholl had any other notice of his discharge than what he mentions in his letter; but he had some reason to expect he should be disrated the 31st of March, as he had then served his complete time as midshipman, and he owns he had heard a report in the ship that Captain Bremer intended to rate young gentlemen recommended to him in order to their serving two years as midshipmen.[3]

By the general muster book, a person whose name is James

---

[1] Nicholl was later commissioned (1772) but rose no further.
[2] Thomas Collingwood: L 1750, C 1756.
[3] While a 'young gentleman' might (as has often been remarked) be rated, let us say, an able seaman on going to a new ship after completing two years as a midshipman, the observation that 'he had some reason to expect he should be disrated' while remaining in the same ship is of interest.

Bremer appears to be rated master's mate; and Captain Bremer acknowledges that he is not more than six years old and says, as he is designed for the service, he took the opportunity, while in his power, of rating him without any view to his wages—and the ship has not been paid since.

In regard to that part of the complaint relative to the false musters, Mr Nicholl says Robert Kirby and John Plummer left the ship in December 1766. They appear, however, on the ship's books, the one till the 11th of May and the other till the 11th of June last, and are then discharged. The ship was mustered by the clerk of the cheque at Kinsale on the 16th and 24th of April when, Mr Nicholl says, they were answered for as being on duty aboard a prize smuggling vessel taken by the *Solebay*. Captain Bremer's account is that two other men, being victualled to do the duty in the room of those absent, answered to the names of Kirby and Plummer, and his clerk says the same thing. Mr Watson,[1] the first lieutenant, does not seem to remember any more of Kirby and Plummer than having watched them with the rest of the ship's company and does not, as he says, recollect any circumstance relative to the musters. Captain Bremer says he kept these men on the ship's books in hopes and expectation they would return to the ship before he left Ireland, and procured two to answer their names to prevent the clerk of the cheque's running them, imagining the service did not suffer thereby...

382. *Admiralty Minute*

23 July 1767

[In 1749, the principle had triumphed that half pay was more of a reward for past services than a retainer. From 1715 to the end of the century, the half pay establishment catered for 130 lieutenants on a higher rate and for 131 on a lower. Until 1767, the higher rate was 2s.6d. a day and the lower rate was 2s.0d. Officers qualified for the higher rate by serving in first or second rate ships of the line.]

Present: Hawke, Townshend, Buller, Brett, Jenkinson.

... The House of Commons having, during the last session of Parliament, presented an address to the King, beseeching His Majesty to make such farther provision for the lieutenants of the Royal Navy on half pay (not exceeding one shilling a day over and above their present half pay for the year 1767) as His Majesty should

---

[1] Thomas Watson: L 1759, C 1780. Died 1781.

think fit, and the time being now come for paying them the half pay due to them to the 30th of last month; resolved that a memorial be laid before His Majesty humbly proposing that a shilling a day be added to the half pay of the said lieutenants,to commence the 1st of January last, to continue till further order, and to be placed on the ordinary estimates of the Navy.

383. *Admiralty Minute*

6 August 1767

Present: Hawke, Townshend, Buller, Brett.

... Mr Samuel Bowen of Georgia having represented by memorial to the King in Council that, having a prisoner in China for four years, he had opportunities to observe the great utility of their sago powder and the several things made from thence in the nature of vermicelli and other gelatinous pastes, which afford great nutriment, are wholesome and easy of digestion, properties very useful in warm climates, tending greatly to preserve the health of the seamen and to prevent scurvy; that when he was released he went to Georgia where, in a plantation of his own, he applied himself vigorously and successfully in cultivating the raw material and perfecting the powder, and that he is now ready and desirous of furnishing the Royal Navy with that ingredient for any term of years at an established price; and the said memorial having been referred to this Board for their consideration; resolved that, as the qualities of this powder with respect to that imported from East India cannot be so properly judged of by any persons as the College of Physicians, a state of the matter be sent to Sir William Browne, their president, with the request of their Lordships that he will lay it before the College and favour them with the opinion of the College whether the aforesaid powder can be safely admitted among the surgeon's necessaries in lieu of that imported from the East Indies.

Resolved that Mr Bowen be desired to attend the College of Physicians with a proper quantity of his powder, that such experiments may be made thereof as shall be judged necessary...

384. *Stephens to Moore*

13 August 1767

Sir,

My Lords Commissioners having taken into consideration your letter of the 27th ultimo [381], containing a report of your inquiry into the complaint made against Captain Bremer of the *Solebay* by Mr Whitlock Nicholl, observe that the manner that Mr Nicholl was discharged is irregular, that James Bremer, a child no more than six years old, is entered upon the ship's books and rated master's mate contrary to the established Regulations and Instructions relating to His Majesty's Service at Sea, and that the four men named in the margin [Robert Kirby, John Plummer, William Saunderson, and John Lisle] are borne upon the ship's books for several months after they left the ship, other men being procured to answer their names at muster, and their Lordships therefore judging it improper to continue Captain Bremer in the command of the said ship, direct me to acquaint you that they have appointed Captain Lucius O'Brien to be captain of her in his room, and at the same time command me to signify their direction to you to cause the said men named in the margin, who have been continued improperly upon the ship's books, to be made 'run' upon the days on which they respectively left the ship; and the name of James Bremer, the boy above-mentioned, to be erased from the ship's books, he not being of a proper age to be entered in any quality on board any of His Majesty's ships; and as, by that means, there will be room to rate Mr Nicholl as master's mate, who appears by your report to have done that duty, it is their Lordships' pleasure that he be rated such from the day he was disrated as a midshipman to the day of his discharge and that care be taken that his pay lists which have been made out for his wages be altered accordingly, their Lordships having directed the Navy Board to pay him his wages in consideration of his being discharged contrary to his inclination. I am etc.

385. *Admiralty Minute*

10 September 1767

Present: Hawke, Palmerston, Yonge, Brett.

... The Navy Board representing that there will soon be room to set up a new 90-gun ship at Portsmouth, a 74 at Deptford, and a 64 at Plymouth, and that the collecting [of] the frames and giving them time to season will increase their duration and create but little expense in this year; resolved that they be directed to do as they propose, transmitting hither draughts and estimates as usual...

386. *Moore to Stephens*

Portsmouth
17 September 1767

Sir,

You'll please to inform their Lordships that a fire broke out last night in the smith's shop in the dockyard, which was extinguished without any material damage.

I beg you'll also inform their Lordships that the officers of the guardships were extremely alert and diligent upon the occasion. I am etc.

Minute: 18 September. Own receipt. Their Lordships are glad to hear that the fire was extinguished without doing very much damage and direct him to signify to the officers and men of the guardships their approbation of the diligence and alertness shown upon this occasion.

387. *Moore to Stephens*

Portsmouth
3 October 1767

Sir,

I enclose you a letter from Captain Marsh[1] relating to a complaint made by Commissioner Hughes against the boatswain of the *St Antonio* [formerly the *San Antonio* (60), taken at Havana in 1762, and now a guardship] for selling a number of the King's hammocks. I was in hopes the boatswain would have impeached some of his accomplices, which possibly might have occasioned our coming to the very root of this evil, but he seems now determined not to do so. I have ordered him to be kept on board with a sentinel over him till I know their Lordships' pleasure therein. I am etc.

Minute: 7 October. Direct him to inquire more particularly into the circumstances of the fact and what evidence there is of it, and report the same to their Lordships for their further information.

[1] Marsh: L 1740, CR 1744, C 1748. He died in 1772.

388. *Moore to Stephens*

Portsmouth
14 October 1767

Sir,

All the information I can get concerning the hammacoes which the boatswain of the *St Antonio* is charged with embezzling is as follows:

An excise officer, in searching two colliers for some run goods, found a parcel of the King's hammacoes, which he carried to Commissioner Hughes. On examining the masters of the colliers, they say they had them from one Hitchens's wife of Portsmouth, who says she had them from the boatswain of the *St Antonio*'s wife. The boatswain at first acknowledged his selling the hammacoes and said that some clerks in the yard were concerned with him, but now he denies all that and says he knows nothing of the transaction...

Minute: 29 October. Let him know that their Lordships have thought fit to dismiss Mason from his employment as boatswain of the *St Antonio* on account of the strong suspicion of his being concerned in selling the hammacoes, and for not having dealt ingenuously in making a full confession of the fact and discovering of persons who were concerned with him.

389. *Admiralty Minutes*

29 October 1767

Present: Hawke, Yonge, Brett, Jenkinson.

... The College of Physicians having reported to their Lordships, in return to their reference of the 6th of August last, that Mr Bowen's sago powder, if it be prepared as he hath represented, is as good as what is commonly sold and may be safely admitted among the medicines of the Royal Navy in lieu of that which comes from East India; and, it appearing to their Lordships that it may be imported from Georgia at a much cheaper rate, resolved, in consideration of saving expense to the public and of giving encouragement to the commerce of His Majesty's colonies, that the Navy Board be directed to contract with Mr Bowen for a quantity of his powder and to issue the same in the usual proportions to such of the surgeons of the Navy as they shall think fit, that proper experiments may be made thereof and their Lordships informed how it is found to answer; and the Commissioners of the Sick and Hurt are also to be directed to purchase some of the said powder and to cause experiments to be made in like manner in the several hospitals...

Their Lordships observing by the accounts sent to this Office that the officers and workmen of the several dock and rope yards have not been paid farther than the 31st of December last, and there having been several reformations made in those yards in the course of the present year and their Lordships having, with a view to encourage the men to a vigorous performance of their duty, promised to use their endeavours that their pay should for the future be as little in arrears as possible; resolved that the Lords of the Treasury be acquainted therewith and desired that the men may be paid as near to the present time as can be done, consistent with other public services...

390. *Moore to Stephens*

Portsmouth
16 November 1767

Sir,

Their Lordships' orders to Captain Collingwood and Captain Bennett of the *Tweed* [(28)] and *Aeolus* [(32)], the former to proceed into the harbour to grave and refit for Channel service and the latter to receive on board His Excellency Hamid Aga, ambassador from the Bashaw of Tripoli, and also Edward Barker, Esq., His Majesty's Consul at Tripoli, with their attendants and baggage, and proceed with them thither, and then make the best of his way and put himself under the command of Commodore Spry[1] [the commander-in-chief in the Mediterranean] are delivered.

And I have also, agreeable to their Lordships' directions, ordered Captain Wilkinson[2] in the *Niger* [(32)] to proceed to Plymouth with a sum of money intended to be sent thither for the payment of the workmen of that yard. I am etc.

391. *Admiralty Minute*

15 December 1767

Present: Hawke, Townshend, Palmerston, Brett, Jenkinson.

[1] Spry: L 1740, C 1745. Left as commodore at Halifax by Boscawen for the winter of 1755. Served off Louisbourg 1757–8 and in the St Lawrence under Saunders 1759. Commodore and c.-in-c., Mediterranean 1766–9. RA 1770 (Document 469). He was an officer of repute but, in private life, a tireless hoaxer. He died in 1775.
[2] Thomas Wilkinson; L 1759, CR 1766, C 1771. Died 1776.

... The Lords took into consideration the late disturbances that have happened [see 375] at the Academy at Portsmouth and, being desirous that the same should for the future be governed and conducted in such a manner as in all respects may answer the end of its institution; resolved that Sir Peircy Brett, Sir John Moore [commander-in-chief at Portsmouth], and Captain Campbell be sent down to Portsmouth to visit the Academy to inquire into the conduct of the persons concerned in the government thereof, as well as the scholars; to make a full report to the Board; and to suggest any alterations or additions in the rules and orders established for the government thereof; and if they should find any scholar who has particularly distinguished himself by good behaviour, to report him to their Lordships that he may be recommended to the King for some particular mark of distinction...

392.   *Stephens to the Navy Board*

15 December 1767

Gentlemen,

My Lords Commissioners of the Admiralty having understood that, agreeable to what was recommended to you in their Lordships' order of the 23rd June last [379], you have visited His Majesty's yards a second time this year; and their Lordships not having yet received from you any report of the state of the yards as it appeared to you on such visitation, or whether you found that the orders and directions you had given on your former visitation, and those you had given in consequence of their Lordships' said order of the 23rd June, had been obeyed, I am commanded by their Lordships to signify their direction that you do forthwith make such report upon the state and condition of each yard severally, and conformably in all respects to their Lordships' directions of the 10th of June [377] concerning the manner of making such reports. I am etc.

393.   *Moore to Stephens*

Portsmouth
29 December 1767

Sir,

You'll please to acquaint their Lordships that in consequence of a court martial held the 16th instant on John Clay Mason, marine, whereby he was sentenced to receive three hundred lashes on his bare back with a cat of nine tails, in such manner and at such time as I should think proper, for deserting from His Majesty's ship *Fowey* [(20)], I appointed yesterday for putting the sentence into execution and ordered a surgeon to attend him, who finding that he was unable to bear more than a hundred and eighty-five lashes of the three hundred without his life being endangered thereby, the punishment was stopped and the prisoner returned on board the *Bellona* [(74)] in the custody of the provost marshal; and I beg the favour to know their Lordships' pleasure whether he is to receive the remainder of his punishment or whether it is to be remitted. I am etc.

Minute: 30 December. Direct him to remit the remainder of the punishment and release the man from his confinement.

394. *Admiralty Minute*

15 January 1768

Present: Hawke, Palmerston, Brett.

... Resolved that Sir Edward Hawke be appointed Admiral and Commander-in-Chief of His Majesty's Fleet, in the room of Sir William Rowley, deceased...

395. *Admiralty Minute*

21 January 1768

Present: Hawke, Townshend, Brett.

... Vice-Admiral Pye having aquainted the Board in his letter of 24th October last from the Leeward Islands that John Wadney, a seaman belonging to the *Chatham* [(50)], had ventured down into the well of that ship at the risk of his own life and did thereby save the lives of several of the crew who were very near suffocation, and that he therefore proposed making him a boatswain for his intrepidity and humanity; resolved that he be acquainted the Lords very much approve of his intention and will take an opportunity of preferring the man in that line.

396. *Admiralty Minute*

22 January 1768

Present: Hawke, Townshend, Buller, Palmerston.

... Vice-Admiral Pye having informed their Lordships in his letter of the 25th October last from the Leeward Islands that the chemical sheathing of the *Scarborough* [(22)] does not produce the effect expected from it; resolved that an extract thereof be sent to the Navy Board for their information...

397. *Admiralty Minute*

10 February 1768

Present: Hawke, Townshend, Yonge.

... The Lords having found by experience of last year the good effects of their order of the 19th February last for restraining the expenses of the Navy within the grants of Parliament, and the honourable House of Commons having voted the sums judged necessary for naval services for the present year, according to the estimates laid before them; resolved that the said order of the 19th February last be enforced to the Navy Board and that they be directed to prepare and send hither, as soon as may be, a plan for the expense of the year, taking care to conform as much as possible in the distribution of the money given by the Parliament to the several services for which it was voted, and in no respect to exceed the whole of the sums granted for the naval service...

398. *Admiralty Minute*

25 February 1768

Present: Hawke, Townshend, Palmerston, Yonge, Brett, Jenkinson.

The Navy Board attending according to order were called in and their report of the 18th December last, concerning the state of His Majesty's dockyards, as it appeared to them on their second visitation in the course of last year being read, it was observed to them that their said report appeared to their Lordships to be too general. And, being discoursed with in respect to the state and condition of His Majesty's several yards respectively, they alleged that, upon their said visitation, they found the orders they had given in consequence of their first visitation had been duly complied with and that each of the yards was in the condition represented in their said report.

It was then recommended to them by their Lordships to visit the yards annually, agreeable to former orders, and to report particularly the state of each at their return...

399. *Admiralty Minute*

10 March 1768

Present: Hawke, Palmerston, Brett, Spencer.

The new patent was read constituting Lord Charles Spencer[1] one of the Lords of the Admiralty in the room of Mr Jenkinson and his Lordship took his seat at the Board accordingly...

400. *Moore to Stephens*

Clifford Street
16 March 1768

Sir,

Being seized with a very painful gout, attended with a violent fever, and my leave of absence from my command expiring tomorrow, I beg you will be pleased to move their Lordships for a month's further leave. I am etc.

Minute: 18th March. My Lords are pleased to comply with his request. Acquaint the senior officer at Portsmouth.

401. *Moore to Stephens*

Clifford Street
16 April 1768

Sir,

I must beg you will please to inform their Lordships that in consequence of my late illness I am still so weak as not to be able to walk across the room and therefore am obliged to request their Lordships' indulgence of a month's longer leave of absence. I am etc.

Minute: 18 April. To be complied with. Acquaint commanding officer therewith.

402. *Admiralty Minute*

20 April 1768

Present: Hawke, Townshend, Brett.

[1] Lord Charles Spencer (1740–1820) was the 2nd son of the 3rd Duke of Marlborough. MP 1761–84 and 1796–1801. A Ld of Ady 8.3.68–16.7.79; held various offices and latterly he was Postmaster General and Master of the Mint 1801–6.

The Lords took into consideration a letter from the Commissioners for Sick and Hurt dated the 25th of February last, representing that in consequence of Vice-Admiral Pye's account of the good effects produced by issuing portable soup to the well men on board the King's ships in the West Indies, they availed themselves of the late slaughter of oxen at the Victualling Office to make such a quantity of the same as could be procured from the offal, with the proportion of mutton, and have now a considerable quantity in store, and therefore proposing to send a farther quantity to the Leeward Islands; resolved that they be ordered to cause a proper quantity to be sent on board the *Jason* [(32)] which is now fitting for those islands at Woolwich, and that Commodore [*sic*] Pye be directed to issue it in the usual manner...

403. *Admiralty Minute*

20 July 1768

Present: Hawke, Townshend, Palmerston, Brett, Spencer.

... The Lords took into consideration a letter from the Navy Board representing the ill effects of copper sheathing in corroding and destroying the rudder irons, bolts, and other iron works under water and proposing that an experiment be made on board the new sloop going to be set up at Deptford by the bolts in her works under water being wrought out of forged copper, instead of iron; resolved that they be directed to make the experiment accordingly...

404. *Instructions from the Lords of the Admiralty to Lieutenant James Cook*[1]

30 July 1768

Whereas we have, in obedience to the King's commands, caused His Majesty's bark the *Endeavour*, whereof you are commander, to be fitted out in a proper manner for receiving such persons as the Royal Society should think fit to appoint to observe the passage of the planet Venus over the disk of the sun on the 3rd of June 1769,

---

[1] Cook, a labourer's son, was at first a seaman in the Baltic trade. Aged 27, he entered the Navy as a common seaman in 1755. Master 1759; won recognition for surveys in the St Lawrence. Through Palliser (p. 445, n. 3) he was appointed to survey the coasts of Newfoundland and Labrador 1762–7. At the prompting of Philip Stephens, he was commissioned on 25 May 1768 so that he could command the *Endeavour* on her voyage. CR 19.8.71 on his return; C 1775. Murdered by Hawaiian natives 1779.

and for conveying them to such place to the southward of the equinoctial line as should be judged proper for observing that phenomenon ... you are hereby required and directed to receive ... Mr Charles Green with his servant, instruments, and baggage on board the said bark and proceed in her according to the following instructions.

You are to make the best of your way to Plymouth Sound where we have ordered the crew of the bark to be paid two months wages in advance.

When they have received the same, you are to put to sea ... to the island of Madeira and there take on board such a quantity of wine as you can conveniently stow...

Having so done, you are to put to sea and proceed round Cape Horn to Port Royal Harbour in King George's Island [Tahiti], situated in 17 degrees and 30 minutes of south latitude and 150 degrees of longitude west of the meridian of the Royal Observatory of Greenwich.

You are at liberty to touch upon the coast of Brazil or at Port Egmont in the Falklands Isles, or at both, in your way thither if you find it necessary for completing your water and procuring refreshments for the bark's company.

We recommend it to you to stand well to the southward in your passage round the Cape in order to make a good westing, taking care, however, to fall into the parallel of King George's Island at least 120 leagues to the eastward of it and using your best endeavours to arrive there at least a month or six weeks before the 3rd of June next, that Mr Green and you may have leisure to adjust and try your instruments before the observation...

You are to endeavour by all proper means to cultivate a friendship with the natives, presenting them such trifles as may be acceptable to them, exchanging with them for provisions (of which there is great plenty) such of the merchandise you have been directed to provide as they may value, and showing them every kind of civility and regard. But as Captain Wallis[1] has represented the island to be very populous and the natives (as well there as at the other islands which he visited) to be rather treacherous then otherwise, you are to be cautious not to let yourself be surprised by them, but to be

[1] Wallis (see also p. 387, n. 1) had been sent, like Byron (p. 126, n. 4), on a voyage of discovery in the Pacific—still a rare European objective—and, by following a novel track, had found Tahiti (King George's Island). Having sailed from England in August 1766, he returned home in May 1768 by way of Tinian, Batavia and the Cape of Good Hope.

constantly on your guard against any accident...

When this service is performed, you are to put to sea without loss of time and carry into execution the additional instructions contained in the enclosed sealed packet.

But in case of your inability to carry these our instructions to you into execution, you are to be careful to leave them, as also the additional instructions, with the next officer in seniority, who is hereby required and directed to execute them in the best manner he can. Given etc.

ED. HAWKE
P. BRETT
C. SPENCER

To Lieutenant James Cook,
commander of His Majesty's bark
the *Endeavour* in Galleons Reach.

Enclosure 1:

404a. *Additional Secret Instructions for Lieutenant James Cook*

30 July 1768

Whereas the making of discoveries of countries hitherto unknown and the attaining a knowledge of distant parts which, though formerly discovered have yet been but imperfectly explored, will redound greatly to the honour of this nation as a maritime power, as well as to the dignity of the crown of Great Britain, and may lend greatly to the advance of the trade and navigation thereof; and whereas there is reason to imagine that a continent or land of great extent may be found to the southward of the tract lately made by Captain Wallis in His Majesty's ship the *Dolphin* (of which you will herewith receive a copy) or of the tract of any former navigators in pursuit of the like kind; you are therefore, in pursuance of His Majesty's pleasure, hereby required and directed to put to sea with the bark you command so soon as the observation of the transit of the planet Venus shall be finished, and observe the following instructions.

You are to proceed to the southward in order to make discovery of the continent above-mentioned until you arrive in the latitude of 40°, unless you sooner fall in with it; but, not having discovered it or any evident signs of it in that run, you are to proceed in search of it to the westward, between the latitude before-mentioned and the latitude of 35°, until you discover it or fall in with the eastern side of the land discovered by Tasman and now called New Zealand.

If you discover the continent above-mentioned either in your run to the southward or to the westward, as above directed, you are to employ yourself diligently in exploring as great an extent of the coast as you can, carefully observing the true situation thereof both in latitude and longitude; the variation of the needle; bearings of headlands; height, direction, and course of the tides and currents; depths and soundings of the sea; shoals, rocks, etc.; and taking of views of such bays, harbours and parts of the coast as may be useful to navigation.

You are also carefully to observe the nature of the soil and the products thereof; the beasts and fowls that inhabit or frequent it; the fishes that are to be found in the rivers or upon the coast and in what plenty; and in case you find any mines, minerals, or valuable stones, you are to bring home specimens of each, as also such specimens of the seeds of the trees, fruits and grains as you may be able to collect and transmit them to our Secretary, that we may cause proper examination and experiments to be made of them.

You are likewise to observe the genius, temper, disposition and number of the natives, if there be any, and endeavour by all proper means to cultivate a friendship and alliance with them, making them presents of such trifles as they may value, inviting them to traffic, and showing them every kind of civility and regard; taking care, however, not to suffer yourself to be surprised by them, but to be always upon your guard against any accidents.

You are also, with the consent of the natives, to take possession of convenient situations in the country in the name of the King of Great Britain, or, if you find the country uninhabited, take possession for His Majesty by setting up proper marks and inscriptions, as first discoverers and possessors.

But if you should fail of discovering the continent before-mentioned, you will, upon falling in with New Zealand, carefully observe the latitude and longitude in which that land is situated and explore as much of the coast as the condition of the bark, the health of her crew, and the state of your provisions will admit of, having always great attention to reserve as much of the latter as will enable you to reach some known port where you may procure a sufficiency to carry you to England, either round the Cape of Good Hope or Cape Horn, as from the circumstances you may judge the most eligible way of returning home.

You will also observe with accuracy the situation of such islands as you may discover in the course of your voyage that have not hitherto been discovered by any Europeans and take possession for

His Majesty, and make surveys and draughts of such of them as may appear to be of consequence, without suffering yourself, however, to be thereby diverted from the object which you are always to have in view, the discovery of the southern continent so often mentioned.

But for as much as in an undertaking of this nature several emergencies may arise not to be foreseen and therefore not particularly to be provided for by instructions beforehand, you are in all such cases to proceed as, upon advice with your officers, you shall judge most advantageous to the service on which you are employed.

You are to send by all proper conveyances to the Secretary of the Royal Society copies of the observations you shall have made of the transit of Venus; and you are at the same time to send to our Secretary, for our information, accounts of your proceedings and copies of the survey and drawings you shall have made. And upon your arrival in England, you are immediately to repair to this Office in order to lay before us a full account of your proceedings in the full course of your voyage, taking care before you leave the vessel to demand from the officers and petty officers the log books and journals they may have kept and to seal them up for our inspection, and enjoining them, and the whole crew, not to divulge where they have been until they shall have permission to do so. Given etc.

ED. HAWKE
P. BRETT
C. SPENCER

Enclosure 2:

404b. *Instructions to be shown by Cook to 'Flag Officers, Captains and Commanders of His Majesty's ships and vessels' encountered on the voyage*

30 July 1768

Whereas we have directed Lieutenant James Cook to proceed in His Majesty's bark the *Endeavour* upon a particular service; you are hereby required and directed not to demand of him a sight of the instructions he has received from us for his proceedings on the said service, nor upon any pretence whatever to detain him, but on the contrary to give him any assistance he may stand in need of, towards enabling him to carry the said instructions into execution. Given etc.

ED. HAWKE
P. BRETT
C. SPENCER

405. *Admiralty Minutes*

Saturday, 30 July 1768

Present: Hawke, Townshend, Brett, Spencer

... The Board being of opinion, from what Dr MacBride[1] has recommended in his *Experimental Essays* on the scurvy and his account of treating that disorder at sea, as well as from the opinions of other persons acquainted with the nature of that malady, that malt made into wort may be of great benefit to seamen labouring under that and other putrid disorders; resolved that a quantity thereof be sent on board the *Endeavour* bark that trials may be made of its efficacy during her intended voyage.

Resolved that the complement of the *Endeavour* bark be increased to 85 men...

406. *King George III to Hawke*

Richmond Lodge
15 September 1768

Sir Edward Hawke,

Having seen by some letters from Sir Horace Mann[2] that the French are uncivil to a very unwarrantable degree to every ship that comes near to Corsica and thinking that my brother, the Duke of Cumberland,[3] might have some disagreeable scene if in his cruise he should meet with any of them, which naturally could not afterwards be so well adjusted between the two courts as the disputes between common ships of war, I desire you will write a private letter to Captain Barrington acquainting him that, in the present situation of affairs, I think it best for my brother to return after the first cruise to Port Mahon. The *Boreas* frigate is detained at Spithead until you have wrote and then you will immediately dispatch that vessel.

---

[1] Dr David MacBride (1726–78) was born in Co. Antrim. Besides his *Experimental Essays* (1764), he published in 1768 a book on treating scurvy at sea.

[2] Mann was British envoy at Florence 1740–86; created baronet 1755. Remembered for sustaining a correspondence with Horace Walpole 1741–85.

[3] Henry Frederick, Duke of Cumberland (1745–90) led an irregular private life and was soon to alienate the King, his brother, by his marriage of 1771. C 1768, RA 1770, VA 1770, A 1778.

407. *Moore to Stephens*

Portsmouth
2 October 1768

Sir,

I have received and delivered their Lordships' orders to Captain Lambert[1] of the *Dorsetshire* [(70)] ... to use the utmost dispatch in fitting his ship for the sea, in order to carry the 25th Regiment of Foot to Minorca...

408. *Moore to Stephens*

Portsmouth
5 October 1768

Sir,

Their Lordships having been pleased to order the *Dorsetshire* to be fitted for the sea with the utmost expedition, I have directed sixty men to be lent her from the [other] guardships to assist therein, which has so weakened them that I have been obliged to reduce the guard boats from three to two; and I beg you'll please to acquaint their Lordships that, if the *Dorsetshire*'s complement is to be completed from the guardships, they will be so reduced as to be unable to carry on the harbour duty. I am etc.

Minute: 6 October. Approve of his having had these men transferred and acquaint him that their Lordships will order men to be brought from the guardships at Plymouth to complete the *Dorsetshire*'s complement.

409. *Instructions from the Lords of the Admiralty to Captain Michael Everitt, commanding officer at Portsmouth*

18 March 1769

Whereas we intend that His Majesty's ship the *Dorsetshire*, lately returned from Minorca, shall do the duty of a guardship again at Portsmouth, you are hereby required and directed to cause her to be put into a proper state ... And you are to cause the men who were lent to her from the ships at Plymouth to be put on board the *Tweed* on her arrival, whose captain is directed to proceed with them to that place. Given etc.

---

[1] Lambert: L 1754, CR 1759, C 1760.

410. *Admiralty Minutes*

12 October 1768

Present: Hawke, Palmerston, Yonge, Brett.

A letter was read from the Navy Board, dated the 3rd instant, representing the difficulties they meet with in procuring sufficient quantities of timber for the frames of His Majesty's ships, and proposing that they may be ordered to collect and prepare the frames of the ships named at the foot hereof, in order to their being set up when the ships now on the stocks are launched, which will not only save time by the timber being out and laid apart to season as soon as it is served into store, but will also be of the greatest advantage to its duration; resolved that orders be given for doing as they propose, transmitting hither the proper draughts and estimates as usual.

Woolwich yard	74-gun ship	On the slip the *Queen* launches from.
Chatham	64.	On the slip the *Reasonable* launches from.
Portsmouth	74)	On the slips the *Elizabeth* and *Worcester* launch
	64)	from.
Plymouth	74.	On the slip the *Royal Oak* launches from.
Sheerness	50.	On the slip where the *Portland* launches from.

In pursuance of His Majesty's Order in Council dated the 7th instant; resolved that orders be sent to the Navy Board to prepare the usual estimates for the ensuing year...

411. *Admiralty Minutes*

26 October 1768

Present: Hawke, Townshend, Yonge, Brett.

A report was read from the Navy Board upon a reference to them of a petition of Elizabeth Neill, widow of Lawrence Neill, late boatswain of the *Coventry* [(28)], praying that the want of his books and papers may be dispensed with in the passing of his accounts; resolved, for the reasons they have given, that her request be not complied with till farther inquiry has been made after the said books and papers, there being reason to suspect he did not keep a regular account of the stores committed to his charge, agreeable to his instructions...

Lord Weymouth[1] having transmitted to the Board copy of a letter from Sir John Goodricke,[2] containing some information he was desired to obtain concerning some timber offered to sale by a Swedish merchant for the use of the Navy; resolved that copies thereof be sent to the Navy Board that they may judge whether it may be advisable to purchase the same...

412. *Admiralty Minutes*

27 October 1768

Present: Hawke, Townshend, Yonge.

... A letter was read from the Navy Board, representing that they have contracted with Messrs Durand and Bacon to furnish North American white pine masts, yards and bowsprits for the use of the Navy, and desiring the King's licence may be obtained for cutting trees in North America, as hath been usual in like cases; resolved that a copy of their contract be sent to Lord Hillsborough[3] and that he may be desired to procure His Majesty's grant accordingly.

A letter was read from the Navy Board, dated the 24th instant, representing that two of the five sloops ordered to be built in merchant's yards have not yet been set up, as money could not be spared for that purpose, and proposing for the reasons therein set forth that they may be set up at Chatham and Portsmouth; resolved that orders be given for that purpose.

A letter was read from the Navy Board, dated the 21st instant, representing that the officers of Chatham yard have acquainted them that the first new dock is in a very ruinous condition and not fit to receive a ship that requires a large repair, and proposing to repair it after the *Antelope* is put out of it next year; resolved that orders be given for doing as they propose...

[1] Thomas Thynne, 3rd Viscount Weymouth and later 1st Marquis of Bath (1734–96) had, as Sec. of State, very recently moved from the northern to the southern dept. He remained there until 16 Dec. 1770 when, at the height of the Falklands crisis, he suddenly resigned (see Document 484). Suppressed the Wilkes riots (May 1768); less effective in foreign affairs. Was again Sec. of State 1775–9. An able speaker and a boon companion.

[2] Sir John Goodricke, Bart., was British Minister Resident at Stockholm 1758–64, and Envoy Extraordinary there 1764–73.

[3] Wills Hill, 2nd Viscount and 1st Earl of Hillsborough (1718–93) was Sec. of State for the Colonies, 1768–72 and for the northern dept. 1779–83. Harsh in his attitude to the N. American colonists.

413. *Admiralty Minute*

Saturday, 19 November 1768

Present: Hawke, Townshend, Palmerston.

... The Board taking into consideration a late letter of the Navy Board representing the difficulties they have lately met with in providing oak timber for His Majesty's dockyards and desiring their Lordships will be pleased to use their influence with the Lords of the Treasury, that every means may be taken for preserving the oak now standing in the King's forests and raising a succession, as also that no oak trees may be felled in the said forests for private use, but that the Navy Board may in future be allowed the preference of pre-emption of whatever quantity can be afforded from thence; resolved that a copy of the said letter be sent to the Lords of the Treasury and that they be desired to give the necessary orders accordingly.

414. *Admiralty Minute*

26 December 1768

Present: Townshend, Palmerston, Brett.

... Commodore Spry representing to the Lords that the [Mediterranean] squadron under his command is in great want of stores, particularly sails and rigging, and that he is apprehensive he must dismantle one of the ships to make the rest fit for service, there being no stores at all at Gibraltar and scarcely any at Mahon; resolved that an extract of his letter be sent to the Navy Board with directions to send out, without delay, a proper supply and to take care that there be no room for any complaint of this nature for the future...

415. *Admiralty Minute*

17 February 1769

Present: Hawke, Buller, Palmerston, Brett.

... Mr Jackson, a chemist, who some time since found out a composition for preserving ship's timber and the staves of casks, of which a trial was ordered to be made in the dockyard at Woolwich, representing to the Board that the workmen and coopers have entertained an unreasonable prejudice against the same, imagining it to be poisonous and destructive to the health of the persons employed in working on the timber, etc., and praying that a strict inquiry may be made into the nature of the composition by the College of Physicians in order to satisfy the workmen and to obviate the attacks and insinuations of persons interested in defeating the success of the invention; resolved that application be made to the College to examine the composition accordingly and to favour their Lordships with their opinion thereupon...

416. *Admiralty Minute*

1 March 1769

Present: Hawke, Buller, Palmerston.

... The College of Physicians having made their report upon the ingredients of Mr Jackson's composition for preserving timber, pipe staves, etc., and declared the same to be innocent; resolved that a copy be sent to the Navy Board to quiet the minds of the workmen in the dockyards employed in working up the timber paid with it and another to Mr Jackson for his making such use thereof as to him shall seem meet...

417. *Admiralty Minute*

3 March 1769

Present: Hawke, Palmerston, Yonge.

... Captain [Charles] Douglas[1] of the *Emerald* [(28)], destined to go to the Barents Sea requesting that, for the preservation of the men's health, the ship may have a bulkhead put up under the half deck, be supplied with fishing gear and a long boat fitted in a particular manner, and that she be furnished with an azimuth compass [to observe the magnetic variation]; resolved that orders be given for doing what he hath requested...

[NOTE. Exceptionally, it was decided to place a document of 18 March 1769 out of its chronological sequence at 409 above.]

---

[1] Charles Douglas's naval career seems to have suffered in its early years from lack of patronage. He was ultimately responsible for important technical advances in British gunnery. Passed for lieut. 1747; L 1753, CR 1759, C 1761. Relieved Quebec May 1776; created baronet 1777. Served at Ushant; testified usefully for Keppel. When captain of the *Duke* (98) he perfected devices for serving and aiming the guns— approved by the Ady 1781. Was Rodney's first captain at the Saints 12.4.82. Commodore and c.-in-c., Halifax 1783–6; RA 1787. He died in 1789.

418. *Admiralty Minute*

30 March 1769

Present: Hawke, Buller, Brett.

... The Council of the Royal Society having represented to their Lordships that, in order to fulfil the King's intentions with respect to the transit of Venus over the sun's disk on the 3rd of June next, it will be necessary to send observers to the northern parts of Europe, particularly to the North Cape of Lapland, and requested that a ship of war may be appointed to carry them thither, to stay for them about two months after the transit is over, and to bring them back again to England; resolved that orders be sent to Captain Douglas of the *Emerald*, which ship has been fitted for this service, to receive on board the two observers ... and bring them back to Sheerness.

419. *Admiralty Minutes*

5 April 1769

Present: Hawke, Palmerston, Spencer.

... There being a very great want of seamen to man the ships fitting out for service; resolved that two lieutenants be ordered up to Town from Portsmouth and one from Chatham to open the rendez-vous to raise men.

Captain Douglas of the *Emerald* applying for an additional quantity of portable soup in consideration of the voyage he is going upon; resolved that his request be complied with...

Dr Knight[1] representing to the Board that he has made some improvements in his boat compasses and desiring that trial may be made of two of them on board the *Emerald* during her intended voyage to the North Cape of Lapland; resolved that directions be given to Captain Douglas accordingly...

420. *Admiralty Minute*

Saturday, 8 April 1769

Present: Hawke, Buller, Brett.

---

[1] Dr Gowin Knight (1713–72) was an Oxford MB (1742) but devoted himself to a study of magnetism. F.R.S., 1747. His improved compass became standard in the Navy after 1752. He was the first principal librarian at the British Museum—from 1756.

... A memorial was read from one Monsieur Girod at Liège setting forth that he has invented a method of preserving timber from the worm and offering to discover the same for the use of the Royal Navy; resolved that he be told, if he will send over to the Navy Board some pieces of wood seasoned with his composition, trial shall be made of them in England and also in the West Indies...

421. *Admiralty Minute*

12 April 1769

Present: Hawke, Buller, Brett.

... Sir Joseph Yorke[1] having sent over some pieces of wood properly paid with a mineral oil invented by Baron Haak which he thinks will effectually preserve them against the worm; resolved that they be sent to the Navy Board with a copy of Sir Joseph Yorke's letter and of one from the Baron on that subject, and that they be directed to cause proper experiments to be made of them and to report the result hither...

422. *Admiralty Minutes*

20 June 1769

Present: Townshend, Buller, Brett.

... A letter was read from Commodore Spry in the Mediterranean, enclosing a list of the Spanish fleet with their present disposition; resolved that a copy be sent to Lord Weymouth for His Majesty's information.

Resolved that Lord Weymouth be acquainted of the appointment of Captain Proby to succeed Mr Spry as commander-in-chief in the Mediterranean, in case His Majesty should have any commands to signify to this Board on that occasion...

423. *Admiralty Minute*

7 July 1769

Present: Hawke, Buller, Brett.

[1] Yorke had, as a youthful soldier, served at Fontenoy and Culloden; and by 1777 he was listed as a full general. However, from 1749 he may be accounted a diplomat. Minister at The Hague 1751–61 (warning Frederick the Great of the impending Austrian attack 1756). Ambassador at The Hague 1761–80; K.B. 1761. Created Baron Dover 1788.

... A letter was read from the Navy Board dated the 30th of May last, in addition to their former letters on the same subject, relative to the scarcity of oak timber for the use of the Navy; resolved that a copy thereof, and of the papers enclosed therein, be transmitted to the Lords of the Treasury and that they be desired to give orders for carrying into execution, so far as in them lies, the several propositions therein set forth...

424. *Admiralty Minute*

Saturday, 15 July 1769

Present: Hawke, Buller, Brett.

Resolved that the *Stag* [(32)] be sheathed with copper and put into condition for a voyage to the East Indies, and that either the *Swift* of *Hawke* sloop, whichever the Navy Board shall judge most proper, be likewise put into condition for the same service.

[This is the whole of the business recorded for that day.]

425. *Admiralty Minute*

19 July 1769

Present: Hawke, Buller, Brett.

... The Navy Board representing to the Lords that they have ordered the *Hawke* sloop to be got ready to proceed to the East Indies in preference to the *Swift*; resolved that they be ordered to cause her to be sheathed with copper.

426. *Admiralty Minute*

9 August 1769

Present: Hawke, Townshend, Buller, Brett.

... Resolved that one of Mr Scott's machines for dressing provisions in salt water and for making the sea water fresh be fitted up on board the *Dragon* [(74)] at Portsmouth by way of an experiment...

427. *Admiralty Minute*

13 October 1769

Present: Hawke, Brett, Spencer.

The *Swift* sloop and *Florida* storeship being intended for Falkland's Islands; resolved that orders be given for supplying them with an additional quantity of portable soup, to be issued occasionally to the well men...

428.　*Admiralty Minutes*

23 November 1769

Present: Hawke, Townshend, Buller, Yonge, Palmerston, Brett.

The Lords took into consideration a report from the Navy Board, dated the 29th of September last, on a reference to them of an application by Captain Bentinck,[1] dated the 20th of July last, concerning the experiments that had lately been made of his new invented pump at Portsmouth, and also a former letter from them dated the 25th of July on the same subject; resolved that they be directed to cause further trials to be made in the manner proposed in their letter of the 25th of July and that they be acquainted their Lordships approve of what they have ordered to be done respecting the further trial of a seven-inch pump.

Resolved that Captain Bentinck be acquainted therewith, and that it does not appear to the Lords by the report from the Navy Board that there was any collusion in the making of the former trials, as he seems to suspect...

429.　*Admiralty Minute*

30 January 1770

Present: Hawke, Buller, Palmerston.

... Sir Edward Hawke having communicated to the Board a letter he had received from the Russian Ambassador, desiring that [in accord with Anglo-Russian policy against the Turks] immediate orders might be given for repairing such of Rear-Admiral Elphinston's [Russian] squadron as might stand in need of it, and the same having been referred to the Navy Board, together with a paper

---

[1] Bentinck was a grandson of the 1st Earl of Portland. L 1757, CR 1758, C 1758. In 1760, when commanding the *Niger* (32), he attacked a convoy bound for Martinique despite the presence of a French 74. A successful inventor of ships' pumps. (The Lords had approved in July 1767 a proposal to test his chain pump.) He died in 1775.

received from Mr Elphinston,[1] containing account of the works thought necessary and proposing to cut down one of the ships from a three decker and make her only two decks and a half; and it appearing by the Navy Board's report that what is requested will give great interruption to His Majesty's service, particularly the cutting down [of] the ship and that the best method of easing her would be to take away some of her upper guns and shorten her masts; resolved that they be directed to do as they propose, and to cause such other ships of that squadron to be docked when defects require it and to be repaired in such manner as to enable them to proceed on their voyage [into the Mediterranean] without entering into considerable repair...

430. *Admiralty Minute*

7 February 1770

Present: Hawke, Buller, Palmerston.

... Two letters were read from Commodore Forrest[2] at Jamaica, representing the very bad condition of the fortifications at that island and the great preparations making by the Spaniards at Havana; resolved that copies be sent to the Earl of Hillsborough for the King's information...

431. *Admiralty Minute*

22 February 1770

Present: Hawke, Buller, Palmerston, Spencer.

... Resolved that the curiosities brought home [in May 1768] in the *Dolphin* and *Swallow* from the new-discovered islands in the

---

[1] Elphinston spelt his name without a final 'e' (D.N.B.). L 1746, CR 1757, C 1758. Led Pocock's fleet through the Old Bahama Channel, thus helping to secure complete surprise at Havana 1762. (See David Syrett (ed.), *The Siege and Capture of Havana 1762*, N.R.S. Vol. 114 (1970) pp. xvii–xviii, etc.) Having joined the Russian navy as a rear-admiral in 1769, he sailed late in the year with a squadron for the Mediterranean but suffered storm damage in the North Sea. The British undertook the necessary repairs. Elphinston fought with great tactical skill against the Turks in July 1770. In 1775 he rejoined the R.N. as a captain; served at Grenada 1779, and in Rodney's three encounters with Guichen, Apr.–May 1780.

[2] Forrest: CR 1741, C 1745. On 21.10.57 he was cruising with three of the line off Cap François and, on encountering a superior force under Kersaint, he fought a very spirited action (See also p. 388, n. 1) In early 1770, he was well placed as commodore and c.-in-c. Jamaica, on account of his planting interests there. However, he died on 26.5.70.

South Sea be presented to the Trustees of the British Museum to be deposited in that place...

432. *Admiralty Minute*

23 February 1770

Present: Hawke, Buller, Palmerston.

... The Navy Board having transmitted to the Lords a plan for encouraging the growth and preservation of oak timber throughout the Kingdom, in consequence of a recommendation from the Board to them for that purpose, grounded on a proposal from the Lords of the Treasury, in order to the same being offered to Parliament if approved of; resolved that a copy of the said plan be sent to the Lords of the Treasury for their recommending it to Parliament accordingly.

433. *Admiralty Minutes*

Saturday, 24 February 1770

Present: Hawke, Townshend, Buller.

... Resolved that orders be given to the Navy Board to prepare and transmit to this office a plan for the expense of the present year, taking care to conform as much as possible in the distribution of the money granted by Parliament to the several services for which it was voted.

A letter was read from the Earl of Hillsborough in return to those from this Board to his Lordship, enclosing some from Captain Forrest, commander-in-chief at Jamaica, relative to the apprehensions he is under for the security of His Majesty's possessions there from the unusual augmentation of the strength of the Spaniards in that neighbourhood and [due] to their injurious and unfriendly treatment of His Majesty's subjects; and his Lordship having suggested the King's pleasure in what manner Mr Forrest should be directed to guide himself and what plan to observe for his proceedings; resolved that a letter be drawn up conformable thereunto and that Mr Forrest be at the same time acquainted what ships are intended to be sent to him...

434. *Admiralty Minute*

26 February 1770

Present: Hawke, Buller, Palmerston.

... The commander of the Russian frigate at Sheerness having taken upon him to fire the evening and morning gun; resolved that the Secretary of State be made acquainted therewith and desired to move the Russian Ambassador that effectual orders may be immediately given to prevent the like irregular proceedings for the future...

435. *Admiralty Minute*

5 March 1770

Present: Hawke, Buller, Palmerston, Lisburne, Holburne, Fox.

His Majesty's letters patent, dated the 28th of last month, were read, revoking the former commission for the Board of Admiralty and appointing Sir Edward Hawke, Knight of the Bath, John Buller Esquire, Henry Viscount Palmerston of the Kingdom of Ireland, Charles Spencer Esquire, commonly called Lord Charles Spencer, Wilmot Viscount Lisburne[1] of the Kingdom of Ireland, Francis Holburne Esquire [who had been a Vice-Admiral of the Red since 1759] and Charles James Fox[2] Esquire, Lords Commissioners of the Admiralty, and they took their seats at the Board accordingly...

436. *Admiralty Minute*

6 April 1770

Present: Hawke, Buller, Palmerston, Lisburne.

... Resolved that the *Dolphin* [(24)] be sheathed with copper and put into condition for foreign service...

437. *Admiralty Minute*

27 April 1770

Present: Hawke, Palmerston, Holburne.

[1] Wilmot, 4th Viscount Lisburne (created Earl of Lisburne 1776) was a Ld of the Ady 28.2.70–1.4.82.
[2] The well-remembered politician and statesman had had his 21st birthday on 24.1.1770. He was a Ld of the Ady till 6.5.72. Already an MP by 1768, he was soon outstanding in debate, while dressing, in those years, as an outrageous fop.

[In September 1768 British authority had been challenged by the refusal of the citizens of Boston to quarter troops sent there to suppress a riot. In March 1770 a brawl between troops and civilians took place there—subsequently called 'the Boston massacre'. The famous 'Tea Party' occurred some three years later.]

Advice having been lately received of a dangerous tumult having happened on the 5th of March last at Boston, in consequence of a fray between the town's people and the military in which several of the former were killed and wounded; resolved, in pursuance of the King's pleasure signified by the Earl of Hillsborough, that orders be sent to Commodore [Samuel] Hood [at Halifax] and to the senior captain of His Majesty's ships at Boston to be very attentive to what passes in that town, and to give the Lieutenant-Governor and other civil magistrates all the aid and assistance in their power for preserving the public peace...

438. *Admiralty Minute*

24 May 1770

Present: Hawke, Spencer, Holburne.

A report was read from the Navy Board, dated the 22nd instant, on a reference to them of a petition from the shipwrights working on the banks of the River Medway, not belonging to His Majesty's yards, setting forth that they are greatly oppressed by the carpenters of His Majesty's ships working at their trade and praying that a stop may be put to the same for the future; and, it appearing by the said report that the carpenters of His Majesty's ships work at their trade only the week they are off duty for the better support of themselves and their families, that it can no ways hurt the petitioners, and that the complaint is frivolous and unworthy of attention; resolved that nothing be done in it and that the Navy Board be acquainted the Lords concur with them in opinion thereupon...

439. *Admiralty Minutes*

6 June 1770

Present: Hawke, Palmerston, Fox.

The *Tamar* frigate and *Florida* storeship being arrived at Plymouth from Falkland's Islands; resolved that the storeship be paid off and laid up at Deptford, and that the *Tamar* be ordered to

Galleon's Reach and to remain there till further order...

A letter was read from Commodore Forrest, dated the 10th of March last at Jamaica, giving an account of the arrival of five French ships of war at Cap François with six battalions of troops on board, and that many more were expected; resolved that a copy be sent to the Secretary of State for His Majesty's information.

A letter was read from Captain Hunt of the *Tamar* frigate, arrived at Plymouth from Falkland's Islands, enclosing copies of letters he received from some Spanish officers at that place and of his answers thereunto; resolved that copies be sent to the Secretary of State for His Majesty's information...

440. *Admiralty Minute*

20 June 1770

Present: Hawke, Buller, Spencer.

... A letter was received from Lord Weymouth, one of His Majesty's principal Secretaries of State, relative to the complaints of the Spanish Ambassador against the conduct of the officers of His Majesty's fleet in the Mediterranean, which have increased so much of late as to endanger in some degree that harmony which subsists between the two nations, and signifying His Majesty's pleasure that Captain Bennett and Captain Ommanney[1] be not again employed in a situation which may give them an opportunity of incurring His Catholic Majesty's just displeasure; and that the four midshipmen and the surgeon's mate, who were imprisoned at Cadiz for carrying on an illicit trade, be dismissed from the service and be not permitted to serve again in His Majesty's fleet; and likewise that it be strongly recommended to Commodore Proby, who commands in chief His Majesty's ships in the Mediterranean, to cultivate a good understanding on every occasion with the officers of His Catholic Majesty and to promote as much as possible a friendly and cordial intercourse between the subjects of the two nations, discountenancing in all those who have the honour of serving His Majesty those mean smuggling arts, which are a disgrace to the service and dishonour the spirit and character of officers as gentlemen; and to endeavour to adjust and accommodate, as far as possible, those disputes and altercations which must necessarily happen between the subjects of commercial nations, and to avoid all rough and harsh methods of

[1] Cornthwaite Ommanney: L 1758, CR 1765, C 1772.

proceeding which will tend to disgust and alienate the minds of the subjects of that crown with which His Majesty wishes to keep up the most cordial and friendly communication; resolved that all the necessary orders be given accordingly.

441. *Admiralty Minute*

16 July 1770

Present: Hawke, Buller, Fox.

The Earl of Hillsborough having signified the King's pleasure that the rendezvous of the ships and vessels of war employed on the North American station should be in the harbour of Boston instead of Halifax, the better to check further violences, prevent illicit trade, and support the officers of the revenue in the execution of their duty; resolved that orders be sent out to Commodore Hood to proceed forthwith to Boston accordingly, and to take such measures and give such directions to the several captains under his command as may be most likely to answer the purposes aforementioned...

442. *Admiralty Minute*

Saturday, 28 July 1770

Present: Hawke, Buller, Fox.

A letter was read from Captain Bentinck desiring, as the trial of his new-invented pump was made against one of a different size and form from those now in use in the Navy, that one of the *Swiftsure*'s pumps, or any other ship's pump now in harbour, may be tried against it; resolved that he be acquainted that the Lords are sufficiently satisfied of the utility of his invention by the trials that have been already made and that they intend to give directions for introducing the use of his pumps on board His Majesty's ships...

443. *Admiralty Minutes*

1 August 1770

Present: Hawke, Buller, Spencer.

... Vice-Admiral Geary [commander-in-chief at Portsmouth 1769–70] having transmitted to the Lords a letter he received from

Lieutenant Biggs[1] of the *Grace* cutter relative to a suspicious French vessel lately arrived in Southampton River; resolved that copies thereof be sent to the Secretary of State for the King's information; also one received from Captain Stott[2] concerning a person supposed to have been employed in carrying secret dispatches to France.

Sir Edward Hawke signified His Majesty's pleasure that Hugh Palliser[3] Esquire should be appointed Controller of the Navy in the room of George Cokburne Esquire, deceased; resolved that the Attorney General be directed to prepare a patent accordingly and that Mr Palliser be ordered to repair to the Navy Office and inspect the books, as usual...

444.   *Admiralty Minutes*

2 August 1770

Present: Hawke, Buller, Spencer.

The Lords took into consideration three letters from the Navy Board, dated the 27th, 30th and 31st of last month, relative to the fire that hath lately happened in Portsmouth yard; resolved that they be directed to cause an exact account to be prepared of what damage is done and to report the most proper steps to be taken for replacing what has been consumed.

And, it appearing from their letters that there is reason to suspect the buildings were purposely set on fire by evil designing persons, they are to make strict inquiry thereunto as soon as possible and report the result thereof to their Lordships...

445.   *Admiralty Minute*

7 August 1770

Present: Hawke, Buller, Holburne.

[1] Biggs: L 1761, CR 1771, C 1778, RA 1795, VA 1795. Died 1803.
[2] Stott: L 1757, CR 1757, C 1758.
[3] Hugh Palliser was a remarkable officer in more than one respect. Born of the Yorkshire gentry in Jan. 1723, he was entered in his maternal uncle's ship in 1735 as a *midshipman*. L 1731, CR 1746, C 1746. Served under Saunders in 1759; also in 1760 and commanded a detached squadron. When Saunders died in 1775, Palliser received from him a legacy of £5,000—an impressive testimony to his proven courage and ability. Served off Newfoundland in 1762 and returned there as governor and c.-in-c. 1764–6. (See p. 424, n. 1 for Cook.) Controller 1770–5. RA 1775; a Ld of Ady 12.4.75–23.4.79. VA 1778; 3rd in command at Ushant. Thereafter, his own actions (together with political circumstances) established him as a highly controversial figure. A 1787.

... Resolved that an advertisement be inserted in the public papers offering a reward of £1,000 to anybody who shall, within three months, discover any person or persons who wilfully set fire to Portsmouth yard, and also His Majesty's pardon to any person concerned therein, except the person who actually set fire to the premises.

446. *Admiralty Minutes*

9 August 1770

Present: Hawke, Buller, Lisburne.

... Several papers having been laid before the Lords proposing plans for buildings and other schemes to prevent the like fatal effects from fire, for the future, as have lately happened in Portsmouth yard; resolved that they be transmitted to the Navy Board for their making such use thereof as they may think proper.

The Lords having received an anonymous letter from Plymouth, giving an account of a fire having been lately discovered among the charcoal in store in that yard; resolved that it be sent to the Navy Board for them to inquire into the truth of it...

447. *Admiralty Minute*

10 August 1770

Present: Hawke, Buller, Lisburne, Holburne.

The Lords took into consideration a letter from the Navy Board, dated the 8th instant, with a copy of a report from the members of that Board who are at Portsmouth, relative to the examination of the ropemakers and others employed near the buildings which were lately destroyed by the fire in that yard and proposing a method which they think advisable to be pursued for restoring the buildings and replacing the stores; resolved that they be acquainted their Lordships approve thereof, and that they be directed to recommend it to the members of that Board aforesaid to endeavour by every means in their power, in conjunction with the Commissioner of the yard, to discover the cause of the fire and to give strict orders that the keys of the storehouses and other buildings be not entrusted to a greater number of such persons than is absolutely necessary; [also] that such persons as are entrusted with them be not permitted to carry them home, but that they be deposited at night in the hands of the officers who from their rank and employment are, and ought to be, responsible for them...

448.   *Admiralty Minute*

17 August 1770

Present: Hawke, Lisburne, Holburne.

... A letter was read from Captain Jervis[1] of the *Alarm* [(32)][2] giving an account of the progress he has made in getting the ship repaired, which their Lordships very well approve of. Captain Jervis is to be acquainted therewith and that their Lordships have ordered a piece of plate to be prepared, in order to be sent to M. Pleville [the port officer at Marseilles] as a public mark of their acknowledgement for the assistance he gave the ship in her late distress.

449.   *Admiralty Minute*

6 September 1770

Present: Hawke, Lisburne, Fox.

... The Navy Board having proposed, as it will be a considerable time before the magazines in Portsmouth yard are put in order again, that the captains of the guardships at that port may be ordered to receive on board their respective sea stores and the rest of their fitted rigging, until convenient storehouses can be built for their reception; resolved that the necessary orders be given for that purpose...

---

[1] John Jervis, later 1st Earl of St Vincent (1735–1823): L 1755, CR 1759; with Saunders at Quebec. C 1760. Commanded the (rebuilt) *Foudroyant* (80) at Ushant, 1778; testified for Keppel. In the same ship, noted for her discipline and efficiency, he was twice at the relief of Gibraltar and, in 1782, took the *Pégase* (74). Made a K.B. RA 1787, VA 1793, A 1795. Was naval commander of a harmonious joint expedition which took Martinique, St Lucia and Guadeloupe 1794. Defeated the Spanish at Battle of C. St Vincent 1797; created an earl. Suppressed all signs of mutiny spreading to the Mediterranean fleet; maintained high efficiency; detached Nelson who proceeded to the Nile. In 1800 he commanded the Channel fleet, reinstituting close blockade. First Ld of the Ady 1801–4; embarked on radical and controversial reforms. Again commanded Channel fleet 1806–7. Adm. of the Fleet 1821.

[2] As captain of the *Alarm* (32), which had been swept ashore near Marseilles in a storm, Jervis had shown great determination and skill in saving the ship from destruction. She was the first British warship to be copper-bottomed (1761). The *Dolphin* was the second (1764).

450. *Admiralty Minutes*

7 September 1770

Present: Hawke, Lisburne, Fox.

The Navy Board having represented to the Lords, in their letter of the 30th past, that all the damaged hemp that remained in His Majesty's storehouses at Portsmouth has been sorted, and such part of it as was proper for twice-laid cordage delivered to the contractor, but there still remains about twenty or thirty tons unfit for that service, and therefore proposed that it may be sold; resolved that orders be given for doing as they propose.

Resolved that the *Albion* at Chatham and the *Prince of Wales* at Plymouth be sheathed and put into a condition to serve as guard-ships.

Resolved that the standing orders for the regulation and well government of the dockyards be strongly enforced by directions to the Navy Board for that purpose and that they be directed to consider whether any further regulations than what are contained in the said standing orders may be necessary and, if so, to propose them to their Lordships ...

451. *Admiralty Minutes*

Tuesday, 11 September 1770

Present: Hawke, Lisburne, Fox.

[This meeting marks the beginning of the Falklands crisis, as far as the Board was concerned. From 11 September until Hawke chaired his last meeting on Saturday, 12 January 1771, the Board met on six days of the week, Monday to Saturday. Hawke presided at all these meetings until mid-November. From then until mid-December illness for the most part prevented him from attending.]

In pursuance of His Majesty's pleasure signified by Lord Weymouth's letter of the 7th instant; resolved that orders be given for the manning [of] the several guardships [all being ships of the line] undermentioned to their highest complements and for victualling and storing them to a three months proportion.

Auguste
Ramillies [(74), launched 1763]   } At Chatham.
Yarmouth

Centaur ⎫
Ajax ⎪
Arrogant ⎪
Bellona ⎬ At Portsmouth.
St Antonio ⎪
Achilles ⎪
Ripon ⎭

Cornwall ⎫
Hero ⎪
Temeraire ⎬ At Plymouth.
Defence ⎪
Belleisle ⎪
Firm ⎭

Resolved that Lieutenant Teer[1] of the *Florida* storeship be ordered to carry out to Falkland's Islands such naval stores and provisions as shall be sent on board by the Commissioners of the Navy and Victualling...

452.   *Admiralty Minutes*

13 September 1770

Present: Hawke, Lisburne, Fox.

... Resolved that orders be given to the Navy Board to cause the [cruisers and frigates] undermentioned to be put into condition for service and to report when they shall be ready to receive men.

Portland ⎫
Minerva ⎭ At Sheerness.

Tartar   At Deptford.
Thames   At Plymouth.
Cerberus ⎫
Kingfisher [sloop] ⎭ At Chatham.

A report was read from the Commissioners of the Victualling on an application of Lieutenant Teer, who commanded the *Florida*

[1] Teer: L 1767, CR 1781, C 1783.

storeship on the last voyage to Falkland's Islands, praying to be allowed credit for 156 gallons of spirits which were leaked out and evaporated by the heat of the ship's hold and the length of the voyage; resolved that he be allowed the same accordingly.

Resolved that the *Cruiser* sloop be ordered to Spithead with new-raised men and then return to the Nore...

Resolved that Lieutenant Samuel Short[1] be employed in raising men in Town...

453. *Admiralty Minutes*

14 September 1770

Present: Hawke, Lisburne, Holburne.

A letter was read from the Navy Board of yesterday's date representing that, if the guardships are ordered to sea, it will diminish the quantity of stores in His Majesty's magazines and proposing to contract for such species as shall be most wanted to supply any deficiency; resolved that they be directed to do as they have proposed...

The King having been pleased to order a squadron of his ships to be immediately got ready for sea and there being no probability of manning them with volunteers; resolved that application be made to His Majesty for an Order in Council empowering this Board to issue press warrants as usual.

454. *Admiralty Minutes*

Monday, 17 September 1770

Present: Hawke, Buller, Spencer, Holburne.

Resolved that orders be sent to the captain of the *Ramillies* at Chatham to send round to the *Royal Charlotte* [yacht, (20)] in the River, in the Commissioner's yacht or some other vessel he shall appoint, four lieutenants, four master's mates, and four midshipmen from the guardships in the Medway and the *Mercury* [(24)] at Chatham in order to be employed in the intended impress...

Resolved that the *Yarmouth* be hastened in her fitting as much as possible and got out to the Nore with all the dispatch that is possible, and that the workmen be employed extra for the greater dispatch...

[1] Short: L 1747.

Resolved that the Navy Board be directed to order two or more vessels to attend on Sir Peter Denis[1] during the intended impress of seamen, and to cause him to be supplied from Deptford and Woolwich with such boats, etc., and at such times as he shall desire...

Resolved that orders be sent to the captains of the [frigates] *Emerald*, *Solebay*, and *Alderney* [sloop] to enter volunteer seamen and bear them on a supernumerary list until farther order.

In pursuance of His Majesty's Order in Council of the 14th instant; resolved that a general impress of seamen be ordered to be commenced on the River Thames under the direction of Sir Peter Denis [and] that lieutenants, petty officers and men be lent him for that purpose from the ships in the River and the yachts.

Resolved that press warrants and proper instructions be sent to all His Majesty's ships and vessels in commission...

455. *Admiralty Minutes*

19 September 1770

Present: Hawke, Spencer, Lisburne.

... Resolved that the Navy Board [may] cause a quantity of hammacoes, bedding, and slops to be sent on board the *Yarmouth* at the Nore for the use of the new-raised men...

Captain Keeler of the *Mercury* desiring to know whether he is to have any marines; resolved that he be directed to complete his ship's complement with seamen.

Resolved that application be made to the Commissioners of the Customs to order their officers at the out-ports, where there are no naval officers, to pay conduct money and subsistence to such seamen as are put on board merchant ships in lieu of pressed men, as usual.

Resolved that orders be given to the several captains to enter such ablebodied landmen as shall offer themselves...

456. *Admiralty Minutes*

20 September 1770

Present: Hawke, Spencer, Lisburne.

... The Earl of Rocheford [Secretary of State for the northern department] in his letter of the 19th instant having signified His

---

[1] Denis (see p. 62, n. 10) had commanded the *Royal Charlotte* yacht since 1761. In Oct. 1770 he would be given his flag (Document 469).

Majesty's pleasure that twenty-two sail of the line, in addition to those already ordered, be manned and fitted for immediate service; resolved that the ships undermentioned be ordered to be got ready for service and that the *Fame* and *Buckingham* be sheathed, and that the workmen work extra for the greater dispatch.

Prudent	At Woolwich.
Barfleur	
Egmont	
Resolution	At Chatham.
Buckingham	
Namur	
Elizabeth	At Portsmouth.
Ocean	
Fame	
Terrible	At Plymouth.
Trident	
Boyne	

... Resolved that the *Glory* [(32)] be ordered to carry to Portsmouth as many new-raised men as she can stow, to be disposed of as the commander-in-chief there [Vice-Admiral Geary] shall direct...

Resolved that the *Glory* be ordered to proceed from the Nore to Spithead with new-raised men and then repair to the Start to procure men from the homeward bound merchant ships.

Resolved that the *Speedwell* sloop be ordered to the Downs to raise men.

Resolved that the *Kennington* [(28)] be ordered to proceed off Portland to raise men...

Resolved that the *Hind* [(20)] be sent off Waterford to raise men...

Resolved that Captains James Kirk[1] and James Shirley[2] be appointed regulating captains in Town and that proper instructions be sent to them for performing that service...

457. *Admiralty Minutes*

21 September 1770

Present: Hawke, Buller, Spencer.

... Resolved that the *Albion* be fitted out at Chatham for Channel service and that the Hon. Samuel Barrington be appointed to command her...

Resolved that application be made to His Majesty to issue a proclamation offering a bounty of 30s. to every able seaman and 20s. to every ordinary seaman who shall enter on board the fleet on or before the 21st of October next.

Resolved that application be made to His Majesty for a declaration of victuals for the ensuing year.

458. *Admiralty Minutes*

24 September 1770

Present: Hawke, Buller, Spencer, Holburne.

In pursuance of His Majesty's Order in Council of the 22nd instant; resolved that orders be given to the Navy Board to prepare estimates in due form of the charge of 25,000 men for the ensuing year.

Resolved that a letter be wrote to the Lord Mayor of London to desire he will give his countenance and assistance to the officers of the Navy employed in raising men, who are ordered to apply to his Lordship for that purpose.

A letter was read from Captain Farmer,[3] late commander of the *Swift* sloop [see 427], and another from Captain Maltby[4] of the

---

[1] Kirk: L 1743, C 1748.
[2] James Shirley: L 1746, CR 1759, C 1762. He died in 1774.
[3] Farmer: L 1759, CR 1768, C 1771. Died 1779.
[4] Maltby: L 1759, CR 1768, C 1771. He died in 1793.

Favourite [sloop], just arrived at the Mother Bank from Falkland's Islands, giving an account of the loss of the *Swift* on the coast of Patagonia and of His Majesty's forces having been dispossessed of their settlement on Falkland's Islands by the Spaniards; resolved that a copy of the said letters be sent to Lord Weymouth for His Majesty's information.

A deputation from the merchants and underwriters concerned in the trade to North America in general attending, were called in and delivered a message from the said merchants and underwriters, returning thanks to this Board for the kind information respecting Falkland's Islands [and] representing that the North American trade in general and that of Newfoundland in particular are now on their return to Europe, many of them bound to different ports in Spain, and requesting their Lordships' attention to prevent loss by captures to the parties concerned. Sir Edward Hawke acquainted them that all due attention shall be given to what they have represented and requested; and they then withdrew.

Resolved that Lord Weymouth be acquainted with the above-mentioned representation and request of the merchants for His Majesty's information and pleasure thereupon.

459. *Admiralty Minutes*

25 September 1770

Present: Hawke, Spencer, Holburne.

The masters of small boats, commonly called 'Peter boats', employed in catching fish for the supply of the city of London, applying to be protected from the impress; resolved that an advertisement be inserted in the *Gazette*, directing all the officers employed in pressing not to molest any of the masters of the said boats, provided they are not seamen.

A letter was read from Captain Salter[1] of the *Lynx* [sloop] at Gravesend, giving an account of opposition that has been made by the men on board the *Duke of Richmond* East India ship and desiring directions how to proceed; resolved that he be directed, as the ship is outward bound and has proceeded as far as Gravesend, and as an application has been made to their Lordships for a protection for her men, to desist from endeavouring to impress them and to proceed to the Nore, agreeable to former orders.

Captain [Alexander] Hood of the *Katharine* yacht [which he com-

[1] Salter: L 1765, CR 1769, C 1776.

manded from 1763 to 1777] desiring leave of absence; resolved that he be acquainted, as there is an appearance of the yacht being wanted, the Lords cannot comply with his request...

Vice-Admiral Geary acquainting the Lords that there are no more marines on shore at Portsmouth than what are absolutely necessary for doing the duty in the dockyard and on shore; resolved that he be directed not to demand any more marines, but complete the ships with seamen and volunteer landmen...

A letter was read from the Navy Board representing that [various] ships, now lying up at Chatham, are in want of a middling repair, which cannot be carried out in that yard for a considerable time, and therefore proposing to repair them by contract in merchant yards as has formerly been done; resolved that they be directed to order them to be brought up to Deptford in order to their being repaired in the manner they have proposed...

460. *Admiralty Minutes*

27 September 1770

Present: Hawke, Buller, Spencer.

... In pursuance of His Majesty's Order in Council dated the 22nd instant; resolved that an estimate of the charge of 25,000 men for the ensuing year be laid before His Majesty for his approbation.

Resolved that an application be made to the King to empower this Board to issue press warrants to the constables within twenty miles of London, that they be allowed 20s. a man for every man they procure, and 6d. a mile for every mile such men travel; and that the Lord Mayor of London be directed to give countenance and assistance to the officers employed in pressing, and to the constables belonging to the city and the liberties thereof.

461. *Secret Instructions from the Lords of the Admiralty to Commodore George Mackenzie, 'Commander-in-Chief of His Majesty's ships and vessels employed, and to be employed, at and about Jamaica and in the Gulf of Mexico from the River Mississippi to Cape Florida'*

29 September 1770

Whereas the Earl of Hillsborough, one of His Majesty's principal Secretaries of State, hath acquainted us by his letter of yesterday's date that the King hath judged it to be of importance that the commanders-in-chief of His Majesty's ships and vessels in the different stations in America should be apprised of the motives for the naval armaments now preparing in the ports of this kingdom, and whereas his Lordship hath in his said letter signified to us His Majesty's pleasure that we should, in confidence of secrecy, acquaint the said commanders-in-chief respectively,

> 'That the King having received advices that the Spanish Governor of Buenos Aires hath thought fit to dispossess His Majesty's subjects of their settlement of Port Egmont in Falkland's Island, so violent a proceeding in time of profound peace will, unless disavowed by the court of Spain and proper restitution made, be considered as an open act of hostility; and therefore the King hath sought fit, with the advice of his servants, to order a number of his ships of war to be fitted for sea, in order to act as the honour and dignity of his crown shall under future events require; that the suspending or increasing this naval armament will probably depend upon the answer which the court of Spain shall give to what has been demanded on this occasion, which answer the King has good reason to hope will correspond with His Majesty's wishes for the preservation of the public peace; but that, in the meantime, they (the said commanders-in-chief) cannot be too much upon their guard, on the one hand to prevent surprise and on the other hand not to give any offence.'

We do, in pursuance of His Majesty's pleasure signified as aforesaid in confidence of secrecy, hereby acquaint you therewith accordingly, and you are also hereby required and directed to proceed without a moment's loss of time to Jamaica agreeable to the order you have already received and, upon your arrival there, to be as much upon your guard as possible, upon the one hand to prevent surprise and on the other hand not to give any offence. Given etc.

ED. HAWKE
J. BULLER
C. SPENCER

[The order was dispatched that day, a Saturday, to Spithead. However, the messenger found that Mackenzie had already sailed, so the orders were sent out to him by the *Spy* sloop.]

462. *Aide-mémoire by Hawke* (holograph)

Sunday, 30 September 1770

To make John Philips carpenter of the *Venus*.

To get the ships round from Chatham to the Nore as fast as possible, and from thence to Spithead, as soon as they have a sufficient number of men to carry them thither.

To hasten the *Conquistador* [(60), taken at Havana] thither. To keep the *Barfleur* [(98), launched in 1768] there for some time.

To hasten the ships round from Plymouth to Spithead the instant they are ready to proceed thither in order to form the squadron.

To inquire how the men come in, and whether seamen enter fast, and what number we have got in the whole, viz. pressed, volunteers, both seamen and landmen. To show to the King.

To consider whether it will be right to send press warrants to the Lord Mayor to give to the constables.

To consider whether it will not be right to apply to the King and Council for to enlarge the bounty for seamen and then to appoint regulating captains to the several principal sea port towns.

To commission the frigates as soon as possible and to consider when it will be proper to send some to cruise off Brest and Ferrol for intelligence.

To dispatch the two frigates away for the Leeward Islands and North America immediately.

To get an old 90-gun ship at Portsmouth, with jury masts, to come round to the Nore to lie there to receive pressed men.

If we should increase the bounty, it will be right to apply for increasing the number of our marines, as likewise to order some frigates to be set up in the merchant yards.

As then it may be supposed that war is inevitable, it will be then right to enlarge our contracts for all foreign stores as well as the principal ones at home. Query: and also to set up some line of battle ships in the merchant yards? But this last need not be done in a very great hurry.

Query: what is to be done about the transports for the troops?

To consider what force we generally had in the last war along the whole coast of North America and whether it will not be right at all events to send a flag officer thither.

To see what force we had at Jamaica and at the Leeward Islands, and also in the Mediterranean, and to show it to the ministry. Then to consider the strength of our enemies in those seas.

To look into the books of the Admiralty to see what force was allowed in the last war for to protect the several different trades at different times, that were bound *out* and *home*, and in what latitude those ships cruised for them, and how far to the westward, and how soon any ships were sent out for the protection of the trade, and as convoys.

To look at my own order book and my Admiralty order book, and for all the orders from the Admiralty which I kept myself;[1] likewise to look at my Admiralty letter book and for my signal books (some of these in my bureau and drawers).

When we increase the bounty to seamen, it will be right to increase the number of the shipwrights and the naval artificers in the dockyards.

To look in my order books for all the orders relative to cruising in different stations to the westward, and how far they are likely to answer.

462a. *Notes of about the same date on a separate sheet*

To give ships to the following captains:

Varlo[2]   ———————— Sir John Moore
Morgan[3]
Vaughan[4]
Saxton[5]
Stott
Balfour...

Query: what is Lord Edgcumbe [at Plymouth] about? What ships at Plymouth are ready for the sea? To order him to send them round to Spithead directly with men to be drafted from the rest, which can be sent back again in frigates...

What are the ships at Chatham about?...

[1] Hawke had most of the instructions received from the Admiralty copied into his 'Admiralty order book', but where they were labelled 'secret' he usually kept no copy. In some other cases (e.g. Doc. 81) he likewise had no copy made. As most of these original instructions have since been lost, only the copies kept by the Admiralty are extant. In consequence, only one reference (the Admiralty one) will be found in the List of Documents and Sources for many of the more important orders received by Hawke.

[2] Varlo: L 1743, C 1759. Superannuated RA 1787.

[3] Jeremiah Morgan: L 1746, CR 1762.

[4] Vaughan: L 1740, C 1746, RA 1775, VA 1778, A 1787.

[5] Charles Saxton: L 1757, C 1760, C 1763. He served under Hawke in 1762 and under Samuel Hood in the American War. Commissioner at Portsmouth 1790–1806; created baronet 1794.

463. *'My own Minutes'* (further holograph notes by Hawke)

Wednesday, 3 October 1770

To consider about Ferrol, and what officer has been there and whether he knows it thoroughly.

To consider all the Admiralty order books from the year 1755 to the year 1761 as to what orders were given to the commanding officers and flag d°., as also to the private captains, whether with convoys or otherwise, cruising in several different stations to the westward. But in ordering ships, single or any number, for convoys, to consider well the force of the enemy, and whether they will be liable to be intercepted. To consider well the force and strength of all your squadrons, before you send them out, and also your commanding officer—for the public.

To look at Sir John Norris's orders when he was sent out with the Grand Fleet to the westward [in 1739–44]...

To bring my order books and letter books [with letters] from the Admiralty up from Sunbury with me, as likewise some of my own order books and letter books from 1755 to 1760, and also the books of private and public signals.

To appoint Sir Peter Denis to the command at Chatham and [John] Campbell to the *Charlotte* yacht at the same time...

Query: will Edwards[1] take the *Mary*'s officers [i.e. those already in that yacht]?

To appoint senior officers of character, capable of doing their duty, and who have not been employed for some time past, to the twelve ships who are first to be commissioned; and to do the same for the frigates and sloops when it's proper to commission them.

To get a particular account from the Surveyor of the Navy [a post jointly held by Sir Thomas Slade and John Williams] of all the different species of stores which now remain in the several dockyards in this kingdom, and how long they will last in peace and how long in war, as likewise an account of the different species of stores which they have contracted for, to make up what is deficient in the yards.

To consider well the strength of the enemies in the different seas where we may send ships or squadrons to, as likewise the commanding officers and captains.

To look at the Chatham, Sheerness, and Portsmouth and Plymouth progresses continually to see how the ships go on in their fitting and to hurry them.

[1] Edwards: L 1740 CR 1747, C 1753; commanded the *Sandwich* (90) in Keppel's division at Ushant. RA 1779, VA 1787, A 1794.

To look in the Admiralty books for precedents of all kinds.

To put upon my list for frigates Captain Charles Inglis,[1] and Captain Farmer, and Captain Onslow.[2]

To get the list of the ships ordered to be commissioned and got ready to receive men from Mr Stephens, and likewise the list of the captains deserving employment. Note: it will be proper to advertise about the lieutenants if we commission those ships.

464.   *Admiralty Minutes*

Saturday, 6 October 1770

Present: Hawke, Buller, Fox.

... A letter was read from Captain Moutray[3] of the *Emerald* [(28)] relating to the subject of impressing; resolved that he be acquainted their Lordships' orders do not warrant his opening a rendezvous on shore, nor do they intend he should do so, but only endeavour to procure the men from homeward bound merchant ships.

The regulating captains representing to the Lords that the volunteer seamen who daily enter are very uneasy at their confinement and anxious to get on board of the fleet, and desiring orders may be given for allowing them a passage to the Nore at 2s. a head; resolved that orders be given for this purpose...

Resolved that Lord Weymouth be acquainted, in return to his letter of the 2nd instant, that the four ships named in the margin [*Achilles* (60), *Ajax* (74), *Bellona* (74), *St Antonio* (64)] are now lying at Spithead ready to proceed on service, except as to men, and that he shall be informed as fast as any of the others mentioned in his said letter arrive there.

465.   *Admiralty Minutes*

12 October 1770

Present: Hawke, Buller, Fox.

... In pursuance of His Majesty's pleasure signified in Lord Weymouth's letter of the 10th instant; resolved that the ships named in

---

[1] Inglis: L 1755, CR 1757, C 1761, RA 1790. Died 1791.

[2] Richard Onslow: L 1758, CR 1761, C 1762, RA 1793, VA 1794, A 1799. Second-in-command to Duncan at Camperdown 1797; broke the Dutch line. Created baronet.

[3] Moutray: L 1744, CR 1757, C 1758.

the margin [*Defence* (74), *Ajax, Arrogant* (74), *Ripon* (60), *Achilles*] be ordered to be immediately got ready to carry two regiments of foot from Ireland to Gibraltar, and that their captains be directed when they are ready to proceed to Cork, in order to receive the said troops on board.

Resolved that the [frigates] undermentioned be ordered to be fitted out at Portsmouth and that the captains against their names expressed be appointed to command them:

Venus	Captains Balfour
Pallas	Laforey[1]
Juno	Stott
Diana	Onslow

Resolved that Lieutenants Joseph Griffiths[2] and Henry Smith[3] be appointed to raise men in Town under the direction of the regulating captains...

An application was read from Lieutenant David Arthur,[4] setting forth that he is appointed chief mate of an East India ship, that all his effects consist in goods he left in the East Indies unsold, and in debts he cannot get in without he goes thither himself, and therefore praying leave for two years, that he may go out in the ship, without which he shall be entirely ruined; resolved, in consideration of these particular circumstances, that he have leave as he desires.

There being still a great number of men wanting to man His Majesty's ships fitting out for the sea; resolved that applications be made to the King to issue a proclamation recalling his seafaring subjects from foreign parts.

To enlarge the bounty offered to able seamen to £3 a man and to ordinary seamen to £2 a man, and to offer to persons who shall discover seamen secreting themselves £2 for every able and 30s. for every ordinary seaman, and to cause the other measures usual on these occasions to be put into practice...

466. *Admiralty Minutes*

Saturday, 13 October 1770

Present: Hawke, Buller, Fox.

[1] John Laforey: of Huguenot family; L 1748, CR 1755, C 1758. Served at Quebec 1759, and at Ushant 1778 (testified for Keppel). RA 1789, VA 1793, A 1795; c.-in-c. Leeward Is 1787–93 and 1795–6 (dying on passage home). Created baronet 1789.
[2] Griffiths: L 1755.
[3] Henry Smith: L 1760.
[4] David Arthur: L 1758.

The [cruisers, frigates] and sloops undermentioned being wanted for immediate service; resolved that the Navy Board and the commanders-in-chief at the ports where they are, be ordered to do everything possible to hasten them in getting ready:

Cerberus
Kingfisher } At Chatham.

Portland
Minerva } At Sheerness.

Diana
Juno
Lizard
Venus } At Portsmouth.
Pallas
Martin

Thames   At Plymouth.

A letter was read from Lord Townshend[1], Lord Lieutenant of Ireland, representing that there is a scarcity of coals in Dublin, that they are all brought from Whitehaven, and desiring orders may be given for protecting all men belonging to the coal ships of that port, as otherwise the city of Dublin will be reduced to the greatest distress; resolved that his secretary be acquainted, for His Excellency's information, that many coal ships of Whitehaven already had protections, and that all the rest will have them as fast as they apply for them, so that their Lordships hope there is no reason to fear the city of Dublin will feel any inconvenience on account of the present impress...

Resolved that a further order be given to all the commanders of His Majesty's ships and vessels with respect to quarantine...

467. *Admiralty Minutes*

16 October 1770

Present: Hawke, Spencer, Holburne.

---

[1] George, 4th Viscount Townshend, commanded the army at Quebec after Wolfe's death. He was a highly controversial Lord Lieutenant of Ireland 1767–72.

... Resolved that orders be given to the Navy Board to take up a vessel offered by Mr Bailleul of Guernsey, and recommended by Vice-Admiral Geary, to be employed in raising men at Guernsey, Jersey, and Alderney...

Vice-Admiral Geary having transmitted to the Lords orders from several impressed men who were sent round to Portsmouth upon the masters of the respective vessels from which they were impressed, for the wages, chests, and bedding belonging to them; resolved that the said orders be sent to the regulating captains with directions to endeavour to obtain the said wages and effects, and dispose of them agreeable to the orders of the parties.

A letter was read from Monsieur Lemesurier of Guernsey containing intelligence from several ports of France [where preparations were in train]; resolved that he be thanked for his trouble and desired to continue his correspondence...

468. *Admiralty Minute*

17 October 1770

Present: Hawke, Spencer, Holburne.

A letter was read from Lord Weymouth, dated the 12th instant, desiring to know for the King's information what progress has been made in the naval equipment lately ordered; resolved that proper lists of the ships and vessels ordered to be fitted be sent to him...

469. *Admiralty Minutes*

18 October 1770

Present: Hawke, Spencer, Holburne.

... Sir Edward Hawke signified to the Board that His Majesty was yesterday graciously pleased to direct that the following promotion of admirals be made, viz.

Hon. John Forbes ⎫
Francis Holburne ⎬   Admirals White -

Sir Thomas Frankland Bart.[1]
His Grace the Duke of Bolton
Sir Charles Hardy, Kt.   } Admirals Blue
Rt Hon. George Earl of Northesk[2]
Rt Hon. Sir Charles Saunders, Kt. of the Bath

Thomas Pye Esq.
Sir Samuel Cornish Bart.   Vice-Admirals Red
Francis Geary Esq.

Sir George Bridges Rodney Bart.
Sir William Burnaby Bart.   Vice-Admirals White
James Young Esq.

Sir Peircy Brett, Kt.
Sir John Moore Bart. & Kt. of the Bath
Sir James Douglas, Kt.   Vice-Admirals Blue
Sir John Bentley, Kt.

Rt Hon. Lord Edgcumbe
Samuel Graves Esq.
William Parry Esq.   Rear-Admirals Red
Hon. Augustus Keppel
[who was actually made a Vice-Admiral of the Blue]
John Amherst Esq.
H.R.H. Henry Frederick,   Rear-Admirals White
Duke of Cumberland

And that the undermentioned gentlemen be made flag officers, viz.[3]

Sir Peter Denis Bart.   Rear-Admirals White
Matthew Buckle Esq.

[1] Frankland: L 1737, C 1740. When commanding a frigate based in the Bahamas 1740–5, he took a number of Spanish prizes (one of them commanded by the man who had, in 1731, separated Captain Jenkins from his ear and another heavily laded with treasure). C.-in-c., Leeward Is 1755–7 (RA after his arrival and after dealing with Pye—see n. 6, page xx). He displayed initiative and ability on the station but was exceptionally forthright in resisting Lord Temple's attempt, when First Lord, to encroach on his patronage (Rodger, *Wooden World*, pp. 307–8). Never again actively employed, but VA 1759, A 1770. MP 1749–84 (when he died) and he was an effective speaker on naval subjects. Succeeded his brother as baronet 1768.

[2] George Carnegie, 6th Earl of Northesk: C 1741. In 1746 he participated in Peyton's unsatisfactory action off the Indian coast. RA 1756, VA 1759, A 1770.

[3] Following the precedent of 1747, the Board awarded flags to these officers on merit and passed over a number of captains. Even so Howe, for instance, had had to wait some twenty-four years since his initial posting. But seven captains protested on grounds of their seniority and they were later back-dated as Rear-Admirals (See Clowes, iii, p. 345 & n., 366.)

Robert Man Esq. ⎫
Richard Spry Esq. ⎪
Robert Harland Esq. ⎬   Rear-Admirals Blue
Rt Hon. Lord Viscount Howe ⎭

Sir Edward Hawke at the same time signified His Majesty's pleasure that the Hon. Captain Barrington be appointed Colonel of
Marines in the room of Lord Howe.

Resolved that Captain John Campbell be appointed to command
the *Royal Charlotte* [previously commanded by Denis] and Captain
Richard Edwards the *Mary* yacht.

Resolved that the captains of the *Juno*, *Venus*, *Diana*, *Pallas*, and
Lizard be ordered to repair immediately on board.

Mr Seddon, the Solicitor of the Admiralty, having been consulted
with respect to four men pressed by Captain Moutray at Leith out of
a brig belonging to that place [see 464], which men were furnished
with Greenland protections agreeable to Act of Parliament; resolved
that Captain Moutray be ordered to discharge them, as well as any
other men he may have since impressed under like circumstances...

470. *Admiralty Minutes*

30 October 1770

Present: Hawke, Spencer, Holburne.

In order to procure men the better to man His Majesty's ships
fitting out for sea; resolved that several captains and lieutenants on
half pay be sent to different parts of England on that service and that
copies of their instructions be sent to the Navy Board for their doing
what may be necessary thereupon, so far as relates to them.

Resolved that the said captains be allowed £5 a week and lieutenants 5s. a day over and above their half pay while employed on this
service; and their contingent disbursements are also to be allowed,
provided they appear reasonable.

Several complaints having been made to the Board of the disorderly proceedings of the press gangs employed in Town; resolved
that directions be sent to the regulating captains to order, in the
strictest manner, the lieutenants employed under their directions
most diligently to attend to their duty, and never suffer their petty
officers or gangs to go out to press men without themselves being
present, and to give as little offence as the nature of the service will

admit...

Letters were read from all the new-made admirals, offering their
service to be employed...

471. *Admiralty Minutes*

31 October 1770

Present: Hawke, Spencer, Fox.

... In pursuance of the King's pleasure signified by Lord Weymouth in his letter of yesterday's date; resolved that orders be sent to
the Navy Board to cause the transports that are to bring the two
regiments from Cork to Bristol, when they arrive at the latter port,
to proceed from thence to Spithead, together with the other transports which were taken up to carry out troops to Gibraltar and
Minorca, and remain there for further orders...

The Board observing a letter in the *Gazetteer* of this day, signed 'a
true Briton', giving an account of the violent proceedings of a press
gang in the house and upon the person of one Mr Lewis; resolved
that the paper be sent to the regulating captains with directions to
inform themselves immediately whether there are any grounds for
what is represented and, if so, to report the circumstances to their
Lordships...

472. *Admiralty Minutes*

1 November 1770

Present: Hawke, Holburne, Fox.

Resolved that Captain Stott of the *Juno* [(32)] have ten days leave
to go to Penzance, where he represents he has a prospect of procuring many men to complete the complement of the ship.

Captain Long[1] of the *Hind* [(20)] having pressed some men from
vessels employed in the white herring fishery, which the masters of
the said vessels represent to be protected by Act of Parliament, and
Mr Seddon, to whom their memorial was referred, having given it as
his opinion that the said men are not liable to be pressed; resolved
that Captain Long be ordered to discharge them and not to molest
any of those people for the future...

[1] Long: L 1740, CR 1756, C 1760. Died 1780.

473. *Admiralty Minutes*

2 November 1770

Present: Hawke, Spencer, Fox.

... A letter was read from the Mayor of Newcastle owning the receipt of the press warrants sent to him to be issued to the constables and promising to give all the assistance in his power to them in the execution thereof, and as he has represented that there are a great many constables in that town; resolved that twelve more press warrants be sent to him to be issued to them...

A letter was read from the regulating captains dated yesterday, in return to Mr Stephens's of the 31st past, relative to the letter signed 'a true Briton' published in the *Gazetteer* of that day, complaining of acts of violence committed by a press gang in the house and on the person of one Mr Lewis, wherein they represent that they find too much reason for the complaint contained in that letter, though aggravated; that the gang therein mentioned belonged to Lieutenant Vitu[1] [recently appointed first of the *Pallas*], who they hope will be able to give such reasons for his conduct as will make it appear more favourable than is set forth in the said paper; also enclosing a paper drawn up by Mr Lewis, giving an account of the fact; resolved that Lieutenant Vitu be sent for, to attend their Lordships immediately...

474. *Admiralty Minutes*

Saturday, 3 November 1770

Present: Hawke, Spencer, Fox.

... Resolved that orders be sent to the senior officer at Portsmouth to hasten the fitting of all the frigates as much as possible and send them out to Spithead.

In pursuance of the King's pleasure signified by the Earl of Rochford in his letter of the 30th past; resolved that Sir Charles Knowles, Admiral of the White, have leave to go into the service of the Empress of Russia, reserving his rank on the list of flag officers, but giving up his half pay and his post of Rear-Admiral of Great Britain...

In pursuance of a letter from Vice-Admiral Geary at Porstmouth; resolved that directions be given to the Commissioners for the Sick and Hurt to cause men who have an inveterate itch upon them, so as

[1] John Vitu: L 1756. Cashiered Nov. 1770 (Document 474).

not to be easily cured on board, to be received into the hospital for cure...

Lieutenant Vitu (who could not be found yesterday before the Board broke up) attending, was called in and, the letter signed 'a true Briton' published in the *Gazetteer* of the 31st past, with the report from the regulating captains of the 1st instant and the enclosed paper drawn up by Mr Lewis, being read, he was asked whether he went out with his gang on the evening these violences are said to have been committed. He acknowledged that, having been very ill all that day, he did order a midshipman to go out with the gang to pick up such seamen or seafaring men as they might meet with, but with orders not to go into any house.

Being asked whether he had not received orders from the regulating captains not to suffer his gang to go on the impress service without himself being present, he admitted that he had and declared that this was the first time he had done so and that it was entirely due to his being unable to accompany them.

Resolved that Lieutenant Vitu, not having paid due regard to the instructions he received from this Office and having disobeyed the orders he received from the regulating captains by suffering his gang to go out to press men without being present himself, be dismissed from his employment as first lieutenant of His Majesty's ship the *Pallas*, and that his name be not inserted in the half pay list of the officers of His Majesty's fleet.

Resolved that the regulating captains be acquainted with what is done and directed to let Mr Lewis know they are much concerned for the violences offered him and how they have punished the lieutenant for his disobedience to orders...

In pursuance of His Majesty's Order in Council of the 1st instant; resolved that orders be given to the Navy Board for causing a ship to be prepared and fitted for the reception of the crew of any ship strongly suspected of infection, agreeable to a proposal of Doctor Mackenzie's, with whom they are to consult on the subject...

475.   *Admiralty Minutes*

5 November 1770

Present: Hawke, Spencer, Holburne.

A letter was read from the Secretary of the East India Company representing that the men on board the Company's ship the *Duke of Richmond* at Gravesend have refused to go to sea unless their wages are increased, and desiring the countenance and assistance of a man of war to compel them to proceed on their voyage, or to press them into His Majesty's service; resolved that orders be sent to the captain of the *Minerva* at the Nore to proceed immediately to Gravesend and anchor as near to the said East India ship as he can, and, if any of her men attempt to escape on shore, to press them into the King's service and lend a sufficient number of men to the ship to carry her to the Nore; but in so doing he is to use the greatest caution and to use no violence so as to occasion bloodshed. [On 12 November the captain of the *Minerva* was able to report that the *Duke of Richmond* had 'sailed quietly away'.]

Captain Maltby of the *Favourite* [sloop] having transmitted to the Board several receipts for the stores left in the possession of the Spaniards at Falkland's Islands; resolved that they be sent to Lord Weymouth, in addition to those already sent to him, for His Majesty's information...

A letter was read from Mr Williams, a surgeon of Wapping, representing that he was called on to attend to a person wounded by Lieutenant Short's gang [see 452] and desiring to be paid for the same the sum of one guinea; resolved that his application be sent to the regulating captains with directions, if Mr Williams did attend the person he mentions, to order Lieutenant Short to pay him and charge it on his accounts...

476. *Admiralty Minutes*

7 November 1770

Present: Hawke, Spencer, Holburne.

... A letter was read from the Commissioners of the Customs that several vessels liable to quarantine may shortly be expected to arrive at Liverpool and requesting that orders may be given to the lieutenants commanding cutters on that part of the coast to examine all such ships and vessels as they may meet with, and conduct such as are liable to quarantine, and are bound to Liverpool, to Hoylake: resolved that orders be given accordingly.

Resolved that the commanders-in-chief at the several ports be ordered to send the state and condition of the ships to this Office three times a week for the future...

Commodore [Samuel] Hood being arrived in His Majesty's ship *Romney* at Spithead from North America; resolved that he be ordered to strike his broad pendant and come ashore...

Resolved that John Bartholomew be appointed acting mast
maker at Woolwich during the absence of Mr Scammell, who is gone
to survey the woods in North America.

477. *Admiralty Minutes*

Saturday, 10 November 1770

Present: Buller, Spencer, Fox [Hawke being absent for the first time
since June.]

... A letter was read from Lord Weymouth acquainting the Board
that, having laid before the King the copy of Vice-Admiral Geary's
letter they had transmitted to him concerning a contagious distemper on board a Dutch vessel at Spithead, with the opinion of two
physicians concerning the same, His Majesty had commanded him
to signify his approbation of what had been done and his pleasure
that the strictest orders should be given to Mr Geary to prevent any
vessel or boat going on board the said ship, or coming from her on
shore, but that every assistance be given her that can be done with
safety and, if she should sail from Spithead while the distemper is on
board, that a sloop may be sent with her to attend on her motions
and give notice if she should touch at any port, to prevent the
infection from spreading; resolved that orders accordingly be immediately sent to Vice-Admiral Geary...

A letter was read from Lord Weymouth, dated the 16th past,
signifying the King's pleasure that Jean Thebaud, the man who has
been some time in confinement at Plymouth on a suspicion of being
concerned in the late fire at Portsmouth yard, may be set at liberty,
provided their Lordships see no reason to the contrary, as there
appears no reason to suspect his being concerned in that unhappy
accident; resolved that orders be sent to Lord Edgcumbe at Plymouth to cause the man to be discharged out of custody accordingly
and that Commissioner Rogers be acquainted therewith...

Captain Ourry of the *Belleisle* [(64)] representing to the Lords that
her quarter-deck guns are so short as to be useless and [having]
desired he may be supplied with six spare guns at Portsmouth in
their room; resolved that application be made to the Ordnance
Board for that purpose.

Captain Ruthven[1] of the *Glory* [(32)] representing to the Lords
that his ship has suffered greatly in the late hard gales of wind and

---

[1] The Hon. John Ruthven: L 1760, C 1762.

that it is necessary to examine into her defects; resolved that the Navy Board be directed to inquire into them and report how they find them.

478. *Admiralty Minutes*

16 November 1770

Present: Hawke, Buller, Holburne.

... Resolved that a copy of Captain Gower's[1] letter from Cadiz, dated the 23rd past, together with some advices from Mr Duff, the Consul at that port, be sent to Lord Weymouth for the King's information.

Resolved that a copy of Vice-Admiral Geary's letter of yesterday with the intelligence of the Spanish preparations at Cadiz be sent to Lord Weymouth for the King's information.

The City Remembrancer having yesterday waited on Sir Edward Hawke with a copy of the resolution of a Common Council held at Guildhall for giving a bounty to encourage seamen to enter into the Navy and requested him, in the name of the Court, to lay the same before the King at a proper opportunity, as an humble testimony of their zeal and affection for his most sacred person and government, and Sir Edward Hawke being unable, through illness, to wait on His Majesty himself; resolved that a copy of the said resolution be sent to Lord Weymouth for His Majesty's information, together with an account of the other bounties that have been granted by other cities and towns for the same purpose...

479. *Admiralty Minutes*

26 November 1770

Present: Buller, Palmerston, Lisburne, Holburne.

[On 14 and 15 November, illness had prevented Hawke's attendance at the Board. From Saturday 17 November to Tuesday 11 December he stayed away. In the interim the Board met usually under the chairmanship of Buller, he being the next most senior, but Lord Palmerston and Lord Lisburne took their turn on occasion. Hawke returned on Wednesday 12 December. On the 13th he was again absent, but reappeared on Friday the 14th. He then continued to

[1] The Hon. John Leveson Gower was the 2nd son of the 1st Earl Gower: L 1758, C 1760, RA 1787. A Ld of Ady 1783–9.

take the chair on six days of the week until his final meeting on Saturday 12 January.]

The *Arrogant* [(74)] and *Achilles* [(60)] being drove back to Spithead and having received great damage at sea; resolved that the *Centaur* [(74)] and *Yarmouth* [(60)] be immediately got ready to supply their places in carrying the troops from Cork to Gibraltar and that the Secretary of State be acquainted therewith.

Resolved that the *Arrogant* and *Achilles* be refitted at Portsmouth for foreign service and that they be sheathed also, as proposed by the Navy Board.

Resolved that Lord Howe be appointed commander-in-chief of His Majesty's ships and vessels in the Mediterranean.

Nine prisoners in Newgate having received the King's pardon on condition of joining the fleet; resolved that directions be given to the regulating captains to receive them on board the tender, and the Navy Board to cause them to be supplied with slops to prevent their carrying any infection with them from the gaol in their old clothes...

480. *Admiralty Minutes*

30 November 1770

Present: Buller, Palmerston, Spencer, Holburne.

Lord Edgcumbe acquainting the Board that the *Ajax* [(74)] is put back to Plymouth, having sprung her mainmast and received other damages; resolved that orders be given for her to be refitted with all possible dispatch, or if the *Hero* [(74)] can be got ready sooner, for her to be fitted for the same service and sent away to Cork with all the dispatch possible.

Resolved that the Secretary of State be acquainted therewith for the King's information...

481. *Admiralty Minute*

Saturday, 1 December 1770

Present: Buller, Palmerston, Lisburne, Holburne.

... Captain Allen[1] of the *Ajax* lately returned to Plymouth having been disabled from proceeding on his destined voyage [from

---

[1] John Carter Allen: L 1745, C 1758; served at the capture of Dominica 1761, and of Martinique 1762. Commanded the *Egmont* (74) at Ushant. RA 1787, VA 1793, A 1795.

Cork to Gibraltar] by a hard gale of wind, having represented to the Board that his rigging was found to be rotten, that none of the spare sails fitted, and that there had been great want of attention in fitting the ship for sea; resolved that a copy of his letter be sent to the Navy Board with directions to make the strictest inquiry into the manner in which the ship was fitted and sent to sea [Documents 451, 464 and 465 refer], and into the conduct of the several officers in their department who had any hand therein, and if it appears there was any neglect in any of them to report their names and qualities to their Lordships, that such directions may be given thereupon as shall be judged proper. At the same time the Navy Board are to be directed to inquire into the manner in which the *Arrogant*, *Achilles*, and *Ripon* were fitted and to report as aforesaid...

482. *Admiralty Minute*

3 December 1770

Present: Buller, Lisburne, Holburne.

... The *Yarmouth* [479 refers] having been found unfit to proceed at present with troops to Gibraltar; resolved that the *Belleisle* [(64)] or any other ship at Spithead (if she should be found unfit) be ordered to be got ready to perform that service, and Lord Weymouth is to be acquainted therewith for His Majesty's information...

483. *Admiralty Minute*

5 December 1770

Present: Buller, Palmerston, Lisburne.

... In pursuance of His Majesty's Order in Council of the 26th past; resolved that orders be sent to the Navy Board to cause estimates to be prepared for an additional number of 15,000 men to serve on board the fleet in the ensuing year...

484. *Admiralty Minutes*

Wednesday, 12 December 1770

Present: Hawke, Palmerston, Lisburne, Holburne. [On Hawke's return to the Board, see the note at the head of Document 479.]

Resolved that application be made to the King to renew the press warrants for the ensuing year.

The Lords took into consideration two letters from the Navy Board, dated the 3rd and 10th instant, relative to the defects of the *Yarmouth* and *Belleisle*, and it appearing thereby that the same must have been owing to some very great neglect or inattention at the time they were fitted as guardships, or when they were lately refitted for Channel service; resolved that the Navy Board be directed to make a very strict inquiry into the matter and to report to their Lordships to whose neglect it was owing that the said ships were suffered to go out of dock in so very bad a condition.

A complaint was read from the company of the *Ajax* for the want of lights to do the ship's duty, of the unjust distribution of the bounty money, and of the ill behaviour of the first lieutenant of the ship; resolved that it be sent to Lord Edgcumbe [commander-in-chief at Plymouth] to make an inquiry into the truth of it...

[On 16 December the Secretary of State for the southern department, Lord Weymouth, who had taken a strong line with Spain over the sovereignty of the Falkland Islands, suddenly resigned. He was replaced by Lord Rochford who transferred from the northern department. This left the way reasonably clear for the crisis to be peacefully resolved. In the sequel, the question of sovereignty was left open with a view to its settlement at some time in the future. Both sides secretly agreed to evacuate the islands. Meanwhile, the naval preparations continued and, according to Document 488, Anglo-Spanish relations remained 'critical' on the last day of the year.]

485. *Admiralty Minute*

18 December 1770

Present: Hawke, Buller, Holburne.

... There being still a great number of men wanted to complete the complements of His Majesty's ships ordered to be got ready for the sea; resolved a general order be issued to impress from all protections, excepting those granted in pursuance of Act of Parliament...

486. *Admiralty Minute*

24 December 1770

Present: Hawke, Palmerston, Holburne.

The Lords took into consideration a memorial from the merchants trading to South Carolina and Georgia, setting forth the apprehensions they are under for their homewardbound trade in case a war should break out with Spain and praying a convoy may be appointed for them to sail from Charleston by the 21st of March next; resolved that a copy thereof be sent to the Earl of Hillsborough for His Majesty's information and directions thereupon...

[On 4 January the same Lords heard a similar petition from the same merchants and decided to assure them that 'all possible attention' would be paid 'to the security of their trade'.]

487. *Admiralty Minute*

Tuesday, 25 December 1770

Present: Hawke, Palmerston, Holburne.

... Lord Weymouth having acquainted the Lords, in his letter of the 15th instant, that the East India Company had sent orders to their homeward-bound ships at St Helena not to proceed from thence without convoy and signified His Majesty's pleasure that a proper one should be appointed to sail from England before Christmas, and their Lordships having accordingly ordered the *Portland* [(50)] to be fitted for that service, which ship will probably be ready to sail from Portsmouth by the 2nd of next month; resolved that the East India Company be acquainted therewith and desired to let the Lords know how long they would wish the said ship should stay at St Helena for the India ships and whether they are desirous of their outward-bound storeship going under her convoy.

488. *Admiralty Minutes*

31 December 1770

Present: Hawke, Palmerston, Holburne.

... A letter was read from Commodore Proby, dated the 7th of last month at Mahon, giving an account of his intentions to remain there till the present differences shall be settled with Spain; resolved that Lord Rochford be acquainted therewith for His Majesty's information and that, as Mr Proby was, in consequence of Lord Weymouth's letter of the 16th of August, ordered to follow such orders as he should receive from the King through the channel of one of his principal Secretaries of State, their Lordships do not think proper to give him any orders relative thereto, lest they should clash with any orders from His Majesty, but that at the same time their Lordships submit whether, in the present critical situation of affairs, it is advisable for Mr Proby to continue at Mahon.

A letter was read from Commodore Byron relative to the number of men that may be spared from His Majesty's ships at Newfoundland to work upon the fort intended to be erected at St Johns; resolved that a copy thereof be sent to Lord Hillsborough for His Majesty's information and that it be proposed that the men should have it in their option whether to work or not and that they should be paid by the Board of Ordnance for the time they do work...

489. *Admiralty Minutes*

Monday, 7 January 1771

Present: Hawke, Palmerston, Holburne.

The Lords took into consideration a report from the commissioners for collecting the sixpenny duties of Greenwich Hospital, on a reference to them of a letter from the Earl of Hillsborough respecting the collection of the said duties from the fishing vessels in North America; resolved that a copy of the same be transmitted to Lord Hillsborough for the King's information and that he be acquainted this Board have not thought it expedient, in the present state of affairs in North America, to give any orders to the said commissioners with respect to the instructions they should send out to their deputy receivers in that country...

Resolved that nine pence a day be paid to each of the Greenwich Hospital pensioners who, by their own desire, were employed in rigging the *Swallow* sloop...

[On Saturday, 12 January, Hawke presided at the Board for the last time. On the same day he was succeeded by the fourth Earl of Sandwich who thus became First Lord of the Admiralty on a third occasion.]

490. *Fragment of a letter from Hawke to his elder son and heir, Martin Bladen Hawke* (holograph)

[1771?]

... for the large grants given last year by Parliament upon a thorough belief it would be war. Another thing this person knows nothing of which is that almost twenty ships of the line are only fit to be broke up and he will never see them repaired as they are not repairable, as also that there was nearly the same number ordered to be set up in slips in the naval dockyards before that gentleman left the Board. All this and much more could be said on the subject to prove what that author asserts is false. But to the point, though all this is true, yet I don't think it is worth while to go so far in it and I only send it for your own information, to the truth of which Mr Chorley [eventually one of Hawke's executors] can inform you.

The late peace establishment will not keep up fourscore ships of the line in perfect repair, especially when it [is] clipped ten or twelve thousand every year by the Minister... All this put into regular form and language is the real true state of thing[s]... No comparisons should be drawn and not a word said, good or bad, in regard to the present First L. Do nothing in this without consulting Mr Chorley.

LIST OF DOCUMENTS AND SOURCES

Where copies of a document appeared both in the Admiralty (Adm.) records at the Public Record Office (PRO) and in the Hawke (HWK) Papers at the National Maritime Museum (NMM), both references will be found below, unless the document was enclosed with a letter from Hawke to the Admiralty. Enclosures with a document have that document's number followed by a letter, for example 265a.

Hawke's letters to the Admiralty (in Adm. 1) are original documents, as are most of the items in Lord Rosse's Papers (RP) or at the British Library (BL). The HWK items are all *copies* contained (except for Document 100) in Hawke's order and letter books. While there are some gaps in these books, the absence in Parts II–IV of a HWK reference for an isolated document often implies that, for reasons of security or confidentiality, Hawke decided to have no copy made. It is likewise notable that there is no copy in the *Admiralty* records of Documents 296, 302 and 316.

1. Instructions:
   Admiralty to Hawke 15 June 1743   Adm. 2/60/25
2. Hawke to Corbett   28 June 1743   HWK/8/1
3. Hawke to Corbett   7 July 1743   Adm. 1/1883; HWK/ 8/2
4. Hawke to Corbett   20 July 1743   HWK/8/15–16
5. Hawke to Corbett   29 July 1743   Adm. 1/1883; HWK/ 8/5 (dated 28 July)
6. Hawke to Corbett   22 Aug 1743   Adm. 1/1883; HWK/ 8/11–12
7. Hawke to Corbett   23 Aug 1743   Adm. 1/1883; HWK/ 8/13
8. Hawke to Burrish 27 Oct 1743   HWK/8/16

	to Faulkner	11 Sept 1747	HWK/2/39
33.	Line of Battle	27 Sept 1747	HWK/2/46
34.	Hawke to Corbett	5 Oct 1747	Adm. 1/88
35.	Hawke to Warren	6 Oct 1747	Adm. 1/88; HWK/9 and HWK/13
36.	Hawke to Warren	11 Oct 1747	HWK/9
37.	Hawke to Corbett	12 Oct 1747	Adm. 1/88; HWK/9 and HWK/13
38.	Instructions: Hawke to the Squadron	15 Oct 1747	HWK/2/76
39.	Hawke to Corbett	17 Oct 1747	Adm. 1/88; HWK/9 and HWK/13
39a.	Council of War	15 Oct 1747	
40.	Hawke to Anson	17 Oct 1747	HWK/9 and HWK/13
41.	Hawke to Warren	17 Oct 1747	HWK/9 and HWK/13
42.	Hawke to Corbett	28 Oct 1747	Adm. 1/88 (undated); HWK/9 (dated)
43.	Corbett to Hawke	30 Oct 1747	Adm. 2/506/24; HWK/9
44.	Chambers to Hawke	30 Oct 1747	HWK/9
45.	Hobbs to Hawke	c. 30 Oct 1747	HWK/9
46.	Corbett to Hawke	31 Oct 1747	Adm. 2/506/18; HWK/9
47.	Corbett to Hawke	2 Nov 1747	Adm. 2/506/23
48.	Hawke to Corbett	4 Nov 1747	Adm. 1/88
48a.	Casualties (14 Oct)		
49.	Court martial of Captain Fox	Nov–Dec 1747	Adm. 1/5291

PART III

50.	Instructions: Admiralty to Hawke	26 July 1748	Adm. 2/72/177; HWK/1/91
51.	Hawke to Clevland	31 July 1748	Adm. 1/917
52.	Hawke to Clevland	4 Aug 1748	Adm. 1/917; HWK/13
53.	Hawke to Clevland	7 Aug 1748	Adm. 1/917; HWK/13
54.	Hawke to Clevland	13 Aug 1748	Adm. 1/917; HWK/13

55.	Hawke to Clevland	16 Aug 1748	Adm. 1/917; HWK/13
56.	Instructions: Admiralty to Hawke	26 Aug 1748	Adm. 2/72/218; HWK/1/100
57.	Hawke to Clevland	28 Aug 1748	Adm. 1/917; HWK/13
58.	Hawke to Clevland	31 Aug 1748	Adm. 1/917; HWK/13
59.	Clevland to Hawke	8 Sept 1748	Adm. 2/508/384; HWK/9
60.	Hawke to Clevland	10 Sept 1748	Adm. 1/917; HWK/13
61.	Hawke to Anson	15 Sept 1748	BL, Add. MSS 15956/46
62.	Hawke to Anson	28 Sept 1748	Bodleian L, Montagu MSS 25446/59
63.	Hawke to Clevland	23 Oct 1748	Adm. 1/917; HWK/13
64.	Instructions: Admiralty to Hawke	22 Nov 1748	Adm. 2/72/326–31; HWK/1/160
65.	Hawke to Corbett	22 June 1749	Adm. 1/918; HWK/13
66.	Hawke to Corbett	5 July 1749	Adm. 1/918; HWK/13
67.	Hawke to Corbett	8 July 1749	Adm. 1/918; HWK/13
68.	Hawke to Corbett	11 July 1749	Adm. 1/918; HWK/13
69.	Instructions: Hawke to the Guardships	13 July 1749	HWK/2/331
70.	Hawke to Corbett	15 July 1749	Adm. 1/918; HWK/13
71.	Hawke to Hughes	24 July 1749	HWK/13
71a.	Stanhope to Hawke	21 July 1749	Adm. 1/918
71b.	Bennett to Stanhope	21 July 1749	Adm. 1/918
72.	Hughes to Hawke	25 July 1749	Adm. 1/918
72a.	Lock to Hughes	25 July 1749	Adm. 1/918
72b.	Statement by T. Brown	25 July 1749	Adm. 1/918

73.	Instructions: Hawke to the Guardships	14 Nov 1749	HWK/2
74.	Admiralty minute	6 Apr 1750	Adm. 3/61
75.	Instructions: Admiralty to Hawke	11 May 1750	Adm. 2/73/284–5; HWK/1 (no p. number)
75a.	Anson to Corbett	16 Apr 1750	
76.	Admiralty minute	24 May 1750	Adm. 3/61
77.	Hawke to Clevland	28 Apr 1752	Adm. 1/918
78.	Instructions: Admiralty to Hawke	31 Oct 1752	Adm. 2/74/183; HWK/1
79.	Hawke to Clevland	3 Nov 1752	Adm. 1/918
80.	Hawke to Clevland	21 Jan 1754	Adm. 1/918

PART IV(a)

81.	Instructions: Admiralty to Hawke	6 Feb 1755	Adm. 2/75/42; HWK/1
82.	Hawke to Clevland	21 Feb 1755	Adm. 1/919; HWK/13
83.	Clevland to Hawke	25 Feb 1755	Adm. 2/512/465–6; HWK/10
84.	Hawke to Clevland	28 Feb 1755	Adm. 1/919; HWK/13
85.	Instructions: Hawke to all captains	5 Mar 1755	HWK/2
86.	Hawke to Clevland	8 Mar 1755	Adm. 1/919; HWK/13
87.	Clevland to Hawke	11 Mar 1755	Adm. 2/512/535–6; HWK/10
88.	Clevland to Hawke	11 Mar 1755	Adm. 2/512/537–8; HWK/10
89.	Hawke to Clevland	16 Mar 1755	Adm. 1/919; HWK/13
90.	Hawke to Clevland	29 Mar 1755	Adm. 1/919; HWK/13
91.	Hawke to Clevland	30 Mar 1755	Adm. 1/919; HWK/13
92.	Instructions: Hawke to all captains	30 Mar 1755	HWK/3

93.	Hawke to Clevland	31 Mar 1755	Adm. 1/919; HWK/13
94.	Hawke to Clevland	1 Apr 1755	Adm. 1/919; HWK/13
95.	Hawke to Clevland	27 Apr 1755	Adm. 1/919; HWK/13
96.	Clevland to Hawke	28 Apr 1755	Adm. 2/513/165–6; HWK/10
97.	Instructions: Admiralty to Hawke	6 May 1755	Adm. 2/75/196; HWK/1
98.	Line of Battle	21 July 1755	HWK/3
99.	Instructions: Lords Justices to Hawke	22 July 1755	RP/H2/25–9
100.	Anson to Hawke	22 July 1755	HWK/22 (iii)
101.	Prize money agreement	23 Aug 1755	NMM/ADL/X/13
102.	Hawke to Clevland	1 Oct 1755	Adm. 1/89 (i)
103.	Clevland to Hawke	7 Oct 1755	Adm. 2/514/172–3
104.	Hawke to Clevland	9 Oct 1755	Adm. 1/89 (i); HWK/13
105.	Instructions: Admiralty to Hawke	27 Feb 1756	Adm. 2/1331/127–9
106.	Line of Battle	14 Mar 1756	HWK/3
107.	Instructions: Hawke to Duff	19 Apr 1756	HWK/3
108.	Hawke to Clevland	18 Apr 1756	Adm. 1/89 (ii); HWK/13
109.	Instructions: Admiralty to Hawke	22 Apr 1756	Adm. 1/1331/137–8
110.	Hawke to Clevland	27 Apr 1756	Adm. 1/89 (ii); HWK/13
111.	Hawke to Clevland	8 May 1756	Adm. 1/89 (ii); HWK/13

PART IV(b)

112.	Instructions: Admiralty to Hawke	8 June 1756	RP/H2/35–9; Adm. 2/1331/139–45
113.	Hawke to Byng	4 July 1756	HWK/13
114.	Byng to Hawke	4 July 1756	RP/H2/45
115.	Line of Battle	10 July 1756	HWK/4

135.	Hawke to Clevland	19 Aug 1757	Adm. 1/89 (ii)
136.	Clevland to Hawke	20 Aug 1757	Adm. 2/520/474; HWK/10
137.	Hawke to Clevland	20 Aug 1757	Adm. 1/89 (ii); HWK/13
138.	Hawke to Clevland	21 Aug 1757	Adm. 1/89 (ii); HWK/13
139.	Hawke to Clevland	22 Aug 1757	Adm. 1/89 (ii); HWK/13
139a.	Thames to Hawke	21 Aug 1757	
140.	Hawke to Clevland	24 Aug 1757	Adm. 1/89 (ii)
141.	Instructions: Admiralty to Hawke	25 Aug 1757	Adm. 2/79/194–5; HWK/1
142.	Notes by Hawke	[Sept. 1757]	RP/H2/66–8
142a.	Draft 'memorandum'		
143.	Hawke to Clevland	4 Sept 1757	Adm. 1/89 (iii); HWK/13
144.	Hawke to Mordaunt	4 Sept 1757	HWK/13
145.	Pitt to Hawke	5 Sept 1757	RP/H2/57–8
146.	Hawke to Clevland	6 Sept 1757	Adm. 1/89 (iii)
147.	Line of Battle	7 Sept 1757	HWK/5
148.	Hawke to Clevland	8 Sept 1757	Adm. 1/89 (iii); HWK/13
149.	Hawke to Clevland	10 Sept 1757	Adm. 1/89 (iii); HWK/13
150.	Pitt to Hawke	15 Sept 1757	RP/H4
151.	Memorandum by Hawke	20 Sept 1757	HWK/5
152.	Instructions: Hawke to Knowles	20 Sept 1757	HWK/5
153.	Instructions: Hawke to Brodrick	23 Sept 1757	HWK/5
154.	Instructions: Hawke to Knowles	24 Sept 1757	HWK/5
155.	Hawke to Clevland	29 Sept 1757	Adm. 1/89 (iii); HWK/13
156.	Hawke to Anson	30 Sept 1757	BL/Add.MSS 15956 48–9
157.	Hawke to Clevland	6 Oct 1757	Adm. 1/89 (iii); HWK/13

157a.	'Minutes of a council of war'	28 Sept 1757	
158.	Hawke to Anson	8 Oct 1757	HWK/13
159.	Hawke to Clevland	8 Oct 1757	Adm. 1/89 (iii); HWK/13
160.	Anson to Hawke	19 Oct 1757	RP/H2/61–2
161.	Hawke to Pitt	21 Oct 1757	PRO/Chatham P 30/8/78 (damaged); NMM/HSR/Z/13 (complete)
162.	Hawke to Clevland	16 Nov 1757	Adm. 1/89 (iii); HWK/13
163.	Hawke to Clevland	15 Dec 1757	Adm. 1/89 (iii); HWK/13

PART IV(d)

164.	Instructions: Admiralty to Hawke	5 Mar 1758	Adm. 2/1331/238–40
165.	Hawke to Anson	7 Mar 1758	RP/'Hawke MSS 1702–1800'/84–6 (and NMM/PST/5, G.7 for photostat)
166.	Hawke to Clevland	7 Mar 1758	Adm. 1/89 (iii); HWK/13
167.	Hawke to Clevland	8 Mar 1758	Adm. 1/89 (iii); HWK/13
168.	Instructions: Hawke to Pratten	8 Mar 1758	HWK/5
169.	Hawke to Clevland	9 Mar 1758	Adm. 1/89 (iii); HWK/13
170.	Line of Battle	11 Mar 1758	HWK/5
171.	Hawke to Clevland	12 Mar 1758	Adm. 1/89 (iii); HWK/13
172.	Instructions: Hawke to ships at Plymouth	13 Mar 1758	HWK/5
173.	Instructions: Hawke to Pratten and Proby	5 Apr 1758	HWK/5
174.	Hawke to Clevland	11 Apr 1758	Adm. 1/89 (iii)
175.	Hawke to Clevland	26 Apr 1758	Adm. 1/89 (iii); HWK/13

175a.	Instructions: Hawke to Keppel	8 Apr 1758	
176.	Hawke to Clevland	30 Apr 1758	Adm. 1/89 (iii); HWK/13
177.	Hawke to Clevland	10 May 1758	Adm. 1/89 (iii)
178 (1).	Draft minute	12 May 1758	Adm. 1/89 (iii)
178 (2).	Admiralty minute	12 May 1758	Adm. 3/66

PART IV(e)

179.	Instructions: Admiralty to Hawke	9 May 1759	Adm. 2/82/527; HWK/1
180.	Instructions: Admiralty to Hawke	9 May 1759	Adm. 2/82/530; HWK/1
181.	Instructions: Admiralty to Victualling Board	11 May 1759	Adm. 2/82/533
182.	Hawke to Clevland	13 May 1759	Adm. 1/92 (i)/136; HWK/14
183.	Hawke to Clevland	14 May 1759	Adm. 1/92 (i)/2; HWK/14
184.	Hawke to Clevland	17 May 1759	Adm. 1/92 (i)/5; HWK/14
185.	Hawke to Clevland	18 May 1759	Adm. 1/92/6; HWK/14
186.	Instructions: Admiralty to Hawke	18 May 1759	Adm. 2/1331/297–9; HWK/1
187.	'A List of the French Navy' at Brest, etc.	[c. 18 May 1759]	HWK/11
188.	Hawke to Anson	[19 or 20 May 1759]	RP/H4
189.	Hawke to Clevland	20 May 1759	Adm. 1/92 (i)/8; HWK/14
190.	Hawke to Clevland	20 May 1759	Adm. 1/92 (i)/7; HWK/14
191.	Line of Battle	20 May 1759	HWK/5
192.	Lockhart to Hawke	21 May 1759	HWK/11

	to Hervey	3 July 1759	HWK/5
214.	Hervey to Hawke	4 July 1759	HWK/11
215.	Hawke to Hervey	4 July 1759	HWK/14
216.	Hervey to Hawke	5 July 1759	HWK/11
217.	Hervey to Hawke	6 July 1759	HWK/11
218.	Hawke to Hervey	7 July 1759	HWK/14
219.	Duff to Hawke	7 July 1759	HWK/11
220.	Hawke to Clevland	13 July 1759	Adm. 1/92 (i)/59; HWK/14
220a.	Hervey to Hawke (extract)	13 July 1759	Adm. 1/92 (i)/60; HWK/11 (complete)
221.	Instructions: Hawke to Geary	16 July 1759	HWK/5
222.	Instructions: Hawke to Clements	16 July 1759	HWK/5
223.	Hawke to Clevland	16 July 1759	Adm. 1/92 (i)/61–2; HWK/14
223a.	Mann to Hawke	13 July 1759	
223b.	Hervey to Hawke (extract)	15 July 1759	Adm. 1/92 (i)/64–5; HWK/11 (complete)
224.	Instructions: Admiralty to Victualling Board	19 July 1759	Adm. 2/83/211
225.	Edgcumbe to Hawke	20 July 1759	HWK/11
226.	Hervey to Hawke	20 July 1759	HWK/11
226a.	Information	20 July 1759	
227.	Hervey to Hawke	21 July 1759	HWK/11
227a.	Report by Hervey	21 July 1759	
228.	Hervey to Hawke	22 July 1759	HWK/11
229.	Hervey to Hawke	22 July 1759	HWK/11
230.	Hawke to Clevland	23 July 1759	Adm. 1/92 (i)/66–74; HWK/14
231.	Hawke to Hervey	23 July 1759	HWK/14
232.	Clevland to Hawke	23 July 1759	Adm. 2/525/561; HWK/11
233.	Hawke to Ommanney	23 July 1759	HWK/14
234.	Hawke to Ommanney	24 July 1759	HWK/14
235.	Hawke to Clevland	24 July 1759	Adm. 1/92(i)/78–9;

			HWK/14
236.	Hawke to Hervey	26 July 1759	HWK/14
237.	Ommanney to Hawke	27 July 1759	HWK/11
238.	Hawke to Clevland	29 July 1759	Adm 1/92 (i)/83; HWK/14
239.	Clevland to Hawke	30 July 1759	Adm. 2/526/27; HWK/11
240.	Hawke to Ommanney	2 Aug 1759	HWK/14
241.	Hawke to Clevland	2 Aug 1759	Adm. 1/92 (i)/86–7; HWK/14
242.	Instructions: Admiralty to Victualling Board	2 Aug 1759	Adm. 2/83/257
243.	Instructions: Hawke to Young	2 Aug 1759	HWK/5
244.	Hawke to Clevland	4 Aug 1759	Adm. 1/92 (i)/89–90; HWK/14
245.	Victualling Board to Hawke	6 Aug 1759	HWK/11
246.	Hawke to Clevland	6 Aug 1759	Adm. 1/92 (i)/88; HWK/14
247.	Duff to Hawke	6 Aug 1759	HWK/11
248.	Hervey to Hawke	11 Aug 1759	HWK/11
248a.	Report by Clements	11 Aug 1759	
249.	Hawke to Clevland	12 Aug 1759	Adm. 1/92 (i)/92–3; HWK/14
250.	Hawke to Clevland	12 Aug 1759	Adm. 1/92 (i)/95–7; HWK/14
251.	Instructions: Admiralty to Victualling Board	13 Aug 1759	Adm. 2/83/284
252.	Clevland to Hawke	13 Aug 1759	Adm. 2/526/87–8; HWK/11
253.	Hawke to Pett	14 Aug 1759	HWK/14
254.	Hawke to Clevland	17 Aug 1759	Adm. 1/92 (i)/100; HWK/14
255.	Clevland to Hawke	18 Aug 1759	HWK/11
256.	Pett to Hawke	21 Aug 1759	HWK/11
257.	Clevland to Hawke	22 Aug 1759	Adm. 2/526/124–5; HWK/11

258.	Line of Battle	25 Aug 1759	HWK/5
259.	Hawke to Clevland	28 Aug 1759	Adm. 1/92 (i)/101–4; HWK/14
260.	Hawke to Clevland	3 Sept 1759	Adm. 1/92 (i)/110–13; HWK/14
260a.	Report by Hervey	30 Aug 1759	
260b.	Hervey to Hawke	30 Aug 1759	
261.	Clevland to Hawke	4 Sept 1759	Adm. 2/526/201; HWK/11
262.	Hawke to Clevland	7 Sept 1759	Adm. 1/92 (i)/116–18; HWK/14
262a.	Report by Bristol	24 Aug 1759	
263.	Hawke to Hanway	8 Sept 1759	HWK/14
264.	Instructions: Admiralty to Hawke	10 Sept 1759	Adm. 2/83/403–4
265.	Hawke to Clevland	10 Sept 1759	Adm. 1/92 (i)/120–32; HWK/14 and HWK/11
265a.	Reynolds to Hawke	7 Sept 1759	
265b.	Minute of consultation	7 Sept 1759	
265c.	Report by Hotham	31 Aug 1759	
265d.	Report by Reynolds	31 Aug 1759	
265e.	Strachan to Reynolds	4 Sept 1759	
265f.	Roddam to Hawke	29 Aug 1759	
265g.	Report by Clements	29 Aug 1759	
265h.	Report by Clements	31 Aug 1759	
266.	Hawke to Clevland	12 Sept 1759	Adm. 1/92 (i)/133–5; HWK/14
266a.	Hawke to Reynolds	11 Sept 1759	
267.	Milnes to Hawke	14 Sept 1759	Adm. 2/526/249; HWK/11
268.	Instructions: Admiralty to Hawke	14 Sept 1759	Adm. 2/1331/322–3
269.	Hawke to Clevland	15 Sept 1759	Adm. 1/92 (i)/151, 138; HWK/14
270.	Hawke to Clevland	18 Sept 1759	Adm. 1/92 (i)/179–80; HWK/14
270a.	Hervey to Hawke	17 Sept 1759	
271.	Hawke to Hood	19 Sept 1759	BL/Add.MSS 35193/96; HWK/14

272.	Hood to Hawke	19 Sept 1759	HWK/11
273.	Hood to Hawke	21 Sept 1759	HWK/11
274.	Hawke to Hood	21 Sept 1759	BL/Add.MSS 35193/97; HWK/14
275.	Milnes to Hawke	21 Sept 1759	Adm. 2/526/278–9
276.	Hawke to Hood	22 Sept 1759	HWK/14
277.	Duff to Hawke	23 Sept 1759	HWK/11
278.	Hawke to Clevland	23 Sept 1759	Adm. 1/92 (i)/171–4; HWK/14
279.	Court martial of Hood	24 Sept 1759	Adm. 1/5298
280.	Swinton to Hawke	24 Sept 1759	HWK/11
281.	Hawke to Reynolds	26 Sept 1759	HWK/14
282.	Hawke to Clevland	26 Sept 1759	Adm. 1/92 (i)/161–9; HWK/14
282a.	Duff to Hawke	22 Sept 1759	
282b.	Reynolds to Hawke	19 Sept 1759	
282c.	Jacobs to Reynolds	16 Sept 1759	
282d.	Minute of consultation	19 Sept 1759	
283.	Hawke to Clevland	28 Sept 1759	Adm. 1/92 (i)/155; HWK/14
284.	Hawke to Anson	29 Sept 1759	RP/H4
285.	Hawke to Anson	1 Oct 1759	Adm. 1/92 (i)/182, 152–3; HWK/14
285a.	Duff to Hawke	30 Sept 1759	
286.	Hawke to Clevland	3 Oct 1759	Adm. 1/92 (i)/183; HWK/14
287.	Clevland to Hawke	3 Oct 1759	Adm. 2/526/318–20; HWK/11
288.	Hawke to Duff	4 Oct 1759	HWK/14
289.	Clevland to Hawke	5 Oct 1759	Adm. 2/526/332–3; HWK/11
290.	Hawke to Clevland	7 Oct 1759	Adm. 1/92 (i)/185–7; HWK/14
290a.	Hawke to Duff	7 Oct 1759	
291.	Hawke to Duff	8 Oct 1759	HWK/14
292.	Instructions: Hawke to Duff	8 Oct 1759	HWK/5
293.	Hervey to Hawke	9 Oct 1759	HWK/11
294.	Hawke to Duff	10 Oct 1759	HWK/14
294a.	Intelligence		

295.	Hawke to Clevland	10 Oct 1759	Adm. 1/92 (ii)/9–12; HWK/14
295a.	Duff to Hawke	7 Oct 1759	
296.	Clevland to Hawke	10 Oct 1759	HWK/11
297.	Hawke to Clevland	13 Oct 1759	Adm. 1/92 (ii)/14; HWK/14
298.	Hawke to Clevland	14 Oct 1759	Adm. 1/92 (ii)/15–16; HWK/14
299.	Clevland to Hawke	15 Oct 1759	Adm. 2/526/371; HWK/11
300.	Navy Board to Hawke	17 Oct 1759	HWK/11
301.	Hawke to Clevland	17 Oct 1759	Adm. 1/92 (ii)/17–18; HWK/14
302.	Clevland to Hawke	19 Oct 1759	HWK/11
303.	Hervey to Hawke	20 Oct 1759	HWK/11
304.	Hawke to Hervey	21 Oct 1759	HWK/14
305.	Hawke to Pett	21 Oct 1759	HWK/15
306.	Hawke to Clevland	21 Oct 1759	Adm. 1/92 (ii)/18A–19; HWK/14
307.	Instructions: Hawke to Young	22 Oct 1759	HWK/5
308.	Hawke to Hervey	23 Oct 1759	HWK/14
309.	Hawke to Hervey	23 Oct 1759	HWK/14
310.	Hawke to Clevland	24 Oct 1759	Adm. 1/92 (ii)/21–30; HWK/14
310a.	Duff to Hawke	18 Oct 1759	
310b.	Porter to Hawke		
311.	Hawke to Clevland	25 Oct 1759	Adm. 1/92 (ii)/31; HWK/14
312.	Lendrick to Hawke	26 Oct 1759	HWK/11
313.	Hawke to Navy Board	29 Oct 1759	HWK/14
314.	Clevland to Hawke	29 Oct 1759	Adm. 2/526/447–8; HWK/11
315.	Hawke to Clevland	29 Oct 1759	Adm. 1/92 (ii)/33; HWK/14
316.	Clevland to Hawke	30 Oct 1759	HWK/11. No copy in Adm. 2/526, but see p.454, Clevland to Hanway, 30 Oct — 'packet'.

317.	Hawke to Clevland	5 Nov 1759	Adm. 1/92 (ii)/35–8; HWK/14
317a.	Hervey to Hawke	2 Nov 1759	
317b.	Lendrick to Hawke	4 Nov 1759	
318.	Instructions: Hawke to Methell	10 Nov 1759	HWK/5
319.	Hawke to Clevland	10 Nov 1759	Adm. 1/92 (ii)/41–2; HWK/14
320.	Hawke to Clevland	12 Nov 1759	Adm. 1/92 (ii)/44; HWK/14
321.	Clevland to Hawke	13 Nov 1759	Adm. 2/526/529–30; HWK/11
322.	Hawke to Geary	17 Nov 1759	Adm. 1/93; HWK/14
323.	Hawke to Clevland	17 Nov 1759	Adm. 1/92 (ii)/45–6; HWK/14
324.	Buckle to Hawke	22 Nov 1759	HWK/11
325.	Instructions: Hawke to Arbuthnot	23 Nov 1759	HWK/5
326.	Young to Hawke	23 Nov 1759	HWK/11
326a.	Report by Willett and Hood		
327.	Hawke to Clevland	24 Nov 1759	Adm. 1/92 (ii)/49–54; HWK/14
327a.	List of the French Squadron		
327b.	Line of Battle	[20 Nov 1759]	
328.	Hawke to Anson	[Late Nov 1759]	RP/H4
329.	Court martial: loss of *Resolution*	29 Nov 1759	Adm. 1/5298
330.	Hawke to Clevland	1 Dec 1759	Adm. 1/92 (ii)/55–8; HWK/14
330a.	Young to Hawke	30 Nov 1759	
331.	Hawke to Clevland	2 Dec 1759	Adm. 1/92 (ii)/63–4; HWK/14
331a.	Keppel to Hawke	2 Dec 1759	
332.	Anson to Hawke	1 Dec 1759	RP/H2/76–7
333.	Clevland to Hawke	3 Dec 1759	Adm. 2/527/76–7
334.	Hawke to Clevland	9 Dec 1759	Adm. 1/92 (ii)/74–5; HWK/14
335.	Hawke to Clevland	16 Dec 1759	Adm. 1/92 (ii)/76
336.	Hawke to Clevland	26 Dec 1759	Adm. 1/92 (ii)/79
337.	Hawke to Clevland	2 Jan 1760	Adm. 1/92 (ii)/81

364.	Clevland to Hawke	30 June 1762	Adm. 2/534/47–8
365.	Instructions:		
	Admiralty to Hawke	1 July 1762	Adm. 2/1332/27
366.	Hawke to Clevland	9 July 1762	Adm. 1/92 (iii) 126–8; HWK/16
367.	Hawke to Clevland	24 Aug 1762	Adm. 1/92 (iii) 133–4

PART V

368.	Chatham to Hawke	28 Nov 1766	RP/H2/116–17
369.	Admiralty minute	12 Dec 1766	Adm. 3/74
370.	Admiralty minute	7 Feb 1767	Adm. 3/74
371.	Admiralty minutes	10 Mar 1767	Adm. 3/75
372.	Admiralty minute	23 Mar 1767	Adm. 3/75
373.	Admiralty minutes	26 Mar 1767	Adm. 3/75
374.	Admiralty minute	3 Apr 1767	Adm. 3/75
375.	Admiralty minute	2 May 1767	Adm. 3/75
376.	Admiralty rules for the Academy	2 May 1767	Adm. 2/94/8–19
377.	Stephens to Navy Board	10 June 1767	Adm.2/541/90–1
378.	Admiralty minute	18 June 1767	Adm. 3/75
379.	Lords to Navy Board	23 June 1767	Adm. 2/541/117–27
380.	Moore to Stephens	20 July 1767	Adm. 1/942
381.	Moore to Stephens	27 July 1767	Adm. 1/942
382.	Admiralty minute	23 July 1767	Adm. 3/75
383.	Admiralty minute	6 Aug 1767	Adm. 3/75
384.	Stephens to Moore	13 Aug 1767	Adm. 2/541/194–5
385.	Admiralty minute	10 Sept 1767	Adm. 3/75
386.	Moore to Stephens	17 Sept 1767	Adm. 1/942
387.	Moore to Stephens	3 Oct 1767	Adm. 1/942
388.	Moore to Stephens	14 Oct 1767	Adm. 1/942
389.	Admiralty minutes	29 Oct 1767	Adm. 3/75
390.	Moore to Stephens	16 Nov 1767	Adm. 1/942
391.	Admiralty minute	15 Dec 1767	Adm. 3/75
392.	Stephens to Navy Board	15 Dec 1767	Adm. 2/541/341
393.	Moore to Stephens	29 Dec 1767	Adm. 1/942
394.	Admiralty minute	15 Jan 1768	Adm. 3/75
395.	Admiralty minute	21 Jan 1768	Adm. 3/75
396.	Admiralty minute	22 Jan 1768	Adm. 3/75
397.	Admiralty minute	10 Feb 1768	Adm. 3/75

398.	Admiralty minute	25 Feb 1768	Adm. 3/75
399.	Admiralty minute	10 Mar 1768	Adm. 3/75
400.	Moore to Stephens	16 Mar 1768	Adm. 1/942
401.	Moore to Stephens	16 Apr 1768	Adm. 1/942
402.	Admiralty minute	20 Apr 1768	Adm. 3/76
403.	Admiralty minute	20 July 1768	Adm. 3/76
404.	Instructions: Admiralty to Cook	30 July 1768	Adm. 2/1332/80–5
404a.	Additional instructions for Cook	30 July 1768	
404b.	Instructions to be shown by Cook	30 July 1768	
405.	Admiralty minutes	30 July 1768	Adm. 3/76
406.	George III to Hawke	15 Sept 1768	RP/H2/136
407.	Moore to Stephens	2 Oct 1768	Adm. 1/942
408.	Moore to Stephens	5 Oct 1768	Adm. 1/942
409.	Instructions: Admiralty to Everitt	18 Mar 1769	Adm. 2/94/532
410.	Admiralty minutes	12 Oct 1768	Adm. 3/76
411.	Admiralty minutes	26 Oct 1768	Adm. 3/76
412.	Admiralty minutes	27 Oct 1768	Adm. 3/76
413.	Admiralty minute	19 Nov 1768	Adm. 3/76
414.	Admiralty minute	26 Dec 1768	Adm. 3/76
415.	Admiralty minute	17 Feb 1769	Adm. 3/76
416.	Admiralty minute	1 Mar 1769	Adm. 3/76
417.	Admiralty minute	3 Mar 1769	Adm. 3/76
418.	Admiralty minute	30 Mar 1769	Adm. 3/76
419.	Admiralty minute	5 Apr 1769	Adm. 3/76
420.	Admiralty minute	8 Apr 1769	Adm. 3/76
421.	Admiralty minute	12 Apr 1769	Adm. 3/76
422.	Admiralty minutes	20 June 1769	Adm. 3/76
423.	Admiralty minute	7 July 1769	Adm. 3/76
424.	Admiralty minute	15 July 1769	Adm. 3/76
425.	Admiralty minute	19 July 1769	Adm. 3/76
426.	Admiralty minute	9 Aug 1769	Adm. 3/77
427.	Admiralty minute	13 Oct 1769	Adm. 3/77
428.	Admiralty minutes	23 Nov 1769	Adm. 3/77
429.	Admiralty minute	30 Jan 1770	Adm. 3/77
430.	Admiralty minute	7 Feb 1770	Adm. 3/77
431.	Admiralty minute	22 Feb 1770	Adm. 3/77

432.	Admiralty minute	23 Feb 1770	Adm. 3/77
433.	Admiralty minutes	24 Feb 1770	Adm. 3/77
434.	Admiralty minute	26 Feb 1770	Adm. 3/77
435.	Admiralty minute	5 Mar 1770	Adm. 3/77
436.	Admiralty minute	6 Apr 1770	Adm. 3/77
437.	Admiralty minute	27 Apr 1770	Adm. 3/77
438.	Admiralty minute	24 May 1770	Adm. 3/77
439.	Admiralty minutes	6 June 1770	Adm. 3/77
440.	Admiralty minutes	20 June 1770	Adm. 3/77
441.	Admiralty minute	16 July 1770	Adm. 3/77
442.	Admiralty minute	28 July 1770	Adm. 3/77
443.	Admiralty minutes	1 Aug 1770	Adm. 3/77
444.	Admiralty minutes	2 Aug 1770	Adm. 3/77
445.	Admiralty minute	7 Aug 1770	Adm. 3/77
446.	Admiralty minutes	9 Aug 1770	Adm. 3/77
447.	Admiralty minute	10 Aug 1770	Adm. 3/77
448.	Admiralty minute	17 Aug 1770	Adm. 3/77
449.	Admiralty minute	6 Sept 1770	Adm. 3/77
450.	Admiralty minutes	7 Sept 1770	Adm. 3/77
451.	Admiralty minutes	11 Sept 1770	Adm. 3/77
452.	Admiralty minutes	13 Sept 1770	Adm. 3/77
453.	Admiralty minutes	14 Sept 1770	Adm. 3/77
454.	Admiralty minutes	17 Sept 1770	Adm. 3/77
455.	Admiralty minutes	19 Sept 1770	Adm. 3/77
456.	Admiralty minutes	20 Sept 1770	Adm. 3/77
457.	Admiralty minutes	21 Sept 1770	Adm. 3/77
458.	Admiralty minutes	24 Sept 1770	Adm. 3/77
459.	Admiralty minutes	25 Sept 1770	Adm. 3/77
460.	Admiralty minutes	27 Sept 1770	Adm. 3/77
461.	Instructions: Admiralty to Mackenzie	29 Sept 1770	Adm. 2/1332/88–9
462.	Aide-mémoire by Hawke	30 Sept 1770	RP/H7
462a.	Notes of about the same date		
463.	'My Own Minutes'	3 Oct 1770	RP/H7
464.	Admiralty minutes	6 Oct 1770	Adm. 3/77
465.	Admiralty minutes	12 Oct 1770	Adm. 3/77
466.	Admiralty minute	13 Oct 1770	Adm. 3/77
467.	Admiralty minutes	16 Oct 1770	Adm. 3/77
468.	Admiralty minute	17 Oct 1770	Adm. 3/77

469.	Admiralty minutes	18 Oct 1770	Adm. 3/77
470.	Admiralty minutes	30 Oct 1770	Adm. 3/77
471.	Admiralty minutes	31 Oct 1770	Adm. 3/77
472.	Admiralty minutes	1 Nov 1770	Adm. 3/78
473.	Admiralty minutes	2 Nov 1770	Adm. 3/78
474.	Admiralty minutes	3 Nov 1770	Adm. 3/78
475.	Admiralty minutes	5 Nov 1770	Adm. 3/78
476.	Admiralty minutes	7 Nov 1770	Adm. 3/78
477.	Admiralty minutes	10 Nov 1770	Adm. 3/78
478.	Admiralty minutes	16 Nov 1770	Adm. 3/78
479.	Admiralty minutes	26 Nov 1770	Adm. 3/78
480.	Admiralty minutes	30 Nov 1770	Adm. 3/78
481.	Admiralty minute	1 Dec 1770	Adm. 3/78
482.	Admiralty minute	3 Dec 1770	Adm. 3/78
483.	Admiralty minute	5 Dec 1770	Adm. 3/78
484.	Admiralty minutes	12 Dec 1770	Adm. 3/78
485.	Admiralty minute	18 Dec 1770	Adm. 3/78
486.	Admiralty minute	24 Dec 1770	Adm. 3/78
487.	Admiralty minute	25 Dec 1770	Adm. 3/78
488.	Admiralty minutes	31 Dec 1770	Adm. 3/78
489.	Admiralty minutes	7 Jan 1771	Adm. 3/78
490.	Hawke to Martin Bladen Hawke	1771?	RP/H2/194–5

INDEX

Highest ranks and titles are given here. Footnotes with biographical details will usually be found under first mention in the text; for example: Watson, V.-Adm. Charles: 16n refers to the text *and* the footnote. An asterisk indicates an article in the *D.N.B.*

Navy Records Society
(Founded 1893)

The Navy Records Society was established for the purpose of printing unpublished manuscripts and rare works of naval interest. The Society is open to all who are interested in naval history, and any person wishing to become a member should apply to the Hon. Secretary, c/o the Public Record Office, Chancery Lane, London WC2A 1LR. The annual subscription is £15, which entitles the member to receive one free copy of each work issued by the Society in that year, and to buy earlier issues at much reduced prices.

The prices to members and non-members respectively are given after each volume, and orders should be sent, enclosing no money, to the Hon. Treasurer, Binder Hamlyn, 8 St Bride Street, London EC4A 4DA. Those marked 'TS' and 'SP' are published for the Society by Temple Smith and Scolar Press, and available to non-members only from the Gower Publishing Group, Gower House, Croft Road, Aldershot, Hampshire GU11 3HR. Those marked 'A & U' are published by George Allen & Unwin, and available to non-members only through bookshops.

The Society has already published:

Vols. 1 and 2. *State Papers relating to the Defeat of the Spanish Armada, Anno 1588* Vols I & II, ed, Professor J. K. Laughton. (£12.00 ea./£40.00 set TS)

Vol. 3. *Letters of Lord Hood, 1781–82*, ed. David Hannay. (*Out of Print*)

Vol. 4. *Index to James's Naval History*, ed. Hon. T. Brassey. (*Out of Print*)

Vol. 5. *Life of Captain Stephen Martin, 1666–1740*, ed. Sir Clements R. Markham. (*Out of Print*)

Vol. 6. *Journal of Rear-Admiral Bartholomew James, 1725–1828*, ed. Professor J. K. Laughton and Commander J. Y. F. Sulivan. (*Out of Print*)

Vol. 7. *Hollond's Discourses of the Navy, 1638 & 1658*, ed. J. R. Tanner. (*Out of Print*)

Vol. 8. *Naval Accounts and Inventories in the Reign of Henry VII*, ed. M. Oppenheim. (*Out of Print*)

Vol. 9. *Journal of Sir George Rooke*, ed. Oscar Browning. (*Out of Print*)

Vol. 10. *Letters and Papers relating to the War with France, 1512–13*, ed. Alfred Spont. (*Out of Print*)

Vol. 11. *Papers relating to the Spanish War, 1585–87*, ed. Julian S. Corbett. (£15.00/£35.00 TS)

Vol. 12. *Journals and Letters of Admiral of the Fleet Sir Thomas Byam Martin, 1773–1854*, Vol. II, ed. Admiral Sir R. Vesey Hamilton. (*Out of Print*)

Vol. 13. *Papers relating to the First Dutch War, 1652–54*, Vol. I, ed. Dr S. R. Gardiner. (*Out of Print*)

Vol. 14. *Papers relating to the Blockade of Brest, 1803–5*, Vol. I, ed. J. Leyland. (*Out of Print*)

Vol. 15. *History of the Russian Fleet during the Reign of Peter the Great, by a Contemporary Englishman*, ed. Admiral Sir Cyprian Bridge. (*Out of Print*)

Vol. 16. *Logs of the Great Sea Fights, 1794–1805*, Vol. I, ed. Vice-Admiral Sir T. Sturges Jackson. (£12.00/£20.00)

Vol. 17. *Papers relating to the First Dutch War, 1652–54*, Vol. II, ed. Dr S. R. Gardiner. (*Out of Print*)

Vol. 18. *Logs of the Great Sea Fights, 1794–1805*, Vol. II, ed. Vice-Admiral Sir T. Sturges Jackson. (£12.00/£20.00)

Vol. 19. *Journals and Letters of Admiral of the Fleet Sir Thomas Byam Martin, 1773–1854*, Vol. III, ed. Admiral Sir R. Vesey Hamilton. (*Out of Print*)

Vol. 20. *The Naval Miscellany*, Vol. I, ed. Professor J. K. Laughton. (£15.00/£20.00)

Vol. 21. *Papers relating to the Blockade of Brest, 1803–5*, Vol. II, ed. J. Leyland. (*Out of Print*)

Vol. 22 and 23. *The Naval Tracts of Sir William Monson*, Vols I & II, ed. M. Oppenheim (*Out of Print*)

Vol. 24. *Journals and Letters of Admiral of the Fleet Sir Thomas Byam Martin, 1773–1854*, Vol. I ed. Admiral Sir R. Vesey Hamilton.

(*Out of Print*)

Vol. 25. *Nelson and the Neapolitan Jacobins*, ed. H. C. Gutteridge. (*Out of Print*)

Vol. 26. *A Descriptive Catalogue of the Naval Manuscripts in the Pepysian Library*, Vol I, ed. J. R. Tanner. (*Out of Print*)

Vol. 27. *A Descriptive Catalogue of the Naval Manuscripts in the Pepysian Library*, Vol. II, ed. J. R. Tanner (*Out of Print*)

Vol. 28. *The Correspondence of Admiral John Markham, 1801–7*, ed. Sir Clements R. Markham. (*Out of Print*)

Vol. 29. *Fighting Instructions, 1530–1816*, ed. Julian S. Corbett. (*Out of Print*)

Vol. 30. *Papers relating to the First Dutch War, 1652–54*, Vol. III, ed. Dr S. R. Gardiner. (*Out of Print*)

Vol. 31. *The Recollections of Commander James Anthony Gardner, 1775–1814*, ed. Admiral Sir R. Vesey Hamilton and Professor J. K. Laughton. (*£15.00/£20.00*)

Vol. 32. *Letters and Papers of Charles, Lord Barham, 1758–1813*, Vol. I, ed. Sir J. K. Laughton. (*£15.00/£20.00*)

Vol. 33. *Naval Songs and Ballads*, ed. Professor C. H. Firth. (*Out of Print*)

Vol. 34. *Views of the Battles of the Third Dutch War*, ed. Julian S. Corbett. (*Out of Print*)

Vol. 35. *Signals and Instructions, 1776–1794*, ed. Julian S. Corbett. (*Out of Print*)

Vol. 36. *A Descriptive Catalogue of the Naval Manuscripts in the Pepysian Library*, Vol. III, ed. J. R. Tanner. (*Out of Print*)

Vol. 37. *Papers relating to the First Dutch War, 1652–54*, Vol. IV, ed. C. T. Atkinson. (*Out of Print*)

Vol. 38. *Letters and Papers of Charles, Lord Barham, 1758–1813*, Vol. II, ed. Sir J. K. Laughton. (*£15.00/£20.00*)

Vol. 39. *Letters and Papers of Charles, Lord Barham, 1758–1813*, Vol. III, ed. Sir J. K. Laughton. (*£15.00/£20.00*)

Vol. 40. *The Naval Miscellany*, Vol. II, ed. Sir J. K. Laughton. (*£15.00/£20.00*)

Vol. 41. *Papers relating to the First Dutch War, 1652–54*, Vol. V, ed. C. T. Atkinson. (*£8.00/£20.00*)

Vol. 42. *Papers relating to the Loss of Minorca in 1756*, ed. Captain H. W. Richmond. (*£8.00/£20.00*)

Vol. 43. *The Naval Tracts of Sir William Monson*, Vol. III, ed. M. Oppenheim. (*£8.00/£20.00*)

Vol. 44. *The Old Scots Navy, 1689–1710*, ed. James Grant. (*Out of Print*)

Vol. 45. *The Naval Tracts of Sir William Monson*, Vol. IV, ed. M. Oppenheim. (*£8.00/£20.00*)

Vol. 46. *The Private Papers of George, Second Earl Spencer*, Vol. I, ed. Julian S. Corbett (*£8.00/£20.00*)

Vol. 47. *The Naval Tracts of Sir William Monson*, Vol. V. ed. M. Oppenheim. (*£8.00/£20.00*)

Vol. 48. *The Private Papers of George, Second Earl Spencer*, Vol. II, ed. Julian S. Corbett. (*Out of Print*)

Vol. 49. *Documents relating to Law and Custom of the Sea*, Vol. I, ed. R. G. Marsden. (*£8.00/£20.00*)

Vol. 50. *Documents relating to Law and Custom of the Sea*, Vol. II, ed. R. G. Marsden. (*£8.00/£20.00*)

Vol. 51. *Autobiography of Phineas Pett*, ed. W. G. Perrin. (*Out of Print*)

Vol. 52. *The Life of Admiral Sir John Leake*, Vol. I, ed. G. A. R. Callender. (*£8.00/£20.00*)

Vol. 53. *The Life of Admiral Sir John Leake*, Vol. II, ed. G. A. R. Callender. (*£8.00/£20.00*)

Vol. 54. *The Life and Works of Sir Henry Mainwaring*, Vol. I, ed. G. E. Manwaring. (*£8.00/£20.00*)

Vol. 55. *The Letters of Lord St. Vincent, 1801–1804*, Vol. I, ed. D. B. Smith. (*Out of Print*)

Vol. 56. *The Life and Works of Sir Henry Mainwaring*, Vol. II, ed. G. E. Manwaring and W. G. Perrin. (*Out of Print*)

Vol. 57. *A descriptive Catalogue of the Naval Manuscripts in the Pepysian Library*, Vol. IV, ed. Dr J. R. Tanner. (*Out of Print*)

Vol. 58. *The Private Papers of George, Second Earl Spencer*, Vol. III, ed. Rear-Admiral H. W. Richmond. (*Out of Print*)

Vol. 59. *The Private Papers of George, Second Earl Spencer*, Vol. IV, ed. Rear-Admiral H. W. Richmond. (*Out of Print*)

Vol. 60. *Samuel Pepys's Naval Minutes*, ed. Dr. J. R. Tanner. (*£15.00/£20.00*)

Vol. 61. *The Letters of Lord St. Vincent, 1801–1804*, Vol. II, ed. D. B. Smith. (*Out of Print*)

Vol. 62. *Letters and Papers of Admiral Viscount Keith*, Vol. I, ed. W. G. Perrin, (*Out of Print*)

Vol. 63. *The Naval Miscellany*, Vol. III, ed. W. G. Perrin. (*Out of Print*)

Vol. 64. *The Journal of the First Earl of Sandwich*, ed. R. C. Anderson. (*Out of Print*)

Vol. 65. *Boteler's Dialogues*, ed. W. G. Perrin. (*£8.00/£20.00*)

Vol. 66. *Papers relating to the First Dutch War, 1652–54*, Vol. VI, ed. C. T. Atkinson. (*£8.00/£20.00*)

Vol. 67. *The Byng Papers*, Vol. I, ed. W. C. B. Tunstall (*£8.00/ £20.00*)

Vol. 68. *The Byng Papers*, Vol. II, ed. W. C. B. Tunstall. (*£8.00/ £20.00*)

Vol. 69. *The Private Papers of John, Earl of Sandwich*, Vol. I, ed. G. R. Barnes & Lt Cdr J. H. Owen. (*£8.00/£20.00*)

Corrigenda to *Papers relating to the First Dutch War, 1652–54*, ed. Captain A. C. Dewar. (*Free*)

Vol. 70. *The Byng Papers*, Vol. III, ed. W. C. B. Tunstall. (*£8.00/ £20.00*)

Vol. 71. *The Private Papers of John, Earl of Sandwich*, Vol. II, ed. G. R. Barnes and Lt Cdr J. H. Owen. (*£8.00/£20.00*)

Vol. 72. *Piracy in the Levant, 1827–8*, ed. Lt Cdr C. G. Pitcairn Jones. (*£8.00/£20.00*)

Vol. 73. *The Tangier Papers of Samuel Pepys*, ed. Edwin Chappell. (*£15.00/£20.00*)

Vol. 74. *The Tomlinson Papers*, ed. J. G. Bullocke. (*£8.00/£20.00*)

Vol. 75. *The Private Papers of John, Earl of Sandwich*, Vol. III, ed. G. R. Barnes and Lt Cdr J. H. Owen. (*Out of Print*)

Vol. 76. *The Letters of Robert Blake*, ed. Rev. J. R. Powell. (*Out of Print*)

Vol. 77. *Letters and Papers of Admiral the Hon. Samuel Barrington*, Vol. I, ed. D. Bonner-Smith (*£8.00/£20.00*)

Vol. 78. *The Private Papers of John, Earl of Sandwich*, Vol. IV, ed. G. R. Barnes and Lt Cdr J. H. Owen. (*Out of Print*)

Vol. 79. *The Journals of Sir Thomas Allin, 1660–1678*, Vol. I, ed. R. C. Anderson. (*£8.00/£20.00*)

Vol. 80. *The Journals of Sir Thomas Allin, 1660–1678*, Vol. II, ed. R. C. Anderson. (*£8.00/£20.00*)

Vol. 81. *Letters and Papers of Admiral the Hon. Samuel Barrington*, Vol. II, ed. D. Bonner-Smith. (*Out of Print*)

Vol. 82. *Captain Boteler's Recollections, 1808–1830*, ed. D. Bonner-Smith (*Out of Print*)

Vol. 83. *Russian War, 1854, Baltic and Black Sea: Official Correspondence*, ed. D. Bonner-Smith and Captain A. C. Dewar. (*Out of Print*)

Vol. 84. *Russian War, 1855, Baltic: Official Correspondence*, ed. D. Bonner-Smith (*Out of Print*)

Vol. 85. *Russian War, 1855, Black Sea: Official Correspondence*, ed. Captain A. C. Dewar. (*Out of Print*)

Vol. 86. *Journals and Narratives of the Third Dutch War*, ed. R. C.

Anderson. (*Out of Print*)

Vol. 87. *The Naval Brigades in the Indian Mutiny, 1857–58*, ed. Cdr W. B. Rowbotham. (*Out of Print*)

Vol. 88. *Patee Byng's Journal*, ed. J. L. Cranmer-Byng. (*Out of Print*)

Vol. 89. *The Sergison Papers, 1688–1702*, ed. Cdr R. D. Merriman, (*£8.00/£20.00*)

Vol. 90. *The Keith Papers*, Vol. II, ed. C. C. Lloyd. (*Out of Print*)

Vol. 91. *Five Naval Journals, 1789–1817*, ed. Rear-Admiral H. G. Thursfield. (*Out of Print*)

Vol. 92. *The Naval Miscellany*, Vol. IV, ed. C. C. Lloyd. (*Out of Print*)

Vol. 93. *Sir William Dillon's Narrative of Professional Adventures, 1790–1839*, Vol. I, ed. Professor Michael A. Lewis. (*Out of Print*)

Vol. 94. *The Walker Expedition to Quebec, 1711*, ed. Professor Gerald S. Graham. (*Out of Print*)

Vol. 95. *The Second China War, 1856–60*, ed. D. Bonner-Smith and E. W. R. Lumby. (*Out of Print*)

Vol. 96. *The Keith Papers*, Vol. III, ed. C. C. Lloyd. (*£8.00/£20.00*)

Vol. 97. *Sir William Dillon's Narrative of Professional Adventures, 1790–1839*, Vol. II, ed. Professor Michael A. Lewis. (*Out of Print*)

Vol. 98. *The Private Correspondence of Admiral Lord Collingwood*, ed. Professor Edward Hughes. (*Out of Print*)

Vol. 99. *The Vernon Papers, 1739–1745*, ed. B. McL. Ranft (*Out of Print*)

Vol. 100. *Nelson's Letters to his Wife and other Documents*, ed. Lt Cdr G. P. B. Naish. (*£8.00/£20.00*)

Vol. 101. *A Memoir of James Trevenen, 1760–1790*, ed. Professor C. C. Lloyd and Dr R. C. Anderson. (*Out of Print*)

Vol. 102. *The Papers of Admiral Sir John Fisher*, Vol. I, ed. Lt Cdr P. K. Kemp. (*Out of Print*)

Vol. 103. *Queen Anne's Navy*, ed. Cdr R. D. Merriman. (*Out of Print*)

Vol. 104. *The Navy and South America, 1807–1823*, ed. Professor G. S. Graham and Professor R. A. Humphreys. (*£8.00/£20.00*)

Vol. 105. *Documents relating to the Civil War, 1642–1648*, ed. Rev. J. R. Powell and E. K. Timings. (*Out of Print*)

Vol. 106. *The Papers of Admiral Sir John Fisher*, Vol. II, ed. Lt Cdr P. K. Kemp. (*Out of Print*)

Vol. 107. *The Health of Seamen*, ed. Professor C. C. Lloyd. (*£8.00/£20.00*)

Vol. 108. *The Jellicoe Papers*, Vol. I, ed. A. Temple Patterson.

(*£8.00/£20.00*)

Vol. 109. *Documents relating to Anson's Voyage round the World, 1740–1744*, ed. Dr Glyndwr Williams. (*£8.00/£20.00*)

Vol. 110. *The Saumarez Papers: The Baltic, 1808–1812*, ed. A. N. Ryan (*£8.00/£20.00*)

Vol. 111. *The Jellicoe Papers*, Vol. II, ed. A. Temple Patterson. (*£8.00/£20.00*)

Vol. 112. *The Rupert and Monck Letterbook, 1666*, ed. Rev. J. R. Powell and E. K. Timings. (*£8.00/£20.00*)

Vol. 113. *Documents relating to the Royal Naval Air Service*, Vol. I., ed. Captain S. W. Roskill. (*£8.00/£20.00*)

Vol. 114. *The Siege and Capture of Havana, 1762*, ed. Professor David Syrett. (*£8.00/£20.00*)

Vol. 115. *Policy and Operations in the Mediterranean, 1912–14*, ed. E. W. R. Lumby. (*£8.00/£20.00*)

Vol. 116. *The Jacobean Commissions of Enquiry, 1608 & 1618*, ed. Dr. A. P. McGowan. (*£8.00/£20.00*)

Vol. 117. *The Keyes Papers*, Vol. I, ed. Dr Paul G. Halpern. (*£8.00/£20.00*)

Vol. 118. *The Royal Navy and North America: The Warren Papers, 1736–1752*, ed. Dr Julian Gwyn. (*£8.00/£20.00*)

Vol. 119. *The Manning of the Royal Navy: Selected Public Pamphlets 1693–1873*, ed. Professor J. S. Bromley. (*£8.00/£20.00*)

Vol. 120. *Naval Administration, 1715–1750*, ed. Professor D. A. Baugh. (*£8.00/£20.00*)

Vol. 121. *The Keyes Papers*, Vol. II, ed. Dr Paul G. Halpern. (*£8.00/£20.00*)

Vol. 122. *The Keyes Papers*, Vol. III, ed. Dr Paul G. Halpern. (*£8.00/£20.00*)

Vol. 123. *The Navy of the Lancastrian Kings: Accounts and Inventories of William Soper, Keeper of the King's Ships 1422–1427*, ed. Dr Susan Rose. (*£8.00/£20.00*)

Vol. 124. *The Pollen Papers: The Privately Circulated Printed Works of Arthur Hungerford Pollen, 1901–1916*, ed. Dr Jon T. Sumida (*£8.00/£20.00 A & U*)

Vol. 125. *The Naval Miscellany*, Vol. V, ed. N. A. M. Rodger. (*£8.00/£30.00 A & U*)

Vol. 126. *The Royal Navy in the Mediterranean, 1915–1918*, ed. Professor Paul G. Halpern (*£8.00/£35.00 TS*)

Vol. 127. *The Expedition of Sir John Norris and Sir Francis Drake to Spain and Portugal, 1589*, ed. Professor R. B. Wernham. (*£8.00/£35.00 TS*)

Vol. 128. *The Beatty Papers*, Vol. I, 1902–1918, ed. B. McL. Ranft (*£8.00/£35.00 SP*)

Vol. 129. *The Hawke Papers: A Selection: 1743–1771*, ed. Ruddock F. Mackay (*£8.00/£35.00 SP*)

Printed in Great Britain by
Billing & Sons Ltd, Worcester